A CENTURY OF THE
SCOTTISH PEOPLE
1830–1950

Professor T. C. Smout was educated at The Leys School and Clare College, Cambridge. He was appointed to a Personal Chair in Economic History, University of Edinburgh, in 1971, and took up his present position as Professor of Scottish History at the University of St Andrews in 1980. Besides publishing various articles in learned journals, he is the author of Scottish Trade on the Eve of Union and *A History of the Scottish People, 1560–1830* (the companion to this volume, also in Fontana Press), and co-author of *Scottish Population History from the Seventeenth Century to the 1930s* and *The State of the Scottish Working Class in 1843*. He was elected a Fellow of the British Academy in 1988.

T. C. Smout

A CENTURY OF THE
SCOTTISH PEOPLE
1830–1950

Fontana Press

First published by William Collins 1986
First issued in Fontana Press 1987
Second impression October 1988

Copyright © T. C. Smout 1986

Fontana Press is an imprint of
Fontana Paperbacks, part of
the Collins Publishing Group,
8 Grafton Street, London W1X 3LA

Set in Bembo

Printed and bound in Great Britain by
William Collins Sons & Co. Ltd, Glasgow

Dedicated with love and admiration
to the memory of Michael Flinn

Contents

Illustrations

ILLUSTRATIONS

Edinburgh Grassmarket
Central Library, George IV Bridge, Edinburgh

Dundee, Powrie Place
City of Dundee District Council, Art Galleries and Museum Dept.

Council housing, ideal
The Blue Blanket, October 1912

Council housing, Shotts
Valentine Collection, St Andrews University Library

Plough teams, Anstruther
The late H. Berstecher, photographer: courtesy of the Salutation Inn, Anstruther

Crofters on Skye
George Washington Wilson Collection, Aberdeen University Library

Steam drifters, Anstruther
G. Cowie, photographer: courtesy of Bill Flett, Esq., Anstruther

Herring fleet, Fraserburgh
Scottish Fisheries Museum

Fish gutters, Peterhead
Scottish Fisheries Museum

Fishing families, Ferryden
Scottish Fisheries Museum

Haymaking, Fife
Cowie Collection, St Andrews University Library

Bothy party, Fife
Cowie Collection, St Andrews University Library

BETWEEN PAGES 154 AND 155

Smiths, Cowlairs
Graham Collection, Mitchell Library, Glasgow

Miners, Fife
Cowie Collection, St Andrews University Library

Coopers
Scottish Fisheries Museum

Shipwrights, Pittenweem
Scottish Fisheries Museum

Railway engineers, Glasgow
Graham Collection, Mitchell Library, Glasgow

Riveters on the *Lusitania*
United Clyde Shipbuilders neg. 123/4, Scottish Record Office

ILLUSTRATIONS

Copwinders, Dundee
Valentine Collection, St Andrews University Library

Weavers, Dundee
City of Dundee District Council, Art Galleries and Museums Dept.

BETWEEN PAGES 226 AND 227

Launch, Stephens of Linthouse
The Bailie, 4 February 1891

Provost Chisholm
The Bailie, 13 April 1902

Football, Southside Park
The Bailie, 15 October 1890

William Struth, Rangers manager
Glasgow Herald Picture Library

Ibrox stadium
Valentine Collection, St Andrews University Library

Muirhead Bone's Glasgow
Courtesy of Mrs Mary Adshead, London (both pictures)

Gladstone's train
Mitchell Library, Glasgow

Reform Bill banner
People's Palace Museum, Glasgow

Rent strike demonstration
Glasgow Herald Picture Library

David Kirkwood batoned
Illustrated London News Picture Library

Glasgow in 1919: demonstrators and tanks
Glasgow Herald Picture Library (both pictures)

Dundee unemployed march
The Dundee Courier

St Andrews unemployed dinner
Cowie Collection, St Andrews University Library

BETWEEN PAGES 274 AND 275

Thomas Chalmers
Hill and Adamson Collection, Scottish National Portrait Gallery

Temperance and Scottish Labour Party membership cards
People's Palace Museum, Glasgow (both pictures)

ILLUSTRATIONS

Pub in Springburn
Graham Collection, Mitchell Library, Glasgow

Pub in St Andrews
Cowie Collection, St Andrews University Library

Ministers, 1840s
Hill Collection, Scottish National Portrait Gallery

School portrait, Anstruther
Courtesy of Mrs Mole, Anstruther

Windmill Brae, Aberdeen
Aberdeen Illustrated in Nine Views (Montrose, 1841)

Union St, Aberdeen
George Washington Wilson Collection, Aberdeen University Library

Boyish elegence, ideal
The Bailie, magazine advertisement, 28 May 1884

Boyish elegence, reality
Graham Collection, Mitchell Library, Glasgow

Children in street, Markinch
Local History Collection, Central Library, Dundee

Evacuees, Dundee
The Dundee Courier

Chartist plate
Courtesy of George Gibb, Esq., Edinburgh

Acknowledgements

It is hard to know where to begin. This book has been a long time in the making, and without the urging of my ever-patient Collins editor, Richard Ollard, and my even more patient wife, Anne-Marie, it would never have seen the light of day. To the Master and Fellows of Clare College, Cambridge, I owe a special debt for electing me to a Visiting Fellowship in 1984 which gave me the space and time to finish it. To the librarians of the Universities of Cambridge, Edinburgh and St Andrews, to the Mitchell Library in Glasgow and the National Library of Scotland I also express my particular thanks for many courteous reader services. Individual scholars have given generous advice and help in tracing references or allowing me to cite their unpublished work: I am especially grateful in this respect to R. Butlin, Sydney and Olive Checkland, Frances Collison, Hamish Fraser, Robert Q. Gray, William Knox, Robert J. Morris, Gwen Neville, Daniel C. Paton, Stephen Patterson, Sylvia Price, Richard G. Rodgers, Roberta Scott, Joan M. Smith, Lorna Weatherill and Donald J. Withrington. None of the errors of fact and interpretation are their fault. From the meetings of the Scottish Economic and Social History Society and the Scottish Oral History Society I have gained more than can be properly acknowledged in the footnotes. Two sections of the book, Chapter I and part of Chapter VII, have appeared, in earlier versions, as the Dow Lecture at the University of Dundee in 1982 and as a contribution to A. A. Maclaran (ed.), *Social Class in Scotland: Past and Present* (Edinburgh, 1976) respectively. I thank the publishers for permission to re-use the material.

The illustrations come from many sources, and locating them proved to be one of the joys of compiling the book. Scotland has had many great photographers from the earliest days. Hill and Adamson's Rembrandt-like portrait of Thomas Chalmers in old age, Thomas Annan's reportage on the Glasgow slums *c.* 1870, George Washington Wilson's study of a couple grinding and winnowing on Skye in 1885 (as remote from ourselves as the Trobriand Islanders): these were examples of the art of acknowledged masters. Before I began my search, however, I knew nothing of the work of Graham of Springburn, Cox of Dundee, Cowie of St Andrews and many others whose portraits and studies—often unattributed—speak to us now so movingly of the men and women of the past. The copyright of the pictures is vested in the following: the Keeper of the Records of Scotland; the Keeper of the Scottish National Portrait Gallery; the Scottish Fisheries Museum; Edinburgh City Libraries; the Mitchell Library, Glasgow; the People's Palace Museum, Glasgow; the Central Library, Aberdeen; Dundee District Libraries; the Museums and Art Gallery Department, Dundee; the University Library, Aberdeen; the University Library, St Andrews; the *Illustrated London News* Picture Library; the *Glasgow Herald* Picture Library; the *Dundee Courier*, the Salutation Inn, Anstruther, Mrs Mary Adshead, Bill Flett, George Gibb and Mrs Mole. Full attributions are given in the list of illustrations, but this is the proper place to thank all the above owners for their courteous permission to allow me to reproduce the illustrations. I would also like to thank the staff of those institutions and the individuals listed above for all their help in hunting down the pictures. Their kindness and enthusiasm has known no bounds, and my debt to them, and to everyone else mentioned here, is incalculable.

T. C. Smout

Introduction

Adam Ferguson, when considering in 1767 the society of the Druids, the Natchez and the Tartars in his *Essay on the History of Civil Society*, wrote that:

> We are generally at a loss to conceive how mankind can subsist under manners and customs extremely different from our own; and we are apt to exaggerate the misery of barbarous times, by an imagination of what we ourselves should suffer in a situation to which we are not accustomed. But every age hath its consolations, as well as its sufferings.

Readers of this book may feel that in some respects the experience of the Scottish people in the century from the start of the reign of Queen Victoria to the close of the Second World War is as remote from their own world as that of the Druids, the Natchez and the Tartars, even though it was the experience of our fathers, grandfathers and great-grandfathers. Who now knows what it was like to be fed only upon three meals of potatoes a day? Or to experience as a child the rigours of the Scottish sabbath, where the highlight was a visit to the cemetery? Or to work as a Glasgow carter a ninety-eight-hour week, rising for five days out of seven at 4.30 in the morning and returning at 9.30 at night, with a thirteen-hour Saturday instead of the usual seventeen hours? If I have dwelt excessively upon the dark exterior of life, it is inevitably so in a book concerned with working-class experience in an age when most Scots were working-class and when their experience was, to the modern eye, bad. What the inner rewards were social history has few means of telling, but, as Ferguson says, 'every age hath its consolations', and we would be arrogant, as well as ignorant, to assume that we are happier people than they were.

If one is to consider, however, simple material wellbeing, the perspectives of the social historian and the economic historian show our century in very contrasting lights. To the economic historian there is a triumphal progression down to the First World War: the success of textiles in the first phase of the industrial revolution is succeeded by the success of iron and coal in the second, then after 1860 by the triumph of steel, ships, jute, tweed and high farming. Only the slump in the staple industries ushering in the interwar depression after 1920 brings this decisively to an end, and the Scottish economy, international leader in so many sectors up to that point, goes into a period of severe crisis that in recent decades has even been described as 'de-industrialization'. To the social historian—or at least to me—things seem rather different. The age of great industrial triumphs was an age of appalling social deprivation, not, certainly without amelioration, but with no solutions for its terrible problems. I am astounded by the tolerance, in a country boasting of its high moral standards and basking in the spiritual leadership of a Thomas Chalmers, of unspeakable urban squalor, compounded of drink abuse, bad housing, low wages, long hours and sham education. I find it unexpected that there should be only such limited improvements in social welfare as late as 1918. What was the point of all those triumphs of the great Victorian age of industry if so many people were so unspeakably oppressed by its operations?

Between 1920 and 1940, there were some clear advances, except in education, but Scotland on the eve of the Second World War was still recognizably Victorian in much of its ethos. The greatest advances in welfare have come since 1950, especially in the 1960s and early 1970s, when the standard of living and the environment were transformed for the better just as people were making the greatest moan about the decline of industry.

My Marxist colleagues, whose labours have done much in recent years to save Scottish economic and social history from tedium, will be inclined to scoff at my amazement at the rigours of the Scottish nineteenth century. For them, it is inherent in the capitalist system that manufacturers should be rich, get richer, and be celebrated as heroes by the bourgeois intellegentsia, while the workers stay poor, or become poorer, as their fate is overlooked in the general triumphalism of economic history. That approach, however, will not do, for at least two reasons. Firstly, many other countries did not follow the pattern of Scotland. For Denmark at one extreme of size, and the USA at the other, the first century of industrialization brought much greater and more widely distributed benefits to the bulk of the population than it did to the Scots, and the beneficent effect of accepting and experiencing basic economic change was evident from the start. The Marxist model fails to explain why this should be so. Secondly, however dismayed the Scottish historian may be at the relatively meagre improvement in the lot of most people in the country between 1830 and the early part of this century, there is no doubt that very substantial gains have been made since then—not gains, certainly, sufficient to iron out much inequality, or to raise society to a level at which every deprivation is abolished, but real gains nevertheless. Since this improvement co-incided with the dismemberment of the British Empire and the clear loss of leadership of the world economy to the United States, it is diffi-cult to maintain that it was financed by what Lenin (faced earlier with the problem of mass immiseration not occurring in the West as Marx had predicted) called 'the super-profits of imperialism'.

To my mind, the Marxist celebration of class consciousness and class warfare as effective weapons in the struggle for the improvement of humanity's lot seems positively perverse in the modern history of the West. Generally, those countries that have achieved consensus in the long term, like Denmark or Norway, and West Germany since the Second World War, have done better in material terms than those that have cherished old notions of class conflict at the work place, like Italy and Great Britain. Not only have their middle classes done better, but everyone has come to enjoy a relatively higher material standard of liv-ing. It may, of course, be argued that there is a current of causality flowing the other way—that Britain has clung to a more militant industrial class consciousness and defensive management only because she has achieved a lower rate of economic growth than her neighbours. It would be blind, however, to argue that there is no causal current at all running from harmony to success: the benefits of an industrial order where the productivity gains from using new technology are eagerly sought by a working class anxious to put them to work and an employ-ing class willing to share their benefits can readily be perceived in the most successful industries of, say, a modern Sweden or Japan.

Scotland after 1830 was never a society of this sort and there, per-haps, lies one explanation for its abiding poverty. In the nineteenth cen-

tury, when the upper classes held the whip hand over a divided and largely unorganized working class, they devised an industrial system predominantly based on one advantage they had over their competitors at
home and abroad—cheap labour in textiles, mines, iron foundries and
ship-building. When, as in the Glasgow cotton textile factories in 1837,
the early unions attempted to resist a round of wage cuts which the
employers had decided upon as their only response to competition elsewhere, they were carefully and systematically broken. At the end of the
nineteenth century, a class consciousness among the workers began to
emerge to match the organized and calculated self-interest already dep-
loyed against them by the employers, and in the early twentieth century that sense of solidarity began to enable the working class to
counterattack. Given the political gains implied by the Reform Acts of
1885 and 1918, the balance of power began to be tipped more evenly.
By then, however, the workers' repeated experience of the employers'
high-handedness, and especially of their almost invariable knee-jerk
reaction of proposing wage cuts or sackings in any position of competitive difficulty, had bred an ineradicable sense of bitterness and mistrust,
manifested in the restrictive practices of the unions and the workers'
more general lack of interest in improving efficiency at the work place.
The industrial depression of the interwar years buried the cheap labour
economy for good, as international demand collapsed and ruined the
old staple industries. But it left a legacy of ca' canny and a lack of moti-
vation that bedevilled the rebuilt Scottish economy for years after the
Second World War and is not dead yet.

The moral justification for the old social view was sought in a mixture of classical political economy and extreme Victorian individual-
ism. On the one hand, workers' combinations were wrong because
they forced the price of labour above its 'natural' level: on the other,
employers deserved their wealth because they considered themselves
finer people than most of their workers—and those among their
workers who had the same qualities would be able (so went the sustain-
ing myth) to become employers in turn. The latter point was very
clearly put in 'Six Lectures Addressed to the Working Classes' by the
Revd William G. Blaikie of Pilrig Free Church, Edinburgh, in 1849:

Working people are sometimes apt to envy capitalists and to speak
very bitterly against them, as if they sinfully monopolised the com-
forts of life. But in what way have capitalists obtained their capital?

Very generally by the plan now described. Industry, patience, self-denial, abstinence from expensive habits and indulgences, delay in entering on the matrimonial state, and other such means, have enabled them to accumulate a capital which has grown by degrees to gigantic dimensions. We know of several cases in point. The way is open for others to go and do likewise.

The middle classes who accepted this myth could feel that those who never made it into their ranks were morally inferior: when the cheap labour was Irish, as much of it was in the west of Scotland and Dundee after 1850, it was possible to add a racial and religious overtone to that feeling of superiority. How could you share decision-making in the work place, or build up a partnership in industry, with a proletariat you considered drunken, ignorant and superstitious? Even in the best circumstances, where there was general respect between employer and employee, as in a small paternalist firm, there was very little mixing at any level. Even today, the most modern electronics firm in Scotland maintains separate dining rooms for salaried and weekly-paid staff, in a way that most Continental or American businesses would consider offensive.

This book is an exploration of that complex world of deprivation and social division: it aims to show what life was like for most Scottish people. I am conscious of much that has been left out that could fairly be considered germane to a larger social history of Scotland. There is little about artistic or intellectual endeavour, though a book could be written about the achievements of the Scots from the *Edinburgh Reviewers* and Thomas Carlyle to the poets of the Scottish Renaissance, from the scientists like Clerk Maxwell and D'Arcy Thompson to the doctors like Simpson and Lister and the divines like Robertson Smith and David Cairns. There is nothing about the Scottish emigrés, either those who permanently sought their fortunes in foreign fields or the colonies, or those who merely went to administer and accumulate wealth within the Empire with a view to retiring to Elgin or Troon. There is not even a fully balanced picture of the Scottish political scene, though I have added two chapters at the close to discuss the politics of the working class, because I believe its ultimate fate explains much of the country's subsequent loss of nerve and the constant dependency on London, both for assistance and to provide excuses for failure, which characterizes Scottish life today. Almost everyone who works on any aspect of the field—and in recent years there have been many excellent scholars, young and old, operating in all its specialities—will feel that I have been overly superficial in their corner. The constraints of space and purpose are to blame. If, however, the volume offers to its readers any understanding of the situations in which their forefathers stood, and therefore of the situations in which they stand themselves today by inheritance, its aims will have been completely fulfilled.

CHAPTER I

Scotland in the 1830s and 1840s

The 1830s and 1840s were decades in European history when much was suffered, much was feared, and much was hoped. The poor suffered: in Great Britain and in Ireland sometimes from shortage of food induced by blight and bad harvests, sometimes, additionally, from shortage of work, induced by the great and increasing magnitude of the trade cycle. The rich feared: feared for political and social stability in a world of Chartist demonstrations in Britain and bourgeois and nationalist revolutions in Europe. The radicals hoped: from Chartist leaders like O'Connor and Lovett to socialists like Marx and Engels, they hoped that out of the suffering and the just resentment of the oppressed would somehow (whether by reason or by violence) come a basic change in human and political relationships: that the poor would inherit the earth in a new, and democratic, dispensation.

From the currents of the age Scotland was in no way exempted. Consider Lord Cockburn, one of the principal architects of the Reform Act for Scotland of 1832, which had been expected by the Whigs to defuse the tension inherent in industrial society by conferring power on a wide spectrum of the middle classes. By 1848, a year of Chartist threats and the trial of some of their Scottish leaders on charges of sedition, Cockburn wrote this deeply pessimistic and sonorously prophetic passage in his diary:

> The man must be very blind who does not see the shadow of the popular tree is enlarging and darkening; and he must see well who can tell us what its fruit will be. Chartism has superseded Radicalism, and draws the whole starving discontent of the country in its train. It is far more a matter of food than of principle. Extension of the fran-

chise is the phrase, but division of property is the object or the expected result; and with a manufacturing population, that is a population of which about a half is always hungry, and the passions of this hunger always excited by political delusion, it is not easy to see how wealth and sense are to keep their feet. The next century will solve this problem, and a few more. Will experience and education change human nature, and men become wise and good? Or shall we go on in this perpetual swelter? Or will manufactures be given up, and the pastoral-poetry state be returned to? Or will they retire from our blighted fields and ruined cities? Or will slavery, with the master's right of the domestic sword, be restored? Or will life, without a capacity to maintain itself, be made a capital offence? Or human productiveness be controlled by physical checks on fecundity? Or population be fitted to the means of subsistence by a regulated system of infanticide, to be executed as a piece of sanitary policy by public officers, under the direction of the Registrar of Births and Deaths? Meanwhile as many passengers as choose are allowed to crowd the vessel, and to eat each other.[1]

It is not the task of an opening chapter to examine the truth or otherwise of this resonant passage as it worked out, or failed to work out, in the following century, but rather to remain in the opening decades of our story and consider the anatomy of that 'popular tree' of the working class 'enlarging and darkening' over the privileges of his own class as Cockburn believed it to be.

Let us begin at the beginning. Queen Victoria ascended her throne in London in 1837: five years later she undertook the adventure of a visit to Scotland, only the second monarch to have done so since the Union of Parliaments in 1707. She came to a country in which the population was growing fast, as Cockburn had implied. At 2.6 millions in 1841, it had doubled since the first enumeration of Alexander Webster in 1755: eighty years of industrialization and agrarian change had conjured up a vastly bigger crew, yet it survived because the ship still somehow found provision for it short of cannibalism. What contemporaries especially feared and commented upon, however, was the growth of great towns. Glasgow, the squalid industrial megalopolis of textiles and engineering, was by far the largest, and was experiencing a headlong rate of increase: at 275,000 it was twelve times as large as it had been in 1755, and between 1831 and 1841 it had grown by more than one-third. Edinburgh, at 138,000, was now only half Glasgow's size, despite its own growth in the New Town and the overcrowding of its slums in the Old Town. Aberdeen, Dundee and Paisley were about half the size of the capital, at 60–65,000. They grew at different speeds. Dundee, prosperous on linen, had grown by 35 per cent in the previous ten years; Paisley, the home of a troubled handloom weaving trade, by only 5 per cent.

Other towns sprang up where there had been villages or green fields before: the iron industry of Lanarkshire doubled the populations of Old and New Monkland parishes between 1831 and 1841 and created Airdrie, population 12,400, but attracting another 10,000 on pay nights from the surrounding mining towns to fight and drink.[2] It had the ramshackle and dangerous character of a frontier town, where rival bands of Orange and Green beat one another up outside the pubs (it had one for every twenty males), the truck-shops and the towering furnaces.

According to Simon Tremenheere, the Government's anxious Mining Commissioner, in 1844, the population of Lanarkshire was without the restraint that 'may naturally be supposed to be exercised by the supervision, authority, and example of the classes of society of a higher grade ... The low animal habits of the uneducated or demoralised receive little check or rebuke from a superior presence.'[3] Such was the typical response of educated middle-class opinion to urban growth and industrialization: whatever the enormous national wealth it had generated, the inhabitants appeared dangerous because uncontrolled—dangerous not only to themselves, but to property, to order, and to the State itself.

Yet—and the point is an important one—only 35 per cent of the population lived in towns of over 5000 inhabitants (the equivalent figure in 1971 was 74 per cent). Two-thirds of the Scottish people were therefore countrymen still—not, admittedly, all in agriculture, for there was much industry diffused through the lowlands in handloom weaving and other occupations: but if they lived in villages and farms they were, at least in theory, the more amenable to the traditional social control exercised by minister, laird and immediate employer. Conditions and relationships were certainly changing in farm and hamlet, but the country still stood for stability, as the town did for insecurity: many believed, with the great churchman Thomas Chalmers, that the salvation of Scotland would lie not merely in preserving traditional rural values but in somehow reintroducing them in the towns. There was a mythological 'Scotch peasant' who figured in much early Victorian writing on social problems: self-reliant, poor and pious, paradoxically at once too proud to accept charity from the rate-payers and too respectful to question the ways either of Providence or of his earthly superiors. He was the imaginary paragon against which real Scots of the lower classes were so often measured, and invariably found wanting.

One striking feature of Scotland in the 1840s was the degree of contrast not merely between town and country but between region and region. Rich tourists (so eminently typified by Victoria and Albert) knew the difference between Highland and Lowland, and believed that outside Edinburgh and a strip of Border country immortalized by Sir Walter Scott, Romance, though admittedly not a peasant virtue, had its abode only in the Highlands, the land of the mountain and the flood. Their Highlands were glamorous, shrouded in the historic mists and poetry of Scott's *Lord of the Isles* and studded with forests and moors where sportsmen could take their game. The Marquis of Breadalbane was impressed and surprised at Prince Albert's consideration in 1842, when at his first Highland shoot at Taymouth he forebore to fire at the roebuck because the bushes in front of the guns were also full of beaters. But tourists saw only selected parts, and those enriched by their very coming. 'When Scott adopted the Highlands as a subject of romantic song and story,' wrote one observer, 'then began a new era of comfort in every spot which his magic touched.'[4] In any case, their gaze fell on the scenery rather than on the Gael. When they did observe the crofter he seemed to them very lazy as well as very poor, transmogrified sometimes into a comical 'Sandy' to parallel the Irish 'Paddy'. In their view he only had himself to blame for the plight he was in.

The real situation in the Highlands was much more complicated than anything the tourist saw or *Punch* caricatured. The eastern and southern districts were better off than the northern and western, but the Highland counties as a group endured a lower per capita income than any other part of Scotland and especially the central industrial core, which held (despite the slums) the main concentration of both middle- and working-class affluence. All sorts of social and economic indicators showed the poverty of the Highlands in the 1830s and 1840s, but perhaps none more tellingly than the squalor of its people's housing and the monotony of their food.

The nature of the Highland house can be judged from the fact that while tax returns of 1842–3 gave a figure for the 'annual' (or rentable) value of the average Scottish house around 12s. per head of population, the figure for houses down the west coast ranged from a pathetic 5d. in Skye and the Outer Hebrides to only 1s. 10d. in western Argyll.[5] Many were described by witnesses to the Poor Law Commission as having literally no value at all, hovels of earth and stone on which no price could be put. This coast and the islands was the *locus classicus* of the 'black houses', which were to prove such ineradicable nesting places for tuberculosis later in the nineteenth century when migrant labourers, returning from Glasgow, brought the bacillus back from their lodgings in the town. The black house was a home of rough stone and turf, its heather thatch pegged to a few roof timbers, without ceiling or paved floor, and without windows or chimney. Animals (cows and perhaps a pony) shared the building for the sake of mutual warmth, but their quarters were separated at floor level from the human living space by vertical deal boarding. Sometimes they were evidently not so separated, as eyewitness accounts from Iona (and indeed from Orkney, outside the Highlands) mention pigs warming themselves before the fire. Probably this was exceptional, however, if for no other reason than that most Highlanders had a superstitious aversion to eating pork.

The staff of Highland life was the herring and the potato, the latter a crop on which the inhabitants relied to a far greater degree than other Scots. The monotony of their fare was all too clearly encapsulated in contemporary descriptions of Highland meals. One from Ullapool speaks of potatoes and salt herring twice a day and oatmeal gruel for supper; one from Gigha of 'potatoes and fish or milk, generally twice in a day, and often three times'. The minister of Morvern told how:

> There are many, it is feared, much in the predicament of a little boy of the parish, who, on being asked on a certain occasion of what his three daily meals consisted gave the same unvarying answer, 'mashed potatoes', and on being further asked by his too inquisitive enquirer, 'what else?' replied with great artlessness but with evident surprise, 'a spoon'.[6]

Potatoes, with or without herring, three times a day, provided calories and vitamins enough for a balanced diet if eaten in sufficient quantity. One estimate, for an able-bodied labourer at Urquhart in eastern Inverness-shire, suggested a daily intake of 8–10lbs of potatoes, plus half a pound of oatmeal and a quart of milk. Another, for the less well nourished Small Isles off Skye, suggested 4½–6lbs of potatoes a day averaged over men, women and children. The lower figure, 4½ lbs, would be enough to keep a person alive even if he ate nothing else. Problems, however, arose every year in early summer when the old stock of potatoes ran low and the cauldron bubbling on the peat was kept going with limpets, root of silverweed, and all kinds of semi-edible refuse.

When the potato crop itself failed, potential disaster faced the population. This happened on a local scale in Argyll in 1833, and recurred again over most of the west coast in 1836 and 1837, threatening mass starvation which was only staved off by prompt charitable action on the part of relief committees organized in London, Glasgow and other towns. Far eclipsing any of these in seriousness, however, was the famine precipitated by the blight of 1846, which simply wiped out the potato crop of the entire west coast: some 150,000 people were at risk—and in neighbouring Ireland between 1,000,000 and 1,500,000 people died as a direct consequence of the same natural disaster. In Scotland there were no such serious demographic effects, because charity again was remarkably quick off the mark in sending relief, and because the London Government (in contrast to its inefficiency in Ireland) organized the distribution of food and seed corn from depot ships stationed in the principal firths. The chief government relief co-ordinator, the effective but lugubriously-named Sir Edward Pine Coffin, cajoled and bullied local landowners to accept at least a minimal responsibility towards their tenants, so that direct deaths from hunger were kept extremely low, and even deaths through hunger-induced diseases such as typhus failed to show much of an increase. It was a remarkable achievement, but the Highlands were never the same again after 1846. It was recognized by both landlord and tenant that the old potato economy was no longer a viable way to enable people to find a living off the land: population was down at the next census in 1851 and continued to drop in every census for the following century.

How could it be that the population of a substantial part of Scotland fell into such desperate straits at a time when, overall, the wealth of Great Britain was increasing so rapidly? The northern and western Highlands were generally agreed by commentators in the 1830s and early 1840s to be the only part of the northern kingdom where the vast majority of the people were worse fed, worse clothed and generally worse off than they had been at the close of the Napoleonic Wars in 1815. The answer is not just that the crofters and cottars had been cleared from the most fertile lands by greedy lairds and sheep-farmers; some had been, but many of the worst clearances down the west coast were yet to come, and those places in the north that had already experienced partial clearances (like Sutherland) escaped much of the destitution in 1846 because population pressure was less acute there. Nor can the problem be entirely accounted for by the population policy of those landlords who had encouraged the concentration and multiplication of the peasantry on some islands to provide labour to gather sea wrack for the kelp industry; it had collapsed in the 1820s, nearly a generation before the famine. At least part of the answer is that the Highlanders contributed to their own problems by their passion for the land they occupied, preferring a life of deepening poverty in an increasingly overcrowded environment to the risk of seeking their fortunes permanently abroad, or in the Lowlands.

To continue our journey round the regions, the economy of the northern Lowland zone that runs along the east coast from Kincardine to Caithness had much in common with that of the Highlands, in that both shared the overwhelming importance of farming and fishing, both endured landlord domination, and both experienced the disadvantages of distance from the largest urban markets, though that was not so seriously felt around Aberdeen. Not that the Lowlanders of these parts felt much sympathy for the Highlanders, or made common cause with them. When the last Scottish famine was raging in the Highlands in 1846–8, the last Scottish grain riots were also taking place in the little Lowland ports from Thurso round to Peterhead: the inhabitants had discovered that meal was being purchased by relief agencies and others for export coastwise and they were obstructing its shipment in case the price rose too much in their own localities. Charity began at home.

The north-eastern mainland had, indeed, its own very strong regional identity and a system of cultural values rooted in what Ian Carter has called the 'peasant' quality of its farming.[7] It was characterized by medium-sized farms cultivated still by the labour of the farmer and his family assisted by wage labour from the unmarried sons and daughters of still smaller farmers, or by crofters, who had holdings on the edge of the cultivated area. Sheer physical effort had made some impact on a harsh environment. 'The country in its natural state is either bogs or stone-covered muirs,' said an agricultural correspondent in 1843. 'No ground has by nature a more poor and sterile-looking surface, or one more seemingly unfit for the purpose of agriculture: and yet such as have gone from Edinburgh to Aberdeen by the mail-coach road during the last twenty years, must have remarked what skill and industry can do in effecting a change in so unpropitious-looking a subject.'[8]

The north-east had its own dietary pattern, in which potatoes actually figured less (but kail more) than in any other part of Scotland. Farmer, crofter and fisherman were far from prosperous: less than a fifth of the parishes reported to the Poor Law Commissioners in 1843 that meat was an item of the diet of the labouring classes, and there were still fewer references to the consumption of tea.[9] They were poor, but they retained a tough, farmstead culture of their own that found expression in the so-called 'bothy ballads' and the secret, quasi-magic society of the Horseman's Word. This region has produced a crop of novelists and biographers, a rich vein running from William Alexander, whose *Johnny Gibb of Gushetneuk* was the finest of the kailyard novels, to Lewis Grassic Gibbon in our own century: common to them all is a sense of the worth of land and community and of the quality of self-reliance, a peasant consciousness found more often in Scandinavian than in British literature. It is quite different from class consciousness and certainly completely different from those expressions of deferential respect towards the upper classes and their values that Chalmers and others assumed would emerge from the world view of their traditional 'Scotch peasantry'.

The richest parts of the Scottish countryside lay south of the great dividing Highland Fault that ran from Dumbarton in a diagonal line over to Stonehaven. This was the area in which by the 1840s agriculture had proceeded furthest along the lines of capitalist change, but even so there were remarkable differences between the various counties. The most sophisticated farming was in the south-east, the Lothians and Berwickshire, where farms were enormous by Scottish standards— four times as large as in Aberdeenshire and employing seven times as much paid labour. 'Lothian husbandry' was the admired apogee of capitalist farming in early Victorian Britain, and famous farms like Fentonbarns outside Dunbar drew students from all over Europe to study agricultural management. This was how an English visitor described Fentonbarns in the heyday of High Farming:

This great farm almost reached the sublime. It went like clockwork. Its fields, of from 20 to 30 acres, were all rectangular. There were no odd corners, no thickets, no hedgerow trees, no ragged, any-shaped pastures. The quickset hedges were clipped low and narrow like those of a garden. No wild rose or old man's beard rambled on them, no may or blackthorn blossom lit them up, neither did the violet or the primrose find a lodging beneath their shade. There were no open ditches, and the plough ran right up to the roots of the fence. The land was as clean as a well-kept garden ...[10]

These modern-sounding ecological deserts, 'factories for making corn and meat', William Cobbett had described them on his Scottish tour of 1830, were cultivated by squads of agricultural workers, or hinds, who formed not a peasantry but a genuine landless proletariat, in the sense that there was no expectation that at any time in their life would they become tenants of land, or be anything other than simple farm labourers. At Fentonbarns there were twenty or thirty of them, living, characteristically, in rows of cottages attached to the steading and away from any village: it kept them in the shadow of the great farmhouse so that their lives could be as clipped and disciplined as the hedges. The permanent labour-force was reinforced, in the summer, by bands of Irish men and women who came in May for turnip-weeding and stayed until the potato-lifting in October. 'In most of the steadings there is a temporary bothy with a fireplace,' explained one parliamentary report, 'some chairs or benches, and wooden bedsteads. In some bothies the beds are arranged like berths on board ship, one above the other. The Irish are allowed the use of these bothies, with straw mattresses, and coarse blankets, get what coals are required, and everything free of charge.'[11] Some farms preferred West Highland workers to Irishmen, though it was agreed the latter were 'quiet, hardworking fellows'.

Of necessity, the hind was also a quiet, hardworking fellow. His family comprised a single work-unit in which each member had his niche. The hind himself was a ploughman: his wife was called the 'bondager' and paid the rent of the cottage by eighteen to twenty days' labour at harvest. The most valuable things a hind could possess, said one East Lothian farmer to the Poor Law Commissioners in 1843, was 'a good wife, a good cow, and a good razor'. The teenage sons were the 'half-hinds' and helped their father with the horses; still younger children worked on the fields weeding turnips or acting as bird scarers.

It was a hard, tough life, but the hind of south-east Scotland was the best-paid and best-fed of Scottish farm workers, a married man's wages being worth £25 or £26 a year in 1843, as compared to £14 to £19 at the other extreme, along the east coast north of Inverness. Very remarkably, considering that capitalist farming was more highly developed in the south-east than anywhere else in Scotland, the hinds' wages were still largely paid in kind—characteristically in oats, barley, peas, the free carriage of up to four tons of coal, free manured potato ground, the keep of a cow and perhaps a little extra cash in lieu of some traditional right to keep sheep or chickens, or to sow a capful of flax seed. The family also generally kept a pig, and their daily meals reflected a greater affluence than further north: everyone began with a breakfast of porridge and milk, often accompanied by tea or coffee; the mid-day meal was dominated by potatoes and broth, but most people also had bacon, ham or pork (or sometimes fish or cheese as an alternative); supper consisted either of porridge or of another dish of potatoes. A farm servant and his wife and four children under twelve years living at Dryfesdale in Dumfriess-shire were calculated in 1843 to consume 14lbs of potatoes and 3lbs of oatmeal and barleymeal a day. Most of the oatmeal was consumed at breakfast as porridge 'from 9 to 10 ounces making a moderate sized dishful for a working man'. No wonder it was traditionally eaten standing, on the grounds that an upright sack fills fullest.

Throughout Lowland Scotland, the character of rural life was very much affected by the proximity of industry and towns; wages tended to be higher where there was competition from industry or an urban labour market, and a higher proportion tended to be paid in cash. The Midlothian hind, for example, was paid in cash rather than in grain because of the proximity of consumer markets where he could shop to satisfy his needs. Many parts of southern Scotland (outside the extreme south-east and Galloway) were themselves deeply penetrated by industry even while remaining essentially rural. Angus, north Fife, and south Perthshire are good examples of this, for there handloom weaving villages were still thriving, and in Angus were still being constructed as planned settlements in the 1830s, despite competition from the factory towns: they were occupied by cottagers who spun flax into hanks of yarn or made coarse cloth in their own homes for sale to local linen factors. Farm labourers in these areas were often bachelors, as many couples, when they married, moved to a village smallholding where they could still combine some cultivation of their own plot with working at the linen trade. This was therefore the classic area of the bothy, constructed not as temporary quarters for Irish or Highland migrant workers, as in the Lothians, but as permanent barracks, segregated from the farmhouse, for unmarried farmhands.

Ayrshire, rural Lanarkshire, and Renfrewshire formed another area of mixed economy where many weaving and mining settlements were interspersed with the farms. The fact that dairy husbandry predominated in the damper climate of the west, however, meant that there was little need for large labour gangs to hoe and harvest: farms were smaller, and to a greater extent cultivated by family labour, like those of the north-east. Such farmhands as there were were often unmarried, some saving up for farms of their own. In places there were relics of steelbow, the old system of sharecropping, by which a capitalist leased stock to the peasantry in return for a share of the returns. An Ayrshire factor to several large estates explained how the unmarried farmhands lived as boarders in the farmhouse but often 'looked forward to having farms of about twenty acres. I could point out a dozen instances of farmers who were originally ploughmen. And these, after having been for a time in the small farms, generally feel inclined to have larger farms.' They achieved their ambition by carefully saving enough out of their wages to begin stocking a farm, and then marrying a female farm servant who had been equally thrifty. On their marriage, both left paid employment and set up as farmers with their joint capital. If they could not attain this, the couple might still marry, the man remaining a farm servant and his wife renting a certain number of cows from the farmer; 'the farmer supplies [the] food . . . the produce becomes her own . . . instead of farming his land, she farms the cows.'[12]

The variations in the long-term expectations of the agricultural community were therefore very very considerable across the face of Scotland, depending on region, soil and circumstances. No generalization is safe, except that the Lowland countryman everywhere lived in too close proximity to their employers, ministers and landlords to escape their surveillance: it was not (and clearly could not be) from them that there arose the open resistance to social superiors or the public questioning of existing institutions that was so worrying to Lord Cockburn and the upper classes.

Of course, the intimacy of rural life could also serve to remind the well-heeled of the needs of the poor. Many a country cottage was rebuilt in the early Victorian years by improving landlords who wished to win commendation from their peers or a prize from the Highland and Agricultural Society, though this did not prevent the general standard of rural housing from remaining deplorably low. The one-roomed house or two-roomed but-and-ben, with earth floors, thatched roof and poor ventilation remained common throughout the century, especially out of sight of the main approaches to the great house. The conscientious Church of Scotland minister was, at least up to the Disruption of 1843, still a regular visitor to such homes; if the old Scottish poor law worked anywhere in the 1830s it was in these Lowland rural parishes, where he could still detect the daily problems of every respectable indigent family and, after judging each case on its merits, either put pressure on their relatives to increase their support or persuade the factor or farmer to offer some small charity in addition to the kirk session's pittance. For Thomas Chalmers this inquisitorial, church-led paternalism was the ideal world he recalled from his ministry in rural Fife, inspiring his vision of the Godly Commonwealth that must be upheld in the country and reintroduced in the city if all the desirable advances of modern capitalism were not to end in anomie and social chaos.

Between town and country lay the many scores of industrial villages of central Scotland, forming a characteristic social environment which was a blend of both. Take the example of Larkhall in Lanarkshire, in 1841 a parish of 2453, mainly colliers, weavers, smallholders and farmers. Thomas Stewart, who wrote the reminiscences of his childhood in 1893, was the son of a small independent coal worker and worked in the mines himself along with his brother and his aunt: he remembered his home as 'a little thatched cottage ... before the door was an orchard, and beyond that a wee burnie'. He went on to relate how 'every householder had a good-sized garden, which was generally kept in a first-class state of cultivation; and in many of them a little byre had been erected where a cow, and sometimes two, were kept'. 'Mrs McGuil', their neighbour, would thresh corn with her daughters in their barn and plough their smallholding, while her husband and sons worked in the mine. Such recollections were not the fantasy of an old man: the census enumeration returns for 1851 record, in the house next to the Stewart family, an Agnes Gold, widow, who farmed eight acres and whose two sons and a son-in-law (as well as a lodger) worked in the mines.[13]

In an environment of this kind, critics of the existing social order were by no means lacking. To Thomas Stewart, the distinguishing trait of the Scottish collier was his independence, which the 'cringing slaves in other trades' envied but could not match. Stewart's father was self-employed, with his own little pit where the coal was worked mainly by family labour and raised by bucket and windlass: when such peasant miners or their sons became employees of some larger coal-owner (as they increasingly did in the iron boom of the 1830s and 1840s), they carried into the new work situation the same pride: they were quick to form unions, quick to assert control over their own working conditions, quick to strike. There was great tension in the iron masters' big new mines round Airdrie and Coatbridge in Lanarkshire between men in this tradition and the initially malleable, raw, immigrant miners, often Irish—a tension which the Larkhall men described as being between 'honourable men' and 'degraded slaves'. In fairness to the immigrants, it was only a matter of time (though it took longer than the 1840s) before they, too, learned to defend themselves from the employer by concerted industrial action.

The handloom weaving villages of the west of Scotland were, more consistently than the coal-mining villages, hotbeds of the Chartist cause. The spirit of their small-town radicalism breathes, for example, in the diaries of James Taylor of Fenwick in Ayrshire, rediscovered and published by his descendant in New Zealand.[14] Taylor was a weaver who approved of political clubs and deplored 'the absurd distinctions that exist in society'; he wrote his own poems in the manner of Burns and belonged to the old Secession Church, which (unlike either part of the newly disrupted Church of Scotland) detested links of any kind between State and kirk. His favourite topics were local scandal, the weather, the harvest, the doings and misdoings of all three of the local ministers, deaths, the state of the nation, the beauty of the sabbath when 'no children are allowed to break from the family circle and run on the street', the deeds of the Fenwick curling club, politics and the pretensions of the gentry. For the last he had a particular and profound contempt. On 27 April 1847, for instance, he described the 'vain show' at the wedding of the local landed family:

Most of the curlers in the parish, along with the Crawfordland tenantry, marched in procession from Fenwick with music and flags, also with mimic plough and harrow and about fifteen of their number bearing torches ... When Mr Crawford and his spouse arrived, the company took the horses out of the carriage and drew the couple from the Green gate up to the Castle, a most loyal display of devotion to wealth, for there was no public merit whatever connected with the parties thus drawn.

This prompted him to a further political reflection:

Men should never lose their dignity so far as to draw their fellow men, however great or good they may be. In fact, no great or good man would allow such a thing to be done to him. It is only the thoughtless, the interested or the servile that will draw on such occasions, and it is only the vain or the childish that will allow themselves to be so treated. When will men learn to be wise? ... When will they cease to be worms for the proud to tread on?

From this mould came the grittiest of emigrants and colonizers, carrying into exile an independence of mind and a disregard for privilege which was to mark the new societies of America and the Antipodes. Their modern citizens are still quick (and correct) to identify as class-ridden the mother country their forefathers left behind.

The society of rural industrial Ayrshire was, despite its spirit, extremely poor in the 1840s. As male weavers' wages fell (by 1842 they were earning only 6s. or 7s. a week, about a third less than a male farm servant in the same county), so they came to rely increasingly on the work of their wives and daughters as muslin embroiderers. The practice of sewing or 'flowering' the fine cotton cloth put out to domestic workers by Glasgow manufacturers came to occupy thousands of women in the west of Scotland and northern Ireland; the largest firm in the 1850s, M'Donalds, had between 20,000 and 30,000 female employees on its books at the height of its prosperity. It was hard work for the girls: it took fourteen to sixteen hours work a day, six days a week, to make 12s.—but if a family contented itself with the woman doing half that and the man getting what he could on the handloom, it could still make a living from cottage industry.

And so we come to the towns, where only a third of the population lived, but which filled the ruling classes with a kind of panic which the quiescence of the agricultural sector or the old-fashioned but essentially small-scale radical spirit of the industrial villages never prompted.

In the towns lived both the richest and the poorest of the labouring classes, with a striking material and cultural difference between the two extremes. The skilled, urban male artisan of early Victorian Scotland, in the thriving occupations, expected to earn in good times anything from 13–30s. a week depending on his trade and level of expertise: anything above the foot of the scale gave him a more or less comfortable margin above subsistence. He could keep his wife at home, send his children to school instead of to work, and accumulate a modicum of solid material possessions—good bedding, furniture, a nice longcase clock, and so on. He had a fair chance of upward social mobility if he was a mason, a joiner, an engineer, or something similar, for from being a skilled craftsman he might aspire with thrift and sobriety to become, later in his life, a small employer or at least a subcontractor. The artisan was therefore the backbone in Scotland of the friendly society movement, the savings bank contributors, and the total abstinence societies. He might or might not be a Chartist, but he often took the closest interest in church affairs, either as a seceder or as a supporter of the Free Church at the moment of disruption.

The artisan also ate well. The beef and mutton of the Highlands and the butter and cheese of Ayrshire, though they might often pass untasted by local working-class producers, appeared regularly on the table of the skilled artisan in Lanarkshire. He was liable, if pressed, to argue that he needed it. This was how a worker earning about £1 a week at a textile-printing factory in Dunbartonshire described his diet to the Poor Law Commission in 1843:

It is to be borne in mind, also, that the occupation of the calico printer is exhausting, and requires a better diet than that of the common agricultural labourer. I myself generally have for breakfast some porridge and milk, a little tea, a slice of bread and ham, and, as far as I can afford it, a little steak. For dinner I generally have broth; sometimes potatoes and milk; and I generally take tea at night, with bread and cheese, or bread and butter, with a slice of toast. This is a fair specimen of what calico printers would like to have; but I should say that a great number of them do not live quite so well . . .[15]

At the other end of the spectrum was the unskilled worker whose earning power lay solely in his muscles, or in his or her ability to endure infinitely tedious work. A male unskilled labourer's wage, across Scotland, could fall to about half that of an artisan, or even less. In north Lanarkshire, Renfrewshire and Dunbartonshire in 1843 the 'lowest class of labourer' (better paid there than elsewhere in the country) was earning about 6s. 6d. a week, in an area where the average farm labourer earned about 10s. and colliers and artisans 15s. Other labourers at the peak of their fitness and earning power could rise to 10s. or even 12s. a week. Even the latter sum hardly exceeded subsistence. The wife of a labourer, like the wife of a weaver, would often have to work at some domestic trade, and the education of the children would almost invariably be sacrificed to the need to send them, at as tender an age as possible, to work in a factory or workshop to top up the man's basic wage.

Unskilled workers and their families, therefore, saved little, accumulated little in their homes, led a domestic life fractured by the treadmill of toiling for a subsistence, and tended to be comparatively illiterate. Their house was in a slum area, their food mainly potatoes and meal unless scrag ends of meat had to be purchased for the man to keep up his strength during a navvying job. Their future was depressing, and pointed downwards to a pauper's grave as their physical energy gave out. In politics, trade unions and kirk affairs, they had, in Scotland in the 1840s, apparently little interest.

In many cases the unskilled workers were recent Irish immigrants, in some, displaced Highlanders. Both these groups were additionally separated from the typical Lowland artisan, and from all other Scots, by ethnic and linguistic barriers, and the Catholic Irish by religious barriers as well. It was hard for them to identify across such a divide, and native Lowland Scots despised both the Highland 'teuchter' and the Irish 'Paddy'. The census of 1841 listed 125,000 Irish-born individuals in Scotland, and in the famine of 1848 there were up to 1000 new arrivals a week from Ireland into Glasgow: such a volume of immigration seemed menacing in itself, but there were other reasons to worry. The vast majority of migrants arrived from the province of Ulster, already accustomed to sectarian bitterness. There is little doubt that the Ulster Protestant immigrant, very often already bearing a Scottish surname, found it easier to integrate than the Catholic, and aggressively asserted his Orange and anti-papistical sentiments as a way of allying himself to the native Scots and dissociating himself from his fellow Irishmen. The Catholic Irish were thereby driven even more firmly into a ghetto mentality, and clung to the bosom of Mother Church to find some kind of comfort and support in a totally unwelcoming environment.

Divide and rule has been a precept for stable government since Roman times. The unenfranchised masses, even in the towns, were so divided by income, life expectancy, culture and creed as to pose, on the face of it, little threat to their governors. True, there had been examples of bloody revolution abroad in the 1790s, but discontent in Britain had been contained for the better part of half a century. Why then, were the rulers so worried? There were repeated comments in the 1830s and 1840s to the effect that the nation was like a powder keg, that class war might break out at any time, that desperate men threatened the state with anarchy. The answer to this conundrum might be that the leaders misperceived the situation, or that there were other factors giving greater cohesion to working-class experience than are immediately apparent. Both possibilities are worth considering carefully.

The elements that would tend to increase the chances of working-class people recognizing a common interest were, firstly, that some of the artisans with the proudest radical traditions, reaching back to the days of the French Revolution and the Friends of the People in the 1790s, had been pushed steadily downwards towards the income level of the unskilled labourer over the previous twenty years, and, secondly, that the cyclical industrial depressions occurring once or twice every decade began to develop such a serious amplitude in the second quarter of the nineteenth century that they threatened to wipe out the savings of many of even the best-paid and thriftiest of artisans. If skilled and articulate workers with a long tradition of literacy, self-help and political self-expression were suffering like this from the system, might they not begin to organize and mobilize the unskilled, who had always suffered from it?

The classic example of depressed artisans was the handloom weavers, who existed in enormous numbers in the towns as well as the villages. The most recent historian of the trade estimates that their numbers grew from 45,000 around 1790 to a peak of 84,560 by 1840, only to fall catastrophically to 25,000 by 1850 (and a mere 4000 in 1880). The collapse was due primarily to the displacement of the handloom by the powerloom, combined with the intolerable destitution so many of them had to face in the depressions of 1841–3 and 1848.[16]

Glasgow and Paisley in the west, Dundee, Perth and Dunfermline in the east were *par excellence* the towns of handloom weaving. What happened in Paisley in the early 1840s was a dramatic example both of the weavers' plight and of the nature of their reaction to acute distress.[17] The town was the fourth or fifth largest in Scotland: its people lived primarily by weaving fine woollen, cotton or silk shawls decorated with patterns of paisley pine imitated from the incomparable textiles of Kashmir. In 1837, there were about 6000 looms in operation, mostly harness looms involved in the fancy trade, each needing the labour of one skilled man and a boy.

Since the 1790s, the community had nurtured a radical, democratic culture of political clubs, debating societies, working-class libraries and friendly societies: but by and large the radical tradition was part of the tradition of the Scottish Enlightenment, embodying both a faith in the ability of man to determine his own destiny and a faith in the appeal to reason and to law. In the highly disturbed years between 1817 and 1820, there had, admittedly, in Paisley as elsewhere in the west, been riots, pike-making, rumours of conspiracy to overthrow the Government by force. Such unrest was not typical. In 1819, between 800 and 1000 of the unemployed had started a process of law to compel the heritors and kirk session of the Abbey Parish to pay benefits to the able-bodied under the old Scots poor law: they had ultimately failed in their intention, but the appeal was a remarkable example both of their organizing powers and of their trust in legal processes. The Provost of Paisley in 1842 was himself a cutler and a former radical: in the year of Peterloo he had to flee the country under suspicion of illegal activities, but now he was a middle-class liberal, involved in the struggle to repeal the Corn Laws and anxious to build bridges with the local Chartist Association in pursuit of a wider franchise. The Chartists themselves were very strong in the town, led by Robert Cochran, 'wee clearhead', himself a weaver, and the maverick Minister of the Abbey, Patrick Brewster. The formal aims of the Chartist Associations were the same throughout Britain: they wanted universal manhood suffrage and annual parliaments of paid MPs elected by secret ballot from constituencies of equal size.

In 1841, trade began to fail in Paisley in a collapse of extraordinary dimensions. Before the spring of 1843, 67 out of 112 businesses operating in the town had gone bankrupt: at the peak of the distress almost

15,000 people—a quarter of the entire population—were dependent on casual charity. The Provost related:

> I have visited a very great number of families and found many of them without any single article which they could dispose of in any form; without anything in the shape of furniture, without anything in the shape of clothes to cover themselves; and several of the petitioners who have come to state their case to me have had to borrow some piece of upper clothing from a neighbour to enable them to appear on the street.[18]

Even the pawnbrokers began to go bankrupt in large numbers as their customers ran out of goods to pledge. The distress was described as the worst ever to have afflicted a British city.

Within six months of the start of the crisis, the relief committee established by the Provost and local worthies showed every sign of running out of cash itself. The Government of Sir Robert Peel was extremely alarmed: if they did nothing, there were fears for law and order from the starving multitude; if they openly intervened with cash, they let the cat of government intervention out of the bag, and every community facing hardship would feel entitled to arrive on their doorstep with a begging bowl. The Cabinet hit on the truly extraordinary device of buying time by donating nearly £2000 out of their own private pockets (and out of Queen Victoria's) to tide the situation over, sending a government agent to Paisley to take over supervision of private relief from the local committee and then launching a national public appeal sponsored by the Queen to channel relief into Paisley and one or two less severely afflicted, but similar, communities in England. The body in London set up to supervise this new stream of charity was ostensibly independent: in fact the Home Secretary, Sir James Graham, secretly kept close tabs on its operations, particularly in respect to Paisley itself.

This action saved the weavers from starvation, but order was kept in the town not because of the Home Secretary but primarily because the local Chartists and leaders of the unemployed wanted it that way. The force at the disposal of the ruling classes was negligible—the Sheriff Depute described the town police as untrustworthy, the rural police as amounting to less than twenty men, and the only alternative using 170 'effective men' in the army contingent in the local barracks. Attempts to raise 'a large force of Special Constables' were frustrated by the refusal of local people to serve. In fact, there was no disorder because the working class identified with the propertied classes within the town: it was seen as a community and not a class problem. They were all in the mess together, and the enemy, if there was one, was not the employer but a distant government unwilling to use public funds to help. Secondly, the leaders of the local radicals were ideologically committed to a moral-force Chartism which utterly eschewed violence. 'By conducting yourselves with decorum,' Cochran told a mass meeting of the inhabitants summoned by tuck of drum on 6 April 1842, 'you will strike more terror to the hearts of your enemies than by any other course you can pursue.' Peel and Graham in London, naturally, were not at all terrified, but they were profoundly relieved.

It might be argued that the handloom weavers, for all their numbers and radicalism, were nevertheless a special case: embedded in an irretrievably dying trade, they constituted a problem which unemployment and old age would solve if the authorities could ride out the present storm. Would there not be more threat in the long run from artisans and semi-skilled workers in normally thriving occupations forced down to the breadline or below in the typhoons of depression? The Poor Law Commissioners in 1843 found plenty of such cases in the towns. For example, they interviewed a mason in Greenock who had formerly earned 12–14s. a week; he had been out of work for thirteen months, and he and his wife lived with three children in a 'bedroom stripped of every article of furniture'. His allowance from the soup kitchen was two chopins of soup and three scones a day: asked how he managed, he replied, 'whiles fasting, and whiles getting meat'.[19] They heard too of a factory worker in Aberdeen found by a witness weeping uncontrollably by the quayside: he had been out of work for eight or nine months and had just been obliged to sell the last of his furniture:

> It would have cost £30. All was packed up to be taken away. He was hopeless of getting anything to relieve himself. He appeared to be a decent man: and if he had had anything like constant employment, even though at reduced wages, he would have been prevented from falling, as he will fall, into the lowest class of destitute characters.[20]

These were respectable people. As one observer put it, in a depression 'the first class which suffers is the improvident, but it goes on until it reaches the provident'.

Nevertheless, there is remarkably little indication that men in this position were driven actively or continuously to confront the political and economic order of the day, or to make a sustained common cause with workers in other occupations and strata of the labouring classes. Certainly there were moments of solidarity: one such was in 1837, when the struggle between the Glasgow cotton-spinners and their employers, with the subsequent arrest and transportation of the union leaders, shook many workers in the west out of their customary class collaboration into sympathetic strikes and protests on the streets. But when many people of this sort became Chartists in the following years, it was generally on the side of a characteristically Scottish moral-force Chartism not so different from that which prevailed in Paisley, which emphasized the need for working-class self-improvement through churches and temperance societies as much as the need for franchise reform.

True, among Chartists, the 'moral-force' influence of Patrick Brewster was nowhere as great as in Paisley: many claimed to follow the militant Anglo-Irish leader Fergus O'Connor, but the latter in turn was appalled at what he considered to be a milk-and-water, toadying approach to the middle class typified by the third annual Scottish Convention held at Glasgow in January 1842. He spoke scathingly afterwards of 'the saints of the Glasgow Chartists Synod': 'There were ten Glasgow preachers, all Whigs—not a drop of Chartist blood in their veins ... Your Synod of Glasgow ... one and all, humbugs ... if you bled them all to death, you would not squeeze out a drop of democratic blood.'[21]

The Chartist movement in Scotland soon split on the basic question of collaboration with the middle classes, for the same sorts of reasons that had impelled the unemployed of Paisley to side with their employers: the basic causes of destitution in the towns were often believed to be not the greed or exploitation of capitalists but external influences which threatened everyone in the community, capitalist and worker alike, with disaster. Of these external influences, the high price of corn was supposed, by the middle-class Whig-Liberal Anti-Corn Law League, to be the most serious, because a tariff on corn was alleged to hold down the demand for industrial goods while forcing up the cost of food. In a few parts of Britain (especially those dominated by large factory employers, like Lancashire) the Chartists utterly rejected this analysis. They proposed a much more class-conscious analysis, believing that the employers wanted cheap food only so that they could depress wages, and that only the achievement of democracy would cure the problem, by delivering control of the economy to the people. In Scotland, where the characteristic unit of production was still the very small family firm, some Chartist leaders were inclined to listen to the proponents of the Anti-Corn Law League, and to join with them in a bridge organization, the Complete Suffrage League. It was never a total conversion, but it caused fatal divisions in the camp. One English Chartist, touring Scotland in 1843, declared that in Edinburgh, as in Glasgow, 'faction has cut the throat of Chartism ... Leaders have been the curse of the cause ... traitors and deserters, still having the unblushing assurance to call themselves Chartists, are the worst enemies to the movement'.[22]

The repeal of the Corn Laws occurred in 1846. Two years later, severe depression returned, sharply but more briefly, to the industrial cities of Britain. 1848 was the Year of Revolutions in Europe, and the revival of Chartism that occurred at this point was fuelled both by foreign political example and by economic problems. Corn Law repeal had not acted as the instant panacea in reducing poverty and increasing employment which the middle-class Anti-Corn Law League had expected, and those moderate Chartist leaders who had shared this hope were discredited. The last heave of Scottish Chartism therefore seemed more desperate and extreme. The English leader Ernest Jones was applauded in the Waterloo Rooms in Edinburgh when he spoke of Chartism as 'a bread and cheese question', and called for 'a struggle against capital'. That struggle would not consist in the destruction of property or of capital, but in the rescuing of industry from its 'unconditional despotism'. In the west, in April, a crowd estimated at between 40,000 and 100,000 met for a demonstration on Glasgow Green, where six weeks before there had been serious riots of the unemployed during which several people had been shot by the police. There was talk of forming a Chartist National Guard, and steps were indeed taken to arm and enrol contingents in Edinburgh, Glasgow and Aberdeen, resulting in the arrest and trial of four local leaders on charges of sedition. But the excitement died away as fast as it had arisen: only 6–7000 bothered to come to the next demonstration on Glasgow Green on a beautiful day in June—as many as would be called forth 'on any occasion by a boat-race or a cricket match'. There were again splits in the leadership, again talk of the advantages of collaboration with the middle class rather than struggle against it, and the entire movement subsided finally into obscurity.[23]

Chartism, then, was not the menace it seemed to Cockburn when he spoke in that year of the 'shadow of the popular tree ... enlarging and darkening'. This was partly due to the deep structural and economic divisions within the working class, but also partly because of the peculiar nature of Scottish artisan culture. Workers had a strong and proud radical tradition, which we shall explore again in Chapter X, totally undeferential in its personal attitude to the ruling classes, but also reformist and rational. They were children of the eighteenth-century Enlightenment and still believed that inequality could and would be overthrown by moral pressure and by reason. This political culture was also affected by a strong and independent religious tradition expressed in widespread allegiance to the seceding churches and later the Free Church—an allegiance shared with many of the employing middle classes. The church connection reinforced their belief in moral rather than physical force, and encouraged them towards the private virtues of self-improvement and temperance rather than the public virtues of solidarity, towards class collaboration rather than class consciousness. Under these circumstances the workers posed much less of a threat to the ruling order than the rulers supposed.

One additional and final factor of great psychological importance in explaining why the upper classes lived in fear of insurrection and suffered from a sense of permanent crisis was physical—the fact of the city slum. The slum was new: poor housing had existed in Scotland for centuries, but never before as a ghetto, with such overcrowding, and on such a scale. Slums in the 1830s and 1840s grew quickly, like a cancer, in the centre of cities which people remembered as having been occupied by genteel people—like Glasgow's Saltmarket and Edinburgh's High Street. Though the middle classes had moved their homes away, they could not avoid contact with slum dwellers in most other aspects of their daily lives. The High Kirk of St Giles and Glasgow and Edinburgh Universities, for example, lay amidst some of the worst housing in Europe.

The reality of the slum was brought home to the public in 1842 by the *Reports on the Sanitary Condition of the Labouring Population of Scotland*, produced under the direction of Edwin Chadwick as a companion to the parallel reports on English towns and cities. In Scotland, the witnesses could not be as precise as in England, since the absence of civil registration until 1855 made it impossible to demonstrate the statistical connection between bad drainage and high mortality that Chadwick used to such devastating and conclusive effect in the south. The Scottish volume was, nevertheless, crowded with telling detail. 'What have you observed to be the general condition of the dwellings of the poorer class?', Dr Alexander Miller, a gynaecologist attached to the Royal Dispensary operating in the centre of Edinburgh, was asked by the investigators. He replied:

> The dwellings of the poor are generally very filthy ... Those of the lowest grade often consist only of one small apartment, always ill-ventilated, both from the nature of its construction and from the densely peopled and confined locality in which it is situated. Many of them, besides, are damp and partly underground ... A few of the lowest poor have a bedstead, but by far the larger portion have none; these make up a kind of bed on the floor with straw, on which a whole family are huddled together, some naked and the others in the same clothes they have worn during the day.[24]

Dr Miller's colleague, Dr Neil Arnott, visited the wynds of Glasgow with Edwin Chadwick himself, squeezing through passages and interlocking courtyards 'occupied entirely as a dung receptacle of the most disgusting kind'. Their inhabitants, 'worse off than wild animals which withdraw to a distance and conceal their ordure', actually hoarded their own dung to help pay the rent:

> The interiors of these houses and their inmates corresponded with the exteriors. We saw half-dressed wretches crowding together to be warm; and in one bed, although in the middle of the day, several women were imprisoned under a blanket, because as many others who had on their backs all the articles of dress that belonged to the party were then out of doors in the streets. This picture is so shocking that, without ocular proof, one would be disposed to doubt the possibility of the facts.[25]

There was nothing in these *Reports* that was sensationalized or stated merely for effect. There was nothing, indeed, that was not corroborated independently again and again by other observers, who were often astonished by the contrast between the horrors of the inner city and the more ordinary hardships of the countryside with which they were more familiar. 'I never knew what destitution was, among the poor in the country,' said one minister who had moved into Edinburgh, 'I never saw a case of destitution that I could not relieve before the sun went down; but here there are thousands of cases that you cannot relieve.'[26]

The very real alarm middle-class people felt when confronted with the slums also extended to all the working-class people who had to live in them, and their fear made them generally unable to see the true nature and remarkable dignity of the majority of the working class even in the most beastly surroundings, so that they readily confused the criminality of some of the poorest with a general political danger to society. Those who came into professional contact with the slum-dwellers—ministers, doctors, poor-law officials—could soon differentiate, but they assumed that the values of the respectable working man would be easily swamped in the deepening morass by the values of the criminal, and conceived that they had a political and social duty to bring help. They must pull the redeemable working man out before it was too late—with better housing, cleaner streets, better schools—and give him better habits and more deferential and orthodox views (for, to them, the idea that a Chartist could be a respectable man was a contradiction in terms). Thus the idea was born that, in one way or another, the urban working classes needed 'social welfare', and that it was necessary for the middle classes to give it. How it was to be provided gave rise to immense controversies about costs, methods and implications which continued throughout the 1840s and well beyond.

To sum up, Cockburn's description of Scotland as a vessel crowded with passengers who ate one another was no bad image: life in Scotland in the 1840s was competitive, unprotected, brutal and, for many, vile. He was right in his prophecies that the coming century would see changes unimaginable to those who, like himself, had hoped to stop the clock in 1832. The Tiger of Change was loose, and society was riding it. But the threat to property was further off than most of his contemporaries believed. Scotland and Britain were not at the point of incandescence, and the story of that coming century is, to no small degree, the story of how the men of Cockburn's class contrived, for better or for worse, that it never should become so.

CHAPTER II

The Tenement City

1

Despite the fixations of the moralists and the politicians on the problem of the slum and the slum–dweller, Scotland in the 1840s was not yet predominantly a country of townsmen: just under a third of the people lived in settlements of 5000 or more. In the next century, however, the situation was dramatically reversed. By 1951, two-thirds of the population lived in towns of 5000 or more; the proportion of those living in large towns of over 50,000 inhabitants had risen from 23 per cent to 42 per cent, and of those living in the largest of all, Glasgow, from 10 per cent to 21 per cent. The town and the city assumed an importance quite unprecedented in Scotland's earlier history.

In the architectural sense, the Scottish city often had dignity and distinction. The capital was admired by expectant visitors tuned to the world of Sir Walter Scott. 'The antique grandeur of the Old Town and the subdued cold classical beauty of the New Town of Edinburgh constitute an aspect *sui generis* so striking and picturesque that we have nothing to compare it with,' said the London *Builder* in 1861, quoting Charlotte Brontë: 'Whoever have once seen Edinburgh, with its *couchant* crag-lion, will see it again in their dreams.'[1] From 'the antique grandeur' the Victorians ultimately subtracted most of the genuine if insanitary ancient dwellings and replaced them by the baronial pastiche of the modern Royal Mile. They added a few notable public buildings, like New College and the McEwan Hall, an array of church spires glorifying sectarian fortunes, flamboyant private schools like Fettes and Daniel Stewart's in the suburbs, and miles of turretage in the middle-class tenements and villas of Marchmont and Morningside. Glasgow, for her part, embarked upon a total reconstruction of her business centre as she grew, along with stately City Chambers, three fine railway termini and appropriate shops and offices. In 'Greek' Thomson's churches and tenements, Charles Rennie Mackintosh's School of Art, and Charles Wilson's towers and terraces on Woodland's Hill, Glasgow found architecture of great originality produced by local talent, and when the time came to rebuild the university, Giles Gilbert Scott threw down a mighty pile of French Gothic on Gilmorehill. Add to that the great monuments of municipal culture, the People's Palace on Glasgow Green, the Kibble Palace in the Botanic Gardens, and the Kelvingrove Art Gallery, and the city possessed by 1914 as fine a clutch of public buildings as any in the land. Aberdeen had her distinctions, too, in Union Street, and Dundee (otherwise a mean city) round the Caird Hall. Even much smaller towns often ran to the grand if austere style, like Rutherglen with its castellated town hall, Hawick with its spired municipal clock-tower and Oban with its hotels along the front. Little was added and little taken away between the end of the Edwardian era and 1950, though ten years of war and twenty of depression added a dilapidation which mid-twentieth-century visitors found unappealing: 'Our hearts sank at the grimness of the towns,' said Simone de Beauvoir of herself and Jean-Paul Sartre on their visit to Scotland in the austere days after the Second World War.[2]

The true grimness of the Scottish town, however, was concealed from the tourist round of monuments and shopping centres, and was revealed only in the patient statistics of the Registrar-General: it lay in the ordinary standard of working-class housing—not in the exceptional slum, though that was bad enough, but in the type of house within the tall, grim, blackened tenement blocks that the average working citizen normally inhabited. The first census to deal with the problem was that of 1861. It demonstrated that 34 per cent of all Scottish houses had only one room: 37 per cent had two rooms: 1 per cent of families lived in houses without any windows: 64 per cent of the entire population lived in one- or two-roomed houses. The 'but-and-ben' and the 'single end' were, in fact, the normal environment in which to bring up a family. In 1886, in Glasgow, a third of families lived in one room:

In some rooms may be found a superfluity of articles—old beds, tables, chairs, boxes, pots, and dishes, with little regard to order or cleanliness. In others, a shakedown in the corner, a box or barrel for a table, a broken stool, an old pot or pan, with a few dishes. In many rooms, no furniture at all; and the whole family, including men, women and children, huddled together at night on such straw or rags as they can gather.[3]

As many commentators were at pains to say, a house of one room (and even a house of two rooms) made domestic life as it was known to the middle classes impossible. There was no privacy, no play space, no work space, no place to get out of the tensions of family life, to think, relax, or sulk. There was not even space to die. As Dr J. B. Russell, the great Medical Officer of Health for Glasgow, said of the children whose deaths were so numerous in this vile environment:

> Their little bodies are laid on a table or on a dresser so as to be some-what out of the way of their brothers and sisters, who play and sleep and eat in their ghastly company. From beginning to rapid-ending the lives of these children are short ... One in every five of all who are born there never see the end of their first year.[4]

The average size of the one-roomed house in Edinburgh in 1861 was approximately 14 feet by 11.5 feet. This did not always prevent the householders taking in lodgers: in the same city ten years later, almost one family in ten in the one-roomed house, and one in five in the two-roomed house, had a lodger, which 'raised very gross problems'.[5]

The situation improved only very slowly. The house without windows had all but gone by 1881. The proportion of houses of only one room had sunk to 13 per cent by 1911, when they provided room for only 9 per cent of the population: but even at that date another 41 per cent of the population lived in houses of two rooms, so that altogether, on the eve of the First World War, half of the total population still lived in houses of one or two rooms. In Glasgow that proportion was still two-thirds. Nor was the situation due to the stubborn survival of old housing stock. Clydebank, for instance, was a small village of 816 inhabitants in 1871 and a brand new town of 30,000 by 1901: ten years later, four-fifths of its houses were of two rooms or less. In Glasgow, between 1862 and 1901, about 18 per cent of all new houses were one-roomed, and 48 per cent were two-roomed. Only with the housing legislation of the 1920s and 1930s was any considerable inroad made

The laird relaxing: an upper-class interior of the late nineteenth century.

Highland housing: ABOVE a home on South Uist about 1885;
BELOW Dunrobin Castle, home of the Dukes of Sutherland.

Lifestyles: ABOVE sportsmen's picnic, Central Highlands, c. 1880; BELOW old couple in Dundee Ovegate, 1929.

Girl in a Glasgow tenement, late 1890s; poverty and its trimmings.

LEFT Girl on a country holiday, c. 1880; wealth and its trimmings.

The Provost of Rutherglen and his lady, c. 1900.

RIGHT A Glasgow couple outside their tenement, c. 1948.

A couple, probably in their forties,
grinding and winnowing grain on Skye, 1885.

into the problem, and even then only in relative terms. By 1951, the proportion of the Scottish population living in one- or two-roomed houses had fallen to a quarter (with only 3.5 per cent left in the one-roomed house): another 31 per cent lived, by then, in three-roomed houses, and a further 25 per cent in four-roomed houses. Less than a fifth, as late as 1951, lived in anything larger than a four-roomed house: the proportion so housed—surely the minimum that could be called well housed—was almost the same as it had been ninety years earlier.

The situation was the more extraordinary by contrast with England, which also correctly regarded itself as having a serious housing problem. In 1911, when half the Scots lived in one- or two-roomed houses, the proportion in England and Wales was 7 per cent; in 1951, when a quarter lived in such houses in Scotland, the proportion in the south was 2.6 per cent. In Glasgow in 1951, the proportion of one- or two-roomed houses was still 50 per cent; in London it was 5.5 per cent. Or, to take the measure of overcrowding devised by the LCC in 1891 of two or more people to a room, one-third of London's population fell into that category, but two-thirds of Glasgow's. The Royal Commission on Housing in Scotland of 1917 disclosed 'an almost unbelievable density':

> There were more than four persons per room in 10.9 per cent of Glasgow's houses, over three persons in 27.9 per cent, and over two in 55.7 per cent, the figures for corresponding English cities were 0.8 per cent, 1.5 per cent and 9.4 per cent.[6]

As late as 1951, again, 15.5 per cent of Scots were still overcrowded at more than two to a room, compared to only 2.1 per cent of English people. To say that the Scottish housing problem was of a different order of magnitude from the English is only the literal truth.

The question therefore arises, how did this situation come about and why was it allowed to persist? There have been innumerable explanations of how the characteristic crowded, high-built stone tenement originated, ranging from the necessity to huddle within a walled town for defence in the unsettled centuries to notions that a French influence gave the Scots a predilection for living high. They are not very convincing when applied to the Victorian age. The ecological and economic arguments, though, may have considerable force. The Scots were a very much poorer people than the English in the late eighteenth and early and middle nineteenth centuries, when the patterns of urban development were established, and could only afford lower rents and fuel costs. To live in one or two rooms in highly overcrowded and ill-ventilated conditions meant substantial savings in heating and lighting in a cold, dark country, especially in stone-built tenements where the contiguous houses (or 'flats' in English parlance) kept each other warm with a minimum of outside walls.

It has also been argued that the Scots have been unwilling historically to spend so high a proportion of their family income on housing as their southern neighbours and most Europeans. Certainly in 1937–8, the household budgets collected by the Ministry of Labour showed Scots spending 8s. 2d. a week on rent and rates compares to 10s. 2d. in England and Wales—9.1 per cent compared to 12.7 per cent of total household expenditure.

Baird in 1954 claimed that in 1911, about 8 per cent of family income went on rent in Scotland compared to 10 per cent in England and Wales, but this depended on a rather optimistic view of equality in disposable income between the working classes of the two countries, which Rodgers has recently challenged. If, as the latter suggests, real wages in Scottish burghs were 13 per cent below those of London and 10–12 per cent below those of the major English industrial districts, but average rent per foot of floor space was 10 per cent higher in Scottish cities than in English, the Scots would not come out of the comparison spending much less on housing than the English.[7]

Nevertheless, since the First World War, the Scots do seem to have spent less on housing than the English, and a general survey of the nineteenth century certainly suggests that the Scots did not put a high premium on trying to secure good housing for themselves. Of course, if a population becomes accustomed to living in small, poor-quality homes (whether as private tenants or, in the interwar years, as council tenants), it may seem a disproportionate sacrifice of other goods to spend more on larger homes—though this does not explain why others have been more willing than the Scots to improve their housing expectations from low levels. However, the Scots, unlike the English, had no nineteenth-century poor law that would, in an emergency, tide an able-bodied man over by outdoor relief during a spell of unemployment. It was therefore more necessary for the Scottish worker to save and to have the smallest possible fixed outgoing payments, to ward off disaster during the inevitable periods without work that affected even skilled men during the downturn of the trade cycle.

To these factors should be added the effect of the Scottish feuing system. In England, houses were constructed by speculative builders on land either sold outright or obtained on long leases. In the south, in the first instance, the landlord selling would demand the highest price and the builder might indeed recoup his heavy initial outlay by building as densely as possible, on the principle that a larger number of poor tenants would provide a bigger sum in rent than a small number of slightly richer ones. In the second instance, the landowner, with an eye to the long-term betterment of the estate on the resumption of the lease, might impose restrictive clauses that would prevent their deterioration into slum property. In Scotland, building land was alienated for ever in exchange for a down payment and an annual feu duty. It was naturally in the interest of the seller to get as large a sum in down payment as he could, just as in the sale of an English freehold; in addition he fixed the annual duty as high as possible; having no possibility of resuming possession, he had no interest in restrictive clauses on building densities in the feus. The builder had little choice but to maximize returns on the land rapidly, since he had to meet not merely interest on money borrowed for the down payment but also a heavy feu payable whether there were houses there or not. In working-class areas this meant as many small houses as possible going up in a tenement as quickly as possible.

Further pressures were built up by the practice of 'subinfeudation', by which a wealthy developer would speculate on the edge of an expanding area, paying a feu-duty himself but then charging others a higher one for permission to build: as the Edinburgh Dean of Guild, James Gowans, himself a builder, explained in 1885, 'A builder ... takes up a lot of land from the superior at £50 an acre, and then by re-feuing or building himself he works it up to £200 an acre. This has been done within this city and large fortunes have been made out of it.' One such fortune was made by Sir James Steel, who bought land at Dalry, the West End, and Comely Bank at the edges of a growing Edinburgh between 1866 and 1894 and became, in due course, Lord Provost and the city's largest ratepayer. He could afford that privilege on a yearly income which, he told a government enquiry, was about £80,000: 'He was informed it was not his capital they wished to know but he reiterated that this was his income.'[8]

It was not, however, very rich men who actually built most of the houses. That was normally done by small capitalists who constructed one or two houses on feus purchased from developers like Steel: only 17 per cent of house-building projects in Scottish burghs between 1873 and 1914 involved three houses or more.[9] The finance for this type of construction was provided by the builder taking out bonds (or loans), payable over a fifteen-year period and yielding 4.5–5 per cent interest: in the 1870s, that was about 1 per cent above the current rate of interest on government stock and attracted investment from trust funds managed by accountants and lawyers who put together little bundles of capital originating from small businessmen, professional people, and their widows. Such bonds could be recalled at three months notice and their interest rate could be varied, which both created great instability in the market and gave the borrower an incentive to complete as fast as possible and sell his tenement off to a new owner. These, too, were very often 'people of moderate means', merchants, craftsmen, retailers and small businessmen of all sorts, who wished a safe investment to provide for themselves and their families in times to come. Sometimes the buyers lived close at hand: sometimes not. Elliott and McCrone cite the example of Graham Street on the expanding northern edge of Edinburgh, where a slightly more prosperous working class was being rehoused at the end of the nineteenth century:

Numbers 1 and 5 were sold by the bondholder in possession (the builder going bankrupt) to a land factor in Argyllshire. This factor appears to have raised bonds mainly from religious acquaintances, £1200 and £1400 being borrowed from Free Church ministers. Numbers 4 and 16 Graham Street were owned by Glen, the musical instrument maker, numbers 6 and 8 by the Beattie family, number 11 by a Leith timber merchant, numbers 13 and 15 by a painter and decorator, number 17 by a clothier, and number 19 by a Free Church minister of Blairgowrie in Perthshire.[10]

The conclusion to be drawn from all this is that an enormous number of middle-class people were involved in making a profit from the construction and ownership of the workers' one- and two-roomed houses, ranging from the wealthiest of land speculators, through the solid divisions of the accountants and lawyers, down to the great mass of the petite bourgeoisie—the Free Church clergy and employer crafts-men who were themselves perhaps just a generation and an income bracket removed from those they housed and whose rents they drew.

It needs to be emphasized that the workers did not love their ten-ements, or live there because they could imagine or desire nothing better. On the contrary, there is much evidence (at least in the twen-tieth century) of their deep resentment at being trapped in the claustro-phobic and often verminous dwellings. According to one oral testimony, the first thing that a Glasgow housewife did on moving into a newly rented house was to go round both rooms with a red-hot knit-ting needle killing the bed-bugs and cockroaches that lived in the cracks in the floor, the walls, behind the range and the fireplace, and in the joints of the fixed box-beds that made up most of the furniture.

The rise of the Independent Labour Party (ILP) in Glasgow was closely connected with John Wheatley's campaign for good houses, which, in turn, seems to have been based on an idea of an immigrant English engineer, John Burgess, who believed that Scottish councils should build English-type cottage homes for the workers and had pre-sented evidence to that effect to the 1903 Glasgow Municipal Housing Commission. The Royal Commission on Housing in Scotland, report-ing in 1917, heard evidence to the effect that only 'for want of a better choice' did the working classes willingly remain in tenements: 'Scottish people who have lived in tenements in Scotland and taken to the cot-tage system in England ... were unanimous in their praise of the cot-tage and condemnation of the tenements.'[11]

The first government-assisted council houses built in the city after the First World War were obviously influenced by this model, though an improved version of the traditional tenement continued to be built by councils because it was cheap. It was, however, still not preferred. Brennan, writing of Glasgow in 1959, found that most people wanted a house with its own front door and, if possible, a bungalow, 'that is, a house as unlike a tenement flat as possible'[12] Whether it was ever prac-ticable in Scotland to build this kind of house in the public sector on a large scale is another matter. Everyone is familiar with the characteristic compromise: the expanse of detached, grey-harled council blocks, three or four floors high, which occur on whatever land the local au-thority could buy on the edge of the existing built-up area between the 1920s and the 1950s. Only by contrast with what they replaced, and with what followed them when councils were persuaded by architectural 'experts' to build the disastrous tower blocks of the 1960s, could they be considered desirable residences.

2

In the 1830s and 1840s, as we have seen, the city-as-slum seemed to be turning into an incontrollable juggernaut, crushing the life of multitudes beneath its path of growth and exploitation. The sense of urban crisis was fuelled by the outbreaks in 1832, 1848 and 1853 of cholera, the terrible new disease from the East, and the more familiar typhus epidemics of 1837 and 1847. It was confirmed by Edwin Chadwick's *Report on the Sanitary Condition of Great Britain* in 1842 and W. P. Alison's *Observations on the Management of the Poor in Scotland* in 1840. The Chartist disturbances of the same years added to the sense that Armageddon might be round the next bend.

In the middle decades of the nineteenth century, as in the 1840s, the Scottish city continued to be recognized by public opinion as a crying scandal of poverty, bad housing and ill-health. As the *Builder* of 1861 said of Edinburgh, every visitor will carry away two impressions, 'a sense of its extraordinary beauty and a horror of its unspeakable filth':

> We devoutly believe that no smell in Europe or Asia—not in Aleppo or Damascus in the present day—can equal in depth and intensity, in concentration and power, the diabolical combination of sulphurated hydrogen we came upon one evening about ten o'clock in a place called Toddrick's Wynd.[13]

Comments of this nature can be found from all quarters. The visiting Danish poet and storyteller, Hans Christian Andersen, found Edinburgh a city of need and despair, as bad as his experience of the worst Italian city.[14] The reporter for the West of Scotland Handloom Weavers Commission said of Glasgow:

> I have seen human degradation in some of its worst phases, both in England and abroad, but I can advisedly say that I did not believe until I visited the wynds of Glasgow that so large an amount of filth, crime, misery and disease existed in one spot in any civilised country.[15]

The middle-class response to this crisis over the second half of the

nineteenth century, though slow and unsteady, was certainly not negligible. The problems, after all, were enormous, and urban growth did
not stand still to be caught and tamed. Glasgow's population between
1841 and 1911 grew from 275,000 to 784,000—nearly a three-fold increase. Edinburgh and Leith over the same period grew from 164,000
to 401,000—much more than a doubling. Aberdeen grew from 65,000
to 164,000, and Dundee from 60,000 to 165,000—a similar rate to Edinburgh. Some small places grew very much faster, especially immediately downstream from Glasgow. Partick and Govan grew by almost
three and four times respectively between 1871 and 1911, and had they
been included within the city boundary would have pushed Glasgow's
population up to around one million.

Furthermore, the administrative machinery for governing the cities
was initially very imperfect, resting on the burgh reform statutes of
1833, which empowered the £10 householders (effectively the middle
class) to elect councils, and in addition allowed them to bypass (but not
supplant) existing councils by adopting a parallel 'police system',
whereby elected magistrates and commissioners of police were given
powers to raise rates for lighting, cleansing, water supply, draining, and
so forth. All the cities and most large burghs worked under their own
'Police Acts', and in 1862 Lindsay's Burgh Police Act enabled communities of no more than 700 inhabitants to make building and sanitary
laws of their own, though it remained 'nobody's official business, until
the nineties, to make sure either that the by-laws which were needed
were made, or that, having been made, they were enforced'.[16] Not
until the Burgh Police (Scotland) Act of 1892 and the Public Health
(Scotland) Act of 1897 was it obligatory to make sanitary and building
by-laws and establish machinery to enforce them. The favourite form
of machinery in respect of building regulations was the revived Dean of
Guild Court. These ancient bodies had been effective in control of
urban development until the middle of the eighteenth century, when
they had gradually fallen into disuse just as the industrial revolution and
concomitant rapid urbanization made their powers most necessary:
there were only 18 left (but those in the largest burghs) by 1868. Under
the stimulation of Lindsay's Act, but still more from the 1892 Act, they
revived in numbers and potency: there were 20 in 1880, 106 in 1898,
189 by 1912. The revived Dean of Guild Courts often took as their
model Glasgow's 'noted and vigorous' court, which imposed high
standards for such things as wall thickness, window size and building

materials: this made a four-storey building in Glasgow 45 per cent more costly than one in London, and, whatever the gain in solidity of construction, inevitably increased the rents of new property for the working class.[17]

In other respects local government was particularly imperfect and muddled in the middle decades of the century. In 1845, the belated reform of the Scottish Poor Law created a Central Board of Supervision and a multiplicity of parochial boards. The former took on the duties of a kind of central sanitary office (though with very feeble powers): the latter had a paid inspectorate that became loaded with all kinds of extra responsibilities—for example, for enforcing vaccination against small-pox in 1855 and dealing with lunatics in 1857. Similarly, there were extended powers for the old, appointed, Commissioners of Supply in the shires, who were given control over county police when they became obligatory in 1856-7, and joined with burgh magistrates in various *ad hoc* bodies, such as district boards of control over lunacy in 1856 and the prison commissioners in 1877. Order was ultimately reimposed at the end of the century, when a series of acts set up popularly elected County Councils to replace the Commissioners of Supply (1889), replaced the Board of Supervision by a more authoritative local government board (1894), and, in town government proper, ended the system of dual responsibility between police magistrates and town magistrates (1892). The coping stone was placed on the process in 1900 when the Town Council (Scotland) Act insisted on uniform constitutions in all burghs, under provost, baillies and elected councillors.[18] Only in the 1890s, in fact, was the framework of local government—and therefore the means of sanitary and housing reform—made uniform and reasonably effective throughout the country. By then, Scotland had fallen a long way behind England, especially in the small towns where the cause of public health had lacked a spur either from civic energy or from a vigilant central authority and where 'only the close proximity of the countryside sometimes made insanitary horrors less horrific'.[19]

The situation was made even more complicated and unsatisfactory by the fact that such laws as mid-Victorian Westminster did make to help to solve problems of urban squalor were often framed in a manner inappropriate for Scotland. Thus the 1866 Sanitary Act was unenforceable in Scotland because those who chose to ignore it could only be sued in the English court of Queen's Bench, whose writ did not, of course, run north of the Border. Similarly the first statutes designed to encourage good quality working-class housing, the so-called Torrens Acts of 1868, 1879 and 1882, were 'practically a dead letter' in Scotland. It is a testimony both to the laziness of London administrations in dealing with Scottish problems and, equally, to the resentment of Scottish local authorities at being ordered about by central government that, once discovered, such anomalies were left unaltered for many years. Again, it was mainly in the last dozen years of the century that these disparities and absurdities were finally cleared up.

In these circumstances, any serious attempts to tackle the urban crisis had to come from energetic councillors using their own powers. Glasgow, with the worst problems, found energy and civic spirit to attempt the most basic solutions—summed up in the contemporary phrase 'municipal socialism', though it was initiated by Liberals and Tories and not by any description of socialist.

The first scheme to catch the public imagination was the Glasgow Corporation Water Works Act of 1855, when for the first time in British history a city hitherto drinking from vile and disease-ridden wells planned to bring fresh water from a country reservoir—Loch Katrine in the Trossachs. It had its opponents, both on the grounds of its unprecedented cost—some £1.5 million—and because some experts were not convinced of its public health benefits. Professor Penney of the Andersonian Institute earned the obloquy of reformers by claiming the water was 'so pure as to act on the lead pipes and poison our people':[20] his evidence was over-ruled, and the hazards to which he correctly drew attention were not rediscovered until the 1970s. The scheme went ahead, and in 1859 Queen Victoria opened the new municipal supply: 50 million gallons of water coursed daily along 35 miles of a great monument to Victorian engineering skills: 13 miles of tunnelling and 'twenty-five important iron and masonry aqueducts over rivers and ravines, some 60 and 80 feet in height, with arches of 30 feet, 50 and 90 feet in span'.[21]

The immediate benefit to health from this great undertaking outweighed the long-term hidden danger of lead poisoning: when cholera returned in 1865–6, only 53 people died in Glasgow out of 400 Scottish victims, though in the previous (and more severe) epidemic it had suffered 4000 fatalities out of a Scottish total of about 6000. The small Fife burgh of Methil lost 63 of her inhabitants in the 1866 cholera outbreak, equivalent to 15 per cent of the total population, which was sufficient indication of the peril that Glasgow escaped. Other towns followed Glasgow's example, Edinburgh obtaining water from St Mary's Loch in the Borders and Dundee ultimately from the Loch of Lintrathen in upland Angus. In the smallest burghs there was often a fierce struggle between those willing to pay for pure water flowing down from a hill reservoir and those who believed it would be sufficient (and much cheaper) to pump it up from the nearest, if generally polluted, river: in Selkirk the town was so divided in a council election contest between the 'Pumpers' and the 'Gravitationalists' that the annual rite of the Common Riding had temporarily to be abandoned. Many small villages and towns long remained in the condition of Lochgelly on the Fife coal-field, where Henry Littlejohn reported in 1867 that there were two WCs for a population of nearly 2000 people, whose sewage was therefore thrown on the surface. Much of it inevitably found its way back into the Mine Well, from which almost everyone drew their drinking water: the supply was, in his words, 'so tainted as actually to predispose to choleraic attacks'.[22]

From the effective provision of decent water, Glasgow branched out in many directions. In 1863 (one year behind Edinburgh), she appointed her first Medical Officer of Health to keep a watching brief on the public health of the city: from 1872 to 1898, the post was held by J. B. Russell, who did more than any man of his age to bring home to the ignorant and complacent the horrible realities of slum disease, the menace of polluted rivers and the evils of insanitary private slaughter-houses. In 1862, the corporation obtained powers to 'ticket' houses, i.e. to fix metal plates to the walls of houses of a certain size indicating how many people were allowed to sleep there, accompanying this by per-emptory powers of police search if overcrowding was suspected. About one in seven of the population lived in ticketed houses by the 1880s. In 1866, the City Improvement Trust was established to carry on the systematic destruction of slum property (which had already begun in an unplanned way when the railway companies cut their way through some of the worst rookeries in Glasgow to build their ter-mini). By 1885, some 30,000 people had been evicted and their homes destroyed, but little was done by the city to rehouse them. Even after 1888, when the corporation became involved in building and owning property on municipal account, the actual number built was very small—2199 houses by 1914, plus 78 model lodging houses (the first dating from the 1870s), housing little more than 2 per cent of the population. It was at least a precedent for the future that the local authority admitted some responsibility for housing the poor among them.[23]

The tradition of public ownership of utilities in Glasgow was extended from the Loch Katrine scheme to the municipalization of the gas supply in 1867, by which the corporation halved the price at which gas had been previously supplied by the private companies, committed itself to the public lighting of courts and tenements, and connected more households to the mains than any other city in the world. In the 1870s the city built the tramlines, and in 1894 took over their management and ran them at a handsome profit. In 1869 the city's first municipal fever hospital was built, with facilities for disinfecting patients' clothes: the concern with cleanliness extended to the provision of public baths and wash-houses from 1878, as well as a municipal laundry service by 1884, providing services for 'all classes of society'. Nor did public ownership stop there. Its ramifications by the opening of the twentieth century were described by one commentator thus:

> [In Glasgow a citizen] may live in a municipal house; he may walk along the municipal street, or ride on the municipal tramcar and watch the municipal dust cart collecting the refuse which is to be used to fertilise the municipal farm. Then he may turn into the municipal market, buy a steak from an animal killed in the municipal slaughterhouse, and cook it by the municipal gas stove. For his recreation he can choose amongst municipal libraries, municipal art galleries and municipal music in municipal parks. Should he fall ill, he can ring up his doctor on the municipal telephone, or he may be taken to the municipal hospital in the municipal ambulance by a municipal policeman. Should he be so unfortunate as to get on fire, he will be put out by a municipal fireman, using municipal water; after which he will, perhaps, forego the enjoyment of a municipal bath, though he may find it necessary to get a new suit in the municipal old clothes market.[24]

Glasgow's municipalization was indeed by then the most extensive in Britain, and it served as an inspiration to other Scottish cities, especially Edinburgh and Dundee. Scottish services of this kind differed from those in England in that municipal enterprises were not expected to make a profit or to subsidize the rates: they were simply expected to make specific services cheaper and better for the citizens.

From time to time, these ventures by the municipality provoked a backlash from ratepayers. Lord Provost John Blackie lost his seat on Glasgow Council in 1867 due to anger at the cost of the Improvement Trust's slum clearance schemes, and a more sustained attack on municipal house-building plans not only unseated Lord Provost Samuel Chisholm in 1902, but brought to a halt all further efforts to extend municipalization. By then a new ideological and party note was entering city affairs. While extension of municipal services had originally been agreed to by a non-political consensus of middle-class opinion, fired by a combination of civic pride and exasperation at the inefficiency of private enterprise, by 1900 municipalization was being plugged by the advanced Liberal and Labour 'stalwarts' as desirable in itself, and angrily opposed by Liberal Unionists and Conservatives as a creeping disease. Opposition was, however, mainly in the spirit of 'enough is enough': nobody was partisan enough to propose privatizing the water, the gas, the trams, the museums or the rubbish disposal services.

3

The success or otherwise of the Victorian corporation in solving or averting the urban crisis that loomed so threateningly in the 1840s can only be judged in terms of what it saw that crisis to be. In part, it was seen as a problem of human suffering, as in this discussion of the Edinburgh slum by a local physician, George Bell:

> What can we do? We return day after day, and night after night, to the scenes of misery, disease and death. We listen to the cry of children, the wail of women, and the deep utterances of men. This awful harmony is in keeping with the picture before us. The pathos of the drama is profound. What can we do? Can we feed the children, comfort the women, and impart hope to the men?[25]

But what was pathetic was also seen to be a menace. What he calls 'the substratum of society in Edinburgh' contained within it 'what is technically called the pauper class ... They are almost, if not quite as wretched; they are as base, taken as a whole; and they are equally dangerous to the country, in every sense of the term.'[26] Therefore an important aspect of policy must be to contain and avert the danger from an uncontrolled and unsocialized class, often identified as being synonymous with the poor immigrant Irish. A third argument was that the economy could not afford the waste of human resources culled incessantly by a great insanitary city. It was eloquently put by Edwin Chadwick in his presidential address to the Social Sciences Association in Glasgow in 1860:

> The primary qualities of those hands whom we are accustomed to call Anglo-Saxon ... which include the Lowland Scot as well as the English, are, as I have elsewhere stated, great bodily strength, applied under the command of a steady, persevering will, mental self-containedness, and impassibility [sic] to external irrelevant impressions, or to distractive pleasurable excitement, that carries them through the continuous repetition of toilsome labour—'steady as time'.[27]

Such men were valuable: two Britons, he said, could do as much work as three modern Norwegians or Danes (and infinitely more than lesser races) so 'it behoves all civic communities to take measures to arrest the insanitary conditions which annually slaughter full two hundred thousand persons by preventible disease'. He suggested that a contractor could, in return for a rate of a penny a week, reduce the Glasgow death rate by at least a third. It was also necessary to ensure that those who did survive in the towns were not maimed and demoralized by their existence there, but were raised to be as capable of work, as 'steady', as those born in the countryside.

Of the three objectives, the destruction of moral and social dangers received the closest attention and achieved the greatest relative success. Hence the priority given to destroying slums rather than building new homes for the inhabitants. In Edinburgh, reported the *Builder* in 1861, nothing had been done for rehousing, but 'Lord Cockburn Street has absolutely ploughed into the vitals of the ancient and gigantic piles of buildings'.[28] The same was true in the next phase of development, which cleared the offensive slums round Chambers Street to make room for the Royal Scottish Museum and the Heriot Watt Institute. In Glasgow the work of the City Improvement Trust was applauded in 1877 as having swept out 'a moral sewer of a most loathsome description, crowded with a population showing by its physique the extent to which the human form divine could be degraded by drunkenness and every attendant form of vice and profligacy'.[29] To cleanse the Augean stables was regarded as much more important than attending to what happened to its inhabitants after the dispersal.

It was nevertheless vital to be able to control the poor, especially as the slums tended to form again in a nearby locality, just as overcrowded as before, whenever an old rookery was pulled down. One way was by the introduction of an effective police force to obviate calling out the military whenever there was a minor disturbance, as when the 79th Regiment of Foot had to be summoned from Edinburgh Castle in 1838 to put down a snowball riot between the university students and a 'mob'. Disciplined and adequate police forces were slowly assembled in every city, though they had their problems. In Edinburgh in the late 1840s, a quarter of the police were dismissed from the force each year for misconduct of one sort or another, and 63 per cent were reported drunk on duty; by the late 1860s the proportion sacked had fallen to under 10 per cent and the proportion drunk to 23 per cent, which was progress.[30] Fear of the mob getting out of hand remained— as late as 1892, the Lord Provost of Glasgow wrote to the Government asking for a regiment of cavalry to be stationed at Maryhill lest there was a riot of the unemployed.[31] By then, however, the crime problem had become easier to contain. Though fear of socialism had replaced fear of Chartism, the anxiety that urban civilization might be suddenly overwhelmed by anarchy welling up from below, so prevalent in the 1840s, had certainly disappeared.

The crime rate fell in the half century before the First World War, though problems remained. The Penny Mob gang of the East End of Glasgow ruled the streets in the 1890s, levying blackmail on the local shopkeepers to pay the fines they incurred as a result of their love of fighting. They were replaced in public infamy by the San Toy Boys of the 1900s, the Redskins and Kelly Boys, who fought with knuckledusters, before the First World War, and the Bridgeton Billy Boys, the worst of the razor gangs of the interwar years. Sectarian and ethnic differences fanned the flames of gang warfare—the Billy Boys were an anti-Catholic gang ready on the fringes of Orange marches and outside the Ibrox Stadium, where Rangers played. A Jewish doctor, recalling a Gorbals childhood in the 1930s, remembers the terror of the challenge, 'Are you a Billy or a Dan or an Old Tin Can?' The third epithet was reserved for the Jews, who were beaten up by both sides.[32] Such mindless violence was bad enough, but as it stayed in and around the slums and did not threaten the wider social order, it was not regarded by authority with much alarm.

Police powers within Scottish towns were extensive, even draconian:

the system of ticketed houses allowed the police to search working-class homes without a warrant, which had more uses than simply checking upon overcrowding. In one year in Glasgow, 55,000 'night inspections' revealed only 7000 houses breaking the overcrowding law, about 13 per cent of those investigated.[33] The rap of authority at midnight curbed and harassed a working-class population, largely Irish, in the dangerous ghettos of the old city centre. The same spirit of discipline tempering welfare determined the treatment of the destitute under the Scottish poor law. Thus the rules of the Glasgow poor-house laid down that 'All the inmates ... shall rise, be set to work, leave off work, and go to bed at such times, and shall be allowed such intervals for their meals as the House-Committee shall direct—and these several times shall be notified by the ringing of a bell.'[34] Similarly, 'morality, sobriety, cleanliness, order, and discipline' were the keynotes of organization in Glasgow corporation lodging houses, where a drill-sergeant from the Third Argyll Rifles was appointed Superintendent in 1878: 'Free Bibles and regular Sunday religious services added a tinge of religion to this panoply of para-military power.' By such means it was intended to inculcate into slum labour those qualities Chadwick had deemed essential to the Anglo-Saxon workman.

The objective of conserving life enjoyed a more limited measure of success, but nevertheless a distinct one. The crude annual death rate in Glasgow reached a dreadful peak of 40 per 1000 inhabitants in the typhus and cholera quinquennium, 1845–9, then fell by degrees to 21 per 1000 in 1901. For Scotland as a whole there are no statistics before 1855, but a fall from 22.3 per 1000 in 1871 to 17.9 per 1000 in 1901 was in line with the experience of the rest of Britain. Most of the fall before 1900 was due to a reduction in deaths from tuberculosis (which remained, however, a very major killer, still accounting for 13 per cent of all deaths in the 1890s), along with the typhus group of diseases and scarlet fever and diphtheria. Cholera, which had seemed most clearly to frighten the middle classes, was extinguished. Otherwise it was the typhus group which was the clearest marker of bad sanitary conditions, accounting for 5 per cent of deaths in Scotland in the 1860s but only 1 per cent by the 1890s. Interestingly, from the 1870s there were relatively fewer deaths from the typhus group in the big cities than in the smaller towns like Motherwell or Port Glasgow, where as late as 1900, in the absence of civic energy and a sanitary crusade, the horrors of the contaminated environment were little changed over five decades.

On the other hand by 1900 there had been virtually no reduction in the infant mortality rate, though among reformers of the early Victorian period it was the appalling waste of life among the young that had called most 'loudly to our leading men' to take measures against 'the unhappy condition of the dwellings' and to dissipate the diseases 'which, courted, entertained and fostered, have, from time to time, carried off thousands upon thousands'.[35] The Scottish infant mortality rate (i.e. the annual average number of deaths under the age of one per 1000 live births) stood at 118 in 1855–9, actually rose to 130 in 1895–9 and was still at 122 in 1900–4. Such overall figures concealed the very close correlation between high infant mortality and bad housing to which John Wheatley, among others, drew attention, by publishing a table of infant deaths in different parts of Glasgow: 'You may see at a glance that the infant death-rate in working-class wards is three, four and almost five times higher than in Kelvinside.'[36] It is surely because the middle classes felt themselves immune from such high infant mortality, as they had not felt themselves immune from cholera or typhoid, that nothing serious was done to combat the scandal and suffering such bleak statistics revealed.

Above all, it was the failure to confront squarely the housing problem that lay at the root of all the other relative failures of nineteenth-century Scottish municipal corporations. True, the one-roomed house declined from a third of the stock in 1861 to a sixth in 1911, and over-crowding, measured by the number of persons per room, fell by one-fifth between 1861 and 1901: but as long as half the Scottish population continued to live in one- and two-roomed houses and overcrowding remained between five and ten times as great in Glasgow as in corresponding English cities, the failure seems close to absolute.

It is generally agreed by economic historians that the only way to cut the Gordian knot would have been to abandon free market principles and either subsidize council-house building from the rates, or by the State, as was done from 1919, or to give some direct aid to the low paid to enable them to rent or buy better homes. That no sustained moves were made in these directions was no doubt due to the vested interests of the very large number of middle-class people who had a stake in the existing ways of building and owning working-class housing. It was a 'Citizens' Union', largely organized by the house-factoring firms, which intervened in the municipal elections in Glasgow to bring down Lord Provost Chisholm and thus put an end to the City Improvement

Trust's plans to build working-class houses on the rates to replace some of the many thousands it had demolished. Those with a direct interest in the building industry, to an even greater extent than at the present day, took care to occupy the commanding heights of the Town Council. Thus in Edinburgh, developers like Sir James Steel and James Gowans sought such offices as Lord Provost and Dean of Guild, and in 1875, no less than 95 per cent of the Lord Provost's Committee, 87 per cent of the Treasurer's Committee (which set the rates) and 86 per cent of the Plans and Works Committee were landlords.[37]

The middle classes lifted the weight of working-class housing conditions from their conscience by adopting a comforting set of interlocking beliefs. One was that the poor could be divided into two parts, the respectable and the unrespectable; it was only the latter (they assumed) that had a serious housing problem, and they were held to be responsible for their own poverty. As the Glasgow Factors' Association told the Church of Scotland Presbytery Commission in 1892, 'the contention of the Association [is] that the root of the evil in the housing of the poor is the thriftlessness, intemperance and want of self-respect of a considerable class among tenant occupants.'[38] The second belief was that interference with the market was intrinsically wrong, a dictum that held for housing as it held for international trade. The third was that philanthropy could cope with cases where the working population really did suffer from bad conditions, though charity had to be discriminating lest it encourage the indigent and undermine thrift and self-help.

The scope and extent of middle-class good works in the Victorian city was indeed extraordinary, ranging from the admirable, like Thomas Guthrie's Ragged Schools and William Quarrier's orphanages for homeless children, to the unwelcome, like the serried ranks of tract-distributing societies, and the useful, like the Night Asylums and Medical Mission Societies. The flavour of piety and medicine in the latter is conveyed by the staff list of a medical mission in the Cowgate, Edinburgh, in the 1860s, which contained the missionary and his wife, 'ten students, three doctors, five Bible-women-nurses, two servants'.[39] Some of the philanthropic societies were directly involved in housing, and helped to build some interesting experimental homes. In Dundee, for example, three housing associations were formed between 1864 and 1874 under middle-class inspiration, their aim being to construct tenements at low cost and to arrange loans to sell them off to working men. In Edinburgh, the operative stone masons themselves formed a Co-operative Building Company, not as a philanthropic venture but as working-class self-help. It built some excellent cottages at Stockbridge and was imitated by others at Fountainbridge and Merchiston, but only the richest workmen could afford to live in them.[40] All these solutions did no more than nibble at the real problem, and concealed for too many years its appalling and intractable nature.

4

The Scottish city that we know today, with its glass and concrete office blocks, its ring-roads, its middle-class suburbs and its segregated and ill-served council estates of dirty harled houses and crumbling high-rise blocks, is the grandchild of the Victorian town. It sprawls over bleak and windy wastes, whereas the Victorian town was at least compact. It lacks amenities except in the centre, whereas the Victorian town was full of shops and pubs in working-class districts. It is often ugly, boring and crime-ridden, but it is not generally verminous or deadly. Infant mortality in Scotland stands now at 12 per 1000, though in the worst districts of Glasgow it is still almost 50 per 1000. To understand the particular problems of the Scottish city today it is necessary to understand its immediate parents, the Scottish towns of the interwar years.

A brand new start was made to Scottish urban history when Lloyd George's Coalition Government of 1919 passed the Addison Act and conceded the principle of state subsidies to local authority housing. The unquestioned rule of the free market came to an end. The origin of this act lay in the Prime Minister's 'Homes Fit for Heroes' election campaign and his perception of a need for 'insurance against revolution'. His mind had been much concentrated on the matter by the stir created by the Glasgow rent strike of 1915, when the working-class women of Govan and Partick had led an attack on the wartime profiteering of house factors in the first effective display of women's political power in Scottish history. More generally, it followed a realization that the working class, having gained a measure of political power from the Reform Act of 1918, was not going to allow the middle class to ignore the central problem of its day-to-day existence for ever. The members of the Royal Commission on the Housing of the Industrial Population of Scotland, reporting in 1917, even welcomed the show of proletarian muscle:

The chief root of industrial unrest is the desire of the workers to establish better conditions of life for themselves and their families ... Bad housing may fairly be regarded as a legitimate cause of social unrest ... So far as housing is concerned, we cannot but record our satisfaction that, after generations of apathy, the workers all over Scotland give abundant evidence of discontent with conditions that no modern community should be expected to tolerate.[41]

Incidentally, it is worth noticing that the occasion for this Royal Commission, one of the most influential and informative in Scottish history, was a complaint by Scottish miners' leaders about the terrible conditions in colliery-owned cottages. Very bad housing had never been a monopoly of the cities. The decaying black houses of the Hebrides, the damp earth-floored cottages on a Lowland estate, and the open sewers between the rows of one-roomed brick houses in the rural coal-fields were as characteristic of Scottish working-class homes as the single-end in the Gorbals.

Addison's Housing Act of 1919 was followed by six others between 1923 and 1938, and by four more between 1944 and 1950. Some, like the Wheatley Act of 1924, subsidized the house and the rent payable by the tenant; others, like the Greenwood Act of 1929, subsidized slum clearance by paying a sum to the council for every person rehoused. The best successes of the overall policy can be seen in the reduction of overcrowding (as measured by the number of persons per room) by one-quarter between 1921 and 1951, and by the fact that by 1951 only a quarter of the population (instead of half) lived in houses of two rooms or less. The shortcomings are revealed by the fact that even in 1951, there were still two people living in one room in 15.5 per cent of houses in Scotland compared with 2.1 per cent in England and Wales. Subsidies worth £80 million paid between 1919 and 1952 had not removed the Anglo-Scottish differential in overcrowding.

Quantitative failures of this sort in the short term are very understandable. The scale of the problems bequeathed by the nineteenth century was so incomprehensibly immense that whatever politicians might promise and people expect, very little could be done quickly. The Acts themselves were experimental, framed with England in mind at least as much as Scotland, and floated out by governments of differing ideological persuasions and budgetary policies. Again, on the local scene, the political commitment varied. Labour did not gain control even of Glasgow Town Council until 1933: Edinburgh remained staunchly anti-socialist under the 'Progressives', among whom building interests remained entrenched. The City Treasurer's main concern in the 1930s, as recorded in his memoirs, was 'to secure public economy and a continuation of the stable rate' against all-comers and all interests.[42] In fact, Edinburgh, because it suffered so much less from unemployment than Glasgow, as well as for ideological reasons, built more private housing than public-sector housing in the interwar years. But in all other cities the shattering impact of the depression severely discouraged the private builder and seriously eroded the rate base on which even local authority housing might hope to expand. The war stopped everything, and from 1945 to 1951 very little building other than of council houses was allowed by the State. This was the Labour Government's response to the Scottish Housing Advisory Committee Report of 1944, which had shown that although 338,000 houses had been built between 1919 and 1939 (only 66,000 without subsidies), half a million new homes were still needed to cater for Scotland's most basic needs. It is no wonder that after the Second World War, and for several decades, councils built hastily: 144,000 houses were completed between 1946 and 1951 alone.

Did they, however, have to build so badly? The characteristic inter-war Scottish housing estate was composed of low-rise, detached, three-storey tenement blocks, containing a clutch of three-apartment houses in the interwar years, and four-apartment houses in the 1940s,[43] placed on the outskirts where land was cheap. These were as removed from the cottage homes envisaged by Burgess and Wheatley as they were from the old terraces near the centre which they replaced. In so far as there was any intellectual inspiration behind them at all they were vaguely related to the garden suburbs proposed by Ebenezer Howard in England in 1898, though they had neither proper gardens nor separate front doors. There were, of course, further essential differences: Howard envisaged his settlements as self-contained towns, with the number of houses per acre about half what was proposed by the Government in the 1930s. The main Scottish exemplar of a 'garden city'—and a singularly cramped one at that—was the Admiralty housing development for the naval dockyard workers at Rosyth, commenced in 1915. In reality, the council estates of the 1920s and 1930s can scarcely be said to have been planned at all, since there were hardly any planners to plan them. Sir Robert Grieve, the doyen of his profession in the 1960s, recalled the situation:

Just before the Second World War, the number of qualified planners in Scotland amounted to not more than six or seven, i.e. members of the Institute [of Town Planning] through some kind of academic training or by setting themselves to sit and pass the examinations of the Institute. The Executive Committee of the Scottish Branch was, in 1937, almost, if not wholly, composed of members who had been admitted on grounds of age and experience.[44]

The municipal authorities consequently spread the estates without much thought on convenient and inexpensive areas. In Edinburgh, the social effect was largely to complete the process that had begun in the mid-nineteenth century, evicting the poor from the old town and moving them even further from the sight of the rich to peripheral estates like Pilton and Craigmillar that became in turn notorious centres for crime and social problems. The capital, with its New Town flats and Victorian villas at Morningside and Merchiston for the wealthy, its new bungaloid growths at Corstorphine and Colinton for the clerical middle class, and its hideous council estates for the workers, became by the end of our period a city of abnormal spatial segregation of the social classes.[45]

In Glasgow in the 1920s and 1930s, there was actually considerable variety in council-house building. Almost a fifth approximated to the ideal semi-detached or terraced cottage model propounded by the ILP, laid out in low densities of twelve houses per acre with their own gardens. Nearly a third were 'flatted' (i.e. in two-storey blocks with four houses in each, two on each floor, with outside stairs going to the upper floor and thus each with 'their own front door'); half were in tenements of two to four stories. The best built houses and the lowest densities were on green field sites, the 'rolling acres' of Knightswood and Mosspark, but the expansiveness of their layout used most of the available building land within the city boundary and made even worse the problem of what to do with those people still crammed in the one- and two-roomed houses of the old centre. The less desirable houses were built at much higher densities closer to the centre at Blackhill. From the start, the council (whether right-wing before 1933 or Labour thereafter) perpetuated the ancient distinctions between the respectable and the unrespectable poor: those whom council officials graded as clean and decent after formal inspection were entitled to 'Ordinary' houses (at Knightswood): those who failed were given 'Rehousing' houses and packed off to Blackhill, which, not surprisingly, rapidly developed a reputation for illness and violence that surpassed even that of the old slums themselves.[46] A family sent to Blackhill was doomed as certainly, and as irretrievably, as a family sent to a Victorian poorhouse.

Was there any alternative to the bleak estates of the degraded Ebenezer Howard ideal? In being critical, it is easy to overlook the constraints of the political and economic conditions under which they were built. The ideas of Patrick Geddes could, however, have been studied with more advantage. Geddes—polymath, eccentric, and part-time Professor of Biology at Dundee—has every claim to be considered as the most original planner of the late nineteenth century. His years of study of the Old Town of Edinburgh from the camera obscura of the Outlook Tower at the head of the Lawnmarket led him to see the city as an organism which, to be understood, had to be slowly and carefully observed from the inside. Geddes did not, like Howard, think of town life as a perversion of the natural, but believed it to be good in itself and even the most desperate city to be capable of being renewed by piecemeal rebuilding and replacement, the introduction of play spaces and gardens in vacant lots, the integration of buildings for housing and buildings for recreation and culture, and the preservation of access to the countryside. He had no time at all for blind demolition and social segregation: he saw ancient communities as rooted in history, organisms to be revived rather than replaced. His masterpiece, the *Report to the Carnegie Dunfermline Trust* of 1904, was a plan (far too extravagant to be practicable) to redesign Dunfermline as a model town for central Scotland. Unhappily, Geddes not only had no eye for economic realities but was also given to ideas so eccentric in detail as to discredit his approach as a whole. He had very little to say in his Dunfermline study specifically about working-class housing except this item, under the heading 'Hygienic and Domestic Improvements':

> The provision of that upstairs balcony which is a main hygienic resource of woman's life in other countries, and next even of the outhung sleeping-cage, has to be henceforth more and more largely considered. The actual immediate gain to our deficient housing accommodation from this easy supply of actual 'outdoor apartments' will only be derided by that section of the public whom the open-air treatment has not yet converted.[47]

It is no wonder that John Wheatley, with an eye to the housewives of

Shettleston who were unlikely to want to spend a Scottish night suspended in a sleeping cage, went for a version of Ebenezer Howard's cottages. Nevertheless, the Geddes principle of integrated urban renewal from the inside had a great deal more to recommend it than the mass building of workers' homes in segregated and distant estates.

Perhaps even more fundamental was the question of finance; firstly, whether the houses built should be for sale (which Addison envisaged as a possibility) or solely for renting (as Wheatley and his successors believed): secondly, whether the subsidy should go to the local authority or be passed on by them to the individual or to a Co-operative Housing Association, either to enable them to buy or to rent. In the event the choices made by government created housing estates owned by the local authority and leased at subsidized rents to working-class tenants. The result was a 'new feudalism' that gave immense power to the officials of corporation housing departments, deprived the working class of the chance to own their own homes ('the greatest of anti-inflationary nest eggs') and often tied people to one spot in a dying local economy.[48] Certainly the experience in other countries, as for example in Scandinavia, which made far greater use of housing associations, was much more favourable, though it must never be forgotten that no other country had housing problems on the scale which Victorian middle-class neglect and self-interest had handed on to twentieth-century Scotland.

In any case, experiments in encouraging working-class collective self-help—along the lines of the Edinburgh operative masons of the 1860s who built their 'colonies' in Stockbridge—became progressively less likely as the twentieth-century labour movement came to rely less on its ancient democratic instincts and more on its trust in what the experts could do for the people. The queue at the Housing Department allocation desk became, in the late 1940s, the main manifestation of the New Jerusalem.

CHAPTER III

Leaving and Staying on in the Countryside

1

As the city rose, the countryside, ultimately, declined. In 1851, 30 per cent of the male employed population worked directly in agriculture: there were still more people, men and women, engaged in farming than in textiles and mining put together, and most rural areas had been enjoying a rising population for a century. By 1901, the proportion of male workers who were employed in farming had dropped by one half to 14 per cent, and by 1951 to less than 10 per cent. At the same time the urban concentrations of the Central Belt drew from the village and the small remote town; a ring of counties on the periphery of Scotland, in the far north and the south as well as in the Highlands, reached their historic peak in the middle decades of the nineteenth century and then steadily fell in numbers while the population of Scotland continued to grow.

The combination of rural depopulation and city growth was not peculiar to Scotland; it was equally to be found in England and Wales and ultimately throughout the whole of Europe, though it occurred earlier in the UK than in other countries. It is what happens when industrialization creates a demand for labour in the town and stimulates the countryside to produce more food with fewer hands, and when the life of the town comes in popular culture to seem more real and desirable than life in the country. Even Norway and Sweden, so often held up as exemplars of how to enjoy economic growth with low social costs, have experienced severe attrition of population in their northern and mountain regions. In Scotland, the modern population of peripheral counties is often much the same as it was in the middle of the eighteenth century, and the decline from 1850 represents the erosion of a surplus that had grown very rapidly only in the previous fifty years. Thus Orkney had a population of 23,000 in 1755 and 21,000 in 1951; Argyll a population of 66,000 in 1755 and 63,000 in 1951; Berwickshire a population of 24,000 in 1755 and 25,000 in 1951—each having been at least one-third higher in the interim. This, however, does not tell quite the whole story: in the middle of the eighteenth century, most people would have lived off the land and all generations would have been well represented; by the mid-twentieth century, more lived in the country towns such as Kirkwall, Oban or Duns, more were involved in occupations other than farming or fishing, and more were elderly. The deserted farmtoun and a scarcity of children at the village school were two signs of the rural problem by the middle of the twentieth century—and this was also true across Europe.

In Scotland there was, however, a very remarkable contrast in people's reactions to the process of rural depopulation. In the Highlands, it was associated with enormous resentment: stamped with the word 'clearance', with overtones of violence, oppression and hopeless suffering. In the Lowlands, there were no such associations: it just occurred, and was accepted. Yet before the 1890s, the fall in population was not more generally pronounced in the rural Highlands than in equally rural parts of the Lowlands. There are eleven Scottish counties that reached the historic peak of their populations between 1831 and 1861; seven of these are in the Highlands and Islands and four (Kinross, Berwickshire, Kirkcudbright and Wigtownshire) are in the Lowlands. In the forty years between 1851 and 1891, during which the law—at least until 1886—afforded no protection against summary eviction, the drop in population of the Highland and Island counties was 9 per cent; the drop in the four Lowland counties was the same. In the forty years between 1891 and 1931, on the other hand, in a period in which it was virtually impossible under Scottish law to evict a Highland crofter from his holding but singularly easy to evict a Lowland farm labourer from his cottage, the population of the seven counties of the Highlands and Islands fell by 26 per cent, that of the Lowland group by only 16 per cent. The law seems to have done nothing to stop the drain of men from the land. If one considers the statistics of men engaged in farming rather than of population, the conclusion is reinforced even more strongly. Between 1851 and 1891, when clearance was still everywhere possible, there was an 11 per cent fall in the Highlands but an 18 per cent fall in the rest of Scotland; in the next forty years, when there was protection for the crofter, there was a 30 per cent fall in the Highlands compared to an 11 per cent fall in the rest of Scotland. These figures make it difficult to believe that the empty glens and deserted crofts that move the modern traveller in the north are primarily the result of clearance.

How, then, can we explain rural depopulation, and the differences between the Highlands and the Lowlands? There is no doubt that many, both men and women, removed themselves voluntarily, and in a spirit of hope: rural life, though certainly not without its powerful compensations in terms of environment, nutrition and security, offered few prospects of high earnings and fewer of social mobility. As the century passed, the culture of the cities came to dominate the culture of the countryside through the popular press and the radio, and rural ways could sometimes seem narrow and dull to the young. Farm work, said one witness to the Royal Commission on Labour in 1893, appeared as 'a rough, dirty, badly paid job with long hours and few holidays'. Furthermore, familiarity with the outside world created by modern communications provided both the self-confidence and the means to leave. Another reporter to the same Royal Commission described the escape of women from the drudgery of field and dairy:

> A young woman will hand over her 'kist' (anglice, chest or box of clothes) to the porter, get her ticket for Glasgow, pull on her gloves, laugh and talk with her parents and comrades, jump into the train, pay her adieu, wave her handkerchief, sit down oblivious to band-box and unencumbered with bundles, and thank her stars that she is at last leaving the *unwomanly* job for domestic service and town society.[1]

The Report was full of comments on the difficulty of obtaining farmhands in the Lowlands at the end of the nineteenth century, and the consequent obligation on employers to provide better cottages and higher wages to compete with the enticements of town life, but equally it was full of comments on how employers reacted to rising costs by introducing labour-saving machinery:

In 1820 ... to cultivate, reap and deliver five different crops ... would have taken 53 days, while in 1892 the same operations would be performed by those using modern methods in 35 days ... the labour displaced in 100 acres of these crops would be one man for every 34 acres.

A modern study has shown how this process continued: in Scotland in 1840 it took 22 man-days a year to tend an acre of barley; by 1914, it was down to 12, and by 1958, to only 3. The tractor and the combine, even more than the horse-drawn mechanical reaper of the late nineteenth century, made the farmer less and less reliant on the sheer muscle-power of his men.[2]

As more and more workers left for the town, rural employers took steps to avoid the rising cost of labour by an injection of capital; the longer this continued, the fewer jobs and prospects were left in the countryside and the more attractive the town appeared to the farmworker. As agricultural operations turned more expensive, becoming a farmer became more difficult, unless the entrant was already rich or at least already in occupation as the son of a large tenant. Price movements in the last third of the nineteenth century reinforced this trend; as first cereal and then animal prices dropped in the face of foreign imports, only the farm with a large turnover and low costs could hope to be efficient enough to maintain its competitive edge. Small farmers as well as labourers found the going more and more difficult: Ian Carter has explained how in the north-east Lowlands of Aberdeenshire and the counties along the southern shore of the Moray Firth, the small tenants operating on the hill edge ('crofters', but not in exactly the same sense as in the west Highlands) were forced by competition with the 'muckle farmers' on the better, lower land either to give up or to attempt to hang on by exploiting to the utmost the unpaid labour of their own sons and daughters, until they, in turn, were driven by desperation and self-preservation to leave for the towns.[3] In these circumstances the old who were left behind could feel disgruntled, bitter and deserted, the last representatives of a vanishing way of life.

It is often asked about migration whether the pull factors are more important than push factors; it is never easy to give a clear-cut answer, because the choice of every individual depends on his subjective preferences and on his personal estimate of the advantages of going or staying. A pull from the cities, always attractive to the adventurous, might become compulsive to many more as their opportunities became better known and the opportunities at home narrowed, or the way of life the country offered seemed less and less to be the only way of life possible. This, broadly, is what happened in the Lowlands. On the whole there was little complaint, partly because it was a very drawn-out process (even before the Industrial Revolution Adam Smith had observed that farmers near the cities had to pay higher wages to prevent their plough-men leaving), and partly because if what you wanted from life was the chance of higher earnings, more fun when you were young, and better prospects of self-advancement (as Lowlanders generally did), it was obvious that the countryside had little to offer, but the town, or the world overseas, had something. There was a choice, and the Lowland countrymen and countrywomen took it in the belief that they were doing something positive with their lives.

2

The situation in the Highlands differed from this at least in degree, though there were many thousands who left in exactly the same spirit as the Lowlanders, and the observations on the Highlanders in the Report of the Royal Commission on Labour in 1892 are similar in tone to the remarks on the Lowlanders:

> In these days of railways and steamboats, places in the very wilds of Ross-shire are brought within easy reach of town industries, and there can be little doubt that the long journey between Beauly and Glasgow does not in the least deter persons so inclined from desert-ing country life for town service.[4]

There were, however, two significant peculiarities in the Highland situation, especially in the first half of our period. One was that, at the very start, the element of force used to divorce men from the land was much greater than elsewhere. The Highland clearances reached a peak in the 1840s and first part of the 1850s, especially in the aftermath of the great potato blight of 1846, which left upwards of 100,000 people in the north-west destitute and dependent on the charity of relief funds to keep them from starvation. When it was over, some landlords, like Macleod of Macleod, found themselves bankrupt as a result of their ex-penditure on famine relief for their tenants; their estates passed into the hands of trustees who endeavoured to maximize returns by replacing crofters with sheep. Others (a more numerous phalanx) simply decided that the time had come to replace men with animals, to avoid the risk of such a famine recurring and further to avoid the danger—as they saw it—of being made legally responsible for the relief of their tenants under a new Scottish poor law. The resultant cruelty and anguish was never better described than by the geologist Sir Archibald Geikie at Suishnish on Skye, where the trustees of Lord Macdonald's estate, anxious to 'make as much money as possible out of the rents' in order to satisfy creditors and hasten the return of the proprietor to possession, 'determined to clear the whole population ... and convert the ground into one large sheep farm, to be placed in the hands of a responsible grazier, if possible from the south country'. The interests of the crofters, he observed, 'formed a very secondary consideration'. This is what followed:

> As I was returning from my ramble, a strange wailing sound reached my ears at intervals on the breeze from the west. On gaining the top of one of the hills on the south side of the valley, I could see a long and motley procession winding along the road ... It halted at the point of the road opposite Kilbride, and there the lamentation became loud and long. As I drew nearer, I could see that the minister with his wife and daughters had come out to meet the people and bid them all farewell. It was a miscellaneous gathering of at least three generations of crofters. There were old men and women, too feeble to walk, who were placed in carts; the younger members of the community on foot were carrying their bundles of clothes and household effects, while the children, with looks of alarm, walked alongside ... When they set forth once more, a cry of grief went up to heaven, the long plaintive wail, like a funeral coronach, was resumed, and after the last of the emigrants had disappeared behind the hill, the sound seemed to re-echo through the whole wide valley of Strath in one prolonged note of desolation. The people were on their way to be shipped to Canada.[5]

Such a description is unusually vivid, but in no way untypical or overdrawn. Nevertheless, the extent and duration of the clearances, as we have already observed, need to be placed in perspective. There were no mass evictions after a particularly heartless incident at Greenyards, Ross-shire, in 1855, which aroused so much rancour and public abuse of the landlords in the press that estate policy began to change towards what Eric Richards has called the 'mainly invisible pressure on the people to ease them out of the region', commenting, however, that there was no *prima facie* case for thinking that such pressure was any greater than elsewhere in Britain.[6] This is certainly supported by the fact that over the next forty years, the decline in Highland population was no greater than the decline in comparable areas of the Lowlands, and was not very great in any case: the 9 per cent fall could be contrasted with a 28 per cent fall in Ireland between 1851 and 1891. This leaves out of the reckoning the fact that well over a million people are thought to have died in the Irish famine of 1845–50, compared to few or none in the comparable crop failure in the Highlands.

It was often noticed that the ultimate fate of those who endured and survived the violence of the clearances was a good deal better than that of those who were allowed to stay behind. The point was well put by an American traveller on a trip to Sutherland, after he had deplored the great statue outside Golspie to the Duke, whom he christened 'Evictor I', responsible for the clearances in the first part of the nineteenth century: 'The sons of the fathers and mothers who had their family nests stirred up so cruelly ... are now among the most substantial and respected men of the Western World ... merchants, manufacturers, farmers, teachers, and preachers, filling all the professions and occupations of the continent.'[7] Those left behind, the American noticed, were still about as miserable as they had ever been. Also telling is the case of the people of Sollas in North Uist, twice evicted before being forced aboard a steamer in 1852 to leave Scotland 'in a blaze of anger and distress'. After appalling sufferings in South Australia, some of those who survived became prosperous, struck up a correspondence with Scotland, and even subscribed a sum of money to buy a ring for the wife of the law officer who had compelled them into emigration, 'as a token of gratitude to me for all the trouble I had from first to last taken in their matters'.[8] Once the break had been made, the Highlander was as capable as the next man of grasping new opportunities and changing old perceptions.

The second distinctive thing about the mid-Victorian Highlander— it was connected, indeed, with the first, the degree of violence deemed necessary to effect the clearances—was that many in the north-west perceived that occupation of a traditional area of land, and not acquisition of new wealth, was the greatest good that life had to offer. Such an attitude was not, however, universal in the geographical area we now call the Highlands: there is no evidence that the inhabitants of the mainland to the east and south of the Great Glen thought any differently about land than those of the rest of Scotland. By the second half of the nineteenth century, this sentiment was probably only intensely felt in a comparatively small area where Gaelic culture was least disrupted, and to which the disturbances known as the Highland Land War, 1881–96, were almost entirely restricted: the Outer Hebrides, Skye and Tiree. It certainly seemed very strange to middle-class outsiders familiar with the *obiter dicta* of classical political economy that an agricultural population should prefer to remain where it was, dividing and subdividing among itself the narrow crofts of unrewarding land in a dismal climate, living off herring and potatoes in good times and off charity in bad, rather than gravitating towards the employment, opportunity and hope afforded to some by the Lowlands and to all by the outside world. Some thought of the Highlanders almost as savages, echoing the sentiments of the notorious sheep farmer and factor Patrick Sellar, who had been responsible for some of the most brutal episodes in the Sutherland clearances in the second decade of the century:

> There is no one thing to be imagined more deeply affecting or afflicting than the absence of every principle of truth and candour from a population of several hundred thousand souls ... [who are] with relation to the enlightened nations of Europe in a position not very different from that betwixt the American colonists and the aborigines of that country. The one are the aborigines of Britain shut out from any general stream of knowledge flowing in upon the Commonwealth of Europe from the remotest fountain of antiquity. The other are the aborigines of America equally shut out from this stream; both live in turf cabins in common with the brutes; both are singular for patience, courage, cunning and address. Both are most virtuous where least in contact with men in a civilized State, and both are fast sinking under the baneful effects of ardent spirits.[9]

Others, more charitably, thought them more ignorant and fearful of the outside world than wicked and idle, so isolated by possession of Gaelic speech and adherence to the traditions of subsistence living that they found themselves unable to cope with any alternative way of life. As was said of the Hebrideans, 'The stranger who appeared amongst them was the infant newly-born, and he who left them was, in general, carried to his grave.'[10]

The more perceptive, however, saw beyond both these views, and were no less amazed. Sir John McNeill, chairman of the Board of Supervision for Poor Relief in Scotland, was sent north five years after the total failure of the potato crop in 1846 to report on the condition of the Highlanders. He was worried to find a population apparently settling down to live off charitable funds, and argued that the only long-term solution lay in encouraging out-migration on a very large scale. What, however, was one to do with the peasantry when the 'tenacity of their attachment to their native soil' was not removed by 'years of intercourse with the more advanced districts'? He could see that on Skye the reluctance of the Highlander to move was due neither to idleness nor to ignorance of the outside world:

> For 20 successive years, one of the crofters had worked for the summer six months in East Lothian with the same master, from whom he had a certificate of character and conduct such as any man in his position might be proud of. At the commencement of each winter, he returned to the small croft in Waternish, at the northern extremity of Skye, on which his family resided, and for which he paid a rent of £5 a year from the wages he earned with Mr Dudgeon, of Easter Broomhouse, near Dunbar. When short of meal or seed-corn in the spring, he applied to Mr Dudgeon, who kindly furnished him with what he required, on the credit of his next summer's work. Here then was an intelligent, enterprising, industrious man, who had lived for one-half of the last 20 years in East Lothian, where he had established an excellent character, and found a kind employer, to whom he was attached and grateful, yet the idea of permanently removing appeared never to have occurred to him. He must have been nearly as familiar with life in East Lothian as with life in Skye; but the attractions of his croft in Waternish continued to be irresistible. He travelled about 600 miles, separated himself from his family and worked hard for six months every year, that he might continue to enjoy his croft and comparative idleness for the other half-year in Waternish. And such was the feeling of every one . . .[11]

What was surprising to men like McNeill was that so many Highlanders refused either to accept their removal as inevitable or to interpret it as a chance for betterment. Had not Adam Smith spoken, in a well-known phrase, of 'the uniform, constant and uninterrupted effort of every man to better his own condition'? It followed that, in pursuit of self-interest, no Highlander should have hesitated to migrate to a locality like East Lothian where there were jobs to be had, and that eviction should never have been necessary. But Gaelic Highlanders often refused to conform to the model of Smithian man. They had their own ideology, which was that possession of land—the tenure (not the ownership) of a croft—was the highest good a man could desire. Other forms of earning a living were possible but less desirable than crofting; a man should only take to them in an emergency, to pay the rent, but not as a lifestyle to help him enrich himself to the maximum extent possible. This is a phenomenon only superficially related to the leisure-preference often discussed by economists, where people prefer (or appear to prefer) time off to higher wages, and thus react to improved wage rates by absenteeism. Sometimes, indeed, peasants appeared lazy; Thomas Pennant in 1772 had described the Sutherlanders as 'almost torpid with idleness . . . the climate conspires with indolence to make matters worse'.[12] However their preference was not really for idleness but for occupying a croft—not leisure-preference but land-preference—and they could work hard and compromise quite readily with the demands of the outside world if they could thereby achieve this preference. And land-preference itself must be partly compounded not merely of love of the soil (real as that was), but also of security-preference: better a subsistence husbandry that is known to produce a living than the chance of a higher income in a situation of higher risk.

It was not that Highlanders were averse to enrichment as such: there was no consumer resistance to better clothes or imported food, and some of the complaints of the 1880s related to their failure to get enough of these good things for themselves over the past half century. But broadly speaking the crofter put home before wealth, the possession of land before the dubious opportunity to gain enrichment through a better income as an industrial worker or even as a landholder overseas. The last option was to many much better than the first, as the emigration societies offering passage to Canada, Australia and New Zealand were quick to realize. But the crofter was prepared to share his holding with his grown-up sons and their families rather than oblige them to leave the settlement for ever, to live on the brink of starvation rather than commit himself to the dangerous currents of urban and foreign life, to commit himself and his family to spending months, even years, as migrant workers, harvesting, fishgutting or labouring in the south. In some respects these sentiments begged almost as many questions as those of the other side, for what would happen if crofting lands were so constantly divided that income levels were driven below mere subsistence? Anyone with a knowledge of what had happened in Ireland could see that the question was not idle, nor was it comprehensively answered by those crofters who simply said that the return of lands under sheep or deer would solve the problem of land-hunger for all time. Gaelic Scotland indeed shared with Gaelic Ireland a cultural view of land in which it was not so much private property as a common resource: the landlord had a right to charge a rent, but not to deprive the population of the use of the land. This utterly conflicted with the landlord's view, which was also that of Scottish law and of Lowland and British society at all levels, viz. that the land was the absolute property of its owner, and that if he wished to maximize his returns by replacing the congested crofts with a sheep run, or to use his grazing land as a deer forest rather than returning it to peasant use, that was no one's business but his own.

To describe the conflict in terms of two irreconcilable ideologies, one of Gaelic peasant values, one of landlord rationality, conceals the fact that by no means everyone subscribed fully to one or the other. Even in remote areas there were always peasants, perhaps especially those with some experience of the outside world through military service, who quietly left for the same ambitious reasons as Lowlanders. There were always landowners whose strong traditional paternalism and conservatism prevented them from running their estates on perfectly 'economic' lines, although the logic of high living and stagnant estate incomes under crofting agriculture generally forced them towards greater rationality in the long run. Again, there was a good deal of talk from church leaders and some journalists about the need in a heartless world for kind, old-fashioned values: the Free Kirk especially tended to moralize on the duties as well as the rights of landed property, mainly because certain Highland landowners had been reluctant to give them sites for new churches after the Disruption of 1843, and also because Hugh Miller, their great publicist and the editor of the *Witness*, was brought up in a needy household and worked for a time as a mason in Cromarty, close enough to the Highlands to gain sympathy for the crofters. In the 1840s and 1850s it had become commonplace among urban Liberals to attack the lairds for heartless disregard of the duties that landownership entailed, and the onslaught rocked the complacency of the landed classes. It put the latter emotionally on the defensive, but not intellectually so, because no one had yet come forth with a reasoned economic argument against clearance.

3

From the mid-1850s, therefore, estate policy was as Eric Richards describes it, not violent eviction, but the quiet encouragement to remove, the easing out, of people who could often pay little in rent and who might become a substantial liability if they stayed. It had mixed success, because of the determination of the crofters not to go easily and their vigorous pursuit of a migrant labour economy that sent the unmarried children to work for the hungry months of the year in service in the south and used part of their wages to satisfy the landlord. Nevertheless, in most regions and islands population had a downward trend, which, though moderate overall, could be locally quite sharp. Tiree under the Duke of Argyll, for example, peaked at 4453 in 1831 and was down to 2773 by 1881; Skye, for much of the period administered by the trustees of bankrupt Macleod and Macdonald chiefs, peaked at 23,074 in 1841 and had fallen to 17,680 by 1881; the county of Sutherland peaked at 25,793 in 1851 (despite the notorious earlier clearances) and fell to 23,370 by 1881. The exceptional case that moved against the trend is worth exploring. The Isle of Lewis climbed from a population of 17,016 in 1841 to one of 25,421 by 1881. Why?

Lewis had been purchased in 1844 from the bankrupt Mackenzies, Earls of Seaforth, by James Matheson, partner in the firm of Jardine Matheson of Hong Kong, opium traders extraordinary, and the possessor on his return to Britain in 1842 of a fortune that any nobleman would have envied. Almost at once he had to reach into his pocket to support the population during the famine of 1846 and the following years: he imported meal on his own account and sold it to the crofters at 25 per cent of the cost; he transported anyone who wished to seek employment on the mainland free of charge in his own boat; he provided work on the island by building roads and quays, enclosing croftland with dykes, and planting marram to prevent sand-blow. In 1851, a baronetcy was conferred upon him in recognition of his exemplary humanity towards a tenantry in desperate need.

A lesser fortune would have been drained by these demands, but Matheson's was merely skimmed. He continued to lay out money on an extravagant scale, apparently spending £384,000 on Lewis between his purchase of the estate and his death in 1878. He became the only large landowner in the Highlands after 1850 who was at once indifferent to financial pressure and not anxious to compel his people to emigrate unless they wanted to. His factors were admittedly strict, dictatorial and unpopular, but there were no removals, except in the case of crofters who themselves petitioned to be shifted from townships of bad land to better.

Lewis thus proves a crucible for testing the question of how the Highland population would have behaved if there had been no pressure on them to leave. The answer is that under similar circumstances they would have stayed and continued to increase as they had done in the first half of the century. This course of action became possible on Lewis, even after the failure of the potato as the traditional staple of life and prop of the economy, because of the growth of the fishing industry based principally on the east coast ports of Scotland after 1854, though with subsidiary activity in Stornoway itself and at Castlebay on Barra. It provided employment for men (on the boats) and girls (on shore) mainly as migrant workers, and it was largely their earnings that paid the rent. Meanwhile, however, on the island, a growing population accommodated itself by subdividing the existing crofts—already small enough—into fragments smaller still. Bitterness grew between the population and the estate because the landowner refused to release back to the crofters any of the land under sheep and deer that had been taken from the crofters by clearance under the Earls of Seaforth before 1844. To the landowner and the factor the request was unreasonable: the men should be glad not to be under the same pressures to leave the island as people were on Tiree or Skye. To the crofters, the estate's policy was intolerable: they were poor, they paid their rents, they did as the factor said, but land was a communal resource of which they were desperately short: its possession conferred meaning to life, and Matheson had no right, in the face of manifest need, to keep them from land which their ancestors had possessed.

It is thus understandable, if ironical, that when the crofters began a campaign of direct action for the return of the land formerly cleared, under the leadership of the Highland Land Law Reform Association, Lewis formed a main storm centre. The most famous incident, the Park deer raid of 1887, involved over a hundred men armed with rifles who took possession of land which originally had been cleared under the Seaforths and which had just been turned by Matheson's widow from a sheep farm into a sporting estate. They shot a large number of deer and ceremonially roasted and boiled them at Stromas, 'the most beautiful of the evicted hamlets'. The rioters did not otherwise behave like left-wing desperadoes:

> When supper was ready, an old patriarch from Marvig rose to say Grace in which he beseeched Almighty God for a blessing on the food which He had so graciously provided, and also on those gathered around him. He hoped that the day would come when a church would stand on the spot where they now stood.[13]

The incident resulted in the arrest of a number of ringleaders, who were subsequently tried at Edinburgh and found not guilty on a charge of mobbing and rioting by a sympathetic jury. Encouraged, the next raid featured a thousand people with pipes playing and flags flying: they tried to occupy the sheep farm of Aignish, killed some of the stock, were confronted and beaten back by soldiers of the Royal Scots and marines from HMS *Jackal* (nicknamed HMS *Jackass* by the locals); this time some of their leaders were sentenced to fifteen months in gaol. Lady Matheson, meanwhile, left the island following threats against her life. The atmosphere was for a time Irish in its Gaelic passion, tension and menace.

The 1880s were a decade of great ferment in the Highlands. On the one hand there was the direct example of Ireland, where the Irish Land League under Charles Parnell and Michael Davitt was organizing the tenants and cottiers behind the slogan of the 'three Fs': fixity of tenure, fair rents and freedom to inherit a holding. The details were well known in Scotland: the government publishers received an order from a remote part of Lewis for the Irish Land Act of 1881, and a group of Skye crofters, 'hearing of the good news from Ireland', said they had a mind to 'turn rebels ourselves'.[14] The problem was compounded by a downturn in the Highland economy after two decades in which good wages for migrant labour and buoyant prices for cattle had done much to repair the damage created by the potato blight: now, industrial depression, poor harvests and several seasons of bad fishing brought about the worst hardship since the 1840s. Riots broke out first on Skye, at the Battle of the Braes in 1882, when a contingent of Glasgow police sent to enforce an eviction order were attacked and routed by a band of infuriated crofters and their wives. The trouble spread rapidly in Skye, and thence to Lewis and Tiree. The Highland Land Law Reform Association (HLLRA) and its political wing, the Crofters' Party, rapidly made inroads on the crofters' allegiance, the latter capturing four seats in the General Election of December 1885. The Government reluctantly bowed to pressure, and in 1883 appointed Lord Napier, former administrator of the Madras Province in the Indian Civil Service, to head a Royal Commission to enquire into the conditions of the crofters and cottars.

The Napier Commission was expected by the HLLRA to be Mr Gladstone's poodle, but it turned out to have a mind of its own. Napier was a brilliant chairman who took infinite pains to win the confidence of the crofters. Three of its members, Charles Fraser-Mackintosh, Alexander Nicholson and Donald Mackinnon, were Celtic intellectuals (among other things), and the first was to become an MP for the Crofters' Party. The remaining two were no more than large landowners, but could be clearly outvoted with the chairman's support. The commission heard evidence from throughout the western Highlands, and in four volumes presented a vivid and detailed chronicle of the wrongs of decades:

11174 *The Chairman*: Were you freely elected a delegate?
Reply: Yes.
11175 *The Chairman*: You produce a written statement?
Reply: Yes:

North Boisdale. We had a great reason to complain. About forty years ago there were twenty-four crofts in this village, and now it is situated on forty-eight, with heavy families. In the month of September the most of our crop will be destroyed with heavy floods, owing to the leading drains being closed up more than twenty years ago. Also the west side, that we called the Macher, are exhausted, and going with the wind, which cannot be made up without the help of the landlord. The hill pasture that we had for grazing our cattle, horses and sheep, if we would have any, are now situated on six or seven tenants. And when we will go out to our grazing place, they are drilling them back with their dogs. The property that we have does not belong to ourselves; it belongs to the men who supply us with food and clothing ... our land is exhausted with the number of people. And about forty-six years ago we used to sell plenty of grain and potatoes, besides keeping up our families, and the place where that was growing is now filled up with Cheviot and oxen . . .[15]

So it went on from island to island, from township to township: the crofters' message was too many people, too little land, but if the land were returned to the people, the hardship would disappear.

The actual findings of the Napier Commission, however, pleased no one. Lord Napier wished to confer security of tenure only on the largest crofters, and to leave the cottars exposed to the risk of eviction as before, on the grounds that the area was already hopelessly congested: this was quite unacceptable to the HLLRA and its supporters, most of whom were cottars in any case. He also wanted to resurrect the traditional Highland township as a kind of peasant commune, with jointly-owned arable and pasture, election of its own officials in township meetings, the right to extract communal labour for public purposes, and with collective responsibility for the payment of rents and taxes: furthermore, he proposed that if the amount of land within their existing boundaries proved insufficient, the townships should have the right of compulsory purchase over adjacent privately-owned land. Land-owners regarded the whole thing as outrageous socialism, and the HLLRA was little better pleased: for all their vaunted respect for land as a communal resource, they had come, in the 1880s, to interpret this as meaning no more than the right of every individual who cared to stay to have absolute security on his own holding.

Not surprisingly, therefore, Mr Gladstone ignored the commission's findings, and in his Crofters' Holdings Act of 1886 reproduced the main provisions of his 1881 Land Act for Ireland which had granted the 'three Fs'. It destroyed the very basis of landlord rights as understood everywhere else in Great Britain by establishing an independent body to fix rents; it conferred security of tenure on peasants who paid the newly determined 'fair' rents; and it provided for the crofters to hand on their holdings to their children by inheritance. It did not, however, take any very positive steps to encourage the reallocation to crofters of land previously cleared and now under sheep and deer, and therefore it failed immediately to allay the hostility of the population: hence the Park deer raid and similar incidents. The possibilities of land redistribution were, however, considerably enlarged by subsequent legislation in

1892, 1897, 1911 and 1919. Between 1886 and the early 1950s (but mainly after the First World War), over 2700 new crofts were created and a further 5160 enlarged: effectively, by the later 1920s, anyone who wanted a croft could get one.

Why did the State so transform its attitude from one of total indifference to the crofters' plight to one of total acceptance of their position, going as far as to give the Highland crofter a uniquely privileged position among all the tenants in Great Britain? Dr Dewey has connected it with an ideological shift in Victorian Liberalism, away from the *laissez-faire* political economy of mid-century to a new 'historicism' of later decades.[16] By the 1880s, the anger and frustration of the Celtic areas was presenting, especially in Ireland, a threat to the very existence of the Union. Men began to doubt if it could ever be removed by the conventional remedy of allowing market forces to take their course, and began to argue that special concessions to peasant groups that took account of their peculiar historical experience would be not merely just but also safe.

Horizons were widening in other ways, too. Gladstone's approach was heavily influenced by a book by George Campbell on how Indian experience of tenures might apply to Ireland. Lord Napier also came to the problem as an administrator accustomed to dealing with Indian views of land that seemed unutterably strange to nineteenth-century Britons whose horizon stopped in the Home Counties or the Lothians. Both Campbell and Napier, however, were also very much influenced by the historical scholarship of the Celtic revival. Napier's key vision of the township commune rested on the picture of archaic Highland society drawn by W. F. Skene in his three-volume *Celtic Scotland*, of which the last part appeared in 1880, 'the greatest work of Scotland's greatest nineteenth-century historian'. If any concession to the Celtic areas was to be based on recognizing the historical differences between their way of perceiving the land and that common to the rest of the United Kingdom, it permitted a breach in the laws of *laissez-faire* political economy which could be fundamental in itself, yet at the same time be firmly limited to those specific areas where peasants had clung to the ideology of land-preference through years when it was thought by most educated men to be inherently absurd, and evidence of mere obduracy or barbarism in the face of modern enlightenment. Conversely, of course, to draw such geographical limits was possible because rural populations elsewhere had given up or never felt the need to cling to a similar point of view. Politically, historicism allowed a remedy to be tailored to a very particular corner of the island without stirring up a hornets' nest of general landlord resentment in Parliament. It was no wonder that the Duke of Argyll, who served in Gladstone's Cabinet, felt himself so victimized by the pro-Celtic land legislation that he resigned and later joined Joseph Chamberlain's anti-Irish-home-rule Liberal Unionists.

The main purpose of the land legislation, for Mr Gladstone and his successors, was political, to still the clamour of discontent in peasant regions. In those terms, in Scotland though not in Ireland, it was a long-term success. Within a decade, the Crofters' Party had rejoined the Liberals. Land raids died out, to be briefly revived after the First World War when the Board of Agriculture seemed to be dragging its feet over processing applications for new crofts and enlargement of old ones in its implementation of the 1919 Land Settlement (Scotland) Act.[17]

These were the circumstances in which the Lewis crofters collided with their landlord in the last classic confrontation between the ways of the great improver and those of traditional society. The island itself, in common with so many rural communities in the north, had been disproportionately savaged by war casualties: from a total population of 29,500, no fewer than 6700 had joined the forces and 1151 had died—about 17 per cent of recruits, and all from the already thinned ranks of able-bodied males. Lord Leverhulme, a soap millionaire with a business empire stretching from Wales to Africa, had bought Lewis from the Mathesons in 1918, in search of a place on which to leave his historic stamp as planner and philanthropist. He expressed his admiration for the 'fine people of the Western Isles', who in exile were 'honoured and respected and filling the highest positions in Canada, Boston, New York and elsewhere throughout our colonies', but who at home were 'living under conditions of squalor and misery'. He proposed to bring employment and high wages by using the resources of his business to introduce modern fishing and fish-processing to Stornoway, to modernize the harbour and to reconstruct the town: 'crofting today is entirely an impossible life for these fine people'.[18] Intrinsic to his plans, moreover, was the retention of the farms in the immediate hinterland, which were to be used as dairy centres to provide milk for Stornoway. Here he immediately fell foul of land raiders, who had gone to serve in the war after Government promises that war heroes would be given more land on their return. Already impatient for the return of these farms to crofting use under the 1919 Act, they took the law into their own hands, as their fathers had done at Park, and occupied some of the farms. Leverhulme's enterprises were then hit by a catastrophic fall in fish prices. Discouraged and offended, he transferred his attentions to Harris, where he had equally little success before his death in 1925. In a final act of generosity, he offered Lewis to its inhabitants as a gift. The crofting townships, however, declined to take the land into ownership, claiming 'that they could not afford the augmentation of rates entailed by acceptance'.[19] It may not have been quite as limp an excuse as it sounded, since the islands were in the grip of bad harvests and shortages that reminded officials of the 1840s; but in any case the Highlander had never seen the point in owning any land outright, providing he could be left secure in the occupancy of a croft paying a modest rent.

The Government, in the person of the Scottish Secretary, Robert Munro, held its breath while all this took place. Munro was always ambivalent about Leverhulme's plans, not because he doubted their economic worth but because he foresaw endless political trouble arising from any backsliding on the promises of 1919: 'If I had chosen that moment to reverse my policy I would have lost any confidence that the islanders still had in me, and my position in the House would have become impossible.'[20] When the plans failed, political peace ensued, and he was presumably relieved.

Though a political success, therefore, it is difficult to see the land legislation as anything but an economic irrelevance, in Scotland as in Ireland.[21] A major part of the justification for the Irish Land Act of 1870 and all its successors was that it would produce a society of active go-ahead small farmers, invigorated by the secure possession of their lands and their protection from rack-renting, impelled into all kinds of innovation and enterprise—behaving like Danish farmers in fact, but in the United Kingdom. That this failed to occur is not surprising. The traditional society of the Gaels, as we have seen, was not very concerned with wealth maximization, and there was nothing in the legislation that would assist them to compete with the capitalist farmers on the mainland, who had much better land, more resources and close contact with the urban market. Crofting remained, therefore, very much a subsistence occupation. On the other hand, since there was so much political demand for it, it might be expected to have provided a framework for retaining a contented population within the Highlands, even if at a low standard of living. In this it failed as well, since population dropped more rapidly in the period after 1891 than it did in the period before.

Looked at in detail, this accelerated demographic decline appears not to be a function simply of a larger number of people leaving the Highlands: actual migration outwards appears to have run at about 50,000 per decade in the last third of the nineteenth century, compared to about 35,000 per decade in the first third of the twentieth. The fall was also due to a declining birth rate, and above all to the selective effects of the migration, as Adam Collier explained in 1945:

In 1881, the population of the crofter parishes was roughly 180,000; in 1931 it numbered barely 120,000, a fall of about 30% in fifty years. Over the same period, the number of children fell by 41% from 55,000 to 32,500; and the number of women of reproductive age (fifteen to forty-five), on whom the Highlands must depend for the maintenance of numbers in the future, declined by 35% to 26,700. On the other hand, the number of persons over sixty-five *increased* by 36% to 28,500. Since 1931 old people have come to out-number children.[22]

In other words, it was the youngest and most reproductive who found the situation intolerable: the old were content to stay.

The explanation for this is found not in the history of crofting legislation, but in the history of fishing and above all of migrant labour. Fishing had particular importance, either as a part-time occupation of a crofter with an inshore boat, or as part of the migrant labour economy where a man might work on an east-coast trawler or a girl as a fish-gutter following the fleet from Shetland to Yarmouth. The Napier Commission itself in 1884 expressed the belief that more income came to the crofters from the sea than from the land; the Walpole Commission of 1891 claimed that three out of four people in the Highlands and Islands were dependent directly or indirectly either on fishing alone or on a combination of crofting and fishing; the Brand Report of 1902 estimated that while the average Lewis family annually derived a cash income of about £3 from the sale of croft produce, they derived £25 from fishing.[23] In the years following the First World War, the entire Scottish fishing industry passed from boom to crisis when the Russian Revolution brought an end to the hitherto vast East European export trade in herring. Rusting trawlers and rotting nets littered the ports from Stornoway to Lerwick, and from Wick to Anstruther. A major prop of Highland life was knocked away.

The fishing economy had been part of a larger migrant labour economy, ranging from the girls who were welcome in the 'female bothies' on Lothian farms, hoeing turnips and reaping in the summer months, to the engineers who sailed the seven seas for the merchant service and the shipwrights who, according to their employer in Greenock in 1886, absented themselves to return to the croft when the season came for sowing, harvesting and cutting peats.[24] This pattern of work had long had fluctuating fortunes, prosperous in the expanding Victorian economy of the 1860s and 1870s, bad in the 1880s, enjoying something of a revival from the 1890s to the First World War; but after 1920 the plunge in employment opportunities of all kinds in the Lowland cities, the final mechanization of the harvest, and the laying up of the merchant fleets brought it effectively to an end. However, at the same time as the remittances home from the young ceased, the unemployment benefits and old-age pensions from the State commenced. The sums, though meagre enough by other standards, seemed gratifyingly large on the islands: as one observer said of Lewis, 'not a few prayed that "employment" would not come inconveniently soon'.[25] Others noticed that old-age pensions relieved the young of their traditional feelings of obligation to remain behind to support their parents at the ancestral hearths. Thus the elderly were happy to stay at home while the next generation increasingly wanted to explore new horizons.

By its very nature, the institution of migrant labour also had an insidious effect on the ethos of Highland life. How long could a peasant land-preference withstand the temptations and rival values of the exterior world? Collier estimated that what happened in the crofting districts of the Highlands was 'on a par with that of other rural areas' like the Lowland south-west and north-east, and that in the half-century before 1914, over half the crofters' children left the area for good. After 1921, young people were actually slightly less prone to leave because employment conditions in the outside world were less promising, but population fell faster than before because comparatively few who were left were of an age to reproduce themselves. In the twentieth century, he concludes, emigration became 'more a matter of choice; there were fewer potential emigrants who found no alternative course open to them'.[26]

4

One may, then, return to the general question of the nature of the allure that led, if not to the start of rural depopulation, then at least to its continuation both in the Highlands and in the remainder of rural Scotland. It was certainly not that the countryside failed to share in the improvement in the standard of living that occurred in the town. Housing, for example, was transformed, especially in the worst areas. In the 1880s, in the Outer Hebrides:

> The typical Lewis crofter's house was built by the crofter himself; it had double low thick walls of loose stone united by a packing of earth or clay ... There was no chimney and often no window ... only one door, used by the cattle and family alike. Inside, the house usually contained three compartments. In the middle was the living room with a blazing peat-fire filling the house with smoke. Rough stones covered with clay made a cold and damp floor. On the one side of this middle compartment was the sleeping room, on the other the byre. The byre had no paving, and the manure liquids percolated into the ground ...[27]

By the 1930s, this type of 'black house' was being replaced 'not for something worse, but far better', still often built largely by the householder and his friends, but with government aid and to government specifications, up to the standard of council-housing elsewhere.[28] Similarly, in the Lowlands, the beastly old bothy housing for bachelor farm hands in Angus, the Mearns and elsewhere finally died out after the First World War, part of a general amelioration in farm-workers' conditions. For married workers the cottage had always been the preferred housing, and this, too, greatly improved, though even as late as 1913, in the Lothians, some cottages were still to be found with one room, tiled and lacking sanitation. Without higher wages, better housing, good equipment and holidays, however, employers found it increasingly difficult to get men at all. As early as 1892, one reporter had observed that 'the cottages must be very good and the horses young and strong' if the farmer was to keep his ploughmen, and another that 'within the last forty years the material condition of the agricultural labourer has been immensely improved ... comfort is written both inside and outside the cottage'.[29]

Among such improvements could certainly be included the decline of labour in the fields by the wives and children of Lowland workers, which had been a prominent feature of Scottish agricultural life at least until the 1880s. It was a function partly of the belief that agricultural work was 'unwomanly', partly of compulsory school attendance after 1872, and partly of rising wages for the man, which enabled him at once to forgo the supplementary earnings of his family on a regular basis and to add to domestic comfort by keeping his wife at home. Wages and earnings in general rose, and though rural wages remained below town wages, there is no evidence that the gap between town and country widened. In the 1840s, the difference in earnings between country workers in different districts was often very large: it was very large between, say, a Lothian hind on the one hand and a Shetlander or a Lewisman on the other. By 1940, the difference in the standard of living between countrymen doing comparable jobs in the Highlands and Islands and the Lowlands was inconsiderable.

Middle-class observers often expressed a general belief that the working class was better off in the country areas. 'I can remember our infant teacher at Linton, Miss Storrar, who had taught in city schools, telling us how well off we were compared with the children in her classes there,' said Andrew Purves, a Border shepherd recalling the 1920s, adding his own verdict that 'as far as I can recollect there was little sign of the grinding poverty and hopeless misery rampant among working folk in the towns'.[30]

There was a lot in that. When the vogue for measuring boys and girls at school got underway in the early twentieth century, country children were always found to be taller and heavier than town children. As early as 1868, R. Hutchison investigated the diet of agricultural labourers across Scotland and pronounced them 'well fed': he cited in detail the food intake of ploughmen, and when analysed by modern standards their diet was not only good but provided much the same energy values as the diets of agricultural labourers studied in the central Lowlands in 1926—and they, too, had large and healthy children. In 1938, Professor E. P. Cathcart and others measured the calorie intake of families on the west Highland coast and in Lewis and found them appreciably above the norm for the rest of the UK—for example, 15 per cent above that of families in St Andrews and 20 per cent above families in Reading. Compared to the families in St Andrews they ate about 40 per cent more protein. This suggests a high standard of living but was partly a function of narrowness of choice: the Highlanders spent 64 per cent of their budget on food (compared to an estimated norm of 40 per cent for industrial households and 48 per cent for agricultural households elsewhere in Britain) because so much of their income was received in kind, as meal, fish and potatoes, off the croft.[31] When the crofters' choice widened, after the Second World War, nutritionists noted a decline in the physique and dental health of Lewismen, because they now spent more of a larger cash income on junk food like ice-cream and sweets, and on entertainment. However, since that was their choice, it would be absurd and condescending to say that their quality of life had thereby deteriorated.

It might be argued that people left the land in the twentieth century because it was more difficult to 'get on' in the countryside. Farming became more difficult to enter as the average size of the farm increased and more and more capital became necessary. Crofting, from the start of the twentieth century, became easier to enter, but it offered no more prospects for social advancement than before. On the other hand, probably only a few farm labourers and cottars ever thought in terms of upward social mobility. An observer in 1892 commented astutely that 'it is not the opportunities for rising in the world that beguile the majority of our young men from the fields, but the desire for a different manner of life'.[32]

The most careful explanation of what such a 'different manner of life' might mean was provided by James Littlejohn after the Second World War, in his classical anthropological study of 'Westrigg', a real parish in the Borders given a fictional name.[33] It was an isolated, upland parish, typical of many in the south of Scotland, the population of which had fallen from its historic peak of 672 in 1851 to 362 in 1951. Littlejohn saw rural depopulation as originally 'bound up with the growth and development of industry', but as only one aspect of the dominance of the town, which could not 'be explained entirely on an economic basis at the present day'. Part of this dominance found expression in what he termed 'the mingled pity and derision' with which a townsman was wont to regard a countryman: as an inhabitant of the local textile centre said of the people of Westrigg, 'We think that they are all sort of daft—I don't mean mental—but just, well, they don't know how to behave properly.' The country people, for their part, were perfectly well aware of this attitude towards them, and knew that it was the attitude of the majority of society: further, they accepted the low value put on isolation which formed the basis of the townsman's attitude towards them, applying it themselves to those parishioners who still lived in the cottages even further from 'civilization' than themselves:

> In the past and even up to just before the war people lived in these out-bye places 'cos they knew no better. They never saw anybody. Before the war when you went to visit them or went near some of the out-bye places you never saw the kids. They all hid when they saw you coming. You saw them keekin' out behind the curtains or somewhere. They grew up shy and backward.[34]

The people who lived in the greatest isolation were, generally, the shepherds; they were well paid and highly regarded for their skills by the farmer, but of all types of rural worker they were becoming in the 1940s the most difficult to recruit, because young men and their wives were less and less prepared to live in this way.

There was thus among the working class a kind of ladder of values which amounted, in Littlejohn's words, to 'a rejection of the status of working-class countryman'. A person in one of the most isolated parts of Westrigg was looked down on by someone from a less isolated part: but everyone in Westrigg was looked down on by the people in the nearest small town; they in turn were regarded as living in a dump by those of the next larger town; and those in the cities thought of the inhabitants of all these country parts as mere ignorant yokels.

This was not, Littlejohn stressed, in any way a middle-class value system: the farmers did not think Westrigg isolated—'it only takes me two hours in a car to get to Edinburgh'—and such immigrants as there were in the parish were upper-middle-class people retiring to enjoy the amenities of the countryside. He also believed that it was 'a fairly recent phenomenon', which is doubtful in view of the very similar views found as far back as the 1890s, though it is probably true that it grew in intensity over the years. It is also evident that this value system came to affect more and more of the countryside until it reached the Highlands and Islands and Lewis itself, competing successfully there with the older ideology of land-preference.

On what was the 'rejection of the status of working-class countryman', this horror of their isolated existence, based? Littlejohn suggested

Street scenes in Dundee before the First World War: notice the bare feet, the bent legs of the children with rickets and (below) the mothers sitting on the pavement. But there is no street litter in a pre-plastic world.

The abiding tenement: LEFT a Glasgow close off the High Street, photographed between 1868 and 1877 before demolition by the City Improvement Trust.
The dim outlines of its inhabitants can be discerned: ABOVE old but inhabited houses in Edinburgh Grassmarket, 1850s; BELOW Powrie Place, Dundee, in the 1920s.

Council housing: ABOVE the ideal artisan dwelling envisaged by planners in 1912: space, greenery and Dutch gables; BELOW the reality, Shotts, Lanarkshire, 1954: no architectural indulgence or trees. The houses in the right foreground are post-1945 'prefabs', the remainder more enduring and typical local authority housing.

Horsepower: two plough teams near Anstruther, Fife, c. 1940.

Crofter power: the men are using the caschrom or foot plough,
and the women fertilizing the ground with seaweed, Skye, c. 1885.

ABOVE steam drifters leaving Anstruther, in the 1930s. BELOW the herring fleet in Fraserburgh, late nineteenth century. There are probably 1000 masts in this photograph.

ABOVE women gutting fish at Peterhead, 1910. Notice the boys minding the baby.
BELOW fishing families at Ferryden, Angus, 1905.

ABOVE haymaking in north Fife in the 1930s; notice how many people are required. BELOW a farm bothy party, Straiton, Fife, in the early 1920s; tea, girls, fiddle and accordion, and bikes with flashy dropped handlebars.

that it had to do with the absence in the countryside of the opportunity to associate with a sufficiently wide range of people, which was also connected both with geographical distance from facilities that mattered, like pub, cinema, football ground, dance hall, and with the lack of fixed free time that country workers like shepherds had to put up with. As one put it to him: 'What happens now is a shepherd goes to town once in a while, meets pals who have leisure at weekends and the same wage or mebbe more, and he knows they have leisure every weekend.'[35] Such resentments, again, were not new. *The Fife Herald and Journal* in 1903 quoted a rhyme about the ploughmen:

Six days shalt thou labour and do all
That you are able;
On the Sabbath-day wash the horses' legs
And tiddy up the stable.[36]

Rural depopulation therefore occurred when the young, in particular, felt their need to associate could only be met by going to town. For them, the rural 'community' had ceased to be a community they cared about.

This process was probably long drawn-out, and associated with the rise of a homogenous popular culture. Among the factors leading to such homogeneity, the spread of compulsory schooling after 1872, with its concomitant of government inspection and a uniform examination system, was very important. The board schools were explicitly intended to equip rural children for life outside and to give them the appropriate linguistic skills to cope away from their own district. In the north-east of Scotland this meant ironing out the local dialect, 'the Doric', from a child's speech: in the western Highlands it meant discouragement of the use of Gaelic within the school and its replacement by English both for teaching and for ordinary communication. There is no reason to think this was not supported by parents: especially in the Gaelic areas, they looked upon the acquisition of fluent English by their children as a prime way to increase their earning capacity in the migrant economy. But seventy years of uniform education, combined everywhere with better physical communications, tended by osmosis to produce a uniform culture in which the ways of the town were given a higher value than those of the countryside. At the same time, the cultural influence of the churches as centres of local life gradually diminished, while after the First World War the influence of the radio and cinema rose in prestige to portray a metropolitan and essentially big-city culture. In these terms, therefore, certainly in the twentieth century, rural depopulation represents the final victory, in the struggle for the hearts and minds of the people, of the town over the country.

CHAPTER IV

A Working Life in Industry

1

The Scottish industrial economy, its foundations firmly laid between 1790 and 1830, rose to its greatest heights just before 1914, and then, in the interwar years, suffered a reverse that cut to the quick the self-confidence of the nation.

In the 1830s and 1840s, the existing predominance of textiles, especially of cotton, was challenged by the rise of the iron industry along with its attendants, coal-mining and engineering. In the final decades of the nineteenth century, ship-building and steel manufacture took the place of the iron industry. The central belt of Scotland became, in the process, one of the most intensively industrialized regions on the face of the earth. By 1913, Glasgow, claiming for herself the title of 'Second City of the Empire', made, with her satellite towns immediately to the east and west, one-fifth of the steel, one-third of the shipping tonnage, one-half of the marine-engine horsepower, one-third of the railway locomotives and rolling stock, and most of the sewing machines in the United Kingdom. Dundee carried out almost all the manufacturing of jute in Britain. Dunfermline was still famous for linen, Paisley for thread, the Border towns for knitwear and tweeds, Edinburgh for a range of consumer goods, Aberdeen for textiles and granite. If the coal-fields of Lanarkshire and Ayrshire were gradually contracting, those of Fife and Lothian were rapidly growing. Scotland, as much social commentary in the first decade of the twentieth century witnessed, knew herself to be a country of squalor, exploitation, bad housing and disease, but she also looked upon herself as rich and successful. The gap in income between England and Scotland, so enormous in 1707 and gaping still in the 1840s, had narrowed substantially by 1914. Then came the collapse of the staple trades in the interwar years, soaring structural unemployment, and depression. George Malcolm Thomson, journalist and member of the recently-formed Scottish National Party (SNP), wrote in 1935:

> The belt of coal mines, blast furnaces, factories, shipyards, docks and railways uniting one grim-faced town to another across the desecrated countryside ... to us it is the outward and visible sign of the labour, the courage, the foresight, the inventive genius of our nation ... But tell us that the great structure is itself in decay, convince us that our place among the thriving and busy of the earth, won at such cost, is ours no longer, show us that the hands of the clock have begun to move backwards, that there are no more high cards left in the pack, and where can we look for comfort? ... Finis has been written to a chapter two hundred years long. A new chapter begins. There are grand dividing lines drawn in red ink across the history of all nations. In Scotland there was the arrival of Queen Margaret in the year 1068, the battle of Flodden Field in 1513. In Ireland there was the Famine of 1846. In England there was the last of the Viking raids in 1066. The turn of the industrial tide in Scotland must inevitably be for the Scottish nation an event of such proportions.[1]

From the perspective of fifty years later, the verdict seems perspicacious. What Thomson could not see, however, was that after the red line had been drawn, it would prove possible to construct a new economy, not so glamorous, perhaps, as the first one, nor so high in the international league tables of output and income, but nevertheless capable by the 1980s of giving those who depended upon it a very much higher standard of living than had been possible in the pre-1914 years. This process had begun, but had not been taken very far, by 1950.

The ebb and flow of sectoral and regional prosperity created and destroyed jobs on a grand scale, as Table 1 opposite indicates. Thus farming and textiles lost half their jobs over the century, and mining, having grown two-and-a-half times in the fifty years to 1901, shrank back by a quarter by 1951. These losses were more than balanced by gains in other sectors of manufacturing, notably in the metal trades, and especially by the great growth of the service industries, which exceeded

TABLE 1

Working population of Scotland by broad industrial group, 1851–1951
(000s employed)

Year	Metals	Textiles & clothing	Other manufacturing	Agriculture & fishing	Mining	Services	Total
1851	60.8	366.4	66.2	347.6	48.1	380.8	1269.9
1901	210.4	299.2	147.7	237.3	127.9	879.6	1902.1
1951	358.2	174.5	255.9	160.7	97.2	1148.3	2194.8

Source: A. K. Cairncross (ed.), *The Scottish Economy* (Cambridge, 1954), table 36, p. 77

manufacturing and mining even in 1901 and accounted for more than half the jobs in Scotland by 1951. In all, the Scottish labour-force increased by three-quarters over the century, but whereas in 1851 it had represented 14 per cent of the British total, by 1951 it formed only 10 per cent. Many people had reacted to the problems of their working environment by leaving.

These processes created industrial working communities of almost infinite variation. Clydeside, for example, was dominated by the image of the skilled male craftsman and time-served apprentice: probably over 70 per cent of the employment in the Glasgow region at the start of the twentieth century could be classified as more or less skilled. But it left room for variety even within the city: for example, while 8300 men worked for the North British Locomotive Company in the traditional furnaces, forges and engineering shops of their three great works, there were over 6000 employees of Glasgow Corporation clipping tickets and driving trams on the 200 miles of municipal track. The term 'engineering' itself could by 1900 cover jobs of totally different skill content and degrees of work-satisfaction. At Singers of Clydebank, for example, 10,000 men and women were employed making sewing machines with the latest American machinery: the division of labour had been carried so far as to make the men feel themselves becoming mindless robots:

I remember Arthur MacManus describing a job he was on, pointing needles. Every morning there were millions of these needles on the table. As fast as he reduced the mountains of needles, a fresh load was dumped. Day in, day out, it never grew less. One morning he came in and found the table empty. He couldn't understand it. He began telling everyone excitedly that there were no needles on the table. It suddenly flashed on him how absurdly stupid it was to be spending his life like this. Without taking his jacket off, he turned on his heel and went out, to go for a ramble over the hills to Balloch.[2]

On the other hand there still existed traditional shops, perhaps backward in the technological sense, where the old premium on the skill and care of the engineer remained, as described by Harry McShane, who, like MacManus, was to play a prominent part in the discontent of Red Clydeside:

> Butter Brothers was a very interesting place. There was very little machinery in the works, and the engineers had to do everything by hand. You were given a wheel and a shaft and the keys for the big cranes and they all came still black from the blacksmiths, not even polished; you had to cut the key-way in the shaft and in the barrel by eye, with a candle at the other end. The key had to be tapered to an eighth of an inch so that it wouldn't slip out, and you had to do that without drawings. Butter Brothers did many jobs like that, with no machinery.[3]

Glasgow, for all its variety, was stamped by a compulsive, male-dominated, working-class culture. Totally different was Dundee, where the jute mills sought to fight off Indian competition by using low-paid female labour. It was a city described by the women's male contemporaries as filled with 'over-dressed, loud, bold-eyed girls', and 'tousled loud-voiced lassies with the light of battle in their defiant eyes discussing with animation and candour the grievances that had constrained them to leave their work'.[4] At the beginning of the twentieth century, there were almost three women to every two men in the city between the ages of twenty and forty-five, and a third of all heads of household (as defined in the census) were women. In 1921, 24 per cent of Dundee married women were working, compared to 6 per cent of married women in Glasgow and 5.6 per cent in Edinburgh. It was a situation considered scandalous by people of many shades of opinion. Glasgow's ILP *Forward* newspaper regarded it as a wicked example of capitalism's propensity to destroy the home: 'The husbands stay at home dry nursing: the woman goes out to earn wages: what an inversion of civilization.'[5] The middle-class Dundee Social Union prescribed not better housing or higher wages, but 'more occupation for men' as the 'crying need of Dundee'. For the women themselves it was just a fact of life; they elaborated their own culture of proletarian female independence, and the husband or son who could not get a job did indeed stay at home to do the housework: 'He used to hae the hoose spotless when she come in, she says, an' ma denner a' made.'[6]

Thirty miles away on the Fife coal-field, the opposite situation prevailed. Here there was virtually no work at all for women apart from picking coal at the bings, a filthy and degrading business only done by a few poor unmarried girls. The labour-force and the community were completely dominated by the miner, whose work on the eve of the First World War was comparatively well paid, demanded absolute physical fitness, and was totally exhausting. When the men came home they expected to be looked after. A perceptive and otherwise sympathetic outsider spoke of the women's 'slavery to the men' at Kelty in these terms:

> Not once can I remember of the women eating their meals with the men ... There were two big easy chairs in the kitchen ... and if either of them chanced to be occupied by one of the girls or women when the men arrived it was instantly left ... I have seen a son of one-or-two-and-twenty order his mother across the room to get his pipe which was on a shelf directly above his head a few inches out of his reach from the chair where he was sitting.[7]

A miner who read through this passage before it was published remarked with indignation to the author, 'Instead of "slavery" you should call it "devotion".'

Apart from the differences imposed by varying patterns of employment in different areas, there were certain basic divisions among industrial workers that were common everywhere. The distinction between the respectable and the unrespectable was of the most crucial significance. It had to do with lifestyles and moral attitudes towards thrift, cleanliness, drink, recreation, sexual behaviour, religion, and so forth; it might be related to work and occupation, but it was certainly not just coterminous with the distinction between the skilled and the unskilled. For clerical and service workers, for instance, the trappings of respectability were often a matter of necessity. As a Church of Scotland committee expressed it in 1894, married clerks and warehousemen were especially prone to be haunted by 'concealed anxieties and difficulties ... needing, on slender means, and with the risk of losing situations as they advance in years, to maintain the outward signs of conventional respectability'.[8] For them it was primarily a matter of clean collars and never smelling of drink. Clerks, indeed, were often suspected by the other workers of hypocrisy and social climbing, though they were also, just as often, rejected by those above them in the social scale as being not really middle class. In Victorian Edinburgh they took their 'respectable' recreation as members of the Bowling Clubs in company with the professional and commercial classes rather than with the skilled artisans in the Bruntsfield Links Allied Golf Club and the Working Men's Flower Show.[9] The latter organizations were, of course, equally respectable, but they were dominated by well-paid manual workers with whom the clerks did not wish to associate.

For the manual worker, respectability was much more a matter of choice, in the sense that an iron moulder or a labourer was unlikely to get the sack merely because his employer found him with a racing newspaper or a bottle of beer in his pocket. Characteristically, the skilled man nevertheless cultivated respectability, joining a friendly society or a co-operative store, perhaps making a deposit in a savings bank, possibly becoming a member of a temperance organization or a church, and certainly making an effort to ensure the regular attendance of his child at school: the tendency was systematically to avoid drunkenness, gambling, swearing and fighting, as far as possible to pay debts on time, and to present a clean and decent home to the neighbours. Such behaviour demanded self-discipline and had a pay-off in material terms: 'respectable' workers could better withstand spells of unemployment and had a better chance of slight upward mobility for their children.

However, this path was easier to follow with a high wage than a low one: friendly societies demanded subscriptions; flower shows presupposed leisure and room to grow flowers; tidy children and a scrubbed stair called for a wife who was not obliged to go out to work after marriage. For this reason, respectability was particularly associated with skilled workers: it was not universal even among them, but it was seen by those who practised it as worth the struggle. 'Touching the lower end of the middle class,' said the Church of Scotland committee, 'there are thousands always and often with difficulty holding the wolf at bay.'[10] Improbable moral tales reinforced respectability's imperative. As late as 1935, David Kirkwood, the Red Clydeside shop steward at Beardmores, seriously told the tale of the 'T.T. Youths', all like himself members of the Good Templars temperance association, and the contrasting 'Jolly Twelve', who worked at the same engineering factory but set out to have a good time:

> We met for lectures, concerts, socials and the rest of it. We also went to night school. We had no money. 'The Jolly Twelve' had money from their mothers. They had the evenings to themselves, went into Glasgow and came home late, often the worse for drink, when they would become noisy, swearing young men. They called it 'seeing life' ... Of the eleven of 'The Jolly Twelve' none lived beyond thirty-six, and eight killed themselves. I know of none that left children, but one committed suicide a week before his son was born. Of the eleven of the other group, all are living except one (who died at sixty-three). Everyone prospered, and their families prosper also.[11]

At first sight it might seem as if those with less income than a young engineer would be even better advised to follow the example of the T.T. Youths, but for the unskilled on low or irregular wages it was much more difficult to keep up a respectable lifestyle however hard you saved, so much more tempting to blow everything on a horse or a night's drinking when there were windfall earnings. Consequently labourers, and the Irish in particular, came to have a reputation for fighting, drunkenness and general 'bad' behaviour, and as they were also obliged to live in the worst housing conditions it was easy for the middle classes, and for many respectable artisans too, to retain the comforting belief that the poor remained poor because they were morally bad. But thousands among the poorest also tried to maintain the canons of respectability as far as they could, eagerly assisted by a Catholic Church that wanted to see the lambs in its flock at least as decent as Protestants. One such was Harry McShane's grandfather, a Glasgow building labourer, 'a well-respected man ... always decently dressed in a blue suit':

> He set his watch every Sunday night by the Edwards clock on Buchanan Street so he would rise in good time for work in the morning: he never missed a minute of work and I never remember him being sick. He made me behave myself, but he couldn't have the kind of influence on me that my father had because neither he nor my grandmother could read or write.[12]

Kirkwood's father was a Protestant labourer in the same mould, so obsessively punctual that his foot was 'probably on the exact step' half way down the tenement stair every day when the factory horn sounded: 'He had a passion for cleanliness. He never smoked. He spent no money on himself . . .'[13] It is no coincidence that both had descendants who made the difficult transition from unskilled work to artisan; and perhaps no coincidence that both descendants made a name for themselves as activists in an emerging labour movement that was obsessed not with individual self-improvement, but with the improvement of a class.

The division between the respectable and the unrespectable might be construed as moral: the division between the skilled and the unskilled was institutional. It formed a deep gulf across the working class, scarcely questioned in the nineteenth century either by management or labour in the manual trades, and only slowly eroded by the rise of semi-skilled grades in engineering and elsewhere at the end of the nineteenth century. Up to the 1950s, it was still a major split, and even today a craft apprentice relaxing in a pub might give his opinion of labourers in language that he would not, even in the company of his colleagues, apply to the boss.

Generally, a skilled worker was one who had served an apprenticeship lasting several years, while an unskilled one had simply walked onto the job. This was true for instance of the ship-building trades, where the riveter was skilled and the holder-on was not; of the building industry (the mason and the builder's labourer); of printing (the compositor and the men or women who fed the letterpress printing machines); and of the railways (engine-drivers and porters). It was not true in the mines, where it was generally thought that the skill of a hewer could be acquired after a relatively short period of practice, and where the unskilled on-cost man, who took the coal and rubbish out behind the hewer, was likely one day (given health and strength) to spend part of his life as a hewer, a transformation of a kind never likely to happen in the apprenticed trades.

In the cotton textile trade in Glasgow and in the jute trade in Dundee the main labour-force was female and there were no proper apprenticeships, but the weavers were traditionally regarded as skilled and well paid and the spinners as unskilled and badly paid. There seemed to be no reason in terms of the difficulty of learning the job why this should be so, but there was certainly a difference in the degree of responsibility expected of the two groups at work: if a weaver spoiled a piece of cloth by negligence in the final stages, all the raw material and labour power invested in the process up to that point was irretrievably wasted; if a spinner was momentarily inattentive it was a simple matter to piece together the yarns and start again. In any case the women maintained the distinctions as fiercely as any craftsmen. In Glasgow, though spinners and weavers both lived in Bridgeton under similar social conditions, there was 'a quite remarkable difference in their appearance and habits' and 'little social intercourse between the two'.[14] In Dundee, a 'greetin' faced weaver' would not dream of speaking to a 'snuffy spinner': 'They wore a hat, an' they wore gloves ... we used tae jist rin wi' wir jeckets on—nae hats or gloves.' Billy Kay recorded a Dundee joke about the weaver who went to the Registrar to fix up her marriage:

> So he says to her, 'Now—you're a spinster?' And she says, 'No look I'm a weaver.' And he says, 'Now look lassie, doon on this form put—you're a spinster.' She says, 'Dinna ca' me a spinster, because I'm a weaver.' So he says to her, 'Look lassie, are you ignorant?' She says, 'Aye, fower month.'[15]

Some industries, indeed, contained no one who was not classified as unskilled—like navvying, the first refuge of the Irish when they came over the sea, and carting, the first refuge of the agricultural labourer come to town. Others, such as bread-making and the pottery industry in Glasgow around 1900, were in the process of being transferred from the province of the skilled to that of the unskilled, due to the adoption of new machinery. It was this kind of technological substitution of capital for skill, already visible at Singers before the First World War, that made the Glasgow engineers so edgy about tolerating the introduction of women onto the shop floor in the munitions factories in the years that followed. They feared, and not without reason, that the new lathes would make their operators mere machine-minders, and that an attentive worker of either sex, if allowed in, would be able to do the job that had kept the male engineer for so many years top of the Clyde-side tree.

Very often, however, a job defined by the outside world as unskilled would demand an extraordinary level of expertise to carry it out successfully. Durland told of two girls in 1904, the youngest aged fifteen, who worked at the brick kilns at Kelty in temperatures of up to 150° Fahrenheit, handling 5–6000 bricks a day, a pair weighing 12 lbs: 'The girls lift them, one in each hand, from the bogey to the pile, setting them down a finger's width apart, working at a high speed that is bewildering ... there are no two men in the brickyards who can handle as many bricks.'[16] They were paid 2s. 3d. a day, 'which is distinctly better ... than the pithead girls'. A miner at the same time was paid 6s. 8d. a day, and a male labourer in the brick-fields 4s. 4d.

The opportunities for intergenerational mobility from unskilled jobs to skilled were not high until the end of the period, though they then apparently improved dramatically. For most of the second half of the nineteenth century, one of the main purposes of the craft unions in the towns was to maintain apprenticeship regulations that would favour their own kin. Labourers, of whom a high proportion were Catholic Irish, had little chance of breaking the barrier. An investigation into the children of the Edinburgh Canongate in 1906 showed that about half the sons of workers in the metal trades went into skilled occupations, but only one in ten of the children of unskilled labourers.[17] A second enquiry, published in 1924, drew on the experiences of the unskilled in Glasgow, Middlesborough and south Wales and found that 450 families provided 313 children for skilled apprenticeships, but that their chances of crossing the great divide depended mainly on the income of the families. The top 10 per cent of the unskilled families provided nearly a third of the apprentices, but they were mostly those in relatively comfortable circumstances, earning £4 a week and upwards in 1920. The bottom third of the families provided no apprentices at all, but they were those 'on the verge of destitution', with casual employment and earnings ranging from 35s. to 65s. The conclusions were, firstly, that the poor were in general obliged to sacrifice the future of their sons (particularly the eldest) for the prospect of the immediately higher wages that could be earned outside apprenticeship, and secondly, that children from very poor homes were also too physically weak and culturally handicapped to be taken on by firms looking for industrial trainees.[18] In 1951, however, an investigation of Glasgow boys found that 'the idea ... that there is almost a caste-system in industrial grades of labour' no longer held. About half the sons of skilled, semi-skilled and non-manual working fathers reached skilled status, but so did 45 per cent of the sons of the unskilled.[19] Presumably the advent of more democratic trade unions, the comparative blurring of craft lines with a proliferation of semi-skilled jobs (just what the engineers had feared), and a general rise in income above the level of destitution during the Second World War at last broke the equation, like father, like son.

2

For the Scottish child, work began young, though the deepest horrors of child exploitation were gradually eliminated in the middle decades of the nineteenth century. Legislation slowly extended from Althorp's Act of 1833, which had laid down a minimum age for the employment of children in cotton mills of nine years, limited their hours to eight in the day up to the age of thirteen, and appointed inspectors: in Scotland the effects were seriously undermined by the absence of civil registration of births until 1855 (so that it was impossible to prove the age of a child) and by the character of the first Factory Inspector, James Stuart of Dunearn, whose inefficiency and partiality for the employers hung a millstone round the effective operation of the law until his death in 1849.[20] The Mines Act of 1842 prohibited the labour of women and young children below ground, and thus terminated the horrible system by which boys and girls of seven or eight worked in darkness and filth drawing tubs of coal from the face for fourteen hours a day. Ashley's Act of 1847 restricted the employment in factories of women and all young persons between thirteen and eighteen to ten hours a day, but it omitted to protect many who did not work in mills: the calender works that pressed and smoothed cloth, for example, employed very young children for twelve hours or more until they were brought under the Factory Act in 1863. It seems likely, in fact, that child labour actually increased in the third quarter of the century as industry itself increased, for many unskilled workers' families simply could not afford to keep their children from working if there was work available, and most employers could find some ill-paid and time-demanding task for juvenile hands. The Argyll Commission, discovering in 1867 that one-fifth of children of school age were not receiving education, attributed it partly to the fact that 'child labour abounded wherever the Factory Act is not in operation'.[21]

It was, ultimately, the reform of the school system that most effectively limited child labour. The Education Act of 1872 made school attendance compulsory from five to thirteen, though with numerous exemptions and provisions for 'half-time' work. In 1883, the leaving age was raised to fourteen, but children over the age of ten (later raised to twelve) were allowed to work as half-timers if they had reached 'Standard III' in reading, writing and arithmetic, and were allowed to leave altogether if they had reached 'Standard V'. The system of half-timers and exemptions was not completely abolished until 1936, and only in 1945 was the school-leaving age for all pupils raised to fifteen.

For many children, the first experience of work, by the late nineteenth century, was, therefore, a part-time job out of school hours. That could be either gruelling or fun. Tom Bell remembered his milk round, about 1890, when he was eight or nine: it involved carrying twenty cans at a time up four flights of tenement stairs for ls. 6d. a week: 'On a winter morning our hands were cracked and bleeding with the frost and cold, and I cried.'[22] Abe Moffat, on the other hand, recalled how around 1908, when he was twelve or thirteen in the Fife mining village of Lumphinnans, he repaid his parents for the present of a violin by taking on a paper-round—'a complete monopoly, as there was no other paper-boy in the place'. He received 3s. 6d. a week and 'lots of tips, and all my school mates, both boys and girls, were always waiting on me coming into school, as my pockets were full of chocolates and sweets'.[23] By the late 1940s, apparently only 10 per cent of Glasgow boys had employment out of school hours, and the proportion did not vary according to the skill of the father: only in that group of boys where the father was dead did the proportion rise to 12 per cent.

In Dundee before the First World War, the continuing employment of girls between the ages of twelve and fourteen raised problems more reminiscent of the early days of Queen Victoria than of the twentieth century. In 1900, there were some 5000 working either as 'half-timers' or as whole-timers exempted from further attendance at school during the day after having passed the necessary standards, but not exempted from school altogether. The half-timers either went to work and to the board school on alternate days, or went to special factory schools run by the largest employers like Buists or Baxters, where they were employed for half the day as 'shifters' in the mill and spent the other half in the classroom. The latter system was much preferred by medical opinion as less exhausting for the children. Far worse was the lot of whole-timers, who from the age of thirteen worked in the mill for five days a week from 6 a.m. to 6 p.m. (with two hours free for meals) and were then, by order of Dundee School Board, made to attend evening school from 7.15 to 9.15 p.m. until they were fourteen. The Certifying Factory Surgeon was extremely critical:

> It is a terrible strain—a long, long day for even a grown woman. If the girl is not very much above the average strength this is sure to tell very seriously. Is it to be wondered at, that they become languid, anaemic and stunted, growing into womanhood with a decided appearance that Nature had intended them to be women of much greater physical strength.[24]

His colleague in the Factory Inspectorate acidly commented that effectively making boys and girls aged thirteen work a twelve-hour day appeared to be legal in Scotland 'while for such children in India a working day above seven hours is forbidden by law'.[25] It was easy to blame the Dundee School Board for granting far more exemptions and permissions for half-time work than any other authority in Scotland, but they were under pressure from extremely poor parents who simply could not make ends meet without the shillings of their own children.

Around the start of the present century, therefore, outside Dundee, work began for most children when they were fourteen. For some, the way ahead was obvious: 'Like every other young boy in a mining village, I knew that my pit clothes with piece-box and flask were ready six weeks before I left school.'[26] For others, it was a matter of finding something to do before a craft apprenticeship, which would not normally begin before sixteen. Tom Bell began as a milkman around 1890, working twelve hours from 6.30 a.m. for 1s. 6d. a week; then he found a better job as van-boy for a mineral water firm, hawking 'Iron Brew' and lemonade round Airdrie and Coatbridge ('the iron-workers in these infernos had a perpetual thirst'); next he entered the bottling factory for a better wage of 16s. a week, and finally became of an age to be apprenticed as an iron-moulder at Beardmores.[27] R. H. Tawney's investigation in Glasgow in 1907 found that half the lads who left school became milk-boys or van-boys, a quarter became unskilled labourers of one sort or another, and only one in eight was immediately taken on as apprentice or learner.[28]

For those not ultimately going forward into apprenticeship, the teenage years were often a succession of jobs with no guarantee of permanent employment at the end. Tawney found that 'It is rare for a boy to pass through less than six places between 14 and 21, common for him to pass through twelve, while in some cases he passes through twenty or thirty.' Many were dead-end jobs, where the boss deliberately took on boys because he knew he could pay them much less than a man's wage, and fired them when they were older in order to hire more boys at the starting end. This was notoriously true in Dundee, where loom-doffers (who assisted with the weaving machinery) were turned adrift at eighteen, trained for nothing, and fit only to enter the army or join the swollen ranks of casual labour. It was true also throughout Glasgow, where Tawney listed among 'almost entirely non-educational employments' such things as 'oven boys in bakeries, rivet boys in boiler shops, drawers off in sawmills, packers in soap works, machine-minders in furniture factories, labellers in mineral-water factories'.[29] Over the next forty years, conditions changed for the better but did not alter out of all recognition. Ferguson and Cunnison's report of 1951 showed that Glasgow boys changed jobs on average once a year in the first three years after leaving school, and that what were now termed 'stopgap jobs' persisted: a third of the semi-skilled and two-thirds of the unskilled did not believe themselves to be permanently settled in their employment at the age of seventeen. The late 1940s provided full employment and considerable competition in the labour-market, and persistence in stopgap jobs was then a feature of the socially deprived—those who had lost a parent, were physically or emotionally disadvantaged, or had been bad at school.[30] The unsteadiness of the young unskilled, which to the Victorians had been a sign of their unrespectability and which Tawney had seen as a manifestation of the inhumane nature of the capitalist system, appeared to his successors as a consequence of the incomplete nature of the welfare state.

Boys hoping to become skilled craftsmen entered an apprenticeship, generally at the age of sixteen. It was a bone of contention between employers and unions what the appropriate ratio of apprentices to journeymen should be. Employers wanted relatively large numbers of apprentices who could be paid very little during their indentures but would do many jobs as well as an adult; unions wanted a low ratio to avoid their trade being flooded by time-served men. The unions had relatively little success. Edinburgh Trades Council reported in 1873 that only two of the twelve trades in the city had any limitation (one apprentice to three journeymen) and the struggles of the 1890s broke the efforts of the engineers and boiler-makers on the Clyde to hold a satisfactory ratio.

An even more serious anxiety around 1900, however, related to the content of apprentice training. An apprenticeship lasted between three and seven years, usually about five years, but instead of the time being used to give a lad all-round experience of the various departments of a workshop, to train a competent engineer or a baker who could turn his hand to anything, there was a tendency to narrow the training to one part of one trade, teach him rapidly, and then use him in effect as an underpaid semi-skilled hand. The great railway shop at Springburn, for example, distinguished between 'premium apprentices', who were middle-class youths moving quickly through the shop floor before entering management, 'privilege apprentices', who, either because they were exceptionally clever and keen or because they were the sons of old employees, were moved from one department to another to learn a range of skills including fitting, erecting, turning and boiler-making, and were possibly even allowed to enter the drawing office, and 'ordinary apprentices', the vast majority, who trained either as fitters, or as erectors, or as turners, but had no experience beyond a certain machine which they could learn to operate very quickly.[31]

'Over-specialization' for apprentices was accompanied by the spread of semi-skilled jobs for which little formal preparation was ever required, and many teenagers drifted in that direction once they had become bored with a long and futile training or impatient with earning so little as apprentices. In the long run, however, there would be a big difference in earnings: a specialized machine-minder around 1900 took home between 22s. and 28s. a week, a time-served craftsman 36s. It was easy to make the wrong choice, and in any case to get a good apprenticeship or a good job generally required 'pull'. The reputation of fathers was often essential. When 'the son of a railway labourer became a clerk in the railway office, and a chemical labourer's son was apprenticed as an analyst in the works' it was because the parents 'had worked there for several years, were steady and persevering and had gained the high regard of the work's manager'.[32] Sometimes the 'pull' was a little more basic, especially if jobs were short: 'At the works out our way you've got to table a pint of beer for the foreman and I can hardly get a pint for myself.'[33] The foreman, indeed, had great powers of hiring and firing. In many Clyde engineering works and shipyards—most famously in John Browns—they were Freemasons, Orangemen and Rangers supporters who thought it part of their calling to discourage the Catholic Irish. Conversely, in many building and contracting firms and at the Greenock sugar refineries, the foremen were themselves

Irish, went to Celtic Park on Saturday, and blackballed Protestant applications to labour in their squad. Overall, however, the sectarian balance at work was definitely on the Protestant side, since the Irish had originally immigrated as unskilled and encountered an entrenched Scottish work force determined, if possible, to keep them that way. It was not until towards the end of the period that being Catholic ceased to mean being at the bottom of the pile in most manufacturing employments.

3

Once trained—however inadequately—and once taken on for an adult wage—however contrived—the worker could then look forward to a lifetime of labour, interrupted no doubt by spells of unemployment. For some, for example steel-workers, coal-miners and jute-workers, most of their life might be spent in one place on the payroll of one firm. For others, a good deal of shifting about was inevitable. An investigation into a Clyde shipyard in 1953 showed that two-fifths of the 300 employees had been there less than a year, and only one-fifth more than five years.[34] This was nothing new. Research on Clydeside before the First World War suggests that half the ship-building labour-force regularly changed their place of work, some because they were forced to when contracts on individual vessels were completed and they were paid off, some because they responded to the lure of higher wages in another yard. The former situation was regarded by employers as a fact of life their workers must put up with, the latter as an evil practice. Thus, in 1880, Charles Connell wrote to Barclay Curle:

> David Law, Angle ironsmith, who has been in our employment for the last four months, informed us this morning, that as he was going home last night, he was hailed from the car by your Foreman and offered larger wages ... Our Foreman, on hearing this offered him an advance to stay, but as the man has not returned from his interview with your Foreman he has seemingly outbid us ... As we think it is most unfair to entice our men away by offering exorbitant wages, we would be glad to know if you approve of what your Foreman has done. We would just like to point out that if once we

begin to outbid one another in this way, it would be the most effectual plan we could adopt to increase the rates of wages all over.[35]

The free market was evidently supposed only to work in one direction.

The degree of mobility on the Clyde varied from trade to trade, being rather low among smiths but rather high among joiners, who had the option of moving into house-building when trade was bad in ship-building. For the unskilled there was a great deal of moving from job to job, not from choice, but from the casual, often seasonal, nature of their work. Thus in the early 1900s there were 30 per cent more labourers needed in Glasgow Corporation Gasworks at the midwinter peak than at the midsummer trough, and the brick-makers and sawyer's labourers who were laid off in bad weather made for the gasworks in December and January. Such neat dovetailing was, however, seldom practicable, and most unskilled workers suffered long spells of unemployment between jobs.[36]

The effects of the Factory Acts that limited the hours of women and children had some impact, in the end, on men's hours. A general gain for most male workers was the arrival of a Saturday half day in the course of the 1860s, though as late as 1865 Gladstone was refusing to allow it for Civil Service clerks. In fact the length of the working day for adults varied considerably from job to job before the First World War. The Royal Commission on Labour, reporting in the early 1890s, revealed enormous differences, depending on custom, union strength, and the nature of the work. Most successful at limiting their working hours were a section of the miners: those in Fife had secured a reduction of the working week from 60 hours to 44 between 1850 and 1890, and were exceedingly proud of their achievement of the eight-hour day (half a day on Saturday) by negotiation in 1871; underground workers in Ayrshire had done even better, at 39 hours, but Lanarkshire miners worked 50 hours. At the other extreme were transport workers. The Glasgow carters reported that they regularly worked a 98-hour week (including the boys), rising at 4.30 a.m. and returning at 9.30 p.m. for 5 days a week, with a 13-hour day on Saturday instead of the usual 17 hours. On the railways, the Caledonian and North British Railways worked their drivers, guards, porters and signalmen as long as possible. Drivers between Perth and Carlisle would leave Perth at 5.00 a.m., arrive at Carlisle at 12.30 p.m., overhaul the engine and start back without a break to arrive again in Perth at 8.30 p.m., doing 15½ hours on duty 5 or 6 days a week. Shunting drivers might shunt for 12 hours without a break, and this was by no means the worst of it:

> On a train in the Dunfermline district an engine driver and fireman were on duty 18½ hours on the sixteenth of July 1892; 17¾ hours on the eighteenth; 22 hours 55 minutes on the nineteenth; 23 hours on the twenty-first and 18 hours on the twenty-fifth, beginning at midnight on Sunday the twenty-fourth.

And for the signalman at Inverkeithing:

> During a 12 hours' shift the number of electric signals is about 5950; entries in the train book, about 1408; lever movements, close upon 1000. The signalman has to attend to all these duties on the spur of the moment and a slight mistake might be disastrous.

It was no wonder that there were sometimes appalling accidents and that the death rate among staff on the railways rivalled, and sometimes exceeded, that in the mines.

Other examples of very long hours included the chemical workers, where three-fifths of the employees were said to work 12 hours a day for 7 days a week, and the employees in various retail outlets where the hours ranged from 83½ a week in bakers' shops down to 69½ a week in china shops. The Secretary of the Scottish Shopkeepers' and Assistants' Union was bitter about the problem: there were, he said, over 16,000 shops in Glasgow employing 98,000 people (many of them women). They were forced to endure conditions like this for the convenience of thoughtless customers: 'The working classes who were in many cases clamouring for an eight-hours day were the worst offenders and seemed to be callous of any interest but their own.' Glasgow Trades Council had declined in the 1890s to support an agitation for early closing.[37]

Other trades at that time fell between these extremes, 50 to 60 hours a week being the norm in, for example, jute mills, iron foundries, and Glasgow Tramways. Even this average day numbed body and soul, as Kellog Durland found when as a young man in 1901, he decided to sample the life of a Fife miner (working 8 hours a day) and of a brickfield worker (working 10 to 11½ hours). The latter was much worse:

Speaking for myself, I found that the last two or three hours took as much out of me as the first eight . . . A man who rises at half-past five (often earlier) and handles sixteen tons or more of stone during the day, getting home between half-past five and six o'clock in the evening, can hardly be expected to encourage many serious interests. I have watched men come home from the brickwork, and as soon as they had finished tea, they would drop into a chair before the fire and drowsily doze away two or three hours, and then tumble into bed. This was about all that I felt like doing after feeding the mill from dawn till dusk.[38]

At the brick-field, he further noticed, 'the old cheeriness of the pit is entirely lacking'.

It is no wonder that the agitation for a statutory eight-hour day was one of the most popular in the labour movement after 1880, or that the socialists, who espoused it most keenly, should have gained support for doing so. Except in the mines, the agitation came to nothing: Parliament limited work underground to 8 hours in 1909 and to 7 in 1919. On the other hand individual unions had much more success in unilateral negotiations with the employers. In 1910, Glasgow railway carters, for example, cut their weekly hours to 60 by negotiation, plus payment for overtime and Sunday work. In 1919, hours were reduced to 48, and, indeed, by the end of the First World War, most organized trades negotiated either a 47-hour week (like the engineers and shipbuilders) or a 48-hour week (like the steel-workers). Probably nothing did more to raise the quality of life for the working class between 1880 and 1940 than this gradual limitation of hours.

People whose daily work was of such eroding length often lived amid insanitary and dangerous conditions. Miners, in particular, generally had no option but to live in company houses which were among the most inadequate and disgusting of all Scotland's miserable housing stock. For example, the Royal Commission on Labour heard in 1892 of the houses provided by William Dixon and Company at Auchenraith. There were 42 single-roomed and 41 double-roomed houses, containing 492 people: there were no wash-houses or coal cellars (coals were kept under the bed): there was an open sewer behind, with 12 doorless 'hen-roost privies' (so called because you could not sit down): there were 2 drinking fountains.[39] When miners left these homes for work they were exposed to industrial disease—even at the end of the period, between 150 and 200 miners died annually from pneumoconiosis alone—and to accidents, which, though they killed far less than disease, were an omnipresent threat in the pit. Terrible incidents, like that at William Dixon's colliery at Blantyre in 1872 which claimed over 200 lives, evoked national sympathy, but it was the everyday tension at work that few outsiders appreciated. Kellog Durland spoke of the 'number of hairbreadth escapes that daily pass without comment; the acts of real heroism that are performed as a matter of course in the day's work ... There are few old colliers who have not met with some accidents in their lives.'[40]

Innumerable jobs less dramatic than mining were also dangerous. In the lemonade factories, 'a mistake in filling or corking would cause the bottle to burst and fly all about the room ... there were not a few bottlers in those days with only one eye.'[41] In the shipyards, riveting was particularly dangerous in a confined space such as the bows: when the union representative complained around 1900, the employers replied, 'Don't tell us any fairy tales. There is no more danger than eating a chop: you may swallow the bone.'[42] In the chemical factories and dye-works, the worst abuses were slowly brought under legislative control. 'Not for years', Dr Alexander Scott of Glasgow Royal Infirmary told the BMA in 1902, 'have I seen women carried home writhing in convulsions from chronic lead poisoning ... not for years have I seen the subject of mercurial tremors totally unable to lift the cup of cold water to his raw and burning lips.' As the twentieth century proceeded, the toll of industrial accidents and chronic bad health slowly declined, and every trade has its own unsung story involving battles and negotiations between employers, officials, doctors and trade union officials.

Even when a job was not particularly dangerous, it was often carried on in conditions that were so disgusting as to stupefy and dehumanize the sensibilities. This was Tom Bell's experience in the 1880s:

The foundry was then the Cinderella of the engineering trade. The conditions under which the moulder worked were vile, filthy and insanitary. The approach to the foundry resembled that of a rag and bone shop, or marine store. The entrance was usually strewn with all kinds of scrap iron and rubbish. The inside was in keeping with the outside. Smoke would make the eyes water. The nose and throat would clog with dust. Drinking water came from the same tap as was used by the hosepipe to water the sand. An iron tumbler or tin can served as a drinking vessel until it was filthy or broken, before being replaced by a new one. The lavatory was usually placed near a drying stove, and consisted of open cans that were emptied once a week—a veritable hotbed of disease.[43]

That could be set alongside Edwin Muir's account of his experiences as a clerk in a Greenock bone factory at the turn of the century. For once, industrial work found a pen that could do it justice:

Sometimes he fancied that the smell always clung to him, that it had soaked into his skin and went about with him like a corrupt aura. He had heard that the men and women who worked in the yard, unloading the bones and casting them into the furnace, never got rid of the smell, no matter how they scrubbed. It got among the women's hair and into the pores of their skin. They breathed it into the faces of their lovers when at night, under the hawthorn bushes outside the town, they found a few moments' sensual forgetfulness, they breathed it out with their last breath, infecting the Host which the priest set between their lips, and making it taste of McClintock's bone factory. A thing so tenacious and so vile had given him at first a feeling of mystical revulsion; but he had got used to it . . .[44]

Under these circumstances, who did the workers learn to hate? Often, and very justifiably, they hated the boss: this did not preclude them, more immediately, from hating another worker, the next person above them in the hierarchy—the skilled plater who shouted at the young, unskilled plater's helper ('I resented this foul, violent language . . . it seemed so unfair and unnecessary seeing that we were all doing our best'[45]), or the foreman who 'used to go round quietly on a Friday night to the men he was going to pay off'.[46] The skilled workers and the foremen—the 'NCOs of industry'—in turn despised and kept in order those below them, a fact that combined with sectarianism to keep the workers even within one occupation from fully developing their sense of a common interest.

Probably, though, it was the miners who first developed something akin to a systematic and unifying class hatred directed against the employers and landowners who lived on the profits and royalties of their industry. The Royal Commission on Labour was told by one of Keir Hardie's associates in the west that 'while the large majority of the miners are socialists that is unknown to themselves'. Durland echoed the thought in 1901, when he described the Fife miners as Liberal voters but 'in a constant state of hatred towards the hard-heeled company'.[47] Robert Smillie found 'a positive hate in my heart' when in 1874, at the age of seventeen, he watched the eviction of strikers from their company home, 'the miners' furniture being piled on carts and taken away to whatever quarters they could find',[48] and the miners, in a rare show of solidarity with another trade, tried to prevent railwaymen in Motherwell being similarly evicted by the Caledonian Company during their strike of 1891—fifty hussars from Maryhill barracks were called out, and a crowd of 20,000 wrecked a signalbox and smashed the glass roof of the railway station.[49]

Formal adherence to socialism did not come until the twentieth century, but it was the miners' continuing iron strength of class feeling and their detestation of their employers that kept them out so solidly in the General Strike and its aftermath in 1926, and sent William Gallacher to Westminster as Communist MP for West Fife in 1935. For many of the miners, when vesting day came in 1947 and the power of the employers passed into the hands of the National Coal Board, it was as though the exploitation of centuries was being brought to an end. The sense of a new dawn was dissipated, however, when it was realized that the Board would be run by the same kind of people who had controlled the industry under private enterprise. It was not industrial democracy but 'expert' bureaucracy that nationalization entailed.

Elsewhere in Scotland, though, it is much more difficult to find traditions of bitter, systematic enmity towards employers thus carried on over generations by the rank-and-file since the nineteenth century. There were many angry individuals in Red Clydeside after 1900, many who increasingly felt the system should be changed, and many who regarded the bosses, in general, as untrustworthy and hypocritical. There was undoubtedly a heightening of class consciousness and solidarity after the turn of the century, when the skilled workers found themselves pressed towards the kind of insecurities that had long been the lot of the unskilled, and this had important political consequences, as we shall see in Chapter XI, where the problem is discussed at greater length.

There remained, however, many workers who were apathetic, or who believed the system to be unalterable at least in their factory, or who hated Catholics more, or labourers more, or who thought that the boss was not a bad chap at heart. The latter was easier to believe when the employer was a patriarchal figure like Charles Connell or William Beardmore who could be seen stalking the shipyard or the shop floor. David Kirkwood—who was perhaps not altogether untypical of a shop steward whose dearest wish was to be allowed to run the factory with the boss—told the following illuminating story about Beardmore. He had been summoned to a bench where a craftsman had misjudged cutting a crank by one thousandth of an inch and had thereby wasted £1000-worth of materials: Beardmore came down, smoking a cigar, looked at the crank and turned to the manager:

'Can we make another?'

'Yes, sir.'

'Then get the thing done.' With that he walked away, 'a very god' says Kirkwood, adding, 'To err is human, to forgive divine.'[50] Autocracy, when clothed in visible, if occasional, benevolence and mercy, could get away with a great deal.

What management did not often achieve in twentieth-century Scotland, unfortunately, was an effective agreement that it was worth everyone's time to work together as hard and productively as possible, since by doing so everyone's income would rise and everyone's conditions would gradually be improved. To have achieved this would have involved trusting the work force with a significant degree of self-management on the job, and sharing with them more readily and generously the immediate returns from new technology. Unfortunately, by upbringing and increasingly by education, the employing class had been taught to regard the working class as irresponsible, inferior, different, another species, whom a manager must learn to 'handle'. So by the 1940s and 1950s Scotland was lumbered with an industrial stalemate: socialists had not convinced their fellow workers of the need to struggle with the bosses for actual control of the economy in the name of industrial democracy, and capitalists had not convinced their work force of the benefits to themselves of working hard for the firm, benefits that would lead to the flexibility of attitudes and high wages of, for example, postwar Germany and Scandinavia. What was left was ca' canny, restrictive practices, suspicion, separate canteens for worker and management, and a general belief that if one side proposed a change the other side should resist it. It is hard to think of a more depressing industrial ethos, or one more likely to guarantee a snail's pace rate of economic growth.

Finally, there is the question of work satisfaction. Could anything of the kind survive the hours, the bad conditions, the enmities and the apathy? It is hard to believe there was much job satisfaction in a Fife brick-field in the 1890s, 'the sluck of despond' as one worker called it, or in the Dundee jute factories, where still in the 1890s children were being beaten to hurry them along to earn a premium known as 'blood money'. But, if oral tradition is reliable, there was still a lot of satisfaction in the skilled craft of the compositor, in the lens grinder's job at Barr and Strouds and in those old-fashioned wood-turning shops where machinery had not yet turned furniture-making into a repetitive chore. There was satisfaction, despite the hours, at the footplate of a great locomotive. In heavy industry, the collier and the steel-worker took a pride in the strength and judgement demanded by their work, and the engineer took satisfaction in his expertise as long as he was left with a modicum of initiative and variety at the work place. A ship-builder might, in the boss's eyes, be prone to absenteeism, slacking or drunkenness (though some of this was reaction to work too intensely heavy to pursue for eight or nine hours without a break): but few did not feel pride in the ship that was taking shape under their hands. At the launch of the most famous of them all in 1934, David Kirkwood, as the local MP involved in getting work on the ship restarted, was among John Brown's special guests in a protected room overlooking the Clyde: 'I looked through the windows and saw the men of Clydebank, thousands of them, standing in the rain, and I wondered what I was doing in the warm covered conservatory.'[51] He did not need to ask himself or anyone else what the men of Clydebank were doing in the rain when the *Queen Mary* went into the river.

CHAPTER V

The Rewards of Labour

1

In the nineteenth century, as the industrial revolution ran its course, the age-long gap between a rich England and a poor Scotland narrowed, and perhaps came close to disappearing. In 1798, when the first income tax was introduced, Scotland paid, per head of population, about 68 per cent of what England paid. In 1867, the Victorian economist R. Dudley Baxter made a much more determined attempt to estimate the differential between the two countries, using both tax data and wage estimates: he calculated that average income per head in Scotland was then about 75 per cent of the English figure. A recent estimate for 1911, which can only be approximate, suggests a figure in the region of 95 per cent.[1]

That probably marks high water. Better estimates became available for the interwar years through the work of A. D. Campbell, who put Scottish national income at 92 per cent of the UK average in the late 1920s, dropping to 87 per cent in the early 1930s, pulling up to 94 per cent in the early part of the Second World War, and levelling out immediately thereafter at 90 per cent.[2] Of course, taking the century overall, the whole of Britain got much richer: Gross Domestic Product per head rose by three-quarters between 1855 and 1905, and by half between 1905 and 1950.[3] Scottish national income per head can be assumed to have risen rather faster than that in the first period and only very marginally slower in the second.

Aggregate figures are one thing: the distribution of the cake is quite another. Victorian Scotland was a very unequal society. Dudley Baxter tried to anatomize the income of 'productive persons' (as he called them) under the general headings of the 'upper and middle classes' and the 'manual labour class'.[4] The result can be seen in Table 2.

Some striking conclusions emerge. The vast majority of the Scots—nearly a million 'productive persons', 70 per cent of the whole—were at the foot of the economic and social pyramid in groups 5 and 6, the lower skilled and unskilled workers. They earned less than £30 a year, partly because of the prevalence among this group of unemployment and low female and juvenile pay. The next 20 per cent were in groups 3 and 4, considered to be the bottom of the middle class and the top of the working class, though in economic terms there was little difference between them, their annual income being £47 2s. to £50. This represents the quintessentially Victorian echelon of the small businessman and the skilled craft-worker, respectable, struggling to keep their economic foothold, feeling that they had much in common with one another but nothing with the poor in the abyss. Above them were the two top groups, the most economically secure, the 10 per cent who received nearly half the national income: group 1 was a small and dizzy pinnacle of 5000 very rich men (wealthy professionals, big businessmen, large landowners) who accounted for a quarter of the national income and enjoyed a personal annual income 200 times as large as the 427,000 people at the bottom of the pile: group 2 was the solid middle of the middle class.

It has been argued that a significant weakness in the Scottish nineteenth-century economy was that there were, in contrast at least to south-east England, too few individuals in these wealthy groups of the middle classes.[5] London's attraction for the highly remunerated bankers, members of the stock exchange and Lloyds, senior lawyers, top doctors, civil servants, and business tycoons of all types, was as evident then as it is now. The relative scarcity of this group in Scotland led to fewer jobs in the service sector, weaker consumer demand and lower incomes all round. As late as 1911, there were only 944 civil servants or government officials in Scotland, and these worked for an average salary of £350 a year. The point is a good one, though Scotland was at least as well provided with a bourgeoisie as most of provincial England, and Edinburgh performed some of the functions of London on a smaller stage. Indeed, using Schedule D income-tax assessments as a measure of middle-class wealth in large towns, in 1880 Edinburgh was the third richest city in Britain, behind only London and Manchester in the tax paid per head. Glasgow came fifth, behind Liverpool but well

TABLE 2
R. Dudley Baxter's estimates of the division of the Scottish national income, 1867

	Number of total 'productive persons'	Percentage of total 'productive persons'	Average real annual income per individual £s	Percentage of Scottish national income going to group
'Upper and Middle Classes'				
1 Higher (incomes over £1000)	4,700	0.33	3,952	25,000
2 Middling and 'upper-small' (incomes £100–£1000)	111,300	7.95	145	21.72
3 'Lower-small' (incomes up to £100)	156,000	11.19	50	10.50
'Manual Labour Class'				
4 Higher skilled (wages over £50)	137,000	9.82	47. 2s.	8.69
5 Lower skilled (male wages £40–50)	558,000	40.02	29.13s.	22.28
6 Unskilled (male wages under £40)	427,000	30.63	20.10s.	11.78

Source: R. D. Baxter, *National Income of the United Kingdom* (London, 1867), p. 56

ahead of Birmingham and Newcastle. Aberdeen and Dundee trailed lower down the table, but nevertheless comfortably exceeded comparable English cities like Leeds and Sheffield. Though they might not have been able to outshine the Londoners, there is no reason to think of the Scottish Victorian middle class as the poor relation of the English provincials. Their finest monuments were their own homes – the sweeping terraces of Glasgow's west end, with gleaming stained glass and art nouveau decoration, and the stolid villas, with their ample gardens of lilac and laburnum, in Edinburgh's southern suburbs.

For the working class the situation was a painful contrast. Undoubtedly, in the middle decades of the nineteenth century one of the attractions of Scotland to a capitalist setting up in business was cheap and plentiful industrial labour, whether provided by lowland craftsman, cleared Highland crofter, or Irish immigrant. It was a situation that altered only slowly, and in the teeth of opposition from employers. In 1860, Scottish wages were often up to one-fifth below those for the same English trades. When Edward Young made an investigation of the international level of wages for the United States Congress in 1872, he attributed 'the great demand for Clyde-built ships' not to their technical superiority but to their low cost, 'owing in part to the cheapness of materials, but chiefly to the abundance of skilled workmen and the low rate of wages paid to them'. More generally, he described Scottish industry as unable to compete abroad without low wages. Masters combined against men to keep down the level of wages, and disputes between the two sides involved all classes in 'ceaseless contentions', but in the end the worker 'must work for a mere pittance, to enable his employer to sell his goods abroad at low rates, or there will be no work for him to do, and he will be left to starve'. The US consuls of the period regularly listed rates for joiners, blacksmiths, carpenters, riveters and labourers significantly below those for London or Newcastle.[6]

What happened next is a matter of some dispute among scholars. In 1886, the first systematic British wage census still showed central Scotland as a low wage area, though apparently not to the same degree as it had been in 1850 or 1860: shipyard-workers, for instance, were paid 8 per cent less in Scotland than in England (£70 a year as opposed to £76), building-workers 6 per cent less (£62 as opposed to £66), print-workers, 13 per cent less (£46 compared to £53 in large works): in other trades, however, for example coal-mining, Scottish wage rates were no different. By the time of the next wage census in 1906, moreover, in four vital fields of heavy industry—iron and steel manufacture, light iron castings, ship-building, and (less markedly) engineering and boiler-making—Scotland in general and the Clyde in particular reported average earnings and wage rates up to or even above the UK average. Professor R. H. Campbell is in no doubt that by the early twentieth century, Clydeside had become a high-wage region in the leading sector industries, and, in the absence of a significant improvement in productivity, that her international competitive situation was threatened as a result. Dr Hunt places the central belt of Scotland as one of the four highest wage regions in Britain.[7]

This finding, if correct, implies that in thirty years industrial Scotland had gone from low wages to high wages, and also that the figure generally accepted for overall improvements in real wages in Britain between 1850 and 1900—about 80 per cent—would be substantially larger in the Scottish case. Before drawing the conclusion that the typical Scottish worker was particularly prosperous at the start of the twentieth century, however, certain other factors have to be considered. Firstly, a great deal of Scottish employment was still concentrated in areas dominated by low-paid female labour (like the textile mills in Glasgow, Dundee and Dunfermline), by juveniles in dead-end jobs (as in much of the unskilled manufacturing and service industry in Glasgow), or by adults in transport (railways and trams paid a good deal less in Scotland) or labouring, where unemployment was chronic and earnings spasmodic and low. Secondly, not all the reported earnings appear to be true: in ship-building, for example, we know that the employers deliberately exaggerated the average earnings of riveters in their reports to outsiders and to the Board of Trade for the wage census, and that in 1906 the average earnings per week were not 47s. 11d. as reported, but 36s. 4d., fully 25 per cent less. Between 1900 and 1910, half the riveters earned less than £2, and a quarter less than 30s.[8] Thirdly, there was a greater inflation in rents in Scotland than in England (an increase of a third as opposed to a fifth, 1876–1910), and the prices of food and fuel were higher in Scotland by 1912. Some of these, and similar, considerations have led Dr Rodgers to a gloomier verdict than that of Professor Campbell or Dr Hunt: he suggests that by the eve of the First World War real wages were as much as '13 per cent below those in London, and 10–12 per cent adrift of those . . . in Lancashire, Yorkshire, the Midlands, Northumberland and Durham.'[9] Whatever the truth of the matter, these considerations knock a great

TABLE 3
Percentage of insured population unemployed, 1927–39

	In United Kingdom	In N-E England	In Scotland
1927	9.7	13.7	10.6
1928	10.8	15.1	11.7
1929	10.4	13.7	12.1
1930	16.1	20.2	18.5
1931	21.3	27.4	26.6
1932	22.1	28.5	27.7
1933	19.9	26.0	26.1
1934	16.7	22.1	23.1
1935	15.5	20.7	21.3
1936	13.1	16.8	18.7
1937	10.8	11.0	15.9
1938	12.9	13.5	16.3
1939	10.5	10.1	13.5

Source: *Ministry of Labour Gazette*

deal of gilt off the workers' gingerbread. They also help to account for the extraordinarily high rates of net out-migration from Scotland, which reached about 50 per cent of the natural increase of the population in the first two decades of the twentieth century. One would not have expected that to occur in a country that was paying high wages to most people.

The years after 1920 were dominated by the slide of the Scottish economy into depression and the concomitant growth of long-term unemployment, affecting not merely the unskilled and lasting not only a few months or a year or two, but affecting whole communities and lasting many years. The depression, of course, was not confined to Scotland, though it was a good deal worse there. As early as 1923, unemployment in Scotland stood at 14.3 per cent compared to 11.6 per cent in the UK as as whole, and at the bottom of the slump, 1931-3, more than a quarter of the work force in Scotland was out of a job, compared to a little over a fifth in the UK. Up to this point, however, it is possible to argue that Scotland was not badly off compared to other regions with a similar dependence on the traditional staples. As Table 3 shows, until 1933, the nearest neighbouring region, north-east England, had consistently higher unemployment. After that date, however, though Scotland approximately halved her unemployment rate to 13.5 per cent by 1939, due largely to military spending on rearming the fleet, her relative position worsened. In Scotland between 1927 and

1929, unemployment had been only about a tenth higher than the UK average: between 1937 and 1939, it was a third higher. Scotland failed in particular to maintain her position compared to the north-east, where unemployment by 1939 had actually fallen below the national average. This suggests that there were particularly serious inbuilt rigidities in the Scottish economy, and that seemed to be confirmed again after the Second World War when unemployment north of the border, though temporarily wiped out as a serious social problem, was nevertheless twice the UK average.

The demoralization of the Scottish work force in the interwar years was enormous, especially in the families of skilled workers with no previous tradition of being out of work for a long time. The investigators of the Carnegie United Kingdom Trust described how the workless . . .

> . . .acquired the art of patience. They had longer and more frequently recurring experiences of unemployment. With drooping shoulders and slouching feet they moved as a defeated and dispirited army. They gave their names, signed the necessary forms and shuffled out of the Exchange. This, twice a week, was the only disciplined routine with which they had to comply.[10]

The same picture was painted in different words by Edwin Muir, driving in 1933 through the desolate urban landscape of Lanarkshire, past groups of 'idle, sullen-looking young men' at the street corners. 'Airdrie and Motherwell are the most improbable places imaginable in which to be left with nothing to do; for only rough work could reconcile anyone to living in them.' In Glasgow he revisited the old ship-building office where he had worked for several years as a clerical assistant: in place of twelve fellow clerks he found six, and those on half-time and half-pay. Outside, the work force stood in the street:

> The weather had been good for several weeks, and all the men I saw were tanned and brown as if they had just come back from their summer holidays. They were standing in their usual groups, or walking by twos and threes, slowly, for one felt as one looked at them that the world had not a single message to send them on, and that for them to hasten their steps would have meant a sort of madness. Perhaps at some time the mirage of work glimmered at the extreme horizon of their minds: but one could see by looking at them that they were no longer deceived by such false pictures.[11]

This was modern unemployment, on the dole, different from the stone-breaking relief schemes by which the Victorians had tried to determine that even the most desperate did not get something for nothing. Its own devastating quality lay in the fact that it became an expectation, and ultimately a way of life, not a singular misfortune. In the past it had been a phenomenon that might be expected to recur from time to time but which would always alternate with far longer spells of work. For many, this was no longer the case.

Those who could do so very often took the road south to the more prosperous regions of southern England: the steel concern of Stewarts and Lloyds moved its entire operation south to Northamptonshire, and the Scottish origins of their work force were still visible in the 1970s in the Rangers Supporters Club at Corby. Many more Scots sought their fortunes abroad. In the 1920s, out-migration became a flood, exceeding the natural increase of the country by 10 per cent, so that Scottish population actually fell between 1921 and 1931. Emigration only declined in the 1930s because there were not many jobs left elsewhere in the world for Scots to go to.

Although unemployment vanished like snow off a dyke with the coming of the Second World War and only returned after 1945 at very low levels, the depression and the two wars between them left Scotland with an outmoded industrial structure. A. D. Campbell estimated that Scottish incomes around 1950 were about 10 per cent below the UK average: the reason was not now lower wage rates, as after the First World War the growth of trade unionism in most trades ensured near uniformity in wage-rate bargaining across the country. Compared to the south there were too many working-class wage earners still in badly-paid jobs, such as the Dundee jute industry or the Border hosiery industry, and in heavy rather than light engineering. In the middle class, similarly, there were too few top salary earners: the concentration of company control outside Scotland, which was a feature of these years, added to all the other forces that had long tended to draw the wealthiest and most ambitious people to London.[12]

On the other hand it was obvious that the years since 1914 had been, overall, a time of rising real incomes in Scotland, for the workers no less than for the rest. The First World War saw an increase, even for the least favoured, large enough to overtake wartime inflation: one calculation suggested that for unskilled workers in Glasgow real wages rose by about 10 per cent between 1914 and 1920.[13] Then, between 1924 and

1948, Campbell's figures indicate that Scottish real incomes rose as a whole by about 40 per cent, half of that coming in the depression and half thereafter. With such an increase, the majority of the Scottish people enjoyed an appreciably higher standard of living by the middle of the twentieth century than had even been imagined at its start, let alone fifty years before that. For all their girning that life, the Government, and the English had let them down, by 1950 the Scots were as well off as Lancashire and Yorkshire, better off than the Welsh, the Northern Irish or the inhabitants of south-west England, and probably better off than at least four-fifths of the inhabitants of Europe.[14] Perhaps the real burden of their complaint was that they were clearly not as prosperous as the envied and distrusted population of the Home Counties. Certainly the ambitious young Scots of all social classes found that the lines of promotion and opportunity drew them to London in a way that had certainly not been true in 1900.

Statistical aggregates of income, however, though they are vital to establishing proper perspectives, inevitably conceal the very different individual experiences of which social history is composed. In Scotland in the interwar years, it all depended who you were, where you lived, and whether the shadow of unemployment fell on your life or passed you by. An Edinburgh working girl of the 1920s found herself in an enclave of service trades little affected by the depression, and provided with opportunities never open to her mother. Instead of working for a pittance as a domestic servant, she could earn a good wage as a typist for a bank, an insurance firm, or a lawyer, like Ellen in Rebecca West's novel *The Judge*. A Fife miner, on the other hand, accustomed to relatively high wages in a dangerous job with full employment, found himself on the rubbish heap, disregarded and virtually starving. Stuart Macintyre cites the example of a mining family which, in 1930, normally earned 41s. 8d. a week with the man working five shifts: of this sum, 33s. 4d. normally went on rent, fuel and food alone. At that time one worker in every three or four on the coal-field was out of a job. The maximum amount of unemployment benefit paid to a man and wife with three children was 32s. a week; the maximum 'transitional benefit' paid in Fife to those whose unemployment benefit was exhausted was 29s. a week; the maximum local relief paid by the county council to the able-bodied unemployed who did not qualify for either of these was 26s. a week.[15] Extreme destitution was inevitably the result for many. Abe Moffat, though a parish councillor at the time, remembered being threatened with eviction from his council house for non-payment of rates when he was unemployed on 26s. 2d. a week; fortunately he won a sweepstake run by the village football team:

> We immediately paid the rates, and the balance was used for the miner's popular diet at that time—fish suppers for the Moffat family to celebrate the occasion. Had it not been for this stroke of luck, I would have had the experience as a Councillor of being evicted, with the furniture lying out in the street.[16]

At least in the interwar years there was a dole, however inadequate and however often cut. Before the Unemployed Workmen's Act of 1904, which was largely a dead letter, and the more effective introduction of unemployment benefit by the Liberals in 1911, there had been no statutory provision for maintaining the able-bodied unemployed in Scotland: the Poor Law did not begin to do so until the 1920s, though it did in England, and charitable organizations or local authorities that organized make-work plans invariably devised schemes which were even meaner and more humiliating than those of the latter-day bureaucracy: for example making people break stones in return for a bowl of soup. The rewards of unemployment have always been designed to be more unpleasant than the rewards of even the nastiest labour.

2

The quality of life is not merely a matter of income. It is also measured by health, perhaps especially by the health of children, and by longevity. Health itself is a function of many things: within the family context it is related to the nature of the house, to the quantity and quality of food consumed, and to the quality of parental care, which are in turn functions partly of income, partly of individual character, and partly of social environment; outside the family, it is related to overall standards of public health, to the advance of medical knowledge, and to the broad social conscience that determines how far a nation will tolerate the avoidable death or sickness of the underprivileged.

The history of the death rate and expectation of life conveys a mixed impression of Scottish social welfare over our century. Good statistics only became available with the establishment of the office of the Registrar-General for Scotland in 1855, but it is fairly clear from earlier, more limited sources that the death rate had risen under the pressure of

118

urbanization in the first third of the nineteenth century and did not fall from its high plateau in the forty years after 1830, although its fluctuations became less wild with the end of the terrifying cholera and typhus epidemics of the 1830s and 1840s. Particularly chilling was the mortality of children under ten years of age, which in 1861 still made up 54 per cent of all deaths in Glasgow. Tuberculosis, 'fever', bowel disease and measles (in that order) accounted for more than half of the mortality in Glasgow, 1836–42, while smallpox in the 1830s still accounted for 5 per cent of deaths, almost all among the children of the poor.

Acquaintance with the deaths of babies and young children was therefore an inescapable fact of Scottish working-class life. Doctors, perhaps, could take it as a matter of course, but mothers were never inured to it simply by other people's familiarity. When, in the late 1880s, a young medical student was working for the Cowgate Dispensary in Edinburgh and attending a pregnancy in a Lawnmarket slum, he and his comrades delivered the girl of an apparently stillborn baby, and as they 'desired to use the body as a subject for dissection', they unceremoniously wrapped it up and took it away in a cab. The cool night air and the jolting vehicle combined to bring the infant to life:

> A Punchinello squeak was heard beneath the seat, followed by an unmistakable cry ... Shamefacedly Hugh and I slowly reascended the turnpike stair, somewhat dubious as to our reception. But we were received with grateful delight, and hailed as wonderful practitioners, the young mother's conviction being that we had taken the stillborn infant away for the purpose of restoring it, and had miraculously succeeded.[17]

It was a story that told as much about doctors as it did about the poor.

In the final third of the nineteenth century, certain types of mortality began to drop. In 1870, the life expectancy of a male at birth was only 41 years, of a female only 43.5 years. By 1950, a boy could expect to live to 64 and a girl to 68. The annual crude death rate in 1870–2 stood at 22.3 per 1000 alive: by 1950, it was almost halved, at 12.5. Most of this dramatic improvement was due to the decline in the killing powers of infectious diseases that especially affected young people and children over the age of one. Table 4 overleaf shows what happened.

A few diseases were wiped out before 1900: the typhus group and smallpox responded to improved sanitary regulations and compulsory vaccination respectively. Others (measles, pneumonia and bronchitis)

TABLE 4

Annual mortality per 100,000 alive from certain infectious diseases

	1861–70	1901–10	1931–9
Tuberculosis	361	209	77
Respiratory diseases	308	277	172
Typhus group	106	10	0.6
Scarlet fever	66	9	4
Whooping cough	66	44	11
Diphtheria & croup	64	17	9
Measles	40	34	9
Smallpox	17	1	–
Total	1053	601	283

Source: M. W. Flinn (ed.), *Scottish Population History from the Seventeenth Century to the 1930s* (Cambridge, 1977), pp. 398–9

did not begin to be brought under control until the twentieth century. Respiratory disease, indeed, had become the main killer in this group by the 1930s, and awaited the wider use of sulpha drugs and the discovery of penicillin to be brought under control in the 1940s. They claimed, however, a high proportion of their victims among the elderly, and so did not affect so seriously the decline of the death rate among the young.

If the elderly are excluded, almost half the saving of life represented in Table 4 came from the conquest, imperfect and incomplete though it still was in the 1930s, of the biggest killer of them all: tuberculosis. It was a disease that particularly affected the adolescent and the young adult and which therefore might have been expected to increase as more survived their childhood years. Like respiratory disease, it was closely associated with poverty and urban squalor (in the 1860s, respiratory disease and tuberculosis together accounted for two-fifths of all deaths in Glasgow compared to a quarter in the rural areas). At the end of the nineteenth century, however, TB invaded the Highland counties which had been free from it earlier, apparently brought back to the black houses by returning migrant workers who had contracted it in the Lowland cities. In many places it proved exceedingly hard to eradicate or even make an impression upon it before the First World War. In Dundee, Edinburgh, and the rural areas, for example, reductions in the death rate were on a very small scale until after 1910. In Glasgow, however, mortality from tuberculosis fell faster than almost anywhere else—though it had further to fall.

The kind of environment in which tuberculosis flourished was indicated again and again in the reports of the Medical Officers of Health W. L. Mackenzie in 1917 described the home of a typical child patient aged five, with rickets, a bad cough and spit, 'and so probably a source of danger to the other members of the family'. The house had two rooms, was 'moderately dirty', the windows opened about one inch: the parents lived there with eight children, the oldest seventeen, the youngest three weeks. Between them they had three beds, with very little bedding: the patient slept alone in a cot. The father was regularly employed, and paid £9 rent in a year: 'The parents have applied for the patient's admission to a home, but it was refused on the ground that the boy had phthisis.'[18]

An effective assault on the disease needed both vigorous action by the public health authorities and a general improvement in the standard of living of the population: it was not possible to treat it by drugs until after 1950. Indeed, the nature of the infection had not been understood at all until 1884, when Koch's paper on the etiology of tuberculosis demonstrated that it was an infectious disease carried by a bacillus. The discovery drove some medical men to hysterical suggestions—for example, that those with what they assumed to be 'a strong hereditary predisposition' to succumb to the bacillus should be prevented from marrying. It was quickly appreciated, however, that there was a link between the disease, congested housing, insufficient fresh air or exercise, and infected food. A vigorous municipality, said Dr J. B. Russell, the Medical Officer of Health for Glasgow in 1896, ought to take effective action on its own account: 'Every public park, and the flowers and music which attract people thither, every open space and children's playground, every cricket and football field, every gymnasium and drillground is a precaution against Consumption.'

There were people with vested interests who opposed reform, like the owners of dark, insanitary cowsheds in country and town. Dr Russell counterattacked the farmer:

... dairy stock is ravaged with tuberculosis. Yet we never hear a farmer or dairyman speak of tuberculosis without speaking of compensation. When he puts windows in his byre, and floods it with light, ventilates it, and ceases to use his cow as a heating apparatus, it will be time enough to speak of compensation. Meanwhile the children of the town are being infected wholesale ...[19]

In 1897, the Public Health (Scotland) Act strengthened the hands of the authorities inspecting for tainted food, and gradually a range of tests and certification were introduced to control the quality of milk. The systematic campaign against the disease can be traced back to the work of Sir Robert Philip at the Royal Victoria Dispensary for Consumption in Edinburgh in 1887: in 1912, the Local Government Board set up a special tuberculosis service along the lines he recommended, to provide sanatoria, hospitals and dispensaries for its treatment. Also in 1912, pulmonary tuberculosis was made a compulsorily notifiable disease, and the State agreed to provide half the cost of treatment of all forms of tuberculosis: by 1934, about 5500 beds had been provided for the specialized treatment. By then, it was on the retreat in all parts of the country, but it was far from beaten: there were, in that year, over 34,000 people known to be suffering from tuberculosis in Scotland, and it accounted for about one-third of the total deaths in the 15–24 age group.[20] As in previous times, it was the poor and overcrowded who were the most likely to contract it and succumb.

Still more intractable, especially in the Victorian period, was infant mortality, the death of children under one year old. It showed no inclination at all to fall after 1870, with the rest of the death rate: indeed, it rose, from 118 per 1000 live births in the late 1860s to 130 in the late 1890s. Then, quite abruptly after 1900, it dropped—to 109 on the eve of the First World War, to 77 on the eve of the Second, and right down to 40 by 1950. Contemporaries (like historians) were as baffled for an explanation of why it stayed up in the nineteenth century as they were for its decline in the twentieth. Certainly, the increase must have been connected with a higher proportion of the population coming to live in the towns, where the unhealthy environment always gave rise to much higher rates. It is quite possible that it was related to the deterioration in the quality of diet discussed later in this chapter. In part, the ability of an infant to survive depends (as that of an older child does not) on its condition at birth, which in turn reflects the health and development of the mother during her own childhood and adolescence. Dr Chalmers, the Medical Officer of Health for Glasgow in 1902, pointed out that over a third of infant deaths in the city occurred within one month of birth and more than half within three months, and so were more likely to be related to 'defective conditions which are antenatal in origin'. He also observed that 30 per cent of infantile deaths occurred among the 14 per cent of the Glasgow population that lived in one-roomed houses.[21]

Similarly, much, but not all, of the improvement in infant mortality since 1900 might be attributed to the gradual decrease, since 1870, in the overwork, malnutrition and serious diseases of girls and young women, assisted in the twentieth century by the introduction of such things as free milk and medical inspection in the schools—in addition, of course, to general improvements in the environment and in medical care during and after the birth itself. But there could be backslidings. Sir Dugald Baird has recently correlated the unexpected surge in certain kinds of stillbirths in the 1950s with the condition of mothers born between 1926 and 1937: childhood malnutrition of girls in families on the dole, he argued, had resulted in damage to their embryos a generation later. Thus not the sins, but the poverty of one generation could be visited upon the next.[22]

Doctors and officials tackling the problem of infant mortality in the twentieth century were disappointed and concerned that it had not fallen as fast or as far as in England. In the nineteenth century, despite lower incomes, the Scottish infant mortality rate had consistently been a fifth or more lower than the English, possibly because of lower levels of urbanization in the north, possibly because in Scotland babies were weaned onto porridge instead of 'a little bit of what Father has'. The two rates began to drop simultaneously, but during the 1920s and 1930s, the English rate fell for the first time significantly below the Scottish one. This was thought to reflect poorer economic and environmental conditions in the urban areas of Scotland. Certainly, in the 1930s, there were rates of 99 per 1000 live births in Glasgow and 80 or more in most of the depressed towns of the west of Scotland, compared to only 39 in Shetland. Country areas were not, of course, areas of high money income: they had, however, other advantages in the quality of life that might count for more in family health.

More generally, the health of children was greatly improved in the twentieth century, but substantial differences due to class, locality and housing persisted in 1950 and, indeed, persist to this day. The position was shown in Glasgow, for example, by the incidence of rickets, a disease which in its extreme form gave children 'legs so misshapen and soft ... that they were as helpless as babies as far as locomotion was concerned'.[23] Rickets also weakened the child and made it susceptible to other diseases—nearly a third of the boys and more than a quarter of the girls admitted to the Belvedere Fever Hospital in Glasgow around 1910 had visible symptoms of previous attacks of rickets, and it was obvious they occurred more often in one-roomed houses than in two-roomed houses, and more in two-roomed houses than in larger ones.[24] Rickets was associated exclusively with urban malnutrition and air pollution, being virtually unknown in the countryside. Overall, however, there was a notable improvement. The percentage of school children in the city suffering from rickets fell from 9 per cent in 1910–14 to a mere 0.3 per cent in 1950–4. Its decline must have helped the simultaneous fall in the infant mortality rate, for it had long been recognized that 'the girls deformed by rickets today became the deformed mothers of tomorrow, and furnish the maternity hospitals with some of their most tragic cases'.[25]

Bad teeth were another problem: in Glasgow the percentage of children reported with 'unsound teeth' rose from 67 per cent in 1914 to an astonishing 87 per cent in 1924, presumably under the influence of a more sugary diet. Then it dropped, by degrees, to 51 per cent in 1944 and 33 per cent in 1954, which was still regarded as extremely high by European standards.[26] Bad teeth, however, were not correlated with low income, as rickets were. The Carnegie investigation into family diet and health in prewar Britain reported in 1955 that the incidence of decayed, missing and filled teeth was the same in all expenditure groups, illustrating the obvious but sometimes forgotten point that some bad health is caused by individual choice and not by the blind impositions of poverty. The children at Gordonstoun school, for example, had as many bad teeth as everyone else, although they had been efficiently treated by conservative methods.[27]

Nevertheless, social inequality could literally be measured by height and weight, which in turn reflected the total healthiness of the child's environment and nutrition. In Edinburgh around 1902, for example, girls aged twelve to fifteen from a local authority school at Bruntsfield, an area where incomes were relatively high, were on average 2.65 ins. taller and 12 lbs. heavier than girls from the decaying tenements of North Canongate.[28] Glasgow evidence shows, however, that such differences could diminish over time: girls aged thirteen from houses of five rooms or more were 3.3 ins. taller and 13 lbs. heavier than girls from one-roomed houses in 1924, but by 1944, the differential had diminished to 1.5 ins. and 5 lbs. There was, moreover, considerable overall improvement: Glaswegian thirteen-year-old girls as a group were 4 inches taller and over a stone heavier in 1950 than in 1910. Even though these class and occupational differences persisted as adults (Glasgow clerks in 1935 were 2 inches taller than metal-workers), and even though Scottish workers in the main cities were smaller than English workers (Glasgow clerks were an inch shorter than London clerks),[29] it was nevertheless clear that welfare and higher wages were slowly making things better (see Graph 1, i–iii, on pages 126–7).

In the twentieth century, a good deal of pioneering effort was devoted by the medical profession in Scotland to analysing diets and trying to discover nutritional explanations for such differences in height and weight. There had certainly been remarkable alterations in diet between the 1840s and the First World War. The investigations of the Poor Law Commission in 1843 showed a striking dominance of oatmeal and potatoes over everything else, in town and country alike: only one parish in ten reported wheat bread or tea as a significant item in working-class diet, and only one in four mentioned meat without a qualification implying that it was in some sense exceptional.[30] Then in the last third of the century there emerged a new diet, initially in the towns, based on cheap imports. Between 1857 and 1903, the price of a sack of 280 lbs. of oatmeal fell only slightly, from 37s. to 31s., while the price of the same quantity of wheat dropped from 46s. to 22s.: the price of an ounce of tea also fell dramatically, by 64 per cent. As one Glasgow trader remarked in 1903, 'Oatmeal is now a luxury and flour a cheap article ... My friend told me that in Centre Street in a morning he would sell as much [flour] as he now sells [oatmeal] in a fortnight.'[31]

The consequence, of course, was that many poor families shifted from porridge to white bread and tea, though some maintained the old ways: David Kirkwood in the early 1880s, while remembering the 'bried and jeely piece' which he took to work as a lad, said that at home, 'Our principal food was porridge and buttermilk. Only on Saturdays and Sundays did we have a hot meal, which usually consisted of broth, made with half a pound of boiling beef and a marrow-bone, and potatoes. We were very fond of broth.'[32]

More generally, however, there was a move towards a new and clearly less nutritious diet, as described in William Mitchell's account of a one-roomed house in 1886:

A loaf of bread is taken from the shelf: an old brown teapot gets a spoonful of tea and is filled with boiling water from a rusty kettle on the hob; a lump of salt butter, wrapped in a piece of dirty paper, is produced, or a little jelly or syrup; two or three broken cups are put

GRAPH 1

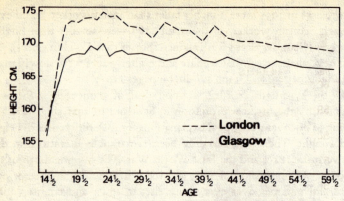

(i) Height of employed men in Scotland (mainly Glasgow) and London in 1938

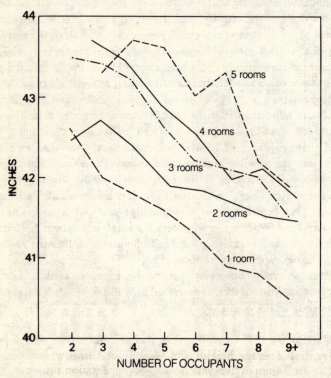

(ii) Average heights of five-year-old Glasgow boys arranged according to number of rooms and of occupants

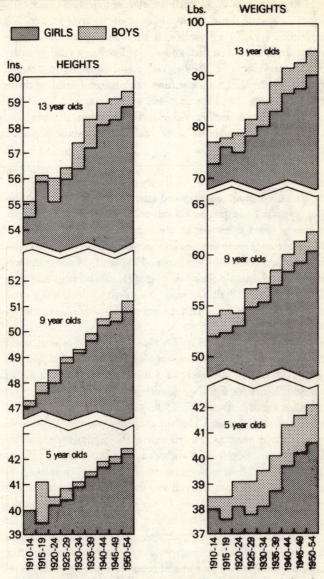

(iii) Average heights and weights of Glasgow School-children in five-year periods since the session 1909–10

on a rickety chair, round which the children cluster, either on stools or squatted on the floor, or on the edge of the iron fender. Sugar is cheap; milk a rare commodity; if the earnings of the family can afford it some ham is boiled; and so, without any kind of order and with a general scramble, they all fall to and quickly consume what is provided for them. This constitutes the principal meal of thousands of poor children, day after day. Tea with sugar and bread without butter is very usual fare. Porridge and milk, broth and beef, may be seen in a limited number of houses, but not where the poorest families reside.[33]

In the better circumstances of the twentieth century, this diet was modified to give more variety, though it remained heavy on carbohydrates, especially sugar, and low on vegetables and fruit. It also slowly spread from the town to the countryside until it reached even the Outer Hebrides—to do devastating damage to their inhabitants' hitherto excellent teeth. In the 1930s, Highland doctors deplored the 'passing of the old staple foods of porridge, salt herring and potatoes, and the substitution of shop bread, tinned foods, tea and sweets and other goods purchased from shops or, more commonly, the traders' vans.'[34]

The early nutritionists, led by Dr Noel Paton and others, attempted to measure diet by its calorie content against a standard, known as a 'man equivalent', that assumed the daily requirement for a male to be about 2750 calories for light work and 3500 for heavy work. Some of their findings are summarized in Table 5 opposite.

Obviously, until around the time of the Second World War, a majority of those investigated fell below the formal standard, though the measurements were rough and ready and the standards themselves only approximate. It was not easy to interpret the results. A family where the father was unemployed and sitting at home needed less food than one where he was involved in very hard labour, so arguably the Glasgow unemployed were better fed than the Stirlingshire miners. Only the St Andrews population was in a relatively good position, because of its mix of higher incomes and the agricultural labourers and crofters who had low wages but still received some payment in the traditional way, as food in kind.

Who was to blame for malnutrition, and how widespread was it? The followers of Noel Paton put a considerable onus on the feckless

TABLE 5

Estimates of calorie intake per man equivalent in Scottish households, 1913–55

Location	Category	Calories
Glasgow	'labouring classes' (1913)	3160
Glasgow	unemployed (1921–2)	2440
Glasgow	employed labourers (1924)	2620
Glasgow	employed artisans (1924)	3070
Dundee	partly employed workers (1924)	2120
Lowlands	agricultural workers (1924)	3220
Stirlingshire	miners (1924)	2910
St Andrews	families of mixed social class (1930)	3119
Highlands	crofters (1940)	3654
Fife	clerks (1952)	3040
Fife	miners (1952)	4030

Source: *Special Reports of the Medical Research Councils*, especially Nos. 101, 151, 242, 289

habits of the urban poor, appearing cross and disappointed when they found them buying tinned beans instead of the porridge oats the medical pundits felt they needed. Ever since the 1870s, it had been the objective of an influential lobby of middle-class women intellectuals to improve the cooking skills of their working-class sisters, but early attempts by ladies' voluntary societies had been rejected as 'a kind of patronage and interference' by the working class themselves. The lobby then switched its attention to trying to get cookery and home-making placed on the official school curriculum, and were rewarded in 1897, when 'domestic science' was officially introduced into the educational code by the Scotch Education Department. Nevertheless, old habits died hard: girls learnt more from their own families' cooking and eating habits than from school lessons, and the middle-class women who believed so firmly in the ideology of good housekeeping seldom knew enough about the constraints of working-class life to make their advice realistic.[35]

It was not until the 1930s that a new approach was made to the whole problem of malnutrition, when John Boyd Orr began his classic survey of the relationship between income and food intake, taking human nature for granted and surveying what people actually ate at different income levels rather than what they ought to have eaten. He reached the startling conclusion, which was at first received with disbelief and hostility, that in Britain 'a diet completely adequate for health, according to modern standards, is reached at an income level above that of 50 per cent of the population'.[36] This applied to Scotland as much as to England, though his later, detailed investigations suggested that the Scots were about as well off as the English for calories and protein intake and a little better off for calcium, but more deficient in Vitamins A and C due to their aversion to fresh vegetables and fruit. In Scotland, though, most income groups were still receiving only half the calcium they needed, which, no doubt, helped the sugar along in its job of dissolving the national teeth. Scottish consumption per head of syrup, treacle, jam and marmalade was nearly three times the English average.[37]

Boyd Orr's scrupulous calculations at the Rowett Institute at Aberdeen, checked by other investigators and a sceptical BMA, ultimately carried the day. In the Second World War, he found a notable ally in Lord Woolton, Churchill's skilful Minister of Food, whose rationing schemes were devised along the lines proposed by the nutritionists, 'that we might even rear a generation healthier and sturdier than its forebears'. In Woolton's words:

> Mothers in pregnancy were taught the proper use of foods and given some elementary idea of the use of vitamins and of the nature of the protective foods. Milk as a food for growing children came into its own, and the school meals service—in which, if local authorities were wise, the knowledge of the dietician was brought into service—completed the task of establishing in the young the foundation of a stamina that would lead to a healthy maturity.[38]

When peace and plenty came at last, some, at least, of this work endured.

Over the period from 1830 to 1940, then, the history of the Scottish standard of living, whether measured as real income or by health and nutrition, is extremely sobering. That there were gains for the majority of the population as well as for the lucky minority is of course beyond doubt, but until about the time of the First World War, these seem to have been remarkably small in terms of family welfare. Most of the gains of the nineteenth century seem to have gone into the pockets of the middle class and adult male workers, whose real wages certainly rose by a significant amount, especially if they were skilled. If the gains for the family as a whole had been as large as the gains in the main breadwinner's earnings, however, one would have expected to find a much better overall health record, a better record in infant mortality, and a better profile of the height and weight of children. It is not clear that the final height of adults improved at all in the course of the nineteenth century, certainly not if military recruitment figures are to be believed: the average height of Scottish recruits to the armies fighting France in 1793 was about 5 feet 5½ inches, very much the same as in the armies fighting in the Boer War in 1900.

What held the working class back in the nineteenth century, if it is accepted that male earnings rose, is an open question. Middle-class commentators said it was drink. Certainly, compared to previous centuries, more workers received much more of their wage in money and less in kind, thus conferring choice, and not all choice was either wise or family-minded. Bad health, however, was continually traced by doctors not to bad people but to bad housing, and to conditions in the towns in which an ever-increasing proportion of the population came to reside. The efforts of the authorities to ameliorate that urban environment, while real, seem only to have been just enough, even in conjunction with rising incomes, to prevent infant mortality from becoming decisively worse before 1900.

Beginning in the first decade of the twentieth century, however, and becoming more general in the years immediately after the First World War, there was a marked upward trend in all the indicators of social amelioration. Further improvement in wages and hours had something to do with this, despite the depression. So, beyond doubt, had increasing state intervention in the housing market, in health provision, old-age pensions and unemployment benefit. Beyond that, there may, in the twentieth century, have been an alteration in consumption habits, so that more of men's disposable income came to be spent on other forms of indulgence than drink, possibly to the wider benefit of their families. It is to this vexed, cloudy, but interesting problem that we must turn in the next chapter. Nevertheless, the material aspects of Scottish life looked meagre by modern standards, even at the start of the Second World War. Throughout the century, from 1830 to 1940, the expectations of the working class were a hard life, a poor house, and few material rewards.

CHAPTER VI

Drink, Temperance and Recreation

1

Drink was important in nineteenth-century Scotland. It was consumed in enormous quantities. In the 1830s, the population aged fifteen and over was drinking, on average, the equivalent of a little under a pint each of duty-charged whisky a week.[1] There was no legal restriction on who might buy drink, and drunkenness among quite young apprentices and women was taken for granted. There was even a recognized problem of children drinking spirits under the age of fifteen. One might imagine, nevertheless, that consumption was very unevenly divided, and that many men drank several bottles of whisky a week while many women drank little or nothing. Legally brewed alcohol was supplemented by considerable quantities of poteen, distilled in the cellar and up the chimney of many a tall urban tenement as well as on the misty shielings of a Highland glen—there were over 700 detections of illicit distillation a year in Scotland in the period 1833–5.[2] The Scots also drank over a pint of beer a week, but as the alcohol content of beer was about one-eighth that of whisky, that was mere mouthwash. The English drank much more beer but much less whisky. It is not clear that they consumed less alcohol.

Scotland nevertheless appeared to her critics a land peculiarly steeped in drink. John Dunlop, Greenock magistrate and pioneer temperance reformer, described a world in which the middle classes vied with the working classes to create occasions for another glass. 'Drunkenness', he said, 'has been reduced into the regularity and prevalence of a general system.' He gave a long list of social usages. A joiner's apprentice had to buy the shop drinks all round when he entered on his indentures: he was put in charge of the fire, and whenever it faltered he had to pay a fine into the drinks fund: the same thing happened if he forgot to extinguish the lights or watch the work at meal times. When he was 'brothered' he had to pay ten shillings for drinks. His first week's wages as journeyman went to the same end. If a workman left his bench, his position was auctioned for drink among the other workers. If furniture was moved, or packed, or carried to a customer's house, the employer bought drink. When it was winter and candles were first used, the employer gave a treat of spirits. So it was in every trade: ship-building apprentices got a 'launch-bowl' when the ship went down the slipway, and terrorized the countryside in a formidable band 'provided with two large stoneware bottles of ardent spirits' which they forced down the throats of any 'inadvertent travellers whom they can lay their hands on'. Maidservants were paid *arles*, or earnest money, on engagement in a new household: 'She has it in her option, however, to drink it with the servants of the house she has left, if she favours them, or with her other friends, if she prefers it.' Birth meant drink—a bottle of whisky for a daughter, and two for a son. Death meant even more drink: 'On the event of a decease, everyone gets a glass who comes within the door, until the funeral, and for six weeks after it.' Dunlop drew the conclusion that 'In no other country does spiritous liquor seem to have assumed so much the attitude of the authorized instrument of complement and kindness as in North Britain.'[3]

That was in 1839. Thereafter the consumption of alcohol slightly but perceptibly decreased in almost every decade. Illicit distilling rapidly declined and ceased to be a problem after 1860. By the end of the century, the amount of whisky consumed weekly per person over fourteen had fallen to rather over half a pint; beer consumption had risen, but not enough to compensate. The major change, however, came between 1910 and 1930, by which time adults were drinking less than a sixth of a pint of whisky a week (about two glasses), and probably under two pints of beer. In 1930, Sir Alexander Walker, speaking for the Whisky Association, told a Royal Commission that the consumption of Scotch whisky was 'almost entirely confined to those of middle age and the aged'.[4] It was a far cry from Dunlop's day. Since the Second World War, levels of consumption have crept upwards again and the age of whisky-drinking downwards, but not, mercifully, to nineteenth-century levels.

Table 6 presents overall data on the consumption of duty-charged

TABLE 6
Drink in Scotland, 1830–1939

	Consumption of spirits (proof gallons) per head of population per year	Publicans' spirit licenses per 10,000 of population at census year	Convictions for drunkenness per 10,000 of population per year	Alcoholic mortality per 1,000,000 per year
1830–9	2.55	72.9	–	–
1840–9	2.38	58.4	–	–
1850–9	2.16	49.5	–	–
1860–9	1.61	38.0	–	–
1870–9	1.93	35.9	–	–
1880–9	1.69	31.2	72	105
1890–9	1.63	18.2	88	103
1900–9	1.60	16.1	103	107
1910–9	1.00	14.2	75	76
1920–9	0.55	12.4	45	47
1930–9	0.35	12.0	27	37

Source: G. B. Wilson, *Alcohol and the Nation* (London, 1940). See also note 1 for this chapter

spirits and shows trends in the changing number of pubs, the alcoholic mortality rate and arrests for drunkenness.

The geographical distribution of public houses varied in an interesting way in early Victorian Scotland. The Scottish Poor Law Commission in 1843 found that in the western Highlands, the Outer Hebrides and Shetland there were few outlets for legal drinking, often only one for every 1000 people: it also heard evidence from Lorne, Islay, Tiree and Skye that there at least, illicit distilling had effectively been suppressed by the excise officers. On the other hand, in the industrial districts of central Scotland from Renfrew to Fife there was a drink outlet for every 150 people or less: in Glasgow and Edinburgh there was one for every 130 people. Even this was beaten in certain small burghs which not only had a thirsty population of miners or fishermen but also acted as a drinking-fountain on market-day to all the dry agricultural parishes around whose landowners and farmers would not tolerate a pub on their land. In East Lothian, for example, Tranent had 52 pubs (one for every 76 inhabitants) and Dunbar 53 (one for every 83). Nowhere else was as sodden as that.

Public houses were of all kinds, ranging from the grand, gas-lit and glass saloons, tempting working man and gent alike into a range of different bars and snugs, down to illegal shebeens and shady clubs where the drink was cheap, or not so cheap, and doctored. One of the few descriptions of a drinking house not written by a temperance foe comes from the manager of just such an establishment in Glasgow. The author incidentally appended to his pamphlet a handy list of recipes for such concoctions as whisky made from meths, sugar, water and 'two drops of the Essence of Prune' (brandy was more demanding):

> In 1855 I was connected with a rattler in the Saltmarket, on the left-hand side going down, it was a licensed house, when I went to it as barman, but three months afterwards it lost the license, and then we started it as an Independent Club, with me as the acting manager, we were open night and day, Saturday and Sunday, never shut at all, we had 13 waiters, and relieved each other in night and day shifts ... There was mighty little fuss about becoming an Independent. If a stranger dropped in we would ask if he saw anybody that knew him in the house, and whether they knew him or not if he could get a proposer and seconder we made him a member on the spot. I gave him a ticket with his name written on it, and he gave me the shilling. A fair exchange that suited me well. It was all fish that came into the net. We kept all sorts of liquors here, including even champagne and sparkling hock—the chief customers for the fiz being the swell English thieves, with so much money flying about I was generally able to give them change for a big note, and they would generally have a bottle over it. We had two kinds of whisky here, the best of it was much like that we used to make in King Street, but the second class was the real kill-me-deadly for choking off the Briggate boys, when we would rather have their room than their company. This business was too good to last ...[5]

Social commentators regarded drink as pre-eminently the problem of the inner city, despite its ubiquitous permeation of Scottish society. The Highlander on his croft, the story went, was over-fond of his dram but could 'hold his drink'. The Lowland farm-worker got blind drunk on feeing day, which was unfortunate and beastly but occurred only once or twice a year. The middle classes avoided setting a bad example to their social inferiors by, on the whole, getting fuddled in the privacy of their own homes. The urban poor, on the other hand, drank publicly, often, and disgustingly.

There was a very large number of descriptions written by outsiders of slum life, with the pauperized spirit drinker almost always forming the central figure. One of the most interesting of these was Alexander Brown's account of a week in Glasgow in 1858, when he went out on different nights as 'Shadow' to take 'social photographs' of the scenes of activity and dissipation around him. Sunday night was calm (this followed the Forbes–Mackenzie Act of 1853 which closed ordinary licensed premises on the sabbath), though the Bridgegate was filled with crowds of men, women and children (and police), preferring the open air of the street to their horrible dwellings. 'Rows of women, with folded arms—scarcely a broken link in the chain for long distances together—line the inner side of the pavement.' The only drink to be had was in an illegal shebeen, where 'the landlord of the private drunkery' gave 'a glass of very good ale' for 'a very good price, too'. On Monday night all hell was let loose: 'the idiotical jeer and senseless laugh of drunkards ... the horrid oaths and imprecations of low prostitutes ... nearly every shop on both sides of the street is a public house ... Rags, poverty, disease and death are the appropriate emblems of the district.'

And so it goes on. Tuesday is quieter than Monday because the compulsory thirst of Sunday has been slaked. Wednesday is market-day and attracts the country visitors, when the prostitutes, 'flaunting in silks and satins ... prowl like vultures after their prey'. Thursday falls between Monday and Tuesday in the intensity of the debauch. Friday is the quietest weekday because the pockets of the workers are empty: payday comes tomorrow. On Saturday, the people flock to the pubs in their tens of thousands:

> One can scarcely realise the enormous number of these houses, with their flaring gas lights in frosted globes, and brightly gilded spirit casks, lettered by the number of gallons, under the cognomen of 'Old Tom' or 'Young Tom', as the case may be, with the occasional mirror at the extreme end of the shop reflecting at once in fine perspective the waters of a granite fountain fronting the door, and the entrance of poor broken-down victims, who stand in pitiful burlesque in their dirty rags, amid all this pomp and mocking grandeur.[6]

That day, shopping and drinking reached their climax, the drinking often coming before the shopping among the poor. The Forbes–Mackenzie Act closed the pubs at 11 p.m., and the King Street Market off the Trongate then enjoyed its busiest hour as the wives got hold of what money was left to replenish empty cupboards: 'Hence the noise and turmoil:—the great blaze of gas-light from the various shops—the camphire lamps of costermongers, in long rows down the street, now and again relieved by the modest rays of a "farthing dip", shadowing forth the scaly brilliancy of stinking fish.'

'Shadow' was in fact a sympathetic observer of the poor, taking the view that the rich differed mainly in their ability to keep their weaknesses out of sight, and that the main reason for drunkenness was that the magistrates allowed too many public houses to tempt the common people with their flashing allure. Another astute observer was Dr George Bell, who anatomized the slums of Edinburgh in two tracts of 1849 and 1850. Though less sympathetic than Brown's, his overall view was nevertheless similar:

> From the toothless infant to the toothless old man, the population of the wynds drinks whisky. The drunken drama that is enacted on Saturday night and Sabbath morning [this was before Forbes–Mackenzie] beggars description. The scene is terrible and the music dreadful. It is impossible to say how much is expended on the chronic drinking, or everyday consumption, of whisky: and how much on the weekly exacerbation, or grand infernal orgie.[7]

Bell calculated in *Blackfriars Wynd Analyzed* that if every one of the 1025 inhabitants drank 4 gallons of whisky a year (likely enough: it is slightly over a pint a week per person over 14), it would cost those 1025 people £2050 *in toto* per annum: but the average income of the inhabitants was only £5 each by lawful means, yielding £5125 *in toto*. Of that sum, £3897 would have to go on food and £650 on rent—to say nothing of expenditure on fuel and clothing. How was this impossible book to be balanced? By crime, was Bell's answer—by begging and theft and prostitution 'in the infamous houses of the wynd ... If we learned that they yield £2000 per annum to the wynd, it would in no degree surprise us.' This was the black economy with a vengeance.

There is no reason to think that Bell was mistaken in making the link between drink and crime; there was also a link between drink and domestic violence, for the battered wife was part and parcel of the whisky culture. It was, though, only too easy for theorists to suggest a series of other links of which the truth was less demonstrable—for example, that drink lay behind all crime and behind most poverty ('whisky makes paupers, that is most certain'), or that as the Irish were

often fond of drink and were generally poor, they were guilty of cor-
roding aboriginal virtue among the Scots.

This approach suggested that the problem of the inner cities could be
cured by stern control of the drink trade, a crusade for the moral recla-
mation of the working classes, repatriation of the Irish, or all three
simultaneously. It took no account of another side of the problem, to
which commentators became more sensitive towards 1900: that drink
was, for the working classes, as much a symptom as a cause of desperate
conditions: 'It offers a transient escape from the miseries of life and
brings the only moments of comparative happiness which they ever
enjoy.'[8] James Devon, the Medical Officer of Glasgow Prison in 1912,
believed that drink, crime and overcrowding in a rented slum went
together: 'The only real substitute for the public-house is the private
house; and when that is fully realised the slums will go.'[9] His point was
made at greater length by his colleague Dr Archibald Campbell, the
Medical Officer of Health for Renfrewshire, in evidence to the Glasgow Municipal Commission on the Housing of the Poor in 1903. He
argued that social life in an ordinary Glasgow two-roomed house was
impossible:

> The man has finished his day's work and has had his ill-cooked tea
> ... His education has stopped short of making reading a pleasure to
> him. The children are noisy, as children are apt to be. There is little
> room to move. Perhaps there is a washing hanging around to dry.
> This might do now and then. He might talk to his wife. Or he might
> play with the children. But for every day, all the year round it is im-
> possible. He puts on his hat and goes out ... The public house is
> warm and bright—and where else is he to go?[10]

The male comradeship of the work place was thus renewed in the pub
in the evening, with the correlation that the wife was obliged to stay
behind in the tiny home to mind the children. The equation made a tradition: drink plus bad housing equalled male self-indulgence and
female isolation.

2

If drink had its devotees, it also had its deadly foes. The temperance
movement was begun in Scotland before there was any equivalent in
England. In 1829, John Dunlop, magistrate and anti-usage propa-

gandist in Greenock, and William Collins, publisher and evangelical enthusiast in Glasgow, founded organizations in their respective towns, mainly to abjure spirit drinking: within a year they had a membership of over 3300. These first societies, however, had only limited impact as they were moderationist and anti-spirit rather than abstinence societies, tending to attract middle-class people and open to the taunt that the members were only too ready to tell the working class to give up whisky while continuing to drink wine themselves.

A new and more effective start was made in England in the 1830s, when the amiable cheesemonger Joseph Livesey started the total abstinence movement at Preston in Lancashire. The movement swept in particular through that band of society composed of the smallest tradesmen and the most skilled workers, and from there spread quickly to Scotland. A fierce battle ensued between the moderationists and the teetotallers, in which Collins drew back, feeling that he could not advocate the complete abjuration of all alcohol use and resenting 'the vituperation used against the old society': Dunlop went forward, trying to bridge the gap by accepting into his organization both moderationists and teetotallers. The conflict ended in total victory for the abstainers. There was then a further struggle among the teetotallers themselves, between advocates of the short pledge and the long pledge, the former swearing merely not to touch drink themselves, the latter not to offer it to other people either. Duncan McLaren, for instance, was a short-pledge man, not using liquor himself but as Lord Provost of Edinburgh feeling unable to ban it from his table.

Finally, though this split did not appear until the 1850s, there was a struggle between the 'moral suasionists' of the Scottish Temperance League, who believed that society could ultimately only be reformed by the mass voluntary abjuration of drink, and the supporters of the United Kingdom Alliance (UKA), who argued that the way forward lay in the compulsory closing of all drink outlets—prohibition. This was not an Anglo-Scottish division but ran deep and wide on both sides of the border, especially after 1857, when a leading light in the UKA, Frederick Lees, accused the star lecturer of the moral suasionists, John B. Gough, of taking drugs: '"The Saint" has been *often* intoxicated with drugs ... once insensibly so in the streets of London, many times in Glasgow, until he was helpless.'[11] The accusation remained unproven, but it illustrated the ferocity and bitterness with which the teetotallers fought each other when not fighting the demon drink.

In the later 1830s and 1840s, the characteristic Scottish teetotaller was respectable, working class, and very possibly a Chartist. The middle and upper ranks of the middle classes were not initially attracted, though they came in later. The churches, too, did not at first give the movement support. Among Presbyterians, the older Moderates distrusted its 'enthusiasm' and the fashionable Evangelicals deplored its emphasis on man's ability to save himself by his own willpower, instead of relying on Jesus. Thomas Chalmers, for all his close friendship with William Collins and his inspiration to John Dunlop, avoided association with temperance until very late in his life. One of the first leading figures to take the plunge was Thomas Guthrie, Minister of Greyfriars and founder of the Ragged School Movement in Edinburgh: he described in his memoirs his fear of having to explain to his middle-class eldership at the first kirk session dinner after he had taken the pledge why he was allowing the bottle to pass his glass untouched. After the Disruption, the Free Church, and still more the United Presbyterians, became much more favourable to temperance, though a proposal in the latter that no one involved in selling drink should be admitted as an elder was dismissed on the grounds that Christ had obviously made no such demand.[12] In 1853, the United Presbyterians had about 150 ministers who were abstainers, the Free Church over 100, but the Church of Scotland only about 20. The shortcomings of the Auld Kirk were a source of sorrow to the Scottish Temperance League: they were shocked that its leader, Norman Macleod, had referred to alcoholic drinks as one of the mercies of the Creator, and still more that the General Assembly had dismissed five ministers in one year for intemperance: 'Year after year the chief business of this venerable court seems to be the deposition of her ministers for the sin of drunkenness.'[13]

Among Catholics, the temperance movement made relatively little initial impact, and was, indeed, very firmly opposed by the Bishop of Edinburgh (himself fond of a glass), who had this to say about teetotallers:

Under the general name of the temperance societies, they are, or may be, spouting and debating societies, political societies, speculating societies, tea and coffee-drinking and dancing societies; in short, anything and everything but what their appellation exclusively implies, viz. *sober* societies ... They seem to me ... exceedingly dangerous in principle ... I myself have been told within my own residence, and by one of the deputation of Catholic teetotallers of my own congregation, that he looked upon me as 'an encourager of drunkenness in Edinburgh'.[14]

On the other hand, the greatest temperance speaker of them all was a Catholic priest, Father Theobald Mathew, whose fame in his native Ireland had preceded him when he came on a visit to Glasgow in 1842. He was met at his hotel by the leaders of the temperance societies of Scotland, Protestant no less than Catholic, greeted by a crowd of 50,000 on Glasgow Green, and appeared with Protestant clergy at a soirée to welcome him in the City Hall. It was a rare moment of respite from the sectarianism and anti-Romanism that marred so much of nineteenth-century Scottish life. In the three days of his visit he received the pledge of abstinence from an army of newly-converted Irish teetotallers from all over Scotland, estimated to be 40,000-strong.

If there was an element in all this of mass hysteria, it nevertheless produced some abiding results. A Presbyterian minister declared that he had been in the habit of visiting a close off Glasgow High Street containing about eighty families, mostly Catholic: 'The people were so uproarious that they almost required a policeman constantly among them.' On the occasion of Father Mathew's visit, however, the population set off in a body to take the pledge from him in the Cattle Market: 'From that day till May 1845, when we left the district, there was not a quieter close, considering the number of inhabitants, in the city. A number are still adhering to the pledge ...'[15]

The leaders of the temperance movement appreciated from the start that the effect of great speakers, even those as eloquent as Father Mathew and J. B. Gough, must be transitory unless an attempt was made to create an alternative to the world of drink. Alcohol, said William Collins, has 'struck its fibrous roots into everything so deeply, that to tear up the spirit-drinking practices is like tearing up the whole social system of society'.[16] But a better life could be constructed without it, given the will at an early age and support thereafter. Thus a children's movement was begun—the Band of Hope—and a friendly society—the Rechabites (motto: 'Peace and Plenty the Reward of Temperance'). There were evening concerts, soirées, and lectures where the evils of alcohol were demonstrated, often in a highly entertaining way by demonstrations of popular science: if alcohol poured on gunpowder caused an explosion what might it not do to the guts of man? There were temperance hotels and temperance tea rooms, including famous ones founded by the Chartist leader Robert Cranston. In Paisley there was a Teetotal Tower with a Rechabite tent in the courtyard, telescopes and a camera obscura for viewing the countryside, collections of paintings, stained glass and curios, a music room with a pianoforte and several refreshment rooms serving tea, coffee, sherbet, tart and cream.[17] The idea was to demonstrate that life without drink could be as full and as sociable and cheery as life focused on the bottle.

The tone of the movement's propaganda is nicely caught in a tale for juveniles called 'the Buffalo Club *versus* the Temperance Meeting'. Fred is tempted to go to the Buffalo Club instead of the Temperance meeting and is upbraided by Harry, who asks him, 'What may not a night bring forth?':

> 'I'll tell you, in this case, what it is likely to bring forth, Harry— twenty as good-hearted fellows as breathe—a good song—some crack speeches—and any amount of fun—that's all.'
>
> 'Are you *certain* that's all?'
>
> 'Well, I–I–almost, Harry.'
>
> 'If you were *certain* that was all, instead of asking you to accompany me to the Temperance Meeting, I might go with you to the Club, for we are as fond of pleasant society, good music and crack speeches as others; but your meeting will also bring forth brain-maddening drinks . . .'[18]

What good did the temperance movement do? It worked on two fronts—self-control and state control. The achievements of self-control can never be measured and should not be belittled: every adult drinker reclaimed and every child persuaded by the Band of Hope to forswear alcoholic beverages for life, was an individual set on a new course, pointed towards an alternative lifestyle and a different pattern of consumer behaviour from that etched out by spirits in the pub. It is clear from the consumption figures, however, that propaganda and moral force alone failed to make a basic impact on the overall problem. In the later 1840s, after two decades of the most fervent campaigning, per capita consumption of duty-paid spirits was about 2 per cent more than it had been in the later 1820s.[19] There was, however, a significant break immediately after that: legal consumption in the early 1860s was a good third lower than it had been in the 1840s. The Forbes–Mackenzie Act of 1853 was a major victory for the temperance cause in Scotland that had no parallel in England. It owed its passage to an alliance of the tee-total interest (now with a larger middle-class involvement) with the evangelical sabbatarians of the post-Disruption kirks. It shut the pubs on Sundays (though so-called 'bona fide travellers' could go to a hotel and drink) and introduced, for the first time, a closing time (of 11 p.m.) on weekdays. Its immediate impact was two-sided, as explained by the Police Superintendent of Leith:

> The Act has done good, and has created evil—while it has dimi-nished drunkenness and tended to the better observance of the Sabbath, it has brought into existence and fostered illicit trafficking in spirits. Though drunk people may still be seen staggering on the Sabbath, parties going to church are spared the pain of witnessing crowds of men and women, with unsteady gait, making their way from the dram shops, cursing and swearing as they go to their wretched homes.[20]

It was, however, followed up by the Methylated Spirit Act of 1855, which hampered the manufacture and sale of meths for consumption, and by the strengthening of the powers of the police to enter unlicensed premises suspected of being shebeens and shady working-class drinking clubs, recommended by the Royal Commission on Exciseable Liquors in Scotland of 1859. All this laid the temperance reformers open to the charge of promoting 'odious class legislation' which affected the pleasures of the poor on their one day off work but did nothing to stop the rich imbibing claret in their own homes and clubs.[21] In addition there was an important increase in spirit duty, which more than dou-bled between 1853 and 1860, making whisky more expensive as well as more difficult to procure: the police in the cities had now become so efficient and powerful that illicit distillation, which had been the citi-zen's recourse under these circumstances in the past, became too diffi-cult and dangerous for most people. One indefatigable character in Glasgow who kept a still under the floorboards was visited by a cus-tomer:

> I asked him what he would do in the event of the authorities coming to the door, and demanding admittance. I'll show you, he says, and

opens the window, and just outside it I saw a rope hanging down from above, which rope he caught hold of and jumping out swung himself into another close for all the world like Myles-na-Coppaleen in the 'Colleen Bawn'.[22]

For all but the most athletic and daring criminals, however, the game was not worth the candle. The State action of the 1850s, the Forbes-Mackenzie Act of 1853, and the associated legislative and fiscal changes did more than anything else to lower overall drink consumption in the nineteenth century.

Though the consumption of spirits rose slightly and fell again in the second half of Victoria's reign, as Table 6 shows, it was much the same in the 1900s as in the 1860s. Since there was no further significant legislative action or change in the level of duty, but a great deal of temperance propaganda on the evils of drink, this underlines again the failure of the movement to influence the character of Scottish thirst. When Arthur Sherwell, perhaps the best-informed English temperance reformer of his day, lectured in Dunfermline in 1903, he observed that while it was 'unquestionably true that temperance sentiment is much more advanced in Scotland than it is in England', the country had failed to make 'any substantial progress during the last forty or fifty years', and in some respects was even worse off than a generation before. He cited the growth in drunkenness convictions and alcoholic mortality (shown in Table 6), and attributed to drink 'the striking increase in insanity during the last half century' (from 205 cases per 100,000 of the population in 1861–5 to 337 cases in 1896–1900). Independent evidence suggested that a quarter of all mental illness in Scotland was caused by alcoholism.[23]

Sherwell favoured municipal ownership of the drink trade—the so-called Gothenburg system, originating in Sweden, in which the local authorities owned the drink outlets and bleakly provided them with as few internal temptations as possible, using the profits to improve amenities in the community. A version of this was tried in a number of villages in the Fife coal-field, and the quite unusually adventurous drinker can still sample 'Goth No. 1' and 'Goth No. 2' in Kelty and the splendidly named 'Red Goth' in Lochore. Kellog Durland described the first Kelty Goth, where a teetotal manager 'walked behind the bar, sometimes stopping to serve a glass of liquor but devoting most of his time to scrutinizing the patrons'. At the end of the first year of operations, the profit permitted a grant of £50 to be made to the village library, a district nurse was employed, 'and there began to circulate rumours of a bowling green, a public park and electric lighting'. But the miners were not sure if they liked it.[24]

The leading temperance reformers of Sherwell's day, though often reflective and expert, had lost a good deal of the flamboyant confidence of the pioneers and some of the smug assertiveness of the post-Forbes–Mackenzie generation. At that time, sensitive to the criticisms of socialists like Keir Hardie that they were putting the cart before the horse, few of them would have repeated the words of Professor Leoni Levi, quoted with disapproving approval by Baillie David Lewis of Edinburgh in 1878:

> What, then, are the causes of the increase of pauperism and crime throughout the country? Not that they [the working classes] earn little, and that they are overtaxed; but that they are greatly given to drunkenness or to an excessive consumption of spirits, which is increasing instead of diminishing.[25]

By 1900, commentators were much more inclined, like Sherwell himself, to attribute drinking, at least partly, to intolerable social conditions in housing and environment, though the previous attitude persisted among those who wanted to believe that nothing could be done to help the multitude due to their innately swinish propensities. The temperance movement in Scotland, while now firmly associated with the churches, continued to have more appeal to the skilled working class than it did in England, a fact that was particularly notable in the ILP. There continued to be a large Scottish membership of organizations like the Band of Hope and the Order of Good Templars: in 1897, six thousand Templars marched in regalia with flags and banners, with ten bands, to the field of Bannockburn to protest against drink, 'More to be feared by the Scottish people than the enemy faced by our forefathers in 1314.'[26]

The movement was still also capable of political fireworks. Due to temperance pressure on the Liberals, the Scottish Local Veto Poll was conceded in 1913, though the first referenda were not held until 1920. The rules were a political curiosity and a testimony to Liberalism's faith in local democracy. A poll could only be held if 10 per cent of the electors requested one; then, for any change to occur, 35 per cent of those on the roll had to vote, and to ensure local prohibition 55 per cent of those voting had to vote in favour of a no-licence resolution. Under these circumstances it is surprising that as many as 584 polls took place in 1920, and that 41 areas voted either for local prohibition or for limitation. Many of these were small towns (for example, Kirkintilloch, Kilsyth, Lerwick and Stromness): some were middle-class residential areas in the cities (such as Cathcart, Pollockshields and Kelvinside in Glasgow). The working-class areas of the inner city with the most licences and the worst drink problems did not vote for local prohibition, which indicates once again the movement's failure to carry the hearts and minds of the masses.[27]

The biggest political bombshell of all was left to last, in the shape of the defeat of Winston Churchill at Dundee by Edwin Scrymgeour, the first and last MP of the Prohibitionist Party, in the General Election of 1922. The vote of the newly-enfranchised working-class women was held to be critical. Even as Churchill packed his bags vowing never to revisit the city, his opponent's cause was being discredited internationally by the obvious failure of prohibition in the USA. Scrymgeour's attempt in 1923 to introduce a national Prohibition Act was warmly supported by the ILP Clydesiders and especially by their fiery leader, James Maxton. They were almost alone. The bill was defeated by 235 votes to 14. The temperance cause had suddenly run out of steam.

The decline in popular interest and support for the movement in the interwar years was, of course, also due to the astonishing decline in drinking. Organized opposition contributed little, in the end, to the dramatic fall in drink consumption, which by the 1930s amounted to little over a quarter of the figure in the 1900s. The true hero was the Chancellor of the Exchequer. The first significant fall came in 1909, when the tax on a gallon of spirits went up by 34 per cent and consumption fell by 18 per cent: the marvel was that the Government had not earlier satisfied both its pockets and the temperance interest by discovering the price elasticity of demand for whisky—i.e. that they could raise more revenue by charging a higher tax per bottle than they would lose by selling fewer bottles to the disgruntled customers. After 1909 there was no stopping. The duty, which in 1860 had been 10s. per proof gallon, and in 1900 was still only 11s., became 30s. in 1918, 50s. in 1919 and 72s. 6d. in 1920. Even allowing for wartime inflation, it turned whisky from a cheap drink into an expensive one, with quite revolutionary effects on Scottish life.

As alcohol became more expensive, so it became more difficult to obtain. At the start of the war, pubs were still open up to thirteen hours a day: the Government was persuaded that the war effort was being seriously endangered by the drunkenness and absenteeism of munitions workers with too much money to spend. The shipyard employers in March 1915 were so concerned that they asked for the imposition of total prohibition: the Mayor of Carlisle reported that in his town and Annan convictions for drunkenness had risen with the influx of 12,000 war-workers from 78 in the first half of 1915 to 800 in the first half of 1916—most of these were from the camps at Gretna. 'Drink', said Lloyd George with characteristic drama, 'is doing more damage than all the German submarines put together.' In response, the State took over the drink trade in a few restricted areas (Carlisle, Gretna, and the naval base at Cromarty) and ran nationalized pubs 'with plain windows and short green curtains' on severe and discouraging lines reminiscent of the Fife Goths.[28] More generally, it imposed draconian restrictions on drinking hours, shortening them to five and a half hours a day with closing time at 9 p.m. on weekdays (the pubs remained shut, of course, on Sundays). The Licensing Act of 1921 extended opening hours to eight hours a day on weekdays and closing time to 10 p.m.: they were still far shorter than before the war, and the number of pubs was also substantially fewer. No longer was it possible for a man to spend his waking hours propped against the bar.

3

As was appreciated by many contemporary observers, the 'drink problem' was also a problem of how the population spent such spare income and non-working time as it possessed. In the century from 1840, both increased: the real wages of the working class grew most markedly in the last thirty years of the nineteenth century and again in the interwar years, provided the breadwinner could stay in employment; leisure time increased with the general adoption of the Saturday half-holiday in the early 1870s and the shortening of working hours in the twentieth century (see Chapter IV). These trends created surpluses in money and time that might have been consumed in drink. Indeed, the renewed rise in whisky consumption between the early 1860s and the late 1870s could well be related to a working class using Saturdays to do the drinking Forbes–Mackenzie had denied them on Sundays, and in the short run it was always noticed that years of full employment and high earnings produced surges in spirit drinking and drunkenness. In 1901, for example, the Prison Commissioners attributed the 'extraordinary rise of the imprisonments last year' to 'the disorderly conduct of the lowest class, who, through an abundance of employment on public works, were placed in possession of wages which they did not wisely expend.'[29] Nevertheless, in the long run drink consumption did not expand in proportion to spare money and time, but declined. The countervailing forces of the rise of modern patterns of consumer behaviour and of modern organized recreation were responsible.

Of the two, consumerism was probably of less importance before 1950, since the size of the house and the propensity of working-class people to share possessions limited the amount of goods a family would own. As long as three-quarters of the population lived in houses of three rooms or less, and three-fifths in houses of one or two rooms, as was the case before the First World War, there was little space for the accumulation of carpets, furniture, knicknacks and all the paraphernalia of the middle class. One of the first modern consumer goods to come into general use was the radio in the 1930s. The Carnegie investigators found it even in the homes of the unemployed:

> The hire-purchase system made it possible for many homes to obtain a wireless set. Little or no discrimination was shown in the choice of items. Very often the set was turned on in the early morning and left running for the greater part of the day. Dance bands and symphony orchestras were alternating backgrounds to the normal activities of home life—cooking, washing and talking.[30]

Plainly the wireless set filled a niche that the television set would take over in the next generation. Until it did so, and until the car finally choked the cities and made the village street dangerous, far more of Scottish life was spent outside the home than is the case today. This too slowed down the rise of consumerism. The street life of the inner city, with poor women standing gossiping outside their homes at all hours and children playing street games in the closes and wynds, was described by many commentators until the 1950s. At Bridge of Earn on the main Edinburgh to Perth road, young children used to stretch their skipping rope right across the main street from one cottage door to another. Not until 1914 was it suggested in the school minutes that playing in the road might be dangerous.[31]

As well as small homes and outdoor life, another factor militating against consumerism was the mutuality of life in the tenements. Glasgow neighbours who lent one another a wringer or a tub on wash days, or borrowed a dark suit from a friend for a wedding or a funeral, as Tom Bell describes,[32] were not exactly developing the mores of the acquisitive society. To buy a friend whisky was mutuality, but it also improved the drink trade's market (the Government actually tried to prohibit this during wartime, by decreeing in 1915 that no person might treat another unless he also treated him to a meal); but to borrow a friend's clothes was a form of mutuality that diminished the market of the textile trade. There is reason to think that as the old communities were slowly cleared away from the 1930s onwards and replaced by council estates, so individual lives became more private and their use of money more personal and more orientated towards accumulating family possessions. Before that time, for example, working-class children had 'very few toys, special children's books, or special sweets and treats'.[33] The cheap toy counter at Woolworth's was the first to put that right.

It was probably the revolution in the nature of recreation in the century after 1840 that did most to counter the pub's appeal. A revolution was indeed hoped for, because the middle classes and the temperance movement had little sympathy for traditional Scottish pastimes, associated with Bachannalian bad behaviour at fairs and annual holidays. Thus one disapproving commentator described a visit to Glasgow Fair through the words of 'Sandy M'Alpine', an imaginary Highlander:

Ther wuz the usual quantity o' shows, cirkuses, an' magic temples, wi' the usual quantity o' undecent strumpery, coorse buffoonery an' brazen-faced quackery exheebited ootside; ther wuz the penny an' the tuppenny theatres, twa or three galleries o' murd'rers and murd'resses … everything o' that stamp did a rowsin', roarin' bizness. The musick salloons an' the whisky palaces … did ther wark bravely.[34]

Reformers of all classes not only supported the movement to provide temperance hotels and coffee and tea rooms but also hoped to elevate the workers by establishing municipal parks, opening existing gardens to the public, endowing museums and building art galleries. Thus in Edinburgh in 1862, the Trades Council gathered over 10,000 signatures in a petition to open the Botanic Gardens to the public on Sundays after church, and the authorities in Glasgow, apart from constructing the Kelvingrove galleries, ran the People's Palace on Glasgow Green as a museum and conservatory for the East End, and erected the elegant glass and iron bubble of the Kibble Palace in the Botanic Gardens at the West End. The public libraries, supported with the assistance of the Carnegie Trust and by other benefactors like Stephen Mitchell and George Baillie in Glasgow, were intended for the same purpose—in the words of Baillie's trust deed of 1863, 'to aid the self-culture of the operative classes, from youth to manhood and old age, by furnishing them with warm, well-lighted, and every way comfortable accommodation at all seasons, for reading useful and interesting books'.[35]

The quality of life was improved for some people by all this activity and benevolence, but in Glasgow most of the parks were too far from the most overcrowded areas, the libraries had comparatively little attraction for an undereducated working population that was also exhausted by long physical labour, and the art-galleries and museums appealed 'to a very limited number ... working class or otherwise'. That shrewd observer of the city, Dr Devon of the prison service, writing in 1912, was critical of the whole idea of 'improving' the workers, and had a respect for their own choice of recreation: 'Perhaps they do not believe that it would be an improvement to conform to our ideals ... Let us remember the monotony of their lives, the numbing effect of the conditions to which they are subject, and be thankful they do not seek worse.'[36]

The benefit of increased leisure fell very unequally between the sexes. It was the male worker who got most from the Saturday half-holiday and the shorter working week: unmarried women in the textile trades also gained, but many female workers were domestic servants or shop hands for whom time off remained exceedingly hard to obtain. As for the married woman with a family, she gained nothing at all: the children still had to be minded, the shopping done, and the house cleaned, for nothing entered the market to save labour for the working-class housewife until the 1950s and 1960s. That air of pinched desperation and the symptoms of chronic illness that doctors and other social workers so often noticed among mothers in poor families surely had much to do with the fact that for them the house was a perpetual prison. Nor were Scottish menfolk famous for their willingness to help: even in the 1950s, when a big-sprung perambulator at last came to the assistance of the working-class housewife and proved a family status symbol, few Scottish fathers would have been seen dead pushing one in the streets.

The recreation which Scotsmen most obviously sought on the eve of the First World War was football. The sport in its modern form was a recent introduction, but in pre-industrial times Scotland had shared with other parts of the British Isles a fondness for a type of mass-football, half sport and half riot, in which one community would challenge another and, with few rules to restrain the competitors, try to kick or carry a stuffed bladder from one point to another. There were complaints about its distracting and disorderly nature at intervals in the sixteenth and seventeenth centuries, and it was said of Sir Walter Scott that he 'would rather have seen his heir carry the Banner of Bellenden gallantly at a football match at Carterhaugh' than hear that the boy 'had attained the highest honours of the first university in Europe'.[37]

The codification of the modern game began in the public schools of England in the early part of the nineteenth century, at Rugby in respect of what became known as 'rugger' and at Charterhouse and Westminster in respect of 'soccer'. Rugger won early converts among expensive private schools in Scotland, especially among that handful of boarding schools which were most imitative of England. H. H. Almond, the headmaster of Loretto School at Musselburgh from 1862, thought football 'an incalculable blessing' since it absorbed the enthusiasm and energies, providing a distraction that was 'worth all the books that have been written on youthful purity'. In addition it taught children how to bear pain, counteracted the influence of 'luxurious and self-indulgent' homes and even 'the tendency of the examination system to make the development of character a secondary consideration'.[38] The heart bleeds for the helpless victims of his mad athleticism. The first international rugby match between England and Scotland was played in 1870. The game continued to flourish among the pupils and former pupils of fee-paying schools but had no popular following except in the Border towns, where it perhaps grafted on to the tradition of mass football of Walter Scott's day. It remained, in Scotland, firmly an amateur game.

The case with soccer was quite otherwise. The first Scottish club was Queen's Park, founded 'by a few happy enthusiasts on the 9th July 1867, at No. 3 Eglington Terrace, Glasgow'; tradition relates that they were associated with the YMCA, which would seem altogether possible as many early football clubs were associated with the fashionable 'muscular Christianity' (Aston Villa grew from a men's bible class). Within the next decade the game took off: Partick Thistle and Ayr were in existence in 1868, Rangers and Third Lanark in 1872, Heart of Midlothian in 1873, Hibernian in 1875. Celtic was a relative latecomer, founded in 1887 by Brother Walfrid, headmaster of the Sacred Heart School in the East End of Glasgow, as a means of raising money to provide free meals for poor Catholic children.[39] The Scottish Football Association was founded in 1873, a year after the first Anglo-Scottish international. By the 1890s, its membership varied between 190 and 130 clubs. It can be no coincidence that the first rage for Association Football came at the same time as the spread of the Saturday half-holiday.

Like rugger, soccer began as an amateur game, but the clubs found it had considerable spectator appeal and began to charge 'gate-money' for the upkeep of their grounds. From this it was a short step to paying expenses and then retainer fees. Scottish players found a ready market for their skills in England; when the mill-workers of Darwen twice held the Old Etonians to a draw in a famous contest for the English Cup in 1878, there were two Scotsmen in the team 'whose presence in Lancashire needed some explanation, though none was ever given'. By 1893, professionalism was formally recognized by the SFA, and of the leading original clubs only Queen's Park kept up the amateur canon. The change aroused disapproval:

> The tendency ... of the last few years has been to drive men of the better classes into Rugby Union football, leaving the Association game to the working classes. These are, unfortunately, mainly incapable of managing the various clubs and associations, and accordingly they elect others, not players, but chiefly publicans, etc., to undertake this duty for them. Under such conditions the future of the game in Scotland is not hopeful.[40]

By then, indeed, soccer was becoming big business, attracting substantial investment by limited liability companies. Celtic in the 1890s constructed a stadium to hold 70,000 people, 'unrivalled in Great Britain'. Whatever the middle classes might think about it, the workers were becoming football-mad. It was the ideal sport for a deprived proletariat, satisfying what Paul Fussell in another context has called 'their need as losers to identify with the winners', and providing them with a fund of bar-room 'dogmatism, record-keeping, wise secret knowledge and pseudo-scholarship of the sort usually associated with the "decision-making" or "executive" or "opinion-moulding" classes'.[41]

The Church certainly resented the rival attraction. In 1891, the Presbytery of Hamilton reported that 'on Saturday afternoons men do nothing but attend or discuss sports', and the Presbytery of Dumbarton that 'the minds of young people and of some old people too are so occupied with matches ... that interest in higher and more momentous subjects is lost ... The Saturday evening sporting paper is the young man's Bible and sermon on Sunday.' Next year the Presbytery of Paisley likewise complained of 'the demoralising concomitants of the all-absorbing game of football', and in 1893 the Presbytery of Brechin had a word of reproach for the disgusting language that was heard at the game.[42]

There is no doubt that football violence and vandalism also existed from the start, though it is difficult to decide how far it varied in intensity over time. Bottles and rivets (from shipyard workers) were being thrown on to the pitch as early as the 1880s, and 'bad blood' was complained of between Celtic and Rangers as early as 1896. It certainly continued. There was, for example, a serious riot at the Rangers-Celtic final of the Scottish Cup at Hampden in 1909, when spectators from both sides invaded the pitch, uprooted the goal posts and tore off the nets, set pay-boxes on fire, broke gaslights all round the ground, and united to throw stones at police and firemen (who threw them back), inflicting injuries on 130 people, 30 of whom went to hospital. With lesser, but still serious, riots involving Rangers in 1905 and 1912, the decade before the First World War may have been one of the periods when crowd behaviour was at its worst.

In the 1920s and 1930s, at least in Glasgow, football violence increased in sectarian content as Celtic began to fly the Irish Free State flag at its matches and Rangers flaunted its Union Jacks and Orange supporters' badges in response. The reply to 'Get stuck intae them Orange-Masonic bastards,' was 'Kill the Fenian shite.' Club management arguably encouraged sectarianism and its accompanying violence as a crowd-puller, so that it became part of the ritual pattern of Glasgow male recreation.[43]

Who, exactly, attended a football match? The only detailed evidence we have comes from the casualty list of the Ibrox disaster of 1902, when a crowd of 68,000 was assembling for the start of an Anglo-Scottish international and part of the wooden terracing collapsed, killing 26 and

Skill and muscle in heavy industry: ABOVE J. Kerr, blacksmith, A. Marshall, hammerman, Cowlairs, 1889; BELOW hewers in a Fife coalmine in the interwar years.

The traditional skills of country towns: ABOVE coopers at work on herring barrels,
c. 1889; BELOW shipwrights at Pittenweem, Fife, 1905.

The industrial skills of Glasgow: ABOVE engineering managers and foremen at a
Glasgow railway works, mid-nineteenth century: every man his own Brunel;
BELOW hydraulic riveters at work on the *Lusitania* at Clydebank, 1906.

Women in the Dundee jute mills; ABOVE cop winders in the spinning department; BELOW the weaving shop. Spinners were regarded as giddy, weavers as responsible and steady, but here the weavers just look exhausted.

injuring 500. The press published the details of the occupations of about half the victims. They ranged from a 'professor of hypnotism' to a milkman; about two-thirds were skilled workers, the building trades, the metal trades, and ship-building being particularly prominent; a third were unskilled; there were only seven white-collar workers, eight men in middle-class occupations, and, tellingly, a solitary housewife. It is likely that all these latter categories would have been somewhat better represented in more expensive seats,[44] though it was a relatively expensive match, the minimum entry being 1s. for an adult and 6d. for a boy, twice the usual sum. Being played at Ibrox, it might also have attracted a high proportion of the traditional Orange supporters of the Rangers, such as the shipyard workers at John Browns. Both these factors would have tended to keep away the poorly-paid Catholic population, but the great popularity of Celtic in Glasgow and Hibernian in Edinburgh suggests that under other circumstances unskilled labour was just as keen on the game as skilled.

There is no doubt that one of the attractions of football was its association with betting, which also absorbed income that might otherwise have been spent on drink—though arguably to no better purpose from the perspective of the spender's wife and family. Gambling ran deep in the industrial tradition. It was endemic among immigrant Irish navvies and rural mining communities. This was how Abe Moffat described 'pitching toss' at Lumphinnans:

> One would throw two pennies up in the air, and all the other members of the group would bet they would come down as tails. If they came down as heads, then the person who threw them up in the air would win all the stakes that were laid down on the ground ... It reminds me of the visitor who came to a mining village and said the miners had a queer kind of religion; a group of miners stood in a ring every Sunday morning and they all looked up at the sky and looked down on the ground and together they would say, 'Jesus, tails again'.[45]

During the third quarter of the nineteenth century, organized betting became a significant urban business. The occasion for this was the Gaming Act of 1853, by which the Victorian Parliament effectively outlawed the working-class betting shops that had grown up in England round horse-racing, but by a characteristic oversight omitted to extend its provisions to Scotland—a fact which appears not to have been appreciated until around 1860, when English bookmakers began to migrate to Scotland like lovers to Gretna Green. Within a few years, the number of betting shops in Glasgow (where there was no race-course) had grown from none to twenty-eight, and Edinburgh also had thirteen.[46] In 1874, the Gaming Act was extended to Scotland, and legal activities by the bookies became difficult. Henceforth, unless you were a rich man who could afford the subscription to an exclusive betting club, or unless you could go in person to place a bet within the boundaries of a racecourse (difficult in Scotland where horse-racing remained under-developed), the only legal way to bet was by using credit and contacting the bookie by letter, telegram or telephone. It was, of course, designed to discourage betting by the lower classes (who seldom had credit), the law remaining unchanged until 1960.

There were two ways round the law. One was by the development of coupon betting—the first pools—which was begun in Glasgow 'in a small office by a man named McCredie in Union Street' in 1899, and in Edinburgh by a twenty-year-old cooper, Robert Spittal, who printed coupons in his own house in 1902 and sold them for 2d. round the city's breweries.[47] By the 1930s, coupon betting was in the hands of large firms and was a generally popular pastime. Football pools were legal because they were conducted by post and involved an element of credit at a humble level. The other was to place bets illegally. The Select Committee on Betting in 1902 heard evidence from the Lord Provost and Chief Constable of Glasgow that the practice prevailed to an 'enormous extent' in the city, despite local by-laws that made it even more difficult to get round the Gaming Act there than elsewhere. News-agents, tobacconists, and hairdressers acted as covers for bookies: there was a well-organized system of street betting, patronized, for example, by shopkeepers, clerks and 'railway officials', and the work place had been penetrated by bookies' agents, especially the ship-building yards and chemical works. It is, of course, impossible to know how much money changed hands, or how many of the population were really absorbed by it. Middle-class contemporaries might have exaggerated both figures. Abe Moffatt observed that in the mining villages you always saw a group playing 'pitching toss' or betting on whippets, but it was always the same small circle of individuals. The Carnegie enquirers said in the 1930s that 'the main excitement of betting was the state of hopeful suspense which occupied the mind for several hours at a stretch', while a few obtained additional satisfaction from becoming experts in the pedigrees of horses and greyhounds and fewer still kept dogs, which 'received as much attention as any child'.[48]

By the early twentieth century, horse-racing was enjoyed at established meetings at Musselburgh and Kelso and also at Ayr, where the suffragettes burnt down the stand. (They also burnt down Leuchars Station and the medieval church at Whitekirk.) Greyhound-racing was popular after the introduction of the electric hare in 1926, with stadia at Powderhall in Edinburgh and Carntyne in Glasgow. A few other sports also attracted betting, such as amateur and professional athletics and cycling. 'Pedestrianism' (professional athletics contests), indeed, probably had a larger following than any other form of racing in the east of Scotland in the latter part of the nineteenth century, 25,000 people attending the opening games at the new Powderhall Stadium in 1870. The sport declined partly because it was even more difficult to prevent the nobbling of human beings than of dogs and horses: at a 300-yards handicap in 1903, for example, 'not one of the runners showed any inclination to win the event . . .', so the promotor disqualified the field and, amidst protests from the contestants and jeers from the spectators, gave the prize money to charity.[49]

In many other ways the Scots developed a culture of recreation in the nineteenth century. Few, apart from the middle classes, could leave home for a prolonged holiday, and seaside resorts like Largs and Dunoon on the west coast and North Berwick and Elie on the east were as exclusively the domain of the professional man, tradesman, and shopkeeper as the Highland grouse moor was of the rich. For the working class, however, nothing was more popular than a trip 'doun the watter' on a Clyde steamer: in 1882, an act was passed extending Sunday closing to passenger vessels plying the rivers and estuaries of Scotland, in view of the 'great evils' that had arisen 'from the sale of intoxicating liquors' thereon. Others enjoyed train excursions: Kellog Durland joined 3000 Fife miners on a jaunt from Kelty to Inverness and thoroughly enjoyed himself: 'The singing and the shouting lasted all day . . . for a trip of that kind there was little intoxication.'[50] Others took to cycling as a recreation: in the early 1890s there was much anxiety expressed in the Church of Scotland about the number of people, especially in the agricultural districts of the north-east, who were breaking the sabbath by using their machine not to go to church but to cycle past it. In the 1930s the Scottish Youth Hostel Association introduced thousands to the pleasures of hiking, and some of the adventurous unemployed (and employed) took up mountaineering:

> You have to understand what Scotland was like in those days. It was a grim place ... It really was grim and you were a youngster in this and you accepted this, you had been brought up to this, this was normal, this grimness, then suddenly to find this escape route, this climbing thing and it absolutely bowled you over ... It was an explosion, it was a wonderful thing.[51]

For all those who took to the Great Outdoors, however, many more took to the Great Indoors. For the young and the courting there was the dance-floor: 'Many young men pass through a phase which has often been described by their parents and friends and sometimes even by themselves as "dancing mad" ... the search for a mate and dancing go hand in hand.'[52] In a similar category came the Victorian and Edwardian music hall, and in the interwar years the cinema. In the 1930s, for example, the Carnegie investigators found that about 80 per cent of their sample of young unemployed attended the cinema at least once a week, and 25 per cent more often: this compared with 15–20 per cent who went cycling and 6 per cent who borrowed books from the public library.[53] Even as late as 1951, the Scots went to the pictures far more often than the population of the UK as a whole—38 visits per person per year as against an average of 29 for Britain as a whole.[54] No doubt it was another side-effect of the small house without room or privacy. However since these things are so obviously part of the strategy of young people for encountering one another, consideration of all that was involved is best left to the following chapter.

CHAPTER VII

Sex, Love and Getting Married

1

There is no reason to suppose that the Victorians were less interested in sex than we are, and certainly not that they were a more moral people. Prostitution was a much bigger problem in the nineteenth-century Scottish city than in the twentieth, illegitimacy was much higher in the 1850s than in the 1950s and the number of girls pregnant before marriage probably not less. Nevertheless, there were undeniably big differences in sexual mores between the two periods, nowhere more obvious than in the middle class. Whereas today girls from better-off homes take the pill at least as readily as their working-class sisters to enable them to enjoy sex with their boyfriends out of marriage, before the First World War they were the least likely to have had any kind of premarital sexual experience or relevant biological information. Medical opinion was unanimous that the daughters of the Victorian middle class were almost never the mothers of illegitimate children or pregnant brides. Absence of formal sex education was, of course, general throughout society, but ignorance of even the most elementary facts was greatest in the middle class. Poor children living in a house of one or two rooms were bound to find something out, despite the minimal privacy of the box bed. Rich children had only the statues in the art galleries to guide them, and most of those wore fig leaves. The daughter of an engineering manager, born in 1889 and married as late as 1917, had this to say to an oral history interviewer: 'I know this, that when I was expecting my first baby I didn't know whether it was going to come out of my tummy or where it was going to come out of. And this is perfectly true, and I was twenty-seven and a half.'[1]

Chastity and ignorance were maintained by the institution of the chaperone, often a married sister or an aunt, whose task it was to maintain a delicate surveillance over the two young lovers, and especially not to leave them unattended for long enough for anything that could remotely be construed as intimacy to take place. The custom became less strict towards the end of the century, and the supervision of courtship in the 1920s and 1930s was generally more relaxed—or even non-existent. Nevertheless, it is safe to say that throughout the century, middle-class girls were unusual, as a group, in upholding the traditional Christian standard that demanded absolute chastity before marriage and complete fidelity afterwards.

The reasons for this were not entirely moral. Since property was transmitted by marriage, a high premium was placed by men on women's virginity: a girl who could restrain herself before marriage could restrain herself afterwards, and the property conveyed through such a channel was bound to go to the right heirs. This was not a specifically Victorian view. Dr Johnson had expressed exactly this in the eighteenth century, when in a conversation at Dunvegan on Skye he observed, 'Consider of what importance to society the chastity of women is. Upon that all the property in the world depends. We hang a thief for stealing a sheep, but the unchastity of a woman transfers sheep, and farm, and all from the right owner.'[2] Thus a woman who refused to conform to the view of sexual morality conventional to her class would make herself a very poor prospect in the marriage market.

However, the same sanctions did not apply to middle-class men, and there was a flagrant double standard in expectations about their behaviour. No doubt many, perhaps most (there is no way of telling), were as chaste as their sisters. On the other hand, a great many were not, either before marriage or after it. 'It appears to be almost taken for granted', wrote one offended Christian moralist, 'that young men should be found in a greater or lesser degree, giving way.' If they needed an excuse they could find it in the fact that couples married late (often in the late twenties), combined with the supposedly hot-blooded character of the human male. It was a peculiarity of the Victorians that they supposed men to have a much greater sexual appetite than women, whereas people in the Middle Ages, with equal lack of evidence, had supposed the reverse. Nineteenth-century doctors were still occasionally prescribing fornication as a cure for tension, and as late as 1918 the Church of Scotland condemned as a 'satanic whisper' the 'widely prevalent notion that strict continence is harmful' to the health of men.[3]

Since, however, the middle-class male was disbarred from seeking sexual relief from women of his own class, where should he go? The maid's bedroom might be the first stop, since she was a girl of another class, living in his own household, and vulnerable to his overtures. The position of Victorian domestic servants was, indeed, often very difficult. They were young: fifteen to twenty-five was the usual age-range for all apart from the cook and perhaps the governess. They were generally unmarried, and sedulously segregated from young males of their own class by employers who provided little time off, insisted on 'no followers', and allowed no opportunity for unauthorized visitors from outside. It is easy to tell which used to be the servants' bedrooms in Victorian villas in Glasgow and Edinburgh because they are the only ones with bars on the windows. The lady of the house was enjoined to 'lock the doors with your own hand and deposit the keys upon your toilet table, otherwise while enjoying the blessings of repose above you may not know what junketings are going on below'.[4] Girls in this isolated situation might fall easy prey to the blandishments or force of a middle-class man already within the house. Many such unlucky servants, made pregnant and then dismissed without a reference, found themselves on the streets. In the later 1850s, four-fifths of those admitted to the prostitutes' refuge, the Edinburgh Magdalene Institution, had once been domestic servants.

It is, however, unlikely that servants were the main objective of males looking for sexual adventures, since it is a foolish bird who fouls his own nest. Seduction carried with it the obvious risk of discovery by a shocked mother or infuriated wife. Most men who wanted experience or variety probably paid cash for it in someone else's home, or working premises. Prostitution itself was not new. In the sixteenth and seventeenth centuries, the penalty for convicted whores in Edinburgh had been a ducking in some horrible pond, whipping and expulsion from the community. In the eighteenth century, vice increased in proportion to the wealth of the capital: William Creech reported that whereas in 1763 there had been five or six brothels and a handful of prostitutes, twenty years later there were 'twenty times' more brothels and 'every quarter of the city and suburbs was infested' with whores.[5] The Edinburgh Magdalene Institute, founded in 1797, and its Glasgow equivalent, founded in 1815, were intended as reformatories, and covered a high percentage of their running costs by putting the girls to work as laundresses, washing other people's dirty linen in private. They were extremely unsuccessful as most of the girls ran away, unable to bear either the discipline or the humiliating unctuousness of their bene-factors.[6]

As prostitution increased, so did both venereal disease and society's anxiety about the peril to body and soul. In 1842, William Tait, a young doctor in Edinburgh, published a remarkable exposé of 'Mag-dalenism' in the capital. He claimed that there were at least 800 full-time girls involved: about a quarter of them lived 'privately' and the remainder were to be found in 200 public brothels, mainly in the Old Town: in addition he estimated that there were about 1200 'sly prosti-tutes'—part-timers driven to vice by poverty or inclination—who operated by hiring a room in 'houses of assignation' where no questions were asked.[7] Ralph Wardlaw in the same year put the number of pros-titutes in Glasgow at 1800 and the houses of ill-fame at 450, estimating even more tenuously that they entertained 36,000 visitors weekly.[8] Even if such figures were partly guess-work, nobody in early Victorian Scotland doubted that the problem was very large, that it was associated with drink and poverty, and that it subsisted on the self-indulgence of men who accepted their right to depart from the Chris-tian ethic as a matter of course.

Some of the girls were drawn into prostitution by the prospect of a glamorous and profitable career as the kept woman of a rich man. Few, however, could either aspire to the top, or, if they attained it, keep the looks and freedom from disease that were demanded by the richest clients. Most were very young: Tait found that of those treated at Edin-burgh Lock Hospital for venereal disease between 1835 and 1840, 4 per cent were under fifteen (including occasional child prostitutes aged nine or ten), 66 per cent were in their late teens, and only 3 per cent were over thirty years. Many of the girls quickly declined into the most wretched circumstances. Take, for example, the description of an Edin-burgh brothel by Isabella Bird, the noted lady explorer and traveller who came to the High Street of her home town in the same spirit that she visited Arctic Canada and the Rocky Mountains: after describing a room about 12 feet square, divided by rotten partitions, the floor heaped with ashes from the grate and the only furniture a bedstead with a straw mattress, a table and a stool, she continued:

A girl of about eighteen, very poorly dressed, was sitting on the stool; two others, older and very much undressed, were sitting on the floor, and the three were eating, in a most swinish fashion, out of a large black pot containing fish. I have shared a similar meal in similar primitive fashion in an Indian wigwam in Hudson's Bay Territory but the women who worshipped the Great Spirit were modest in their dress and manner and looked *human*, which these 'Christian' young women did not.[9]

The customers of the brothels were any men who were prepared to pay, not just the urban middle class. The army and navy, as always, were important in the trade. In 1858, 'Shadow' noted that Wednesday night in Glasgow was farmers' night: the girls gravitated towards the corn exchange and cattle markets as the day's business drew to a close. John Dunlop described the Edinburgh prostitutes as 'the chief relievers of the pockets of the operatives on pay night', and William Walker said that Edinburgh girls came over to work the great proletarian celebration of Glasgow Fair. In Stranraer, one of the few country towns with a prostitution problem, the clients were Irish navvies flush with cash at the port of embarkation.[10]

In these circumstances the girls (with their attendant ponces and madams) were extracting a small temporary surplus from the working class, but it was the people with money at the top of society who provided the best pickings. William Logan, Glasgow city missionary, in 1871 classified brothels like railway carriages. First-class establishments, he said, were supported by 'noblemen, wealthy merchants, military officers, sea captains and *gentlemen* who move in the higher circles of society'; second-class brothels 'are chiefly supported by men in business, clerks, warehousemen, shopmen etc.', as well as by many medical students and some theological students; third-class houses 'are chiefly frequented by persons from the country, mechanics, apprentices, soldiers, and sailors'.[11] Dr Tait in Edinburgh in 1842 noticed that the whores were one-third fewer in summer than in winter, and fewer still in autumn: he attributed this to the migration of the wealthier families to their country houses, and to the university vacations. He believed that 'perhaps a fourth part of the rising population' was thus ruined and depraved (this can only have been a guess) and that those particularly at risk were 'lads who come from the country to learn businesses in town,

163

or to receive a College education', young men with too much wealth for their discretion, and those who 'pursue the paths of literature and science': 'The young lawyer, physician, and general student, view this kind of relaxation as indispensable for their health ... the pulpit is not even exempted from the inroads and consequences of these habits.'[12] From the early nineteenth century to the early twentieth, there was an Edinburgh tradition that the brothels of Rose Street were never so busy as during the General Assembly, but this may be no more than an amusing calumny about the clergy. The more secular assemblies at Musselburgh races certainly drew the silks and painted faces to tempt the swells.

As time passed, prostitution declined, but it did not disappear. The authorities at least tried to make it less flagrant. Individual burghs took advantage of the power granted by the General Police and Improvement (Scotland) Act of 1862 to close brothels and drive prostitutes from the streets. William Logan thought that this strategy partly worked, and that by 1871 the business was conducted 'with less ostentation and attractiveness to the outside world': he said the number of brothels had fallen to about 85 in Edinburgh, with a similar decline in Glasgow. In 1901, Edinburgh police reported 424 notorious prostitutes and 45 brothels in the capital, but in 1911, only 180 prostitutes and 29 brothels. Shady institutions, however, could come in a variety of unexpected guises, and the Parochial Inspector of Glasgow in the same year drew attention to 'the existence of ice-cream shops which were merely cloaks for indecency'.

Legislative measures, in fact, did nothing to touch the factors of supply and demand. As long as there were girls forced by the poverty and dangers of city life to consider prostitution as their best economic option and men frustrated and irresponsible enough to pay for their services, it was likely to remain a problem. Many observed how the downturn of the trade cycle, which destroyed the meagre earnings of many women in casual work, such as milliners and seamstresses, increased the number of 'sly prostitutes' on the streets. Patrick MacGill, the immigrant Irish navvy who in 1914 wrote an autobiographical novel describing how he lost his girl to the seduction of a Scottish farmer and found her again by accident walking the streets of Glasgow, blamed prostitution not on faulty morality but, after the fashion of the new century, on 'employers who pay starvation wages, and the masters who fatten on sweated labour'.[13]

After the First World War, there seems to have been a further decline in prostitution, due perhaps to economic factors that gave steadier employment to more women outside the spheres of domestic service and the sweatshop, and to the start of the welfare state, which began to relieve the margins of desperate poverty. Within the middle class, the more relaxed attitude to contact between men and women, though far from permissive, was probably also a factor. Nevertheless, Edwin Muir in 1934 found the prostitutes still an enduring part of the Edinburgh scene: 'They live, as members of the proletariat, in the poorest districts, but their main beat is Princes Street, and it has in their eyes the prestige and familiarity of a business address.' Since the Royal Mile was still a semi-slum, and Princes Street regarded as the socially exclusive shopping precinct of the city, the whores appeared as the only people truly comfortable walking in both parts of the capital.[14]

Similarly, the attitude that middle-class men might have a go at working-class girls to gain experience but should leave their own kind alone, long continued. Dr Verney, the much respected founder of Edinburgh University Medical Health Service, startled a student debate at the end of his long career by adhering, in the 1960s, to the moral attitudes which had served his profession so long:

> Dr Verney replied that to prescribe the pill for unmarried girls would be contrary to the dictates of his conscience . . . It is necessary to the male student to prove their manhood by the experience of sex. Earlier they had found this outlet outside the university, but now found it within the university, with an associated rise in illegitimacy and venereal disease in the student population. This Dr Verney attributed to a decline of moral principles among the young women—in his day young women came to the university for education not for fornication. In the tense and claustrophobic silence which followed . . . the sense of most of what he had said previously was forgotten.[15]

The students can never have heard the double standard expounded so clearly. They were right to be shocked.

2

So far we have considered the sexual mores of the middle class and of those of the working class who chose either to earn a living by prostitution or to go with prostitutes. What of the rest of society?

Commentators had little to say on the matter until the 1850s, when the Registrar-General for Scotland published, for the first time, the statistics of illegitimate births. These showed three salient and remarkable features. Firstly, illegitimacy was on average higher in Scotland than in England and most of Europe. Secondly, it was generally higher in the countryside than in the towns, which was unusual in a European context. Lastly, it was very much higher in some parts of the countryside than in others. In 1861–5, for example, the proportion of illegitimate births was 16.6 per cent in Banffshire compared to 4.2 per cent in Ross and Cromarty; close analysis of the returns for 1855 (the only year for which this exercise is possible) shows that a teenage girl in Banff was more than twenty times as likely to have a bastard as one in Ross, and the risk even for girls in their twenties was between four and six times greater in Banff than Ross. Such extraordinary statistical disparities obviously showed that there were real differences in what was regarded as acceptable sexual behaviour among the working classes in different parts of the country. It was easy to see this but difficult to explain it, though many made the attempt.

The discovery of a high rate of illegitimacy in Scotland was received by reformers of different persuasions as ammunition for their various causes. The Revd James Begg, for example, was attempting to stir the Free Church to agitate for better housing for city artisans and for reform of the rural bothy system. He claimed that illegitimacy was caused by overcrowding and the consequent brutalization: 'Jesus says to his people, "When thou prayest, enter into thy closet and shut thy door." This evidently supposes a state of things to exist in regard to the dwellings of the people which in many districts of Scotland is not at present realized.'[16] He was infuriated when told by the Registrar-General for Scotland that bad housing could not be the cause of illegitimacy since housing was most overcrowded in the cities where illegitimacy was comparatively low. Furthermore, the areas with the highest rate of bastardy, the north-east and the south-west, did not house farm servants in bothies, comfortless sheds set apart from the main farmhouse and occupied by many men together, but in 'chaumers', rooms in the farm and near the kitchen accommodating only one or two men. Similarly, temperance reformers who wanted to associate illegitimacy with drink-maddened passion were informed that in Banffshire almost all the illegitimacy occurred in the agricultural community and virtually none among the fishermen, although 'our country labourers and small farmers are as free from intemperance as our fishermen are from abstinence or even moderation'.[17] Educational reformers who thought that high illegitimacy must be caused by defects in the school system were confounded when the Registrar-General pointed out that the north-east had one of the highest literacy rates in the country, but Ross and Cromarty one of the lowest.

Some picked up the stick from the other end, and attributed the low rate of bastardy in the Highlands to a lack of 'natural forces' among the Celts: but how could a racialist explanation be reconciled with the fact that the vigorous Vikings of Orkney and Shetland had almost as low an illegitimacy rate as the listless inhabitants of Ross and Cromarty? Could religion be a factor? The Roman Catholics of Glenlivet had a very high rate, those of South Uist and Barra a very low one; the Presbyterians of Galloway (the heartland of the old Covenanters) had a high rate, those of Lewis (where the modern Free Kirk and its offshoots were strictest) a very low one. In the north-east it did not seem to make any difference if you were a church attender or not. A Free Church Minister in 1888 had this observation: 'A woman once said to me with reference to her erring daughter, "It was not so bad as if she had taken twopence that was not her own." That woman was a fair type of the average church member in this district, neither better nor worse.'[18] None of these approaches seemed to suffice.

Investigators perhaps drew closer to the heart of the matter when they considered the economic context of marriages in the agricultural community. They noted the absence of any stigma on a girl who lost her virginity before marriage, or even on a woman who had borne a bastard: abortion and infanticide were not practised as there was 'no pressure on the woman to commit any crime' and, among her own class, 'no feeling of indignation aroused in consequence of what they would call her "misfortune"'.[19] They associated it in the Borders and south-east Scotland with the hinding system, whereby a ploughman was expected to bring with him to employment a female helper called a 'bondager' (if he was not married he had to hire the girl), and only reached the peak of earnings for the family group when he also had children available to work as weeders, herds and 'half-hinds' at his side. The young farm servants would therefore sleep with their girls before marriage to test their fertility. Bridal pregnancy was alleged to be universal: as one Lanarkshire minister put it, 'I really do not remember when I last married a young woman who was not in the family way,' and another added, 'I seldom, if indeed ever, perform the service where it should not have been performed long before.'[20] Illegitimacy arose either because there was a proportion of rascals who slept with the girls with no intention of going through with the marriage, or because some men delayed marriage until after the birth as a matter of convenience. Under Scottish law, unlike English, subsequent marriage legitimized a bastard.

Although the institution of hinding was confined to the south-east, the explanation could be generalized to cover other areas on the assumption that it was always in the interests of farm-workers to ensure that their future wives were capable of having children who would add to the family income and look after the couple when they got old. It became a widely accepted explanation, bitingly summarized by R. B. Cunninghame Graham: 'Our sexual immorality, and the high rate of illegitimacy, we explain thus. No thrifty man would buy a barren beast. Therefore, as we cannot buy our wives and sell them if they prove unprofitable, 'tis well to try them in advance.'[21]

Where this approach seemed inadequate, however, was in accounting for differences between one part of rural Scotland and another. What was it about the north-east and Galloway that produced far more bastards even than the Borders? What was it about the Highlands and Islands that produced far fewer? And how did an explanation along the lines of fertility-testing square with another observation often made in counties with high illegitimacy—that it frequently ran in families, 'to a very large extent a hereditary sin', and that multiple illegitimate births by different fathers were common? A study of Minnigaff in Kirkudbrightshire, 1880–93, showed that 28 out of 42 bastards had come from 9 families. In the north-east, a reporter remarked that 'the only thing they seem to feel is if the father does not acknowledge the child. A woman who had five illegitimate children said to me that her mother said she was just the one to have them, as she always got a father.'[22]

To unravel this skein of problems it is useful to ask two questions—how far was parental control exercised over courtship in different parts of the country, and on whom did the economic burden of looking after an illegitimate child fall? Control over courtship was apparently quite different between the rural Lowlands and the Highlands, although in both cases a couple would court with a degree of freedom and physical intimacy unknown to the middle classes. In a series of remarkably frank articles published in the *Scotsman* in 1870, Dr J. M. Strachan of Dollar observed that it was 'especially difficult to make the two classes understand the immense difference that exists between them. Working men will not believe that it is possible to court a wife without stolen interviews, with the lady sitting on the gentleman's knee, or enfolded in his arms, for hours in the dark; and they are totally incapable of conceiving that a kind look or a gentle pressure of the hand will yield delight a thousand times more exquisite than the coarser feelings in which they themselves indulge.' He explained to his middle-class readers how it was unusual for working-class lovers in the Lowlands to meet in public: the ordinary thing was to meet after dark, at the back of a haystack, in a barn or an outhouse, or, 'especially in the case of servant maids', in the girl's bedroom. Each meeting lasted for two or three hours and was repeated weekly, a girl perhaps having several such lovers and a boy not regarding it as wrong to visit different girls after this fashion. As for their parents, 'not even the most particular thinks there is anything wrong in this manner of courtship'. He was careful to stress that such visits did not necessarily imply sexual intercourse: 'the upper classes would be astonished if they knew how long such visits were continued without a fall from virtue. In many cases they are so continued for years. In some ... no fall from virtue takes place.' The Kinsey Report would have described it as heavy petting. But in too many cases, Dr Strachan goes on, by this activity, the 'outworks are dismantled, the citadel [left] defenceless', and the girls 'learn, when it is too late, what a woman can never learn too early or impress too strongly on their minds—that a lover's encroachments, to be repelled successfully, must be repelled and negatived at the very outset'.[23]

It was sound and timeless advice. What Strachan observed as a general practitioner was entirely confirmed by what other writers had said about the midnight prowling of farm-workers out of their bothies, and by the ballads and folklore of the countryside:

> 'Twas a young apprentice boy
> Came courting his dear.
> The moon was shining bright
> And the stars were twinkling clear;
> He went to his love's window
> To ease her of her pain;
> His darling rose and let him in,
> Then went to bed again.[24]

The significant point is not only that love was very physical, but that parental control over the behaviour of the couple was minimal. It was in any case difficult to assert control, since the children left home as teenagers and went to work at farms where the employer was generally very unwilling to stand *in loco parentis*. And was it ultimately in anyone's interest to prevent a girl having sex with her lover if that was the way to get a husband, start a family, and set up a household when they were both young and strong and at their peak earning levels as wage labourers?

Courtship in the Highlands and Islands was scarcely less intimate: it fell into the category that social historians call 'bundling', found historically over a wide area from Wales and Norway to New England, in which the couple spent the night together, either indoors or under the stars on a summer shieling, but wrapped up under separate blankets or plaids, or with a bolster or board between them. Accounts of Orkney and Shetland tell of the 'lang bed' into which all the unmarried couples would climb after a wedding party, the 'members of each sex being alternately ranged along the floor on a huge couch of straw', but 'nothing immoral occurs'. There was also individual bundling on the islands: 'You know in other parts of the country except for Shetland, if a girl and a boy go to bed together it's for one purpose and one purpose only. But here in Shetland a girl and a boy would go to bed together as they might go for a walk.' In Orkney and Shetland there was a very low nineteenth-century illegitimacy rate, but parental surveillance of courtship does not appear to have been particularly close. The restraint seems to have been self-imposed.[25]

In the Outer Hebrides the general customs were much the same. An outsider who stayed for a long period on Lewis wrote in 1874:

> Most of the unmarried young men pass the winter nights with their sweethearts. The want of light in most dwellings, the numbers of dark corners even in daylight, and the general habit among the people of throwing themselves down on the straw simply divested of their outer garments, gives every facility for courtship in the Hebridean fashion. As the girls are, at the same time, 'very kind', courting assiduously, and are possessed of far greater energy than the men, they acquire a great hold on their affections.[26]

Oral accounts of what went on in the Western Islands describe it as very carefully controlled. Hebridean homes had only one room: with

mother knitting in the corner, it was impossible to do too much. (A di-
lemma arose when island houses began to be built with two or three
rooms: was it polite to sit next door or polite to stay?) Similarly the
girls who went up the hill on the summer shielings to tend the animals
and were visited at night by the boys of the township were always
accompanied by a few older women who acted as group chaperones. In
the Hebrides, bundling seems to have been a more acceptable courtship
custom than walking out, for walking removed the control of other
people from the lovers. On Barra there was a moral precept, 'If you go
with anybody to any lonely or out of the way place the Devil is the
third person.' Such strict parental control brought the illegitimacy rate
down to extremely low levels: in rural Lewis in the last two decades of
the nineteenth century it was under 2 per cent, which was half the rate
for Shetland and one-seventh of the rate for Banff.

Why, though, should parental control vary in this manner? The key
is to consider who would bear the economic burden of an illegitimate
child, and how. The areas with highest bastardy rates were also areas
with much year-round employment for girls around the farmhouse
and the cowsheds. If a girl had an illegitimate child she could often
hand it over to her own mother to look after in her cottage, and pay
over part of her wage for its keep. Then, perhaps, when she found a
man who would marry her, she could bring into the new household
one or more children old enough to start a little field-work—for, as Dr
Strachan said, 'Previous unchasteness, even with another individual,
does not form a very serious bar to marriage.' In the north-east, an
unmarried mother would sometimes come to the altar with her children gathered round her skirts like a hen sheltering her chicks, to sym-
bolize that the man was marrying a ready-made family.

In the Highlands and Islands, however, a completely different economic context surrounded illegitimacy. Wage labour was rare: there
were no options for the young except to help their parents on the crofts
or boats in return for their keep, or to leave on seasonal migration for a
job in the Lowlands to provide the extra money on which their parents
depended to help pay the rent, which in any case only lasted for a few
months every year. If an illegitimate child was born, it was the
mother's parents who would have to find the wherewithal to feed and
keep it: there was no way the mother could turn over anything extra to
her parents to help, for (unlike in the Lowlands) she had no independent income. Since there was no local wage labour, the child could

contribute nothing until it was old enough to become a migrant. Furthermore, in the second half of the nineteenth century, land was extremely congested and society extremely close-knit—nowhere more so than in the Hebrides. On the one hand, if a boy made a girl pregnant it was much more difficult for him to escape the consequences of being found out and held responsible than it was for a footloose Lowland farm-worker who moved from farm to farm on yearly hirings; on the other, he could not go to the girl's father, offer to marry her and to set up separately as a crofter on a piece of land of his own. He had to wait for land to become vacant, and the average age of first marriage in the Highlands was higher than elsewhere in Scotland. Hence it was in everybody's interest to show, and to impose, restraint.

The same sexual ethic of self-control and submission to the guidance of parents was visible among Irish families in Scotland, though certainly not among the navvies, whose reputation for fathering bastards and frequenting brothels was notorious. More typical of the immigrants were the families observed by a Scottish tailor who acted as voluntary baillie in the village of Raploch in Stirlingshire:

> About the beginning of May they go with their families to the bark peeling ... They stay out about two months and sleep in wooden sheds, lying together as thick as bees, but there's no immorality among them; indeed they just behave to each other like a wheen children, you would not think they had the same notions as other folk. I have only known two or at most three Irish girls go wrong, and it was always with Scotchmen.[27]

Perhaps the restraint originated in a similar situation of land shortage and later marriage back home in Ireland, reinforced by the great strength of the Catholic Church among the working class in the close-knit immigrant community.

Most Irish went to live in the cities or in smaller industrial towns in the west of Scotland. Most of the evidence about sexual behaviour in the mid-nineteenth century, however, is drawn from the countryside. It is unlikely that there was one single working-class attitude to sex or courtship in the Victorian town, but rather a wide variation from the chaste Catholic Irish families through to those Scottish 'mechanics' and others who frequented brothels with almost as much avidity as students. The skilled artisans and clerks, according to Dr Strachan, in 'feelings and manner approximate to the class above them'. Part of the disorienting experience of the rural immigrant must have been encountering new sexual customs without knowing their different and varying rules. No wonder that girls from such localities as Orkney and Shetland, where bundling traditions were matched by self-restraint on the part of the island boys, were regarded as particularly at risk from seduction in the very different moral atmosphere of the town.

3

It is extremely difficult to trace alterations in working-class sexual ethics after around 1870, because the levels of anxiety and discussion about them of the 1850s and 1860s were never reached again. Alterations in the illegitimacy rates, demonstrated in Table 7, may, however, provide a clue.

TABLE 7
Illegitimate births as a percentage of all live births

	1861–5	1886–90	1911–15	1936–9
Scotland	9.79	8.04	7.21	6.26
Urban and industrial counties:				
Lanarkshire	8.40	6.47	5.90	5.46
Renfrew	7.62	5.36	4.93	4.05
Fife	8.08	6.00	5.18	5.16
Lowland rural counties:				
Berwickshire	10.75	10.88	10.28	8.53
Banffshire	16.62	15.31	13.44	11.98
Wigtownshire	15.65	16.80	15.71	14.91
Highland and Island counties:				
Shetland	4.36	4.28	5.78	6.86
Ross and Cromarty	4.24	5.08	7.10	8.35

Source: M. W. Flinn (ed.), *Scottish Population History from the 17th Century to the 1930s* (Cambridge, 1977), pp. 350–1

Illegitimacy declined in Scotland as a whole and especially in urban and industrial counties, where more of the population came to be concentrated. It also fell in Lowland rural areas, though the old habits of the north-east and the south-west died surprisingly hard. Only the Highlands and Islands moved against the trend, illegitimacy there rising to meet the national average as land-based peasant societies declined and parental control slackened.

Generally, the national decline in illegitimacy paralleled the decline in births legitimately conceived after marriage: whereas there had been 36 live births per 1000 of population around 1871, there were only 19 around 1931. Artificial contraception could have made some contribution: from the 1880s, the use of the rubber sheath in particular became better known, as a consequence of the much-publicized trial of Charles Bradlaugh and Annie Besant for distributing 'neo-Malthusian' propaganda. Contraception was evidently first practised by the middle classes, among whom the birth rate fell first and fastest. Already by 1911, there was a well-marked class difference in family size, as Table 8 shows.

TABLE 8
Average size of families in different occupations in Scotland, 1911

Physicians	3.91	Agricultural labourers	6.42
Lawyers	3.92	Coal-heavers	6.61
Schoolmasters	4.25	Miners	7.01
Clergy	4.33	Crofters	7.04

Artificial contraception was sternly denounced by all the churches, not least by Presbyterians, who spoke of 'the withering blight cast over humanity' by its practice and demanded that the manufacture and sale of anti-conception materials should be 'rigorously repressed'. The Revd Norman Maclean believed that the future of the Empire depended upon it: 'If the British race refuse to multiply and develop the resources of its vast empire, other races, not yet weary of life, will inevitably displace it. If Australia and New Zealand are not occupied by the British, the yellow man cannot be shut out.'[28] The opposition of the Roman Catholic Church was even more stern, and more relevant, given its continued following among those of Irish extraction in the less skilled echelons of the working class: in the interwar years, the Catholic lobby successfully extracted promises from ILP candidates to oppose birth-control in return for support at the polls. There is, in fact, little evidence that artificial birth-control was widely used within the Scottish working class before the Second World War, though the birth rate soon began to decline for all groups in society. It seems at least as likely that births were limited by increasing physical restraint between the sexes, both before and after marriage, as by contraception. But the evidence is admittedly inconclusive and indirect.

By the interwar years, descriptions of courtship are quite different from the midnight prowling, bundlings and clandestine meetings in bedrooms that distinguished at least the countryside of Victorian Scotland. Dance-halls, once regarded by Dr Tait and others in the 1840s as disreputable, frequented by sly prostitutes and attached to 'houses of assignation', attained respectability and importance as a meeting place for working-class teenagers: the Carnegie Trust investigators of the 1930s said that many of the young unemployed went through a phase of being 'dancing mad', saving all their spare cash for the entrance fee and the decent clothes which were expected of the patrons. For those who could not afford the dance-hall, walking certain known streets provided 'the second best way of meeting with girls' and was an activity 'to be seen at its height on Sunday evenings ... Usually both lads and girls went about in twos and threes, and some colour was added to the evening by their casual encounter'.[29] Edwin Muir put it more graphically:

> Nowhere that I have been is one so bathed and steeped and rolled about in floating sexual desire as in certain streets of Glasgow and Edinburgh. This desire fills the main thoroughfare and overflows into all the adjacent pockets and backwaters: the tea-rooms, restaurants and cinema lounges. The only refuges from it are the pubs, which convention forbids women to enter, but which, nevertheless, are always well attended. There, like sailors after a difficult and nerve-whipping voyage, the men put into harbour and wrap themselves in a safe cloak of alcohol.[30]

Lovers in the 1930s encountered the old problem of finding a place to cuddle, for, despite the slightly bigger houses, 'there is no "spare" room in the average working-class home where the young people can ever be alone'. Those who definitely meant to marry, said the Carnegie investigators, 'spent quite a large part of their time visiting relatives and friends, going for walks and attending the cinema'.[31] The cinema, with its warm darkness and romantic images on the screen, held all the advantages in a cold wet country, and, as we have seen, the Scots went to the pictures more often than anyone else in Britain. It was said that opening a cinema in Stornoway ended bundling for good on the island of Lewis, since it was more private and more fun at the flicks. Some will remember with nostalgia the double seats certain cinema proprietors installed in the back row of the stalls for advanced courting couples.

Whatever it was that determined the choice of marriage partner it was obviously not always and everywhere the same as that which operated among farm labourers in the Victorian age: the need to find a strong, fertile woman accustomed to farm life and able to breed a family to work alongside the husband. In many other sectors of Scottish society, however, there had long been traditions of marrying mainly within an occupational community. In a Fife mining village, for instance, a hewer's daughter needed to know all the ways of the place: she was brought up by her mother to make herself absolutely subordinate to the needs of the men when they were in the house, yet to learn the crucial responsibility for running the budget on which the happiness and viability of the household ultimately rested. The father and the working sons often made over their pay packets to the mother and received spending money in return. Stuart Macintyre summarizes the situation of the married woman in Fife in the 1930s thus:

> The lot of the housewife was extremely arduous. Cramped accommodation required constant tidying and cleaning, all laundry had to be washed by hand, water had to be heated and food cooked over a coal stove and there were no nursery facilities for children. The burden on the miner's wife was especially heavy as she waged a constant battle against the coal dust that invaded her house and the smoke that begrimed her washing. Working clothes had to be dried or washed daily and when the men of the house worked double shifts, she had extra meals to prepare and extra bath water to boil for the end of the shift.[32]

Men were more likely to look for miners' daughters to do all this than to turn, for example, to the daughter of a local carter or clerk.

Similarly among fishermen the sense of looking only to one's own kind was deeply engrained. A fisher-girl had, in addition to innumerable household tasks, to mend the nets, bait the hooks, gut the fish, wash the offal from the street, and, after marriage, run the family single-handed while the man was away from home for long periods at sea. It bred great independence of character, and it was not thought that a farmworker's daughter could ever learn what was required. The Essex University oral history interviewers found, for example, that intermarriage between country families and Buckie fishing families was practically unknown before the Second World War; nine-tenths of those interviewed in Buckie had found their wives either from within the town itself or from similar villages along the coast. There was such a sense of apartness that farm children were held by fisher children to smell bad.[33]

In the cities, exclusiveness in the search for marriage partners was never carried to such extremes, but there had once been tendencies in the same direction. In Edinburgh in 1865–9, for instance, some 60 per cent of the brides of printers had been the daughters of skilled or white-collar workers, only 7.4 per cent the daughters of semi-skilled or unskilled workers. Among building labourers, only 15 per cent had married the daughters of skilled and white-collar workers, and 52 per cent married into the semi-skilled and unskilled. Thirty years later, the proportion of building labourers marrying into skilled and white-collar occupations had doubled. By the end of the nineteenth century, 'analysis of intermarriage confirms the impression of a weakening of social segregation and cultural distinctions within the working class'.[34] In the interwar period, the growing anxiety of the Presbyterian Church regarding intermarriage with Catholics (because the rules of the Catholic Church insisted that the offspring were raised in their faith) was a further sign of a breakdown in occupational, as well as sectarian, barriers to marriage, since the Irish, or their descendants, were still disproportionately concentrated in the less skilled occupations, and religious intermarriage thus often also implied a marriage between people of different social standing. It was this factor rather than any real danger of a renewed flood of immigrants from the other side of the Irish Sea that led the Church of Scotland in the interwar years to establish a committee to investigate 'the threat to Scottish national identity' posed by Catholic immigration. In fact, however, it was Cupid's darts fired across the boundaries of sect and social strata that did as much as anything else to harmonize race relations and prevent the west of Scotland becoming a second Ulster.

Perhaps it is as impertinent to ask the question as it is vain to expect a proper answer, but what, exactly, determined the selection of marriage partners in the twentieth-century working class? Brides did not bring property with them, but they could bring the reputation of being 'from a good home', i.e. a home where a girl had had a steady family background and a thorough training from her mother in the innumerable necessary household skills. Such training began young, and might involve gruelling chores even for a child. A docker's daughter described herself to an interviewer as 'washing and everything at twelve and thirteen years old', and a miner's daughter recalled having to scrub the floor and do the washing while her little sister was outside skipping. It was out of the question for the boys to help out with the grind of housework, as a stonemason's daughter explained: 'They didn't have to do anything in the house. We used to have to wash out their white gloves and clean their patent shoes to let them away to the dancing. They were the apple of my mother's eye. Nothing could go wrong with the boys.'[35]

Some little girls, though, apparently loved it. Mollie Weir's classic description of an upbringing in the Glasgow tenements in the interwar years dwells on all the tasks that she was taught to do by her grannie while mother worked to support them painting railway wagons. These jobs ranged from assisting in the weekly ritual of polishing the big black range until it 'gleamed like dusky satin', to returning bad eggs to a grocer who would not refund the money without physical proof of the smell, from judging the quality of a cheap cut of meat, to brushing a senile neighbour's hair. She had a sharp eye for all women's work, not least for the heavy task of washing:

> I loved when the white things were judged to be ready, for then came the scene I liked best of all. The heavy boiler lid was lifted right off, and leaned carefully against the back wall of the wash-house. Clouds of steam rushed everywhere. Up the chimney, out of the open door, into every corner. The washer, a long pole held in both hands, bent over the seething mass in the boiler, fished out a load, expertly twirling the steaming clothes to keep them safely balanced, and then ran with the laden pole across to the tub of clean water.[36]

The older women in the tenements were 'all experts. This was their world'. Their praise of a young housewife, 'Aye, she hangs out a lovely washing,' was an accolade: their disparagement, 'She's hangin oot her *grey* things,' came close to social ostracism.

It was important therefore, in a world with no modern household appliances, that a potential wife should be physically robust, and that she should have the skill to make do on a small and possibly irregular income: 'The success of the housewife in coping ... would determine how the family would weather hardships brought on by unemployment or illness, and her household management was an important criterion of "respectability" in the conventional sense.'[37] Certainly, both sexes gave themselves plenty of time to look around for a suitably experienced partner: the mean age of marriage in Scotland in 1861, 28.6 for a man and 25.6 for a woman, had risen in 1931 to 29.4 for a man and 26.4 for a woman. Over the same period, illegitimacy and, apparently, prostitution, declined rather than increased, which surely indicates increasing sexual restraint during the long delay.

It is indeed likely that the quest for respectability became more pervasive in the working class in the first half of the twentieth century, with the decline of drink, the clearance of the worst slums, the spread of white-collar occupations (not least for women), and the first glimmerings in the 1930s of modern mass consumerism, heralded by contemporary advertising images of a healthy family of four drinking cocoa and listening to 'His Master's Voice' on the phonograph. If so, the ethos of the old labour aristocracy, whose 'feelings and manners approximate to the class above them' would become general throughout the urban working class. That would certainly help to account for the decline of illegitimacy, because nothing was more likely to hinder a girl in a search for a good marriage than having had someone else's baby out of wedlock. In particular, a bastard would damage a girl's chance of upward social mobility, and, with the weakening of social restrictions relating to skill or occupation in the search for a marriage partner, an attractive girl who was careful to keep her reputation now had a good chance of marrying higher in the working class, or even of rising above it altogether. In the early 1950s, James Littlejohn's study of 'Westrigg' had shown that while it was still more common for couples to choose partners of equal status, the cases in which a man married a girl of lower status outnumbered those in which the man married a girl of higher status by seven to one. A woman was 'lowered' by marrying 'beneath herself', but a man never was.[38] Certainly the enhanced chance of mobility would further help to generalize the ethos of respectability and was likely to enhance the allure of beauty over strength in the marriage market, since a girl who married into the middle class would find servants to assist her with the washing and cleaning the house.

Finally, the selection of a marriage partner was subject to the imponderable influence of the mass media in ironing out cultural distinctions and imposing its own stamp on custom. Edwin Muir considered that the levelling influence of the radio, the press and the system of public education had by the 1930s made Scotland much more like the rest of the United Kingdom than it had been before the First World War, and the Carnegie Trust investigators similarly concluded that there were few distinctive characteristics in the life of the young unemployed in Glasgow compared to the other unemployed groups they studied in England and Wales. Neither was thinking specifically of courtship, but the influence of the cinema, which played so large a role in the life of Scottish lovers, must have been a significant one. Maybe it also helped to make both physical attraction and virtue more important. The 1920s and 1930s were the heyday of Hollywood's code of ardent romance tempered by strictly moral conclusions: to every boy, one true girl, very attractive and responsive, but never quite carried away before the chime of the wedding bells; to every girl, one square-shouldered boy, pressing his case, driving off libidinous villains, and ready to give his all after the ceremony. We can never know how many hearts were melted because in the dark the girl in the next seat seemed to look like Ginger Rogers, and the boy like Douglas Fairbanks.

CHAPTER VIII

Churchgoing

1

Where do we come from? Where do we go? How should we behave on the journey, and who should be our guide? The Middle Ages had decided that religious problems were for priests. The centuries from the early sixteenth to the late nineteenth, on the other hand, stand out in European history as the age when the Churches, Protestant and Catholic alike, made their most strenuous effort to persuade the entire lay population of the importance of being actively and continuously religious, while according professional religious leaders even greater attention and prestige than before.

In Calvinist Scotland, the seventeenth century saw the first climax of this great attempt, and the Victorian period the second and final one. The leaders of the Presbyterian churches were central figures in nineteenth-century public life. Thomas Chalmers was acclaimed in a manner seldom accorded to any Scot in his own lifetime, and in 1847, his funeral cortège was attended by tens of thousands of mourners. The names of lesser leaders, like Thomas Guthrie, James Begg, Norman Macleod or Robert Rainy, were as familiar as those of any contemporary politician. Church affairs were a focus of national interest and feeling within Scotland: the twists and turns of the Ten Years Conflict that preceded the Disruption of the Church of Scotland in 1843 were followed with the closest attention and mounting excitement by the upper and middle classes, and by at least a portion of the working class. Scarcely less marked was public interest in the trial of Robertson Smith for heresy by the Free Church in 1881, and in the case before the House of Lords in 1900 on the division of the property of the Free Church following its union with the United Presbyterians. Scotland, if not religious, was at least fascinated by religious affairs.

How deep did religion go? According to their admirers, the Scottish Presbyterian churches gave the nation a distinctive and excellent social flavour: 'the most moral churchgoing people in the world', said an American visitor, stating the approval that most of his countrymen found for the Scots.[1] Chauvinist clerics at home, following the opinions of the seventeenth-century Covenanters, still sometimes portrayed Scotland as a new Israel, its inhabitants a second chosen people of the Lord. The commands of the Church were assumed by churchmen to be the standards which the population strove to follow in their daily behaviour, and the message of salvation that they preached from pulpit and tract was the frame in which people saw the drama of their lives.

Of course the Church criticized and castigated. Chalmers in particular developed a critique of contemporary industrial society as dehumanizing, tending to make the employer greedy and uncompassionate, the worker depraved and mendicant. The tenets of modern political economy he believed to be true laws, like the laws of natural science, yet he equally believed that the undesirable side-effects of their operation could be counteracted by an alliance of the State and the Established Church. He called for the State to support the Church in building new churches and financing extra ministers in the heart of the industrial towns where the Church had lost its grip. The old parochial system, which had served the kirk so well in the rural past, needed re-invigoration for modern conditions. He appealed for the construction of a new godly commonwealth of restored community values, where the rich would personally discharge their social responsibilities among the poor as benefactors and as elders and deacons, while the poor in their gratitude would learn to know and keep their place. It was all very conservative. The alternative he saw as social chaos, upheaval, bloodshed, war. His leadership of the Church of Scotland from 1832, however, culminated ten years later in the catastrophic Disruption, and few thereafter heeded the fullness of his message. Philanthropists with chequebooks nevertheless abounded, and the rich seldom saw any conflict between getting on in this world and succeeding in the next. 'The gospel of wealth', declared Andrew Carnegie, Scotland's best-known emigrant, 'but echoes Christ's words.'[2]

To natives and foreigners alike, the Scottish Victorian sabbath was the outward and visible sign of the Church's inward and spiritual sway.

A universal stillness fell over Glasgow and Edinburgh (except in the unredeemed slums) at the time of divine service, and pervaded small towns and villages from dawn to dusk. The Church complained of sabbath breakers: a Glasgow minister, for example, informed the Board of the Edinburgh and Glasgow Railway when they first proposed allowing Sunday trains in 1842 that they were 'infidels, scoffers, men of unholy lives, the enemies of all righteousness, *moral suicides, sinners against light, traitors to their country, robbers and murderers*'.[3] What is astonishing today, however, is the degree to which observance was upheld. On Sundays the churches held the country in thrall for Christ. This was how it was recalled by the son of a small businessman born in 1865:

> Sunday at home was a dismal ordeal for the younger generation. All newspapers and books of a secular character were carefully put out of sight. After breakfast, preparations were made for the Church. Black clothes were taken from the wardrobe and carefully brushed, clean linen was taken from the chest of drawers, boots were polished, and when everything was ready the whole family was marched to Church for the eleven o'clock service. After a meal (usually prepared on the Saturday) was served on our return from the Kirk, we were marched off again for the afternoon service at two o'clock. The evenings were long and dreary. Sometimes we would read Bunyan's *Pilgrim's Progress* or *Good Words* or, in summer time, we had a sedate walk to a Cemetery . . .[4]

This was followed at 9 p.m. by Bible study, sometimes by 'an attempt to sing a verse or two from the Psalms of David', by prayer, and by bed at 10 p.m., 'some of us, I fear, thankful that this dreary monotonous "Lord's Day of Rest" was over'.

Even in the hour of the Church's apparent triumph, however, there were those who discerned on the walls the faint outline of a different script, which by the end of the century had become plain. By 1900, churchmen were on the defensive. The Church had not collapsed: on Sundays the whistle of trains and the rattle of trams past the windows of city churches and the bells of cyclists in the villages became more persistent every year, but the sabbath was not dead. Commentators spoke of a drift away from church attendance, but it was difficult to prove that attendances were very different from what they had been half a century earlier. There was, however, a quite unmistakable conviction that the Church had less meaning in the lives of men as religion became less interesting and less important to them. The age had commenced, not of unbelief, but of indifference, rising at best to what Principal D. S. Cairns of Aberdeen United Free Church College called in 1919 'the dim and instinctive theism which is the working faith of perhaps the majority of the youth of this nation'. By 1940, Scotland still appeared more devout and Sabbatarian than England, but even in the remotest and sternest corners things had changed somewhat. Thus a visitor to Lewis in the Second World War found an army hut used by the island youth for monthly dances: 'When I asked a young crofter invalided from the Navy whether the Elders of the Kirk made no protest, he replied that they had, but had to give it up: "They see that we won't stand for it." This would have been unthinkable during the First World War, or after it.'[5]

To understand what happened, let us begin with the formal history of the Church, or rather of all the different churches and sects which together ministered to the natural or induced spiritual thirst of the nation. At the start of the nineteenth century, the established Church of Scotland was in a position of substantial numerical superiority. There were also various Presbyterian seceding bodies, remnants of eighteenth-century quarrels, boasting some 300 congregations in all. These were particularly strong among the lower classes in the central belt and in the west (it was said in 1819 that as many as 40 per cent of the people of Glasgow were seceders), but the proportion was much smaller outside these areas. There were small numbers of Congregationalists, though they had an increasing reputation due to the evangelical fervour of their leaders; Episcopalians were widely scattered and fashionable among the well-to-do but nowhere enjoyed a broad popular following; Roman Catholicism dominated a few Highland parishes in the southern Outer Hebrides and Aberdeenshire and Irish immigrant communities in the towns, but before 1830 the main inrush of Irish Catholics had scarcely begun. Methodists, Baptists and Quakers were present in minute numbers, usually in towns where the artisans were strong, like Paisley, Dunfermline and Dundee. Methodism became, however, one of the main denominations in Shetland in the first half of the nineteenth century.

Within the Church of Scotland, the first decades of the century were dominated by ideological and party struggles between the Moderates and the Evangelicals. The Moderates were the party of the ecclesiastical and political establishment whose dominance over the Church in the 1790s had finally been assured by their political subservience to Henry Dundas, into whose hands the Westminster Cabinet entrusted the management of Scotland. They stood, broadly, for a rational, impersonal and unenthusiastic religion, outwardly orthodox in Calvinist theology yet tolerant of intellectual deviation, and overwhelmingly polite and conformist in social tone. The Evangelicals were men of a less accommodating nature. In the mid-eighteenth century their strength had lain mainly among pietistic town clergy and old-fashioned country ministers, but the party was transformed into an aggressive force by leaders who had come directly or indirectly under the twin influences of English revivalists like William Wilberforce and Charles Simeon and of the new political economy in the Scottish universities. Evangelicals in the Church of Scotland were, of course, also orthodox Calvinists and Presbyterians. Their distinguishing mark was their fervour for the religious life, narrowly defined. Thomas Chalmers, while still a Moderate and country minister at Kilmany in Fife in 1805, had declared two days a week quite sufficient for the discharge of his duty: the other five were for 'uninterrupted leisure, for the prosecution of any science in which his taste may dispose him to engage'. After his conversion to Evangelicalism in 1811 following an illness that brought him to death's door, he worked on pastoral business to the point of exhaustion, and his ministry became a model of evangelical service which all young enthusiasts tried to emulate. The core of their faith was a burning conviction in their personal salvation through the merits of Jesus, a conviction often reached only after a period of profound psychological agony: to 'bring to Jesus', to bring men and women to the same spiritual climax they had experienced themselves, became the ultimate aim of Evangelicals, to which all secular and intellectual values had to take second place.

Many of the Scottish Evangelicals looked back to the seventeenth-century Covenanters for their spiritual predecessors and made heroes of those intolerant and persecuted men who took to the hills after the Restoration. In many ways the Evangelical and Covenanting ethics were similar: both were fervent, both were puritanical, both in their heyday were anxious to see their ideals adopted by society as its norms. But the seventeenth-century zealots wished to transform society as a corporate act, to alter the ways of the world, if necessary by legal compulsion, in direct preparation for the second coming of Christ. Most nineteenth-century puritans first wished to transform individuals, to help each man personally to make his way to the throne of Grace, and only secondly wanted to reform society in order to make the individual's path to God an easier one. Chalmers' own social vision was larger than that. The State, he thought, must give financial backing to Church extension. While eschewing legal compulsion as a way to make men good, he did believe that a godly commonwealth in the seventeenth-century sense could be created by individuals with this state backing if the upper and middle classes dedicated themselves to the service of their fellows and if the working class practised the traditional country virtues (as he saw them) of thrift, sobriety, continence and self-help. Indeed, it was only by the creation of such a Christian society through a vigorous programme of Church extension, sessional schools, and poor-law reform (to discourage the scroungers) that he saw any hope for the redemption of industrial society from moral and political disaster.

It was this call to action which made Chalmers' preaching so magnetic to the urban middle class in the 1810s, 1820s and 1830s. On one level, his values were their values. He stressed the correctness of the laws of political economy, the futility of trade unionism and democracy, the divine origins of a hierarchy where rich and poor had their obligations and their place, and the prime responsibility of the individual for his own material well-being and spiritual health. At times he came close to saying that all the sufferings of the clotted slums were due to the moral failings of their inhabitants, a belief that remained ingrained in the Scottish middle-class mind until the twentieth century. The other part of his message, that possession of wealth and power was ignoble without equivalent philanthropy and a sense of personal responsibility, was the inspiration to generations of soul-searching men to give generously of their money and time to the community. That Victorian Scotland was as world-famous for serious philanthropists—like William Collins of the temperance movement and William Quarrier of the children's homes—as it was for drunkenness and bad housing was due in no small degree to Thomas Chalmers. What was ultimately forgotten was his insistence that without affirmative action by the State to back the Church in the creation of a godly commonwealth, industrial capitalism would continue to degrade society.

In the first third of the nineteenth century, the Evangelicals went from strength to strength. Thomas Chalmers became Moderator in 1832, but only after two decades in which his pastoral work in Fife and

Glasgow and his tenure of university chairs at St Andrews and Edinburgh had established him as the overwhelming personality in the Church of Scotland. Evangelical institutions—Sunday schools, missionary societies, and Bible Society—all flourished. A great surge of lay and clerical enthusiasm in the north carried the Highlands into the fold of fervent personal religion, with the need for a sense of conversion its central tenet. By 1834 Evangelicals had achieved a majority in the General Assembly, and thereafter they set the dominant key in nineteenth-century Scottish spiritual life: even their enemies were affected by its tone.

The following years were overshadowed by the events leading up to the Disruption. The conflict was basically about patronage: who was to have the most say in the appointment of the minister—the congregation, or the patrons (usually landlords) whose rights of nomination had been re-established by the statute of 1712. In 1834, a General Assembly asserting the rights of the people and of Christ over the patrons and the State and dominated by the Evangelicals passed a Veto Act giving congregations the right to reject a nominee. The Act was in due course declared unlawful by the Court of Session, as conflicting with Parliament-made law. The House of Lords upheld this decision, successive Whig and Tory administrations declined to alter the statute, and various nominees brought forward by patrons were duly rejected by congregations and by the Church. A further rebuff for Chalmers had come when Melbourne's Whig administration declined to give government funds to build new churches for the Church of Scotland, cutting the ground from beneath the projected godly commonwealth.

The stage was set for a direct clash, and when it occurred, in 1843, it took the form of a secession led by Thomas Chalmers and followed by two-fifths of the ministers, who walked out of the General Assembly and set up a new church, a Free Church of Scotland, where the law of Christ would be unimpeded by the claim of the State. In doing so they cast their bread upon the waters, for the new body would have to build its own churches and schools and finance its own ministers entirely from voluntary contributions without any support from traditional funds which the established church enjoyed. Those who had walked out had initially expected to be in the majority and thereby to force the hand of the Government without any prolonged secession, perhaps without a secession at all. Nevertheless it was an act of remarkable courage:

They walked in procession down Hanover Street to Canonmills ... through an unbroken mass of cheering people and beneath innumerable handkerchiefs waving from the windows. But amidst this exultation there was much sadness and many a tear, many a grave face and fearful thought, for no-one could doubt that it was with sore hearts that these ministers left the Church, and no thinking man could look on the unexampled scene and behold that the temple was rent without pain and sad forebodings.[6]

The Disruption did indeed rend the temple, and with such shattering force that the Church in Scotland lost all its monolithic character for the remainder of the century. The Established Church—the Church of Scotland—looked for a time as if it might shrivel into a mere rump, as the majority of its finest and most active leaders, along with 39 per cent of the ministry and a third of the congregations, had left it. In Aberdeen every minister had gone over to the Free Church: over much of the Highlands defection to the Free Church was also almost complete, both by ministers and congregations: those who remained were almost inevitably tarred by the accusation of being cowards and time-servers, toadies of the lairds. In Glasgow and Edinburgh, however, the division between those who stayed in and those who left was much more equally balanced, and in the Borders the Church of Scotland retained the loyalty of most of its members.

The Free Church, meanwhile, had the ball of self-imputed righteousness at its feet, and very large sums were contributed by its membership for new buildings and for the salaries of clergy and teachers: a fund was established from which support could be given to poor parishes in the Highlands and elsewhere where there was great enthusiasm but little cash. In the early days, the Free Church drew on a wide spectrum of support in the middle classes and among many artisans. In 1851 the religious census taken by the Government indicated that the numbers attending the Church of Scotland and the Free Church were almost the same. A third great Presbyterian church, the United Presbyterians, had come into being in 1847, with the union of two of the largest groups of the eighteenth-century seceders: in 1851 they were about half the size of each of the two halves of the old church, but had a membership which, while beginning relatively humbly in terms of social class, contained many followers who were strongly upwardly mobile. The notion that Christians had a civic duty to become involved in the government of their towns and in the moral, social and physical well-being of their communities was particularly strong with the United Presbyterians at the end of the century.

As time went on, however, the Church of Scotland enjoyed an unexpected revival. This was partly due to its own virtues, especially the leadership of men like James Robertson, Professor of Ecclesiastical History at the University of Edinburgh, and Norman Macleod, noted liberal and former disciple of Chalmers, who had a substantial popular following in Glasgow: both were inspired by the belief that only an established church could be a national church and carry out its moral and spiritual duties for the whole people. The Free Church meanwhile began to suffer from internal weaknesses. Dependence on voluntary sources of funds made it increasingly dependent on rich middle-class benefactors who alone could meet call after call to enable it to compete with its rival at home and abroad. Those who paid the piper called the tune, and the artisan supporters of the Church began to find themselves increasingly in the cold. Some of those who at this point left the Free Church returned to the Church of Scotland, especially when the old bitterness over the Disruption began to fade. Chalmers himself was so distressed by what he saw as the voluntarist tendency in the Free Church (and its failure to compel the State to recognize it as the true Established Church by moral force) that he withdrew from active leadership within two years.

The Free Church, however, was caught up in a series of institutional changes which partly masked what was happening to its support in other directions. In the second half of the century, it absorbed two smaller but important groups of eighteenth-century seceders who had remained outside the United Presbyterians, and after lengthy negotiations in 1900, it also joined the United Presbyterians, forming the United Free Church. This was at a certain cost: in 1893 a group of Highland congregations seceded to form the Free Presbyterians, and in 1900 a minority of the Free Church who would not join with the United Presbyterians were also left as a remnant church. But the effect of this barn dance was to leave Presbyterians in the early twentieth century in two main blocks instead of three, and thereby to prepare the way for the final fusion of 1929, when the United Free Church and the Church of Scotland were at last reunited.

Meanwhile, non-Presbyterian churches were gaining steadily in numbers: by the 1870s, they had won the allegiance of perhaps one in five of the population, by the 1940s, about one in four. This was especially due to the great increase in Roman Catholics: in the eighteenth century they had amounted to only 20,000 or 30,000 souls, mainly in rural enclaves, but by 1851 Ireland was pouring a famine-stricken people into all the Scottish towns and the Catholic population is estimated to have amounted to about 146,000 (5 per cent of the population), increasing, largely by intermarriage, to 750,000 (15 per cent of the population) by 1951. From 1829, it had become legal to hold Roman Catholic services in Scotland; in 1878 the Catholic hierarchy was restored in Scotland and the first bishops with Scottish territorial titles were appointed. All this exacerbated the existing urban racism, bitterness and bigotry, partly sublimated but partly perpetuated in football. The Episcopalian Church, too, was successful: it became a popular country church in the north-east after the Napoleonic Wars, and later, under English Anglo-Catholic influence, made a great effort to extend its congregations in the towns, though its churches in the slums remained more beautiful than full. The Congregationalists were the third denomination to make a major advance, partly because James Morison led a breakaway liberal group, the Evangelical Union, from one of the old Presbyterian seceding churches in 1842, and it soon became a small but devoted church of artisans and miners: in 1896, the Evangelical Union joined with like-minded sects to form the Congregational Union of Scotland, a body about as large by 1950 as the Episcopalians. Baptists and Methodists continued to hold their own small place in towns, joined before 1900 by the Plymouth Brethren and faith missions of several kinds, strong especially in the fishing villages of Buchan and Banff. There was therefore no shortage of different flowers in the garden of the Lord when the twentieth century began.

Probably the best way of measuring how many people reckoned themselves as belonging to the various churches is to examine the Registrar-General's return of where couples chose to be married. Table 9 opposite shows the result. Such figures say nothing about the intensity of religious allegiance, and for many people, being married by clergy may have been an act of deference towards their parents' feelings or the only formal religious act they undertook in their lives between their Christian baptism and their burial. The bottom line shows the rise of 'non-religious forms', or irregular marriages undertaken by declara-

TABLE 9
Denomination of weddings in Scotland

	1861–70 %	1881–90 %	1901–10 %	1921–30 %	1941–50 %
Church of Scotland	44.3	46.2	45.3	44.5 ⎫	
Free Church	23.5	20.3 ⎫	26.6	20.5 ⎭	60.6
United Presbyterians	14.3	11.6 ⎭			
Roman Catholic	9.2	9.9	10.5	11.6	13.1
Scottish Episcopalian	2.1	2.8	2.9	2.8	3.1
Other religious forms	5.9	6.7	8.3	8.8	8.0
Non-religious forms	0.2	2.5	6.4	12.7	15.1

tion before witnesses, which were (until 1940) the Scottish equivalent to civil marriage before the Registrar in England. Such marriages had always been perfectly legal in Scotland: the growing willingness of some people to do without the benefit of a clerical blessing at the most crucial moment of their private lives demonstrates the trend, but probably underestimates the true extent, of an explicit drift away from the Church.

According to the religious census of 1851, a third of the entire population attended morning service in Scotland and a fifth attended afternoon service (no doubt many attended both), and this when contemporaries believed that only 58 per cent would ever be in a position before witnesses, which were (until 1940) the Scottish equivalent to civil marriage before the Registrar in England. Such marriages had always been perfectly legal in Scotland: the growing willingness of some people to do without the benefit of a clerical blessing at the most crucial moment of their private lives demonstrates the trend, but probably underestimates the true extent, of an explicit drift away from the Church.

2

Was the falling-off of faith which so many people noticed around 1900 perhaps a consequence of the sectarian storms that swept Victorian Scotland? It is often said by churchmen today that the Church is taken less seriously because the Body of Christ lies in so many pieces. But in Scotland the years of bitterest division were at the time of the Disruption, when religious enthusiasm was also at its peak: by 1900 old wounds were beginning to be forgotten, the movement towards amalgamation of churches was underway, and a spirit of tolerance unknown in earlier years was abroad. This was not unnatural. When men are deeply stirred, the heat of their ardour fuses small differences into great stumbling blocks; when they are less certain, they become more humble in their dealings with other men.

One great change in the second half of the century was the erosion of ancient certainties regarding heaven and hell. Old Calvinism, for all its party divisions, had been intellectually monolithic: Moderate and Evangelical, establishment churchman and seceder alike had all held that man was predestined to everlasting bliss or to everlasting fire, that hell would take the majority and heaven the minority, and that the division between sheep and goats had been immutably decided in advance by the divine Election of a chosen few out of the damned masses. Hell was no harmless metaphor. It was said of the English Evangelicals, 'Hell and heaven seemed as certain to them as tomorrow's sunrise, and the Last Judgement as real as the week's balance-sheet.'[7] In the eighteenth century, Thomas Boston had taught that even little children and helpless infants might go to hell, and that it was wrong to presume they were protected by innocence. God would crush them like the eggs of the cockatrice, for unless he did they would grow into devils. Such a doctrine was compelling and terrible. It was hard to accept it and remain sane without deciding that one was oneself already numbered among the Elect, and so destined to escape the everlasting fires. If so, it was clear that one would try to live a good life, to be obedient to the commands of the church, and to be a devoted church-goer. It was unthinkable that a member of the Elect would not be zealous in these matters: if he was not, then he could not be so sure that he really was counted among them.

This doctrine was demolished in the nineteenth century in two main stages. The first was a theological step which undercut the doctrine of Election. In 1831, an Argyll minister, John McLeod Campbell, was expelled from the Church of Scotland for heretical views which he later developed in his book *The Nature of the Atonement* (1856): he has been described as 'his country's greatest modern theologian and the forerunner of a milder, more loving, more truly evangelical understanding of the faith'.[8] John Morison was expelled from the United Secession Church in 1841 for similar ideas. Both suffered for expressing the view that salvation was freely available to those who wanted it and were willing to accept the assurance that Christ died for all men. It was just possible philosophically to reconcile this theory with Election, but it was seen more and more clearly that the doctrines of Election were irreconcilable in practice with active Evangelicalism. The theology of Campbell and Morison worked like leaven even on those who had expelled them, and by the end of the century it had become orthodox in most branches of Presbyterian belief. At the same time, men took a milder view of the damnation of children. In 1872, William Logan, the Glasgow City missionary, edited a popular book of essays, *Words of Comfort for Parents Bereaved of Little Children*, in which a common theme was that children provided God with most of His angelic recruits for heaven, adults being generally too corrupted to get in. Nevertheless, the change in the theological climate initiated by John McLeod Campbell was only a small step. As long as the Bible continued to be regarded as the inspired word of God it was very difficult to avoid the conclusion that He was eternally hellbent, dooming to everlasting torment most created souls.

The destruction of the literal interpretation of the Bible was accomplished by twin European intellectual movements, in science and history. The scientific movement was started by Sir Charles Lyell and other geologists who were puzzled to explain the existence of the strata of the earth if it had been created in seven days: the tragic suicide in 1856 of the great amateur geologist and Free Church journalist Hugh Miller has been supposed to be connected with his inability to reconcile his scientific knowledge with his belief in Genesis. Although it was Charles Darwin's theory of biological evolution which most famously eroded a fundamentalist reading of the Bible and caught the popular imagination in the following decades, the subjection of the Bible to higher criticism on historical grounds which began in Germany in the middle of the century was no less damaging to the old simplicities. The first scholars influenced by the German school began to hold positions of power in Scottish theological colleges from the 1860s. In 1863, Andrew Bruce Davidson, described by an admiring contemporary after his death in 1902 as 'the finest teacher of his land and time', was appointed to the chair of Hebrew at the Free Church's New College in Edinburgh. He was the first person in Scotland to examine the scriptures with the tools of literary and historical criticism, and his influence on two generations of divinity students was incalculable. In 1881, his most brilliant disciple, William Robertson Smith, was expelled from his chair in the Free Church College at Aberdeen for suggesting that the Pentateuch might have been written by different hands: he withdrew to Cambridge University and pursued his interest in Oriental languages and relative cultures, to become, in due course, one of the founding fathers of modern anthropology. In the long run it became evident in Scotland even to the Free Church that Smith had been 'a martyr for the cause of Biblical scholarship'. But not at once: further heresy trials—of Professor Marcus Dods of New College and Professor A.B. Bruce of Glasgow College—took place in 1890, and only through them did it gradually become clear that a literal interpretation of the Bible was open to all manner of scientific and historical objections. Quite ordinary men, in the pews and outside, and not merely theological experts, were made aware of the main lines of the argument, and honest leaders within the church could not merely put their heads in the sand and pretend they did not exist.

The last of the heresy cases was conducted against another distinguished scholar, George Adam Smith of the United Free Church, in 1902. He was tried for suggesting, among other things, that the early chapters of Genesis were not historical but owed much to Babylonian myth, and that the lives of the patriarchs, as depicted in the Bible, had their 'fanciful' side. He was found not guilty, and the Presbyterian tradition in Scotland has continued to produce intellectuals to debate the central issues of biblical scholarship with openness and integrity.

In these circumstances, what happened to the popular conception of hell? If God was the God of love, did He really condemn most people to damnation? If He was good, was it logical that He would thrust His own children for ever into eternal fires? 'I call no being good', John Stuart Mill had said, 'who is not what I mean when I apply that epithet to my fellow creatures.' If Genesis or the date and authority of the four Gospels could be questioned, the terrible problem of hell might also be open to examination. Some Presbyterians slid by degrees into a much milder view of eternal life. A noted liberal Evangelical minister, Norman Maclean, had this to say in the interwar years:

Man's place in eternity is not fixed unalterably in death; if he carry with him the power of choice and will; if in the depth of hell it be still in his power to say 'I will arise and go to my Father' ... It cannot be contrary to His will that He should wish that the souls banished by their own deeds far from Him may find their way back to Him . . .⁹

He was not far from propounding a Presbyterian purgatory, a half-way stage to hell, where people could decide a second time whether to go on or turn back.

Others had less courage to break with the past and simply ceased to preach on heaven and hell, having themselves no conviction, or feeling it a subject too complicated or too uncertain for treatment in the pulpit. But without a conviction of hell, what was salvation about? From what were you saved, if sinning had no penalty? What was the Evangelist talking about?

Men began to notice the faltering tones of the Church, wavering between the old dogmas of the conservatives, which became increasingly unbelievable in the light of science and scholarship, and the new doubts and silences of the liberals, which lacked all compulsive power. 'The Church', said Norman Maclean, 'gives no answer to the question "Where are our dead?" . . . No wonder pews become increasingly empty.' Christianity since the beginning had centred on the life after death. If the Church was vague about it, men reached their own conclusions: if there was a God, He was good: if He was good, He would send you to heaven or at least give you a second chance if you had made a mistake; if He would give you a second chance, it could not matter tremendously if you were a bit of an agnostic here and now, or didn't go too regularly to church. God was good. It would all come right in the end. As a piece of homespun logic this had considerable strength and consistency. It caused the death of hell, the liberation of many from psychological terrors, and the cooling of much fervour among the laity. The Church of Scotland by the mid-twentieth century still gave the impression of not quite knowing what had happened, or what it should do about it. How could a Protestant religion survive in its traditional forms if God was truly Love?

3

Who were the church attenders? In the late eighteenth century, and earlier, it is fair to assume, at least in rural areas, something like universal involvement in the church on the part of all the families in the parish, and probably regular attendance by most who were not too young, or too old, or too ill, or living too far from the building to come each Sunday. The parish church was central to the life of the community in a secular as well as a religious sense. This was how an Aberdeenshire man remembered the sabbath in his youth, before the Evangelicals had transformed it into the stern thing it later became:

> At an early hour on Sabbath morning, dogs, men, and lasses assembled in the churchyard, each for purposes of their own: the elderly portion squatted on gravestones, or, leaning with their backs against the walls of the church, smoked, snuffed, and talked, of markets, crops and the farmers' prospects, while the younger portion collected in groups, said 'soft things', simpered, laughed and talked scandal. Seldom a Sabbath passed without the dogs winding up their gambols by a fight, either in the churchyard or in the church itself, during the service. No sooner had the minister pronounced the benediction than the congregation flocked to the door ... Advertisements of 'bargains', 'lost property', 'roups', and so forth were then made by proclamation, at the church doors, on dismissal of the congregation.[10]

In the towns, the church had never been the centre of social life and amusement in quite this way, and even in the countryside the Victorian Church in all its branches soon came to discountenance such worldliness on sacred ground. But had town populations ever had the same apparently universal church attachment as rural areas? For the eighteenth century we just do not know, but by the 1820s it was obvious that there was already an enormous amount of religious indifference among the working classes in big cities. Thomas Chalmers uncovered the extent of this during his ministry in Glasgow. He estimated that around 60 per cent of the population ought to be in church on Sundays if every family were conscientious Christians, but in Barony parish, with an immense population of 52,000, only 20 per cent were coming to church; this was a notoriously poor area, but it suggested that two-thirds of the working class in the slums had little or no connection with the church even before the Victorian era began. As a proportion of total urban population, the number of the indifferent would have been smaller, but still substantial. It was estimated in Edinburgh, for example, that one-third of the population 'had no fixed connection with any Christian church'.

Chalmers' generation believed the answer to be the building of more churches. It was assumed that the poor stayed away because there were not enough places in which to worship: in Glasgow, at St Johns, there were only 1640 seats in all the churches for 8000 inhabitants, and in Calton and Bridgeton only one chapel of ease for 29,000 inhabitants. William Collins was an elder of St Johns, and in 1834 became inspired by Chalmers to make himself the leading lay spirit in the early church extension movement, which absorbed most of his philanthropic energy once he had wearied of the temperance cause: with Chalmers himself as convener, the Church Extension Committee of the Church of Scotland built 222 new churches in 7 years, adding one-fifth to the existing stock.

Chalmers embarked on a crusade to persuade the Government to back the Established Church by providing the finance for the re-Christianization of Scotland, and to rouse the working classes to demand new churches. On both counts he failed. The Whigs were not inclined to imperil their electoral support by favouring an Established Church over the seceders, and Chalmers, as a known Tory and friend of Peel, was heard with some scorn by the urban working class when he claimed to be 'labouring for the unenfranchised population', and, trying to use their language, claimed that 'more resolute, more determined, more out-and-out radicals than the Church Extensionists of Scotland are not to be found in the Empire'.[11] It was a measure of the social gulf between them, and of the identification of the Church of Scotland with the ruling orders, that the man whose oratory could so often move a middle-class congregation to tears and action left working-class audiences sullen and hostile. Chalmers admitted in private to feeling uncomfortable when addressing audiences of labouring men: it was a disability he shared with most of his colleagues.

In the event, the real solution to the apparent shortage of church seating came with the Disruption, when Free Church congregations needing to accommodate themselves in a hurry erected everywhere churches to duplicate the parish churches of the establishment. By 1851 there were seats for 63 per cent of the population. Not all churches were well placed to catch the indifferent Christians of poor areas, however, and church extension was continued by most denominations, Catholic and Episcopalian as well as Presbyterian. Unfortunately it was seen to have little effect except in Catholic Irish areas, as the new churches remained substantially empty or simply drew congregations away from the older ones: by the 1890s there was a widespread appreciation that providing water could not of itself make horses drink.

In the second half of the nineteenth century, we know slightly more about who would and who would not attend church. A religious census was held in 1851, to ascertain how many attended worship on a given Sunday; there were further statistical investigations around 1870 and in 1882 (less complete, and not free from sectarian bias by those who compiled them); and in 1890 the Church of Scotland set up a Commission on the Religious Condition of the People which sat for six years and reported in detail from each presbytery on the state of church attendance. From the last-mentioned in particular, we can build up a more detailed picture of late Victorian religious life.[12]

In the Highlands and the western and northern Islands the situation was rosy, for here the population still possessed a zeal for the active religious life that by 1900 was elsewhere becoming rare. The conversion of the Highlands to evangelical Presbyterianism had been the work of a series of missionaries and zealots from the closing decades of the eighteenth century on: the Highlanders above all had accepted the Free Church with joy after 1843, partly because the Church of Scotland was tainted by its close relationship to the lairds in the decades of the Clearances. At the end of the century, the Highlanders still clung with the greatest tenacity to the early principles of that church, and in many cases rejected its flirtation with liberal theology and with the United Presbyterians even at the cost of new secessions. By then, however, there was somewhat less bitterness between the Free Church congregations and the rump of the local Church of Scotland and even some revival in the membership of the latter. In any case, people were 'decidedly church-going': even in the poorest parts of Inverness in the 1890s, only 32 out of 200 families had no church connection.

In the agricultural Lowlands, the churches at first sight also had relatively little to worry about. The 1851 census and the 1883 investigation had both shown that the best attendance was in rural areas. In the 1890s, many country presbyteries in the south of Scotland reported that virtually all the families still had a church connection, and that people came to worship with a fair degree of regularity. Beyond the Forth there was more doubt, especially in those areas with much migrant labour, where the bothy system prevailed, or where farm-hands were housed in attics. Here the young men at least had slipped out of the habit of regular church attendance: 'There is scarcely one farm-servant who attends in my parish,' said a minister in the north-east, and many echoed him. Some blamed the new craze for the bicycle, that carried the men past the church on Sundays instead of to it. Others blamed laziness or, worse, the young farm-hands staying in their rooms all day reading 'political newspapers'—'the old respect for the House of God is decreasing'. Ministers tried in vain to get at the bachelors by pastoral visiting and other forms of encouragement, but in many cases they had given it up as a bad job and now never went near the bothies from one year's end to another. Even so, the Church was not deeply worried: inattendance was partly a sin of thoughtless youth, and it was noticed that when the young ploughman married he often acquired again his forefathers' habit of church attendance.

In the fishing villages of the east coast from Berwickshire to Banff, the position was different again. Here in many places the Church of Scotland was finding its membership sapped by other bodies, particularly the Plymouth Brethren and faith missions of various kinds. Like Highlanders, fishermen had not been very pious in the eighteenth century; the first evangelical shock seems to have arrived with the preaching and singing tours of Sankey and Moody from the United States in the 1870s, and many families and even whole communities lived in a haze of religious excitement for years to come. Others, however, remained unaffected: as the Presbytery of Dalkeith put it, fisher-folk were 'either earnestly good or utterly irreligious'. But as a group they could not be considered indifferent.

The miners were another target for the missionaries, like those who swept down on Fife and Kinross in 1888 in a 'Hallelujah Chariot' and risked the occasional broken head for their witness:

> The publican filled the drunkards up with drink, and sent them in to disturb the meetings. Night after night the open-air meeting was broken up, sometimes with volleys of stones and rotten eggs, sometimes by a drunken cabby, who, brandishing his whip, would drive his horse and cab right through the crowd.[13]

This, however, was at Milnathort, beyond the edge of the coal-fields. Within the mining areas the evangelists seem to have been hard put to arouse any kind of response for or against, though in Cowdenbeath the missionaries received a reward described in their own words as 'mud, rotten apples, etc., victory, war with the devil, peace of God possessing our hearts and minds'. In the reports of the 1890s, these places are recognized as strongholds of indifference. In the Presbytery of Hamilton one-fifth to one-half of the Protestant families did not attend church: 'In the congested mining centres of Lanarkshire there is an average of more than a fourth of the Protestant portion of the population living apart from Christian ordinances.' In the Presbytery of Haddington, 'indifference prevails to a great extent'; though the native miners were fairly regular in attendance, the incomers were 'utterly impossible to get hold of'. The same was true in the Presbytery of Dunfermline, where in one mining parish three-quarters were said to have lapsed from the church. This, of course, still left considerable numbers as formal attenders, but enthusiasm for religion seemed to be lacking even among those who went to church. There was thus no equivalent in the Scottish coal-fields to the nineteenth-century religious fervour of miners in South Wales, Durham and Northumberland, though why this should have been so is not very clear.

It was in the large towns that the churches could expect to encounter the biggest problems. There was, however, little formal inattention to religious ordinances there by the middle class, though in the 1890s, ministers noticed a cooling interest in those religious activities the Evangelicals had been enthusiastic about in the middle of the century: family worship in the home was dying out, and many seemed to be in church from convention rather than conviction. At the bottom end of the scale those with bourgeois pretensions, such as clerks and shop attendants, could usually be relied upon at least to keep up appearances, but in 1896 the Church observed even here 'a kind of Bohemia of younger manhood' which was not bothering to maintain any religious connection. In the 1830s and 1840s, despite the reception afforded to Chalmers, skilled manual workers and artisans had been the backbone of many town congregations, especially among the various seceding churches and other non-conformist bodies like the Evangelical Union. When Morison, founder of the latter, stood trial at his Secession Presbytery in Kilmarnock, 'it seemed as if all the shoemakers of Darvel had struck work for the day'. Again, the rise of scores of ephemeral Chartist churches after 1838 was a symptom not of infidelity but of devotion to the religious ideal: artisans left the organized churches in frustration over the political views of the clergy, but they wanted to form churches of their own. Most returned to the fold after the excitement had subsided. Active artisan participation in church life did not disappear suddenly or completely, and many Scottish labour leaders of the first part of the twentieth century had as young men enjoyed a powerful church connection, especially with the United Presbyterians. The life seemed to go out of the tradition, however, as the twentieth century proceeded.

Other urban workers with smaller or less regular wages than the skilled were less committed from the start: it was these, apparently, whose absence from church had saddened and alarmed Chalmers in Glasgow before 1820, and there is no indication that the position improved at all in the course of the century. Thus in 1891 it was reported in one area of Glasgow 'occupied by unskilled workmen' that three religious censuses in seven years had come up with the same result: five out of seven of the non-Catholic population had no connection with any church. Catholics enjoyed greater fidelity than Protestants, but even they felt the cooling of ardour, especially among single men parted from their culture and from their families in Ireland. It was also noticed in both Glasgow and Paisley that the migrant Highlanders, so devout at home, were strikingly indifferent to the church in the towns.

It is extremely difficult, for any period in the nineteenth century, to form an accurate idea of the overall number of those who had the church-going habit. In 1851, investigators claimed that on census Sunday 33 per cent of the population attended worship in the morning, 21 per cent in the afternoon, and 6.5 per cent in the evening, but this threw no light on how many people went twice, or how many people with a regular 'church connection' had not gone at all on that particular day. In 1874, James Johnston reckoned one-fifth as the correct figure for people with no church connection at all. The commission of the 1890s reached very much the same conclusion but revealed many interesting details in the pattern. In Glasgow, for instance, it was thought that at least half the young men had no connection with any church, yet attendance at Sunday school by children was far more general than this might suggest. The ecclesiastical authorities were always surprised and upset by the degree of indifference to religion, but in the circumstances we might be surprised so many went to church at all. In the 1890s it was not the fall in actual numbers that disturbed commentators but the dying fires of enthusiasm among those who still gave formal allegiance: there were many presbyteries like Kinross which could report general attendance but 'a decided lack of interest in the Church and its work'.

4

The Church often asked itself why it was failing to hold the interest of the working class in particular. One explanation was that the system of pew rents discouraged the curious visitor and the man with little money. Undoubtedly it could: we hear of proprietors who padlocked their pews to prevent strangers using them at services they did not attend themselves, and of the free places in the church clearly set at the very front or at the very back so that anyone who sat in them seemed to be marked with a stigma of pauperism. But when the pew-rents were eventually done away with, there was no flood of workers back to the church. Some people blamed the long working hours, which so exhausted the toilers at the furnaces or behind the shop counters that they were too weak to come to worship on their one morning of respite: but evening services, often tried, were poorly attended, and when at last, in the 1860s and 1870s, more and more workers began to get Saturday afternoons off there was again no rush to church. Others blamed the general conditions of urban life, where the foul housing, poor food and the problem of drink had demoralized the poor to a point at which they could not even begin to think of association with a church. It was a saying of Keir Hardie that you could not be a Christian on a pound a week. But when the tide of poverty began to edge back in the twentieth century, there was no corresponding religious revival. For that matter the eighteenth-century countryside had been a world of pew-rents, hard work, bad housing and poverty, but that never kept the poor from church.

At the end of the nineteenth century many blamed football, cycling, modern literature, or even socialism for diverting the attention of the workers. Ministers were especially jealous of football, for it above all aroused exactly the heart-warming zeal and total devotion which they themselves had tried so hard, so painfully and so totally unsuccessfully to arouse for God. Undoubtedly football was the new opiate of the people. But such observations, however true, all begged the question of why these new activities were more addictive than church. In all the investigations there was one hard and unattractive fact which ministers kept striking: the working class could no longer see the point of the kind of church they were faced with in the towns and villages of Scotland.

Part of the explanation was the loss of the secular aspect of church life. In the late eighteenth century, the rural churchyard was a trysting place and a market place for a scattered country population. The nineteenth-century Evangelicals threw the courting couples, the gossips, the rouping beadle and the town crier out into the streets and pubs. Towns had more and flashier pubs, and increasing numbers of theatres, music halls and football grounds, so there was much more to do in any case. Again, in the eighteenth century, the schools had been indissolubly linked to the Church: after 1872, the tie was dissolved and schools were run by elected school boards. Poor relief had depended on the charity of minister and kirk session: from 1845, it was the prime duty of an elected Poor Law board. It was even possible to use the Registrar-General's facilities to get married and buried, and to register the names of the children outside the framework of the Church. The State and the amusement industry between them had taken away much of the significance of the Church in everyday life.

But the loss of the ability to identify with the Church also operated at a deeper and more psychological level. Workers found ministers a people hostile or incomprehensible. 'No reflection is more sad than the apparent inability of the regular ministry of the Church to reach the lower depths of the population,' it was reported to the General Assembly in 1896. The clergy were regarded by many with aversion. Of the miners in the Presbytery of Dunfermline, for instance, it was said, 'A great many of those who do not attend church had socialistic tendencies and looked upon ministers, if not as their natural enemies, at least as pillars and supports of the presently existing state of matters,' and at the Presbytery of Meigle the same phrase cropped up: 'The ploughmen look on the ministers as their natural enemies,' because, in this case, they opposed union requests to borrow school premises for meetings. A hundred years previously, these words would not have been used, though at that time the clergy upheld establishment values at least as strongly as they did in the 1890s. Nothing could have been more outspoken than the kirk's condemnation of the peasant levellers in the 1720s or of the weaver radicals in the 1790s.

But the eighteenth-century minister, like the laird, personified the community, and when the congregation listened to him it identified him with the parish, a division more meaningful in the rural world than the division of class. He personified also the ideology of God the Father, an image of great meaning in a society arranged in households where even employers regarded themselves *in loco parentis* to their servants and apprentices. By 1890, industrialization and migration had weakened the old idea of community but strengthened that of class. No one thought of himself as belonging to this or that *parish* of Glasgow, though a sense of locality might still identify an inhabitant of Cowcaddens or Bridgeton. The minister, however, personified nothing but his obvious middle-class background. Even in rural districts where the idea of the parish community was still alive and the Church was stronger than in the towns, the old paternalism was dead: it was said in Kirkcudbrightshire, 'If they were spoken to about going to church they would answer to the effect that the farmer had no business with them in that respect.'

There was a change, too, in the position of the artisan: for most of the nineteenth century the small craftsman and artisan found sense and relevance in a social teaching which emphasized thrift, restraint and self-improvement. The Church itself was instrumental in setting up savings banks where thrifty servants and artisans could salt away their money; it ran the schools and encouraged the mechanics institutes where self-improvement was taught to the masses. But by the early twentieth century, changes in industrial structure and the rise of welfare provision made these values seem irrelevant. What did it profit a man to scrimp and save all his life like the Church said, if he was to end up as he began, a wage-slave? And if the welfare state would provide at least something for old age and illness, was there the same need for unremitting thrift? The old doctrines made most sense where they helped the artisan to climb from journeyman to small master, as was still possible in Victorian times, and where there was particular need for a self-help ethic to avoid the pit of pauperism.

The working class, and artisans in particular, also found themselves excluded from positions of influence in the churches such as the eldership. This was most noticeable in the urban Free Church, where artisans had shown some enthusiasm for the principles of the Disruption in 1843, and thereafter there had been an ebbing away by working men as the church came to depend more and more on large middle-class subscriptions to keep going. It was least noticeable in one-class areas such as the Highlands and fishing villages. Churches in these areas—the Free Presbyterians, the Evangelical Union, the Plymouth Brethren—were often dominated by working-class people even in 1900. At the other extreme, middle-class areas of the towns often had churches where anyone of lower class was clearly unwelcome even in the congregation. 'The class church is a great evil,' said the Church of Scotland commission of the 1890s, but it had undoubtedly come to stay.

By the end of the nineteenth century, therefore, there was no doubt at all that the Church was ceasing to be at the forefront of most people's lives. For many in all classes it had lost its intellectual compulsiveness. For very large numbers in the working class it was profoundly identified with a middle-class ethos for which they could feel less and less enthusiasm. This was true despite the notable role of early Victorian churchmen like James Begg in pressing for better housing for the working classes: he was the minister of an Edinburgh Free Church kirk who was equally noted for his extreme anti-Catholicism and for his opposition to any movement to reunite the divided Presbyterian churches. A more attractive personality was his Disruption colleague, Thomas Guthrie, whose campaign for the 'street arab', the child vagrant of the industrial city, deservedly earned him almost universal admiration in his own lifetime and after death a fine statue on Princes Street. The early social reformers generally gave as their motives the salvation of souls and the preservation of social order. The next wave, urging the Church towards a new social conscience concerning housing and the plight of the working classes in the 1880s, the 1890s and at the beginning of the twentieth century, was both more sensitive and more secular:

We attack intemperance when we should attack the wretched house, the bad atmosphere, the unwholesome surroundings, the weary grind, which take the pith and uplook out of the man ... We are suspicious of trade unions, yet they are the labourers' protection, they provide for security, they apply the principle of cooperation, they educate a sense of self-respect.[14]

Without doubt they were spurred to their new sensitivity towards social questions by fear of agnostic socialism: and they found respite from their own theological uncertainties in a gospel of action: 'It is practical religion, not theological disquisitions, that can fill the churches or keep them full.'[15] Sometimes 'practical religion' took on an overly competitive edge. In the Grassmarket of Edinburgh, for example, the beggars and the destitute who swarmed in the worst slum of the city in the 1890s found that they could get relief every day of the week if they switched from Church of Scotland, to Free Church, to United Presbyterian, to Episcopalian, to Catholic, depending on who gave out the free soup and old clothes each day.

To a limited but important degree, the churches at the turn of the century had some success. Their efforts, especially those of the United Presbyterians, were sufficiently strong and sincere to influence the emergent ILP and suffuse its efforts with a glow of Christian morality. The labour leaders of early twentieth-century Scotland very often saw their fight in terms of a struggle between good and evil, like that of the old Covenanters to whom they often referred, rather than a class struggle between capital and labour. On the other hand, the new Church reformers certainly failed to 'fill the churches or keep them full'. The public's indifference was seldom expressed in open anti-clericalism, but in what contemporaries termed a 'canna-be-fashedness' or a 'scepticism—not absolute infidelity, but a scepticism which showed itself in a flippant spirit and tone towards the Christian verities'. The churches, even the established Church of Scotland, felt themselves becoming congregational, giving up the larger pastoral mission to the whole parish and the whole nation which had been the vision of Thomas Chalmers and the Evangelicals, and concentrating instead on the welfare of its members and their families, so that church-membership ultimately became only the hereditary habit that it largely is today.

But we must not exaggerate the degree of decline that had set in at the end of the Victorian age: the decline was slow, and even in 1940 not as marked as in most European countries. People at first sensed it rather than saw it, and many hoped it was a temporary phase, a passing weakness which more vigorous mission, more lively services, a new church here and a new hall there, would soon dissipate. Only gradually did they come to sense that the change was permanent, and apparently irrevocable. John White, more than anyone the architect of the reunion of 1929, spoke around 1930 of the alteration he had witnessed in his career as a minister from 'an unquestioning acceptance of the orthodox message of the Church', to 'a secular rationalism, Hedonism and the New Psychology'.[16] He believed that the rot had set in well before the First World War. Probably that war had accelerated it, through the shock many people experienced on the discovery of the incompetence of the generals and politicians: religious leaders, who blessed the guns and criticized pacifism in the name of Christ, rightly shared in the general odium.

It was also difficult to feel that, despite the good intentions, the Protestant churches in the first half of the twentieth century ever tore themselves away from the general outlook of their middle-class membership. The decline of the sabbath was self-evident: it was described in these terms in 1960:

> Though it breaks out from time to time, one cannot say that Sabbath Observance is currently a very burning issue. Even among church-folk the feeling is forming that a Sunday bus or car-ride to the coast after church, a bathe or a game of cricket on the beach on a holiday Sunday, maybe even a quiet non-holiday hour on the tennis courts between services—that these and similar diversions are not the last word in pagan indulgence.[17]

Nothing here about a sneaked visit to a pub as a 'bona fide traveller', a game of football or a peep at the *News of the World*.

'Church extension' was tried again after the reunion of 1929: the 1950s were a decade of 'Mission' in the new working-class housing estates, and with some success, for the Church of Scotland membership actually stood higher in 1961 than in 1931. Nevertheless, that success proved ephemeral, and church membership has dropped steadily ever since to well below its nineteenth-century levels.

It would be most unfair to say of the Church of Scotland that it completely failed on intellectual grounds, or that it ceased to say anything of relevance to the modern world. In the twentieth century it bravely strove to reconcile philosophy, science and biblical scholarship with religion, and its most noted theologians, especially John Baillie, who held chairs in the USA and Canada as well as in Scotland, had a world-wide reputation among those who still cared for such things. Again, the Church and Nation Committee of the reunited Church of Scotland from 1929 actively pursued a policy of confident pronouncement on national affairs—anything from communism to rural depopulation, from atomic warfare to the effect of television on public morals. The last occasion on which it swayed government policy on any matter was in its liberal views on African self-determination in the 1950s. However, its intellectual and political views increasingly fell on deaf ears. The Church of Scotland never did find a solution to the other and more fundamental problems posed by the death of hell, the rise of class, and the spread of other entertainment.

CHAPTER IX

The Aims and Failures of Education

1

In the first part of the nineteenth century, the Scots were extremely proud of their universities and schools, and not without certain reason. The Universities of Edinburgh and Glasgow, in particular, had been the crucibles of the Scottish Enlightenment of the late eighteenth century, and their reputations still rang around the world. The influence of the pupils of Dugald Stewart, Professor of Moral Philosophy at Edinburgh and disciple and interpreter of Adam Smith, was felt widely and deeply in the corridors of British power, not least through the *Edinburgh Review*, founded by Francis Jeffrey and his friends in 1802 and soon the most influential journal in the United Kingdom. Simultaneously, the system of parish and burgh schools, substantially supplemented by private 'adventure' schools, produced a population renowned for its literacy and what middle-class contemporaries called 'intelligence'. The Scots, indeed, had developed an attitude towards mass education significantly different from the untrusting and hostile attitude still dominant among the rulers of England. The English view, which went back at least to Bernard Mandeville's *Fable of the Bees* of 1724, was exemplified in the hostile speech by which Davies Giddy helped to defeat an attempt in Parliament in 1807 to introduce a Scottish-style rate-aided parochial school system into the south:

> However specious in theory the project might be of giving education to the labouring classes of the poor, it would be prejudicial to their morals and happiness; it would teach them to despise their lot in life, instead of making them good servants in agriculture and other laborious employments. Instead of teaching them subordination, it

would render them fractious and refractory, as was evident in the manufacturing counties; it would enable them to read seditious pamphlets, vicious books, and publications against Christianity; it would render them insolent to their superiors; and in a few years the legislature would find it necessary to direct the strong arm of power against them.[1]

The Scottish attitude, which was destined in the course of the nineteenth century to win the day in Britain as a whole and thus to form an interesting and little-recognized case of the scotticization of England, was articulated, but not invented, by Adam Smith. He spoke, in *The Wealth of Nations*, of the need to overcome the 'gross ignorance and stupidity which, in a civilized society, seem so frequently to benumb the understandings of all the inferior ranks of people'. For him, 'a man without the proper use of the intellectual faculties of a man' was 'mutilated and deformed' in an 'essential part of the character of human nature'. Education, however, was to Smith not only a basic civil right: it was also a necessary social insurance. The State derived from it the safety of an intelligent consensus of the governed:

> The more they are instructed the less liable they are to the delusions of enthusiasm and superstition, which, among ignorant nations, frequently occasion the most dreadful disorders. An instructed and intelligent people, besides, are always more decent and orderly than an ignorant and stupid one. They feel themselves, each individually, more respectable and more likely to obtain the respect of their lawful superiors, and they are therefore more disposed to respect those superiors. They are more disposed to examine, and more capable of seeing through, the interested complaints of faction and sedition, and they are, upon that account, less apt to be misled into any wanton or unnecessary opposition to the measures of government. In free countries, where the safety of government depends very much upon the favourable judgement which the people may form of its conduct, it must surely be of the highest importance that they should not be disposed to judge rashly or capriciously concerning it.[2]

It is important to realize, moreover, that neither Smith nor anyone else in Scotland believed in thorough-going democratic equality of opportunity in education. The common people, in Smith's scheme, 'cannot, in any civilised society, be so well instructed as people of some rank and fortune', though they should be assisted 'to read, write and account' at an early age, in publicly-aided schools 'where children may be taught for a reward so moderate that even a common labourer may afford it'. It was never intended that formal education for the vast majority should go beyond the three Rs, though provision was always made for a select few even of the common people to go to burgh school and university.

In practice, the Scottish system in the early nineteenth century did allow most working men to acquire basic literary skills, and a small number of boys (never girls) to go forward to more advanced study. More to the point, it began to win recognition from English intellectuals for achieving Smith's second purpose, social control. Thus Thomas Malthus contemplated Scottish working-class education in these words:

> The knowledge circulated among the common people . . . has yet the effect of making them bear with patience the evils which they suffer from, being aware of the folly and inefficacy of turbulence. The quiet and peaceable habits of the instructed Scotch peasant compared with the turbulent disposition of the ignorant Irishman ought not to be without effect upon every impartial reasoner.[3]

From 1816, the leader of the campaign for popular education in England was Henry Brougham, student of Dugald Stewart and co-founder of the *Edinburgh Review*. From his efforts there arose ultimately in England and in Scotland the principles that govern modern policy towards education: those of capital grants from the State to establish new schools where needed, conceded in 1833; of government inspection of schools as a prerequisite for grants to help meet running costs (and hence State control of education through Privy Council) in 1839; and the pupil teacher system of 1846, by which the State tried to ensure a cheap, adequate supply of schoolmasters for the future. The coping stone was placed on these early efforts by the creation of publicly-managed board schools in England in 1870 and in Scotland in 1872. The aim of the board schools was famously summed up by Robert Lowe in a speech before the passage of the Second Reform Bill: 'It will be absolutely necessary that you should prevail on our future masters to learn their letters.' It was identical to one of the aims of education adumbrated by Adam Smith. It is in that sense that the English became converted by the Scots.

On the other hand, because English thinking was focused so sharply on trying to bring elementary education cheaply to a large and relatively neglected working class, and to do so under guidance from a Committee of Privy Council located in London, Parliamentary legislation for both countries tended to be fixated in these directions. Consequently Scottish critics in the later nineteenth century often felt that their education was being anglicized—made to concentrate on the simplest needs of one class and controlled from London—rather than being developed along the Scottish tradition of an education that opened a wider range of opportunities for some, at least, in all social classes, under local control. The difference was succinctly expressed by a Scottish teacher in evidence to the Argyll Commission: 'The object of the Privy Council grants is to effect the education of a class, the object of the parochial schools was to overtake the education of a people.'[4] That, however, was to overstate what the parochial and burgh schools, even at their best, had ever done or set out to do. Their aim since the sixteenth century had been to give all people enough literacy to read the Bible and to inculcate a set of rules about acceptable social behaviour— and in addition, to pick out a very small elite for further training in Latin as a preparation for higher education. It was in being meritocratic rather than democratic that the Scottish tradition proved itself the forerunner of what has come to be the dominant ethos in British education in the present century.

No one showed greater anxiety for the traditions of Scottish education than the leaders of the Evangelical party in the Church of Scotland—Thomas Chalmers, pre-eminently, along with others like Henry Duncan, founder of savings banks for the rural working man, for whom 'the universal diffusion of knowledge' was 'the surest and most powerful instrument for the protection of society', and George Lewis, author of the influential polemic, *Scotland a Half-Educated Nation* (1843). Lewis regarded 'our parochial churches and parochial schools' as 'the only remains we can show the stranger of the ancient excellence of our country ... the only institutions round which linger Scottish feelings and attachments': it would not be the last time incipient nationalist feeling was used as a defence of traditional Scottish schooling.[5]

The church in the early part of the nineteenth century had reason to worry, both about the general health of Scottish education and about its own control over it. In the Lowland countryside, the single school in each parish, funded partly by a tax on landowners and partly by the pupils' own fees and supervised by the Church of Scotland presbyteries, still worked well enough to provide basic literary skills to a high proportion of the population, but in the industrial areas the parochial schools and more ambitious burgh grammar schools simply could not cope. Nearly two-thirds of all the schoolchildren in Scotland in 1818 were found to be outside these public institutions and mainly in small private schools known as 'adventure' schools where the parents bore all the costs and in which the Church had no say.

There followed a remarkably effective counterattack by Thomas Chalmers and his allies in the Church of Scotland. In the 1820s, 1830s and 1840s a crusade to supplement the parochial schools with Church 'sessional' and 'General Assembly' schools in the towns attracted generous donations from the congregations, greatly assisted by public finance after 1834, when the Government began to give grants to schools in Scotland. The proportion of pupils in private schools, i.e. those that depended entirely on fees, fell to one-quarter in 1851 and declined still more thereafter. Contrary to what has sometimes been averred, the normal experience for a Scottish working-class child even in the early Victorian period was to attend a school where his or her parents did not have to meet the total cost of education.[6]

After the Disruption, however, the position became so complex that the ultimate fate of Church-assisted and Church-controlled education was called into question. The Free Church initially set up many hundreds of its own schools to supplement and rival those of the Church of Scotland, but soon found the strain on its funds to be such that it could not cope without government grants and government inspection: the United Presbyterians were a third force, the increasing bands of Irish Catholics a fourth, and the Episcopalians, on a minor scale, a fifth. The situation was a mess, with only a small minority going to the parochial schools of the Church of Scotland, and in any given area many overlapping, small-scale institutions of different kinds competing where one on a larger scale would have sufficed. Repeated attempts by Lord Advocate James Moncrieff to establish a system of non-sectarian, publicly-financed schools to be controlled by a central authority sitting in Edinburgh came to nothing. The bills which he sponsored in 1854, 1855, 1856, 1862 and 1869 perished because MPs south of the border feared that any move in Scotland to deprive the Established Church there of its privileged position in the parochial schools would become a stalking-horse for a similar attack on the

Church of England. In 1854, two-thirds of Scottish MPs had voted in favour of the bill, but it was still rejected in the House of Commons by the weight of English votes. It needed the authoritative Argyll Commission on Scottish school education in the 1860s and the passage of the English Board Schools Act in 1870 before the Scots were allowed an equivalent measure of State control and help. Even then, Young's Act of 1872 was inferior to Moncrieff's various bills in two respects, making no good provision for State-supported education above elementary level, and (after a short interim) passing control of the popularly elected local school boards to London: the so-called Scotch Education Department that it established existed for many years 'only as a name painted on a door in Whitehall'. This altered with the establishment of the Scottish Office in 1885, but only in 1939 did the SED complete its move to Edinburgh.

The quality of Scottish education, and the number of children it reached, was already causing anxiety in the three decades before 1872. The situation in the countryside was reckoned to be better than in the towns and industrial districts. John Gordon, the first government school inspector in Scotland, noted in his report on four Lowland counties in 1844–5 that 'the period of attendance commonly terminates among the agricultural population at 13 or 14 years of age; in manufacturing and mining districts it is very often cut short at 8 or 9'.[7] Even in rural areas, however, all was not well. In the north-east, where traditional standards of education were held to be particularly high, schoolmasters in 1870 complained that 'two-fifths of the children of agricultural labourers in these counties are uneducated' on account of 'their being too soon withdrawn from continuous attendance'.[8] Perhaps the significance of that verdict hinges on what they meant by 'educated', but the minute books of country schools constantly testified to the pressures of harvest, weeding and parental poverty in keeping the children away from school.

Above all, however, it was the demand for child labour in industry that was the enemy of school attendance, and despite the Factory Acts there are indications that the extent of such employment grew rapidly at the start of our period. In Clackmannanshire, for example, male child labour increased by 53 per cent and female by 78 per cent in the five years between 1857 and 1862. According to Robert Somers, in Glasgow in 1857, under half the population aged between five and ten was attending any school at all:

Every branch of skilled labour as well as our shops and warehouses, offer employment to little boys who can read and scrawl their names. For a still less educated class, there are the factories, the bleachfields, the tobacco-works and a host of minor manufactures. Making matches, stringing beads or bugles on ladies' dresses, and a hundred other trivial occupations, absorb the labour of multitudes of children of both sexes, irrespective almost of age and totally irrespective of their instruction.[9]

Glasgow's problems were compounded by the fact that many of the poorest children were also Catholic, for whom little provision was as yet made: Somers found that only 13 out of 213 schools in the city were Catholic, and though these were of good quality they could cope with only a small percentage of the immigrant Irish population.

The quality of the teaching was also highly variable. It was at its worst, in the opinion of the Argyll Commission, in the remaining private adventure schools in the cities, the last resort of the very poor, where teachers of low character and little education taught for a pittance. One census-taker, asking for the master at such a school in Glasgow, was told by 'a small boy, who appeared to be in charge for the moment' that this was the day the children paid their fees, and that the master was in 'the shop next door': he was located 'combining porter with penmanship and geography with Glenlivet'.[10] On the other hand, there was a confidence in the real achievements of the majority of the schools under Church control, confirmed in many areas by the continual attendance of middle-class children. In the countryside and the smaller towns it was still the case that all but the richest received their earliest education in the same classroom. In the 1880s, John Boyd Orr, the son of the local quarry owner, went to the village school at Kilmaurs in Ayrshire from 9 a.m. to 4 p.m. with an hour off to eat his 'piece' in the school shed. His recollection that in such schools 'the children of the poor were probably as well educated as those of the wealthy in rudimentary subjects like reading, writing and arithmetic', holds true also for the earlier period.[11] In the large towns there was more social distinction. Partly this was due to segregation of residence—a school in a poor quarter full of unskilled labourers was likely to have a very different tone from one in a district dominated by shopkeepers. Partly it was due to the absence from any school of the very poorest children: in 1872, when attendance to the age of thirteen was made compulsory by the State, the number of pupils in Glasgow jumped by 23 per cent within a year.

It is not surprising, therefore, that on the eve of Young's Act there were significant regional variations in the ability of the population to write (we know nothing of reading). One primitive way of testing this ability at the lowest level is to discover who could write his own name. The 1871 census showed that 89 per cent of men and 79 per cent of women marrying in the previous decade had been able to sign the register, the percentage in the Lowlands varying from 99 per cent of men and 97 per cent of women in Selkirkshire (the other Border counties and the north-east were nearly as good), down to 83 per cent of men and 69 per cent of women in industrial Renfrewshire (Dunbartonshire and Lanarkshire were much the same). In the Highlands, the situation was very much worse even than in the industrial cities, ability to sign falling as low as 65 per cent for men and 49 per cent for women. Neither the parochial schools nor a century and a half of charitable effort by religious bodies such as the SSPCK and various Gaelic societies could overcome the problems posed by geographical remoteness, very large parishes and a non-English-speaking population. Comparing Scotland as a whole with England, however, the superiority of the Scottish system is seen to be real: male illiteracy (again measured by inability to sign the marriage register) in Scotland in 1871 was only half the English figure, and female illiteracy was one-quarter less.[12]

On the other hand, considered as a whole, Scottish education at mid-century was extremely inegalitarian, mainly because the economic pressures on the great mass of the population put anything apart from the acquisition of the most basic literary skills far beyond their reach. It was true that Scotland had, relative to population, quite good provision above that level. In the 1860s, the Argyll Commission found that Scotland had one university place for every 1000 of the population, compared to 1:5800 in England, and that in 'secondary' schools the Scottish ratio was 1:140 and the English 1:1300. Nevertheless, the typical Scottish secondary school—the burgh school—was tending already to become the preserve of the middle classes, 'tradesmen and shopkeepers at the one end, and professional men and the less wealthy landed proprietors at the other, but having few or no representatives of the lowest or highest classes on their benches'.[13] The highest had been creamed off by the English public schools. The lowest were mainly at work. Detailed figures showed that the famous High Schools of Edinburgh and Glasgow, and Perth Academy, had no working-class children at all in 1866, and that in five secondary schools in Aberdeen, Inverness, Ayr and Dumfries the average was about 10 per cent.[14] On the other hand, many of the parochial schools in rural areas were involved in providing something of what we would now regard as secondary education for their most senior pupils.

The universities certainly did better than that, to give a semblance of truth to the myth of a democratic tradition in Scottish education. In the early 1860s, they received no fewer than 23 per cent of their Arts Faculty intake from children of manual workers, many coming straight from parochial schools at the age of thirteen or fourteen. However most of those of humble origin who went to university were the sons of traditional craftsmen—'neither the rural poor, nor the majority of factory workers, nor the unskilled workers of the towns had more than a token representation'.[15] The son of a minister was 'about a hundred times as likely to go to university' as the son of a miner. No entrance examination was necessary to get into a Scottish university, and a relatively generous provision of bursaries for poor scholars allowed the 'lad o' pairts' his chance to enter the hallowed portals. On the other hand there was a price to pay for the open door in terms of academic standards: the universities themselves were often regarded as alternatives to the burgh schools, not making much higher demands and catering largely to a similar age-group in the mid-teens. By the 1880s, there were many complaints that Scottish graduates had to go to England for any kind of higher training, and that their own universities put them at a competitive disadvantage in the job market, 'the hand-loom weavers of the intellectual world'.[16] Working-class entrants usually came as mature students into Arts or Divinity, aiming at some qualification to raise them out of the rut. Many were among the enormous number who failed at the end of their first year. In the Glasgow University junior class in Latin in 1889–90, for example, 200 candidates failed out of 255. The presence of working-class undergraduates, however, enabled national spokesmen, in a self-congratulatory mood, to maintain the delusion that any Scotsman could, through the tradition of national education, raise himself to any height he cared to aim for, if he had brains and was capable of effort and self sacrifice: 'The great Napoleon used to say that every soldier carried his Marshal's baton in his knapsack: so every Scotch peasant, when he goes to school, carries in his satchel a minister's gown, or other emblem of a learned profession, and it is his own fault if he lose it.'[17] That so few of humble origin, out of the great multitude, actually succeeded in climbing the class ladder on the rungs of educational opportunity tended to confirm the middle class in their other comforting delusion, that it was moral weakness that kept the poor where they were.

2

Generally, the history of Scottish education since the advent of the SED has been written either as a denunciation of anglicizing practices (like George Davie's celebrated work on the universities) or as chronicles of progress under difficult circumstances (like the texts of H. M. Knox and James Scotland).[18] Such perspectives are defensible, but it is more important to realize that the general ethos of education did not change: it continued to aim firstly at providing, as cheaply as possible, the bulk of the population with the bare minimum of elementary education combined with adequate social discipline, and secondly, at giving a small number of children of all classes, but especially of the higher classes, a more respectable academic education, to qualify them for their role as a controlling elite.

In these aims, in the view of its critics, it has been successful only at crippling psychological cost. As long ago as 1919, A. S. Neill criticized the dominie who beat the children to teach them to fight the battle of life: 'The discipline of the school gives each child an inner sense of inferiority ... And the working-classes are suffering from a gigantic inferiority complex, otherwise they would not be content to remain wage slaves.'[19] More recently, H. M. Patterson has described how the schools uphold both 'the ferocious stress on social conformity so characteristic of Scottish civil society' and its complement, the 'easy acceptance of a ruthless search for advancement to some position of reward, power and station within the undeniable social hierarchy—in the Kirk, in business, in politics, in sport, or in the professions'.[20] Such verdicts are harsh, but they may nevertheless strike a chord among those who have to live with the cultural realities of twentieth-century Scotland. They also accurately indicate the enduring nature of the schools and universities as servants of a state in which the political and economic requirements of the upper and middle classes have always maintained an easy precedence over all other considerations.

Nevertheless, the early board schools under Young's Act had some striking successes in elementary education that had been denied to their predecessors under the parochial system. Within thirty years, illiteracy, for both sexes, had been virtually eliminated in Highland and Lowland alike. The problems of attaining satisfactory educational standards in the Highlands remained immense, not least because the factors of the local lairds succeeded in maintaining control as dominant members of the school boards and because the unrelieved poverty of the area made it impossible to raise an adequate school rate except with generous contributions from the estates. However the new schools, which here as elsewhere rapidly subsumed the old parochial schools and most of the different independent schools, at least provided the population for the first time with the essential ability to read and write in English. In masterminding this the SED has been accused of serious crimes against the Gaelic language, especially by resisting the recommendations of the Napier Commission in 1884 that in Highland schools, instruction in the native language 'ought not merely to be permitted but enjoined'. In fact, throughout the nineteenth century, as Dr Durkacz has observed, 'the Highlander himself was strongly and consistently against the use of Gaelic as a school language',[21] on the grounds that what was needed to get on in the world was English—as an HMI said in 1899, 'The language is beautiful ... but the people do not want it.' The contrary view was expressed by the activists of *An Comunn Gaidhealach*, but their attempt to introduce an amendment into the Education Act of 1908 to make Gaelic compulsory resulted only in a crofters' backlash in the school board elections, when the vote went, in the contemporary phrase, overwhelmingly 'anti-faddist' and against them. Ten years later, the 1918 Act called upon the new local education authorities to provide 'adequate provision for teaching Gaelic in Gaelic-speaking areas', without specifying either what it meant by 'adequate provision' or defining a 'Gaelic-speaking area'. In the continuing absence of popular enthusiasm at the Gaelic grass roots, very little happened to encourage further Gaelic education before the Second World War. But Highland boys and girls did become completely literate in English.

In the Lowlands, an ambitious crusade against illiteracy was necessary only in the great cities, and it was nowhere conducted with more vigour and success than by the school board in Glasgow. The 1872 Act had made education compulsory for children between the ages of five and thirteen: the board found that there were 87,000 children of this age-group under their jurisdiction, but only 53,000 on the total roll of the existing schools, of whom, on average, 10,000 were absentees— 'putting the most generous interpretation on these figures only about 60 per cent of children ever went to school at all'.[22] In the first decade, the board found it impossible to do much more than absorb into new buildings the children from earlier schools which closed down with some relief and made their work over to the new body as soon as it came into operation. Most schools followed this course, apart from those under Catholic supervision. By the end of the century, however, attendance was successfully enforced by the Glasgow school board on all children except for the five-year-olds, and there were places for everyone. An HMI in 1897 spoke in admiration of the Glasgow board's 'Herculean labour': 'One who has visited the fine schools in those grim streets that fringe the great arteries of traffic, and has seen the pale, pinched and joyless faces of the children can form some idea of the difficulties of the situation.'[23]

Glasgow's achievement, and those of the other school boards, were only made possible by a transformation of the teaching body from a predominantly male profession into a predominantly female one, though men continued to occupy the headships, the most prestigious teaching posts and the positions of power within the teachers' organization, the Educational Institute of Scotland. In 1851, 65 per cent of the teachers had been men; by 1911, 70 per cent were women. Women predominated because they were cheap to employ, willing and plentiful, and the school boards needed an immediately augmented supply of inexpensive labour. The average salaries of male teachers, 1872–1900, varied between £121 and £143 a year, but those of female teachers only between £62 and £72—half the cost. Initially, lower remuneration might be justified on the grounds of lower average qualifications, but when in 1905 the Presbyterian churches finally relinquished their hold over the teachers' training colleges to the SED, there was a rise in the number of women seeking the certificate until, in 1914, they amounted to 65 per cent of the whole certified teaching staff in Scotland. Efforts to claim equal pay for equal work were then countered by the male teachers' argument that women were not the main breadwinners in the family and so did not deserve equal pay. It was, moreover, not in the financial interests of the SED or the school boards to heed any counter-argument that might increase the bill for elementary teaching, so the inequality was effortlessly perpetuated.[24]

Developments within the non-elementary sectors revealed most clearly the true orientation of late nineteenth-century Scottish education. Following English thinking, the 1872 Act had not regarded secondary schools as a matter of any priority in the state system. The management of the old burgh schools was indeed transferred to the new boards, but by the 1870s, the majority of them taught most of their pupils little other than the three Rs and were easily converted into new, essentially elementary board schools. Thirteen burgh schools which did have an extensive interest in an advanced curriculum—they included such famous names as Glasgow High School, Ayr Academy and Montrose Academy—were designated 'Higher Class Schools' and allowed to continue advanced teaching, though at first denied both grant aid and rate aid from the public sector. They became dependent on expensive school fees, and in practice scarcely different to the numerous private secondary schools, calling forth from Sir James Grant, the historian of the burgh schools, the acid comment that 'Poor people ... are thus debarred for the first time in the history of their country from taking advantage of the grammar schools ... They are no longer national schools open to all classes but select schools for the upper middle class.'[25] The Act also made provision (until 1899) for ordinary board schools to add a little extra to the elementary curriculum in designated 'specific subjects', but the opinion of most school inspectors was that tacking bits on to the end of primary schooling was worse than useless. Thus Kilmarnock Academy, which had not been designated a Higher Class School, tried to teach such 'specific subjects'; 'the presentation [for examination] in the first stage of Latin is 70 or 80, it falls in the third stage to three or five ... There is often only a single pupil in the third year of French or German.'[26] It seemed like mere tokenism.

Opportunities were further narrowed, as far as the working class was concerned, by the alterations in the law respecting the old endowed schools. In Edinburgh there was a concerted campaign, in the interests of the professional middle classes, to capture for their own purposes the funds of such institutions, especially the long-established Merchant Company schools and those of the Heriot Trust. The old residential 'hospitals' were turned into large fee-paying day schools which the working class could not afford and which directed middle-class children from the earliest age towards preparation for a different kind of education from that of the workers. It was a total negation of the philosophy of everyone at least starting from common ground. John Marshall, Rector of Edinburgh High School, put the implications of the new creed only too clearly in 1886, when he said that secondary education was not 'something added on mechanically at the end of a previous education called Elementary: the two are from the first organically different . . . just as a workman's two or three-roomed dwelling is not at all to be likened to a slice out of a rich man's house, but has an organic unity and completeness of its own'.[27] The Trades Council of Edinburgh strenuously opposed this view, especially in relation to Heriot's Trust, arguing that the intention of the seventeenth-century founder had been 'to raise up a respectable, thinking, able class of artizans or citizens', not to favour an already pampered elite. Their view did not prevail. The upshot was that Edinburgh School Board later found it hard to develop decent secondary education in its own publicly-financed schools, as the influential people in the city took the view that there were already sufficient good secondary schools for appropriate purposes. The children of the working class in the capital clearly suffered as a result.

Glasgow developed differently, with the encouragement from 1886 of an SED under Sir Henry Craik that was evolving a much more positive view of the need for publicly-financed secondary education to fill the gap between state schooling and university education. The school board, in a city with few endowed schools on the Edinburgh model, began to extend secondary education under its own auspices in so-called 'Higher Grade Schools' (not to be confused with the 'Higher Class Schools'). These were ordinary board schools which children entered at the age of five, but which had been selected to carry education to a higher level than Standard VI and a later age than thirteen years. The board did not act out of regard to the working class, but in order to encourage the Glasgow middle class to take a greater interest in educating its own children past the elementary level:

> While the working classes in Scotland, to their lasting honour, have been till quite recently more alive to the advantages of education than are the corresponding classes in England, the reverse proposition holds true when you reach the middle classes . . . As a rule in the middle and upper classes English parents are more concerned about their children's education and willing to spend more money on that education than are Scotch parents.[28]

The board, indeed, was at first accused of misusing the rates paid by the working classes to subsidize the middle classes, since large fees were charged in 'Higher Grade Schools' throughout their age range and well-to-do parents were thus 'relieved of the discomfort of the presence of the poorer classes'. To some extent this criticism decreased after 1892, when all elementary and much secondary education became free, and when bursaries were more widely available for those secondary schools where fees were not abolished. But there was not a great rush to the secondary schools in any case—even in the late 1890s, only a few hundred children of any class in the immense city of Glasgow were staying on after the age of fourteen. For most, here and elsewhere, the counting house and the factory still beckoned more insistently than educational opportunity.

3

In the twentieth century, Scottish education has been marked by the same attitude that branded it in the nineteenth, which regarded it as a matter of low social priority once the perceived needs of the middle classes had been attended to, and once a channel had been opened for a limited number of working-class children to use secondary school and university as a means of upward social mobility. Neither the Scotch Education Department (rechristened the Scottish Education Department in 1918), nor the teaching profession, nor the public at large, expressed much interest in achieving high standards for the bulk of the population, or even in discovering what the world outside Scotland considered high and appropriate standards for an efficient, modern nation.

What happened in the universities at the top of the educational ladder was an interesting illustration of how all kinds of reform might be introduced except opening higher education to as many people as possible. Throughout the second half of the nineteenth century, the universities had been under pressure from within and without to revise their curriculum and set higher academic standards, to adapt themselves to a situation where the middle classes needed to pass the new entrance examination to the British Civil Service, and in other ways to come to terms with the vocational needs of an elite in the modern world. The ordinances of the Scottish Universities Commission, which sat from 1889 until 1897, achieved most of what the reformers had been demanding for decades. A four-year Honours degree (on the Oxbridge model but taking an extra year) was introduced alongside the three-year Ordinary degree, which gradually declined in significance. New subjects and new chairs were introduced. Women were admitted on an equal footing with men, though only after a prolonged campaign in which it was suggested that St Andrews (desperate for money as usual) might find a new role as a segregated women's university for Great Britain.[29] For all universities in Scotland a compulsory entrance examination replaced the old system of open access; passes were necessary in English, mathematics, Latin or Greek, and a fourth approved subject, at the standard set by the Leaving Certificate that Craik had introduced into the schools in 1888. This did, indeed, close the universities to many mature students, but it conversely made them the logical destination for secondary-school leavers needing a higher qualification. The modern three-tier system came into being, and the average age of university entrants rose to about seventeen or eighteen. From that time forward, the Scottish universities again grew steadily in academic prestige in the international community, though as late as the 1960s they could still be criticized by the Robbins Commission for being backward in research.

The universities grew in size as they revived in academic standing: from 4400 places in 1830, they developed modestly to 6000 in 1900, then leapt to 10,000 by 1938, and 15,000 by 1950. This rate of increase was slower than the equivalent in England, but England still had a long way to catch up: in Scotland in 1950, the ratio of places to population was 1:318, in England 1:641. As for the participation of the working class in the Scottish universities, there was probably some progress in the fifty years up to the First World War because of the availability of national bursaries, and, from 1901, of the munificence of Andrew Carnegie in founding the Carnegie Trust for the Universities, which by 1910 helped with the fees of about half of all university students in Scotland (and 70 per cent in the Arts faculties). This was more than sufficient to offset such factors as the institution of an entrance examination and a higher school-leaving age. At Glasgow, always the most working-class of the Scottish universities, the proportion of male students from the working class in all faculties rose from 18.6 per cent in 1860 to 24 per cent in 1910, though there had been no improvement over fifty years for the children of the semi-skilled or unskilled. Then, however, the situation stagnated: the social composition of the intake was virtually unchanged in 1910, 1934 and 1960. The extent of continuing inequality was clearly brought out by Adam Collier in his study of Glasgow in 1938:

> In the post-war period 1926–35 there was roughly one entrant to every 20 children born in Social Class 1; in Social Class 2 (Artisan) the figure was one in 212; and in the lowest Social Class it was one in 550 ... Whereas in Social Class 1 the number of children born per entrant for law was of the order 200 to one, in the lowest social class this ratio was of the order 20,000 to one. In the case of medicine these ratios were approximately 70 to one and 6,000 to one.[30]

The characteristic ambition for a child of working-class parents entering the university at this time, in fact, was to take an Ordinary MA in Arts and to aim to be a teacher. This was especially true of girls. In the interwar years, however, the drive by government and local authority to economize on education and reduce the salaries and numbers of teachers during the depression caused a steep drop in the recruitment to the Faculty of Arts at Glasgow, from 969 students in 1928–9 to 492 in 1934–5. Among other things, therefore, the effect of the crisis of the 1930s was temporarily to reduce the main opportunity for working-class upward mobility in the west of Scotland. More depressing in the long term was the failure of the working class to win a much larger proportion of university places for itself than it had already achieved a century earlier.

Much of the responsibility for the nature of Scottish education in the present century can fairly be laid at the feet of the SED under Henry Craik and his successor, John Struthers, who ruled the department from 1905 to 1921. There was in this period no shortage of complex administrative and statutory attention. The school-leaving age had been raised to fourteen in 1883, but with provision for 'half-time' after ten: it was not effectively raised to fifteen until after 1945. After the Education Act of 1908, the Higher *Class* Schools, both public and private, came to be known as 'secondary schools', and became the five- and six-year secondaries of later decades. The Higher *Grade* Schools were widely developed after 1899 by local school boards, and those with five-year courses also became recognized as 'secondary schools' by 1920. In addition, there were provisions from 1899 under which children staying on in board schools after the age of twelve could take supplementary courses for a year or two, usually of a vocational nature related to future employment in commerce or industry. The problem of the Catholics (still poor, but with an echelon now starting to rise into the middle class) was tackled by the 1918 Act, under which voluntary religious schools were still allowed to come under the state system, but the Church was allowed both to vet new staff for appropriate beliefs and to maintain the former level of religious instruction. To militant Protestant enemies (widespread and successful in local elections, especially in Glasgow, in the interwar years), this was 'Rome on the rates'. To John Struthers of the SED it was a necessary step to bring into the state network of socialization what he called 'a pariah class and a growing national danger'.[31] In any event it perpetuated sectarian education and thereby helped to keep alive religious animosities within the cities. Finally, the system of local control by elected school boards was replaced in 1918 by *ad hoc* county education authorities, which in turn made over their powers to county councils and the town councils of the four cities in the Local Government Act of 1929. The old boards had sometimes been penny-pinching and parish-minded but there was an immediacy of democratic participation about them that was sacrificed in all later arrangements.

The basic philosophy of the early leaders of the SED between 1885 and 1921 was to make available public secondary education to those whom they felt could benefit by it, and to make it appropriate for the future career needs of the pupils. In the hands of Craik and Struthers this admirable aim came to involve two less admirable assumptions. Firstly, in the school system that emerged after 1900, it was taken as axiomatic that pupils could, at the age of eleven or twelve, instantly be classified as 'academic' or 'non-academic'. Secondly, it was assumed that the former would be mainly, but not entirely, middle class, destined for government, the professions and business, and that the latter would be, and would remain, working class. In 1903, post-elementary school education was therefore divided into three streams (upper, lower and intermediate) effectively narrowed to two by the changes of 1920. A small number of exceptionally gifted poorer children might, if spotted young enough and given an unusual degree of support by their parents and teachers, make it to the top stream, but it was assumed that most would remain, and should remain, in the social class into which they had been born.

These assumptions did not pass without criticism. Ramsay Mac-Donald was one of the few politicians who saw the new system for what it was: 'A scheme for helping a few individuals to rise from one

Dignitaries at a launch at Stephens of Linthouse, 1891.

Provost Chisholm on his visit to London in 1902 extolled Glasgow's civic enterprises; the lower half of his escutcheon refers incidentally to his campaigns against bookies and barmaids.

Football as recreation: the amateur game in Glasgow, 1890.

Football as business: William Struth, manager of Rangers since 1920,
receives his portrait on his retirement in 1954.

Football as escape: Ibrox in its urban desert,
seen in an early air photograph, 1921.

Muirhead Bone's Glasgow: ABOVE the barrows near Albert Bridge, 1910;
BELOW mounting a great gun, 1917: 'a glow of pride is always felt in a gun shop
when one more masterpiece like this is ready at last to go out to its work'.

Gladstone's Scotland: ABOVE the campaign train; note the thistles flanking the bust; BELOW banner carried by the stonemasons in the Third Reform Bill demonstration in Glasgow.

THE NATION AND THE QUEEN ARE AT YOUR BACK
THE FEW MUST BOW TO THE MANY WILLIE;
AS THEY DID BEFORE IN DAYS OF YORE
IN 1832 WILLIE.
YOU'LL GET YOUR NAME CUT OUT IN STANE
IN HONOUR OF YOUR FAME WILLIE;
IT'LL MAKE THE TORIES A' THINK SHAME
OF 1884 WILLIE.
(THIS POLE CARRIED A BANNER IN 1832)

Protest and repression on the Red Clyde;
ABOVE LEFT the rent strike demonstration, 1916;
BELOW LEFT David Kirkwood, engineers' leader, batoned by police in 1919 as he leaves
the City Chambers to attempt to quieten the crowd outside.
The picture was published under the caption, 'a striker struck'.
ABOVE the strikers in George Square, 1919: did it look like Petrograd?
BELOW tanks in the Cattle Market a few days later: the Government thought it did.

ABOVE the start of a march by the Dundee unemployed, 1930s.
BELOW dinner given by the British Legion for local unemployed men at St Andrews, 1937.

class into another ... nothing to do with the improvement of national education.' He went on to say that the system 'would fail and ought to fail, if its effect was to form a new series of classes and sub-classes, of servants and masters, of subordinates and superiors, determined by the schools through which they had gone'.[32]

A. S. Neill, as a young teacher in a village board school, was oppressed by the overwhelming sense of futility of what he was set to do by the regulations of the Scottish Education Department:

> Tonight after my bairns had gone away, I sat down on a desk and thought, What does it all mean? What am I trying to do? These boys are going out to the fields to plough; these girls are going to farms as servants ... I can teach them to read, and they will read serials in the drivelling weeklies, I can teach them to write, and they will write pathetic notes to me bye and bye; I can teach them to count, and they will never count more than the miserable sum they receive as a weekly wage ... My work is hopeless, for education should aim at bringing up a new generation that will be better than the old. The present system is to produce the same kind of man as we see today.[33]

Such reflections, however, were remote from the calcifying orthodoxy of the SED, encapsulated in 1920 in the reply of Struthers' deputy and successor in office, George Macdonald, to the criticism by its own advisory committee that the proposed dual classification of children was too rigid:

> They have ignored the fundamental fact that the school population falls into two parts—the majority of distinctly limited intelligence, and an extremely important minority drawn from all ranks and classes who are capable of responding to a much more severe call ... Education must be adapted to their capacities, and matters will not be helped by ignoring the difference between them.[34]

He dismissed as utopian the committee's alternative scheme, based, he said, on the untenable proposition that 'all save a few backward children are capable of profiting by the same sort of education'.

The consequence of this thinking was a new division, worked out by stages, between what came in 1940 to be called 'senior secondary schools', which provided for the minority five-year courses and led to the Leaving Certificate at seventeen or eighteen, and 'junior secondaries', which provided inferior three-year courses for 'the majority of distinctly limited intelligence'. How enormous the majority proved to be can be seen from the figures of school-leavers in 1951: 87 per cent of the occupied population aged twenty to twenty-four had left school at fifteen or younger: a mere 5 per cent had left aged seventeen to nineteen. It was a less favourable proportion even than in England. The system had defined the overwhelming majority of the population as stupid, and reaped the miserable consequence.

It is difficult to tell what the Scottish population thought of their education. They had long been conditioned, in a spirit of 'here's tae us, wha's like us', into accepting it as the best in the world. By the 1950s, however, external observers and incomers were seldom as enthusiastic about the traditions of Scottish education as the native teachers. Their professional body, the EIS, was demonstrating its complacency by refusing to allow those trained elsewhere to teach in Scottish schools in the public sector. Thus a Frenchman trained in France was not allowed to teach French in a Scottish school without taking a Scottish teaching qualification, so very few Scottish children attained any fluency in foreign languages. Almost everywhere there was an absence of 'child-centred education'. Whereas elsewhere since the 1890s—in Scandinavia, France, America, even England—there had been rapid development of techniques that worked through the psychology of the pupils to develop their personality and capture their interests, the approach in the Scottish classroom remained, at least for most of the first half of the twentieth century, grimly authoritarian and narrow. This was perhaps due in part to the underdeveloped character of infant teaching in nineteenth-century Scotland, where despite having Robert Owen and David Stow as the early British pioneers in the field, there was little popular response to the idea that young children could benefit from early schooling: in 1861 about 2 per cent of the under-fives were at school in Scotland compared to 16 per cent in England and Wales, and though the figures were higher the gap was not narrower by the end of the century. Infant education elsewhere, as Dr Roberts points out, was 'almost inevitably associated with free, child-centred, and progressive methods of instruction': where it was weak, as in Scotland, a strong lobby for the child-centred approach was lacking.[35]

Above all, at the top, in the SED and in the Scottish training colleges, formalism reigned supreme: the theories of Continental and European reformers were treated with a smug indifference, and the ideas of the Scottish educational dissidents A. S. Neill and R. F. Mackenzie, though accorded wide respect abroad, were regarded at home either as fads or as subversion. Even the theories of John Dewey, propounded in the United States at the end of the nineteenth century and universally accepted elsewhere, only began systematically to enter Scottish schools in the 1950s. Dewey had, for example, stressed the importance of technical training as an indispensible part of the liberal curriculum: 'In Scottish schools the result [by the 1930s] was a tiny handwork department, consisting often of a single room, in which a few elementary processes in working with wood were taught to a handful of boys, generally those too poorly endowed to tackle the stiffer "academic" subjects.'[36] In short, anything but the most basic curriculum taught in the most traditional way was regarded as superfluous in most schools until after the Second World War: most education was what it had always been, a drilling in the three Rs. If the child could not understand the lesson, the tawse was on the desk.

Perhaps, then, it is in the history of the school more than in any other aspect of recent social history that the key lies to some of the more depressing aspects of modern Scotland. If there are in this country too many people who fear what is new, believe the difficult to be impossible, draw back from responsibility, and afford established authority and tradition an exaggerated respect, we can reasonably look for an explanation in the institutions that moulded them.

There were many ordinary individuals in the teaching profession itself, of course, whose attitude was different from that of officialdom, who were puzzled by the shortage of resources in the face of great need (as they still are), and who urgently wished to begin something new, and more child-centred. Such, for instance, was Janetta Bowie, who arrived in a Clydeside school in the 1930s to teach a class of seven-year-olds and found on the teacher's desk, apart from the register, 'only two other articles ... a Bible and a strap'. The headmaster, 'who seems to merge fittingly into the background of this dingy school as with a protective colouration', measured out the cardboard for the primary modelling class to the last inch. Let her have the last word:

There are fifty children. It seems strange that I should have fifty to teach when all the time there are teachers with nobody to teach. The unemployed teachers could all be employed if we had a reasonable number each. Of course, they might need some more schools, and that would supply employment for some of the queues at the Labour

Exchanges. But this line of thought is altogether too reasonable. Human beings are not actuated by reason—only by emotion, and expediency.[37]

Indeed, the more it changes, the more it remains the same.

CHAPTER X

The Working-Class Radical Tradition
to 1885

1

Political and social change in Scotland, over the century from 1830 to 1950, was gradual, reformist, constitutional. In the end it was considerable, though perhaps less sweeping than in most European countries. In the end, as at the beginning, Scotland remained a capitalist country: 'property' was intact. In the end, as at the beginning, effective power and wealth remained in the hands of a small circle of people, though not necessarily the same type of people, and not often the descendants of the same people as those Lord Cockburn and his friends had known in the 1840s. In the end, as at the beginning, Scotland remained British: the Union was intact.

The path from 1830 to 1950 (and beyond) passed through several thickets where the rulers, unable to see their way, cried out in alarm—as they had done in the 1830s and 1840s: Chartism was followed by Keir Hardie's Socialism in the 1880s, then by the Red Clydeside of the 1914–20 period, then by the 1930s, with their concatenation of a revived nationalism, mass unemployment and left-wing politics. These were each milestones in that they marked, or led to, changes in attitude, moderate shifts in power: they were also false alarms, in the sense that they seemed to portend much more basic alterations—revolutions, cataclysms—that never took place.

In accounting for the relative conservatism of Scottish social and political change it is not enough to credit governments with wisdom, duplicity or infinite cunning: Scotland (and Britain) was not ruled by particularly subtle men. It is necessary above all to understand the nature of the opposition. What did those who stood for basic change actually want, and how did they propose to set about it? Our two final chapters address these problems.

The first monster petition of the Chartists, bearing 1,200,000 signatures from all parts of Britain, was presented to the House of Commons on 14 June 1839. Its demands, the 'six points' of universal suffrage, payment of MPs, abolition of property qualifications, equal electoral districts, the secret ballot and annual parliaments, were rejected by Parliament in the ensuing debate by a contemptuous majority of 235 to 46. Joseph Hume, opponent of the Corn Laws and ally of trade union rights, the most distinguished Scottish proponent of radical electoral reform in the house, was one of a tiny number who spoke eloquently in its defence. Nothing happened. Property was shaken but unmoved, as it was to be by the even larger petitions of 1842 and 1848.

At the time of the Chartists, the radical tradition in Scotland already had half a century of agitation behind it: that is to say, ever since the foundation of the Scottish Friends of the People in 1792, groups and individuals had been pressing for basic reforms of the constitution that would give one man one vote, in the belief that democratic representation of this sort could be equated with human liberty. The earliest radical societies perhaps made no great appeal to the bulk of Scottish wage-earners—urban labourers, colliers, seamen and the like: their membership was characteristically drawn from the ranks of small shopkeepers, small handicraft producers and their social equals, but with an all-important leavening from skilled labour, the numerous and influential handloom weavers, for whom the doctrines of Paine did have something like mass appeal. An unsympathetic versifier expressed it thus in 1793:

> The worthy members of these worthy meetings,
> Are cobblers some, some brewers to their trade,
> Weavers are some, some finely thrive by beatings,
> And some by their smart feet do make their bread.
> Old toothless schoolmasters, and furious tanners,
> Tailors, hair-dressers, deep-read butchers too,
> All list with zeal under fair Reform's banner,
> And that they will be great men vow.[1]

It was expected by some that economic growth—or what

eighteenth-century writers more elegantly termed the 'increase of opulence'—would decrease the number of those who worked for wages and increase those who worked for themselves, and in doing so lessen the servile dependence of the poor upon the rich. As John Millar, Professor of Civil Law at the University of Glasgow and later himself a radical sympathizer, put it:

> When the arts begin to be cultivated in a country, the labouring part of the inhabitants are enabled to procure subsistence in a different manner ... instead of becoming servants to anybody, they often find it more profitable to work at their own charges and to vend the product of their labour. As in this situation their gain depends upon a variety of customers, they have little to fear from the displeasure of any single person ...[2]

As the eighteenth century merged into the nineteenth, however, it became obvious that the employed proletariat, far from withering away under the forces of the industrial revolution, would greatly increase; as it did so, the appeal of the radicals—the appeal of democracy itself—bit more deeply into the wage-earning echelons of society. Agricultural labourers, it is true, remained uninflammable, but the urban work force was increasingly involved as it grew in size and complexity. The period between 1816 and 1820 was particularly dangerous, with weavers and demobilized soldiers taking to the streets in organized demonstrations, open drilling with arms, and rumours of an Anglo-Scottish radical alliance to bring the Tory Government to its knees by force. At the time of the so-called Radical War in 1820, many tens of thousands came out on strike in the west of Scotland in response to a placard calling them 'to desist from their Labour, from and after this day, the first of April; and attend wholly to the recovery of their Rights'.

A decade later, during the agitation preceding the Scottish Reform Act of 1832, the huge processions of operatives marching peaceably behind the symbols of their trades in Glasgow, Edinburgh and elsewhere sent shivers even down the spines of those Whig middle-class reformers who were using them for their own ends to bring pressure on Tory opponents: 'a gratifying yet fearful spectacle', Cockburn called the thousands who marched with their 'groves of banners' through the centre of Glasgow.[3] The Act increased the Scottish electorate from 4500 to 65,000 but did nothing whatsoever for the remaining 400,000 or so other adult male Scots who were left without a vote: it was this situation the Chartists set out to remedy seven years later.

It was natural, therefore, that by the 1830s, political radicalism should have a working-class character more pronounced than that of its eighteenth-century progenitors. Part of its support came from workers in occupations either greatly enlarged by the industrial revolution or called into being by its inventions—like the Lanarkshire miners, or the textile spinners of the Glasgow and Aberdeen factories (where the women as well as the men played a part in the agitation). It has to be said, though, that such 'new workers' often tended to be more passive than active in their support, more ephemeral than constant in their loyalty, and more in the rank-and-file than in the leadership compared with older groups. Part of the support came, as before, from the tens of thousands of handloom weavers, whose lot was becoming ever more desperate as competition with the factories and the Government's refusal to assist them drove them to the wall. Part came from tradesmen in other overcrowded and declining sectors like shoe-making and tailoring, and from people in low middle-class positions who were no nearer the vote than before—those lineal descendants of the 'toothless schoolmasters and furious tanners' of 1793. It was they in particular who often provided local leadership for Scottish Chartism in the 1840s, which thus remained, despite everything, conservatively rooted in the values and traditions of the independent craftsman and small producer that would have been familiar fifty years before.

The radical tradition embodied in the Chartist cause in Scotland indeed owed its being to the great eighteenth-century ideals of the American and French Revolutions, as subsequently sifted and restated by such Englishmen as Tom Paine, William Cobbett and Thomas Attwood. It retained, however, a native flavour that made the Chartist of Glasgow or Aberdeen distinctly different from the Chartist of Oldham, and another political animal altogether from any Paris *sansculotte* or *communard*. As noted in Chapter I, the Scottish Chartist characteristically retained a deep faith in the virtues of moderation and the power of reasoned argument, combined with a marked reluctance to condone violence as a means even to a good end and a belief that co-operation with the middle classes could still ultimately pay higher dividends than the class struggle. This 'moral force' streak in the Scottish tradition, though it clearly went back to the moderation and constitutionalism of the Friends of the People, was probably stronger in the 1830s and 1840s than it had been in the interim: in the years leading up to the Radical War, inflammatory talk of 'death or liberty' and pike-making in the weaving sheds had not been uncommon among the radicals of the west of Scotland, but when in 1830 an Englishman from Preston endeavoured to rouse the Glasgow operatives 'in the style of 1817 and 1820' he was rebuked in their newspaper, the *Herald to the Trades Advocate*, in these words:

> Mr Johnston does not seem to be aware that a great change has been effected in the mode of thinking and speaking among us, since those days. We do not now require the aid of vulgar or violent personalities, in pointing out the abuses which we are subjected to, from the system of misgovernment. It is bad measures, not men, that must first be exposed and removed, and against which all our energies should be directed.[4]

On the other side of the fence, despite talk by the upper class of the immediate danger of revolution, experienced and responsible politicians sometimes compared the mood of the 1840s favourably with earlier years: Peel, in a speech on the European disturbances of 1848, invited Parliament to consider the peaceful spirit prevailing in towns like Paisley, 'where in former periods—in such times as 1818 and 1819—social order has been shaken to its foundations'.[5] Despite this, however, it is important not to over-emphasize the class-collaborationist element in Scottish Chartism. For one thing, the most eloquent spokesman for moderation and moral force was regarded by many local Chartist societies with distrust. The Revd Patrick Brewster's efforts, from his power-base in Paisley, to persuade the movement to form 'New Moral Force Associations' that would formally disavow violence under all circumstances had very limited success; such bodies were indeed established in Paisley itself, in Edinburgh and Perth, and in five small towns, but even in Paisley and Edinburgh the Chartists did not consistently endorse this policy. The moral force men were partly balanced by a handful of smaller Chartist associations, in Forfar, Renfrew, Elderslie and the Vale of Leven, that even went so far as to declare it necessary for free citizens to possess arms and to be willing to use them in the defence of liberty. Most Scottish Chartists adopted a central position, represented by the Glasgow Association, which began by declaring that the oppressors would never heed moral force unless there was physical force behind it, but went on to say that violence should be used only as a last resort and in response to violence first used against the working classes.[6] Again, the efforts of middle-class Anti-Corn Law Leaguers to build up Complete Suffrage Associations as a bridge between themselves and the Chartists sometimes seduced individual Chartist leaders, but was largely repudiated by the rank-and-file. Even those most to the fore in the creation of Chartist Churches and Total Abstinence Societies—distinctive characteristics of Scottish Chartism and comparatively rare in England—yielded nothing in their call for a democratic society: 'Interests in such issues', says the historian of Aberdeen Chartism, 'never distracted the Chartists from their primary task of building up support for political reform.'[7] And Patrick Brewster himself, when suspended by the General Assembly for a sermon whose 'drift and tendency' was 'to excite the humbler against the higher classes of society', responded that Scotland's social health needed 'not purity, gentleness, peaceableness, and all that beautiful train of virtues ... but only a single virtue, the virtue of JUSTICE.'[8] He gained few friends among his own class for plain speaking.

Strangely enough, especially in view of the gales that were rending Europe in the 1840s, that 'Springtime of Nations', nationalism was never a conspicuous part of Scottish Chartism. It is doubtful if it had been much stronger earlier in the Radical tradition. Thomas Muir, the exiled leader of the Friends of the People, had, it is true, addressed a series of appeals from France couched in stirring nationalist language, but they were perhaps intended to appeal more to his hosts than to his countrymen, on whom, in any case, they had little obvious effect. English radical writers, especially John Cartwright and William Cobbett, often made appeals to a mythic English past, with reference to an imaginary Anglo-Saxon democracy, the 'Norman yoke', King John and Oliver Cromwell. Sometimes the Scots adopted this, quite unhistorically, as their own, the strikers of 1820 coming out in response to a placard on the streets that referred to 'those rights consecrated ... by Magna Carta and the Bill of Rights'. More often, they supplemented the English tradition by finding instances in their own past of popular resistance to tyranny and celebrating them with an enthusiasm that sometimes made the authorities nervous. Thus in 1814, 15,000 people came to Bannockburn to commemorate the 500th anniversary of the defeat of Edward II, and next year a Strathaven radical organized a demonstration of 10,000 'democratic people' to march 'to the place where the Covenanters defeated Claverhouse, and from thence to a cairn of stones or tumulus on the farm of Allanton, Ayrshire, about two miles from the field of Drumclog, and where they imagined Sir William Wallace had fought his first battle with the English'.[9] Significant, too, was the use of 'Scots wha' hae', Burns' resounding patriotic song, as a rallying call for radicals in the period 1817-20. This so infuriated the magistrates of Paisley, for example, that they considered making it an offence to tap out the tune on a drum. However the song was also popular among the cotton spinners of Lancashire, not because they were expatriate Scots but because it carried, for them, the universal message about resistance to tyrants, 'death, or liberty'. In exactly the same spirit, presumably, the Scots in 1820 responded to the reference to Magna Carta.

From such patriotic seeds as these, in other European countries under union with a powerful neighbour, like Norway or Portugal, passions grew, and ultimately independence and separation from the union partner was reaped. This was not to be the case in Scotland, which developed instead a kind of dual ethnic consciousness, composed partly of loyalty to the actuality and opportunity of modern Britain, and partly of loyalty to the memory and tradition of Scotland. It was a consciousness that working-class radicals shared with other parts of society, for Scots of all classes and political persuasions certainly cherished a sense of their past distinctiveness. The appeal of the historical novels and epic poems and ballads of Sir Walter Scott to the middle classes was one manifestation of this, though their patronizing tone towards the 'commonality' irritated working-class readers.[10] No one else could have been more loyal to the Act of Union or opposed to radicalism than Scott, a convinced Tory of the old school, but no one did more to further the study of the history of pre-Union Scotland, by founding clubs devoted to rescuing and publishing the key documents. He was the archetypal patriotic Scot who accepted being British as a matter of course.

A writer of more plebeian roots was Hugh Miller, son of a Cromarty skipper and himself for a time a working mason, in many ways a nonconformist but no friend of Chartism either. He recalled another facet of popular nationalist feeling:

I first became thoroughly a Scot some time in my tenth year; and the consciousness of country has remained tolerably strong within me ever since. My uncle James had procured for me from a neighbour the loan of a common stall-edition of Blind Harry's 'Wallace', as modernized by Hamilton ... I was intoxicated with the fiery narratives of the blind ministrel, with his fierce breathings of hot, intolerant patriotism, and his stories of astonishing prowess; and, glorying in being a Scot, and the countryman of Wallace and Graham, I longed for a war with the Southron, that the wrongs and sufferings of these noble heroes might yet be avenged ...[11]

Boyish loyalty in 1812 did not, however, lead the mature Miller to adult rage in the Springtime of Nations, but rather to a sensitivity about the distinctiveness of Scotland in a British society. He became a leading lay figure in the Disruption of the Church of Scotland in 1843, partly because he believed the State was interfering in an ignorant and unwarranted way in the internal affairs of the Scottish kirk; but it never occurred to him, or to the Free Church, to repudiate the ideal of a link between the Church and the British State.

The Scottish Chartists in the 1830s and 1840s were in exactly this position. At the start they followed the lead of London, Birmingham, and the north of England without question, but argued with the General Convention about the wisdom of backing the Charter with a general strike or 'sacred month' that might slide into violence or a revolution. They called a Scottish delegate conference in Glasgow to express their dissent, and established a Central Committee for Scotland. But Scottish Chartism remained part and parcel of the British Chartist movement, seeking reform of the Parliament at Westminster, and British rather than simply Scottish liberty.

Such dualities of consciousness—of being Scottish and British, of being Breton and French, of being Catalan and Spanish—have been much commoner in European history since 1800 than is often acknowledged; they are difficult for historians and political scientists to accommodate into their schemes, because there is always a temptation either to denigrate the 'lesser' consciousness (Scottish, Breton, Catalan) as mere regionality, unlikely to have serious leverage as a political force, or alternatively to mistake it for the powerful inner passion of a submerged nation that must, in the end, break out in rebellion or independence. In fact the duality of consciousness represents a real emotional tension, a contradiction within the citizen that is never resolved. In happy times, when opportunity knocks for the inhabitants of the dual state and when the sensitivity of the larger unit to the needs of the smaller is not too blunted, the lesser consciousness exists as an important part of the cultural and spiritual support of the Scot, or the Breton, or the Catalan, but does not exert itself except in sentimental expression of regional loyalties. In less happy times, when an empire falls or an economy receives a jolt to its accustomed patterns of growth, the lesser consciousness may grow obsessionally powerful, and form a weapon in the hands of the peripheral nation to extract concessions from the seat of government in London, Paris or Madrid. It is an irony of Scottish history, however, that every effective concession by the centre to the periphery—for example the establishment of the Scottish Office in 1885 to meet the needs of Scotland to have properly framed legislation, or the establishment of the Scottish Development Agency in 1975 to direct government assistance into the Scottish economy—has resulted in the tightening of bonds between the centre and the periphery. It is a type of nationalism which, since it seeks special consideration for Scotland without ever rejecting the loyalty towards the larger unit, leads ultimately to greater dependency, not to separation.

2

This, however, is to digress: the early Victorian world was still far from thinking in terms of any sort of government intervention as being a good thing, except in exceptional circumstances. Chartism was about liberty, about the political self-help of the people acting collectively. It failed, dealt a mortal blow in 1842 by the rejection of its second monster petition to the Westminster Parliament and by the subsequent failure of sporadic political strikes, and finally extinguished by the collapse of the 1848 revival. By 1852 the movement was a memory. It is, however, possible to trace the working-class radical tradition that began with Tom Paine and reached its apogee in Chartism, continuing as a thread through Scottish political life for the succeeding century. Despite the infusions between the 1880s and the 1920s of socialist ideas relating to the common ownership of the means of production and the notion of a class war that were very alien to Paine, some of the older radical tradition's most characteristic attitudes and values remained prominent in Scottish political life almost until the Second World War. In their emphasis on individual dignity and liberty, on self-help, and on the possibility of all men working together for the common good, these older traditions could only partly be accommodated either with Marxist-Leninism or with twentieth-century theories of the welfare state.

The immediate beneficiary of the failure of Chartism from 1850 was the Liberal Party, which for the next seventy years was to owe a great deal to the support of the working classes. In every election down to 1922 (except for the 'khaki election' during the Boer War in 1900), the party won an outright majority of Scottish seats; in some years of Gladstonian triumph, like 1868 and 1880, there were fifty-two or fifty-three Liberals and only seven or eight of their opponents returned for the Scottish seats. The towns and cities were particularly loyal: the Glasgow voters, for example, only once returned a Conservative MP for any of their seats between 1832 and 1886.

The Victorian Liberals were, in effect, a consortium of three different social and political groupings—the Whigs, the so-called 'radical' middle-class Liberals, and the 'Lib-labs' of the working classes. The Whigs were the heroes of the first Scottish Reform Act in 1832, aristocrats like the Duke of Argyll, patrician lawyers and intellectuals like Lord Cockburn and Thomas B. Macaulay in Edinburgh, wealthy merchants like James Oswald in Glasgow: they were reluctant to extend reform further, intolerant both of sectarianism in religion and of the rights of trade unions. The middle-class radicals were represented by men like Joseph Hume, successively MP for Aberdeen and Montrose burghs, and, later, Duncan McLaren, the Lord Provost of Edinburgh, MP for the city and John Bright's brother-in-law. They were, characteristically, enthusiasts for the further extension of the franchise to most urban householders by the Second Reform Act in 1868, doctrinaire free-traders, and believers in anti-drink legislation; they opposed the factory acts, any generous reform of the poor law or further extension of the rights of trade unions, and they were especially strongly against the privileges of the established Church of Scotland after 1843, being members of the Free Church or the United Presbyterians to a man. The Scottish Lib-labs scarcely ever walked the corridors of power at Westminster but were nevertheless a distinctive and important pressure group. They welcomed every step in the extension of the franchise, believed in the need for factory acts and unions, and, although personally often teetotal, would in the early days mainly have preferred moral persuasion to law in limiting the drink traffic. They deplored all sectarian politics that got in the way of improving educational facilities for the working classes, as squabbles about control of the schools so often did. On the other hand they were at one with middle-class Liberals in wanting to keep down the poor rates, believing hardly less fervently than Duncan McLaren that a man should take care of his own social security by the systematic practice of thrift.

With such divergences in the troika, the unity of Liberalism was often in danger of being overturned, especially in the absence of a strong Conservative enemy. Middle-class radicals frequently opposed Whigs, or ran candidates pledged to disestablish the Church of Scotland, or were themselves opposed by Lib-labs who resented their hostility towards legalizing trade union picketing. The party eventually split, of course, over the question of Gladstone's support for Irish Home Rule in 1886. Until then, what held it together in Scotland was a common belief in the virtues of self-help, a dislike of hereditary privilege as enshrined in the values of the Conservative Party, and a certain identification with patriotic Scottish or nationalist sentiment within the framework of the United Kingdom. All these things appealed to the skilled workers, often themselves ex-Chartists in the 1850s, who formed the rank-and-file of the Lib-lab sector of the party.

It was, for example, certainly not difficult for middle-class and working-class Scots to share a wide range of values relating to self-help and thrift, particularly at the social interstices where a skilled artisan might in some circumstances hope to pull himself up by his bootstraps to the status of a small employer, or a small independent businessman fear the danger of being dragged down by bankruptcy into the morass of the proletariat. For such people, total abstinence made sense: the marginal pounds spent on drink and the marginal hours spent being drunk could determine the course of a man's whole life. Such men also believed, with scarcely less fervour, in the virtue of saving, supporting the thrift institutions of savings bank, friendly society and co-operative movement. The foundation of the Scottish Co-operative Wholesale Society in 1868 was a milestone in this respect. No doubt the exceptional meanness of the Scottish Poor Law, even after the reform of 1845, in refusing relief to the unemployed made the practice of thrift even more necessary to the Scottish working man. He saved his pennies not because he was duped by middle-class propaganda into believing that saving was a respectable bourgeois virtue, but because his savings were all that stood between his family and destitution during the repeated downturns in the trade cycle.

The humble shopkeeper, the small employer and the skilled worker also shared a profound belief in the value of education as a good in itself, and as a ladder to a more secure position for their children. Thus the lower middle class and the Edinburgh Trades Council were allies in the long and ultimately unsuccessful struggle, lasting from 1870 to 1885, to save the ancient Heriot's Hospital and its associated outdoor schools (which the parent institution had established in poor quarters of the city) from being taken over or closed down by the professional classes, who wanted to divert the endowment fund to make a select school tailored to their own needs: 'It was not', said the Trades Council, 'so much the wish of George Heriot to turn out great, and learned, and shining men, as to raise up a respectable, thinking, able class of artizans or citizens, and to do so more especially by helping those who had not the means to help themselves.'[12] In Edinburgh itself this sort of argument was lost, due, in part at least, to the great power of the rich men of the Merchant Company. In Glasgow it had a good deal more success, and the secondary education provided by that city's school board at the end of the nineteenth century was much more widely available to the upper working class and lower middle class than its equivalent in the capital.

Concern over education and struggles for control of the town schools merged with a further shared value, civic pride. We noted in Chapter I how readily an alliance was forged in Paisley between the Chartist unemployed and the Anti-Corn Law Leaguers on the town council, based on a strong sense of locality rather than class, anti-central government rather than anti-employer. Pride in one's town remained an intensely strong community bond, bringing political rewards and personal satisfaction to those in all walks of life who were generous with time and money. Thus MPs like the Liberal members for Dundee sought to win the approbation of the electorate by donating land for civic parks. Lord Provosts like William Chambers of Edinburgh sought to leave their mark on a city by an impressive building or a slum-clearance programme such as that commemorated in Chambers' Street. And former Chartist notables also did their bit for the community, as instanced by Robert Cranston's private ventures in a teetotal coffee house and two temperance hotels in the capital, or James Moir's public-spirited work as a town councillor in Glasgow:

> His untiring efforts to preserve and improve our public parks, and the introduction of the 'Urinal' by him, in spite of sneers and opposition both in and out of the town council, opened up other sanitary improvements not to be credited now, except by those who remember the indecencies and filth of the closes and stairs in ancient Glasgow.[13]

The civic radicalism of middle-class and working-class leaders was also expressed in their shared hatred of aristocratic landowners who maintained in certain country constituencies island fortresses of Tory patronage and power against the eroding Liberal sea. To radicals of all origins and shades, ex-Anti-Corn Law Leaguer and ex-Chartist alike, the landlord was the evil dragon of the old regime, wounded in 1832, yet still a menace to those who lived in its proximity, and still awaiting its chance to sally out once more against the heroes of progress. Whig leaders with their own broad acres, like the Duke of Argyll, naturally saw things rather differently, but Gladstone himself did not hesitate to describe the political conflict between the Liberals and the Conservatives as a battle between 'the class', by which he meant all who enjoyed hereditary privilege, and 'the masses', everybody else. 'You are opposed throughout the country', he cried in a good rabble-rousing speech in Glasgow, 'by a compact army, and that army is the case of the class against the masses.'[14] It was the language of open class war, albeit not drawn up on Marxian lines, and it rang a bell for urban men every time they heard of a Tory landowner refusing a site for a Free Church congregation or sweeping crofters out of the glens and into their own labour market.

Opposition to hereditary power had a long radical ancestry and could lead to outright anti-monarchical principles. Tom Paine himself had exclaimed, in a devastatingly sardonic passage, 'Kings succeed each other not as rationals but as animals ... to be a king requires only the animal figure of man ... an hereditary governor is as inconsistent as an hereditary author.'[15] Republican sentiment after mid-century was still powerful among some Scottish radicals in the working class, though not in the middle class. In some circumstances it could merge with working-class anti-clericalism equally rooted in the eighteenth-century thinkers of England and France. In Scotland this might find expression in scepticism about the *obiter dicta* of the great kirk leaders, in particular of Thomas Chalmers' schemes for a powerful revived ecclesiastical authority that would force the common people, in the words of one critic, 'to submit like the serfs of Muscovy ... or the bestial of a Highland laird'.[16] It did not, however, normally result in an attack on Presbyterian beliefs *per se*, which were comfortably assumed to be rational. On the other hand, radicals of all shades might on occasion be drawn into no-popery campaigns which also fed on nationalist and racial tensions between the Irish immigrant and the native population.

One of the channels into which the energies of working-class radicals might flow in the 1850s and 1860s was illustrated by the papers of John McAdam, organizer of the 'Black Flag' pro-Reform demonstration in Glasgow in 1832, emigrant to Canada and the United States in 1833, and participant in the last days of the Chartist excitement on his return in 1848.[17] The next quarter of a century he devoted to the cause of European liberation movements as a close friend and correspondent of Garibaldi, Mazzini and Kossuth, bringing with him a radical thirst for liberty, a republicanism, an anti-clericalism and even a nationalism that the ruling powers in Britain might well feel happy was directed to affairs outside Scotland. 'From my boyhood I had warmly sympathized with the oppressed Peoples in their death bondage to despot and priest,' he wrote in his autobiography. In his letters he referred to Queen Victoria's predecessors as 'the beastly sons of old mad George', and the efforts to commemorate her husband as 'vain memorials for doing nothing'. He described his own efforts to establish free libraries and reading rooms in Glasgow in 1876 as 'opposed by the Catholic Priests in the interests of ignorance, nor will we get more help from our Protestant Priests now than we did when we tried them on behalf of the Protestant College of Eperjes.' The construction of the Wallace memorial outside Stirling owed much to his initiative and energy, and he persuaded Garibaldi, Mazzini, Kossuth, Karl Blind, and Louis Blanc each to send messages to be placed in the tower within a frame made from wood of the Wallace Oak of Elderslie. He explained in his letter to Garibaldi that this would assist the 'cause of Nationality' in Europe by making 'our aristocracy and the trading class "who care for none of these things"' aware of the relationship between what he plainly regarded as a historical struggle for freedom in Scotland which had in some sense already been won long ago, and the contemporary struggle abroad which had yet to taste the fruits of success.

McAdam's enthusiasm for liberty in a foreign field was very widely shared among the Scottish working class. Kossuth, 'with his large lustrous eyes and almost theatrical posture', received a rapturous welcome 'amidst deafening cheers and the waving of handkerchiefs' when he appeared at the City Hall, Glasgow,[18] and his wife, amid comparable scenes, was presented with a specially commissioned shawl by the weavers of Paisley. Thanks largely to McAdam, he was followed within a few years by Karl Blind lecturing on Poland, and Louis Blanc on France. Scottish volunteers went to serve with Garibaldi, each 'with two sets of tartan shirts and bonnets with the Scottish thistle to show their nationality'. They were not called upon to fight. When a lecture tour of Scotland by the great Italian hero had to be called off in 1863, there were 200,000 disappointed applicants for tickets to be placated by the organizers.

All this political activity in an international cause ultimately helped to generate an atmosphere in the late 1860s in which the working classes turned with renewed enthusiasm to the cause of British Parliamentary reform itself. When the bandwagon started to roll again, it culminated first in the passage of the Second Reform Act in 1867–8 (giving the vote to ratepaying male householders and ten-pound-a-year lodgers in the towns, and to small owners and middling tenants in the countryside), and then to the Third Reform Act of 1884–5 (further extending the vote, especially among rural householders, to bring in such groups as crofters, miners and farm-labourers).

The passage of each Act was preceded by great demonstrations in the main cities, no whit less impressive than those of 1832. These processions were pure street theatre, encapsulating more than anything else in the nineteenth century the character of proletarian Liberalism, and emphasizing its civic and craft pride, its class feelings against landlords, its sense of belonging to a coherent tradition of reforming zeal that stretched back at least a century, and its loyalty to the Liberal leaders felt to be its modern standard bearers. The Glasgow demonstration of 1884, intended to put pressure on an obstructive Tory House of Lords, involved (according to the press) 64,000 in the procession and another 200,000 gathering to greet them on Glasgow Green. They carried countless pictures of Gladstone and many of Bright, a flag from as far back as 1774, banners from 1832 and from Chartist days, and models and mottoes old and new. The French polishers, for example, carried a miniature wardrobe first borne in 1832, and a flag inscribed, 'The French polishers will polish off the Lords and make the cabinet shine.' The upholsterers had a sofa first carried in 1832, the potters a model kiln with the words, 'We'll fire them up,' the sawyers a banner with the device of two circular saws and the words, 'The crooked Lords—we'll cut them straight.' The executive of the Scottish Land Restoration League passed with the motto, 'God gave the land to the people, the Lords took the land from the people.' The employees of Charles Tennant carried a dozen flags and banners, with a model of a cooper at work made in 1754 and borne in the demonstrations of 1832, 1866 and 1883. The fleshers simply led an ox with a placard round its neck, 'The House of Lords.' The basic message was clear—the 'class' obstructed reform, the 'masses' were here to demand it.[19]

The Third Reform Act has been described as 'a bold and logical measure granting manhood suffrage in town and country alike'.[20] Had it achieved this end, or been intended to do so, working-class radical support for the Liberals might appear totally justified in the perspective of its own tradition, Gladstone giving what Paine sought. Unfortunately, due to the continued existence of groups who were not enfranchised (servants living-in, sons living at home, soldiers in barracks, those in receipt of poor relief, and those who had not paid their rates), and to the complexity of the laws relating to voter registration (admittedly better in Scotland than in England), the Act left some 40 per cent of adult males in the United Kingdom still unenfranchised in 1911, clearly concentrated in the poor and younger working class.[21] In truth, Paine and Gladstone were very different animals. For Paine, the right of a man to participate in political government was innate, resting on his nature as a human being, a sentiment rendered in Robert Burns' paean to democracy, 'a man's a man for a' that'. For Gladstone, by instinct more Whig than democrat, the right to vote was a moral privilege to be extended to a respectable class as and when it showed itself capable of acting responsibly. His was a train of thought that also went back to the eighteenth century, to the preoccupations of the thinkers of the Scottish civic humanist tradition, musing on the problem of how a private citizen could retain virtue in a corrupt world: the Victorian political mind transmuted it into a problem of how the proven virtuous citizen could be granted citizenship without destabilizing the social order.

The Liberal solution was progressively to extend the franchise while maintaining handicaps in the way of those least likely to be respectable and independent in the working class. They thus deliberately penalized those with insecure employment, who had either to move house frequently or to be lodgers with consequent difficulty over voter registration, and the poverty-stricken, who were unable to pay their rates or to support themselves without recourse to poor relief. In so far as the Scottish working-class radicals in the mid-Victorian years allowed themselves to be hoisted onto a Whig and middle-class Liberal bandwagon that made respectability rather than humanity the criteria for a vote, they abandoned a great deal. If it was always possible to respond to that criticism by maintaining that one step in reform implied another, that Liberalism was a gradualist and progressive movement towards a true democracy that could not be regarded as properly finished by the Third Reform Act, then it was also up to the working-class Liberals to be energetic in urging the rest of the party down that path when it showed signs of becoming complacent after 1885. That the local Liberal working-class leadership generally failed to do.

The reason is not hard to find. There is no doubt that most working-class radicals and trade union leaders revelled in their reputation for respectability in the third quarter of the nineteenth century, and they were not at all averse to the Gladstonian idea that by their manifestly excellent qualities they had 'won' the vote. The emphasis on respectability was a divisive element within the working class, too, for it gave a moral dimension to the craftsman's feeling that he was a cut above the labourer in more than just his level of skill. For instance, when slightly higher wages enabled Edinburgh artisans to move away from the old slums of the decaying inner core to the area round Gorgie-Dalry and Easter Road in the last third of the nineteenth century, they were as dismissive as any middle-class observer about those they left behind. 'In a moral point of view these localities will never contain a well-conditioned population,' wrote an 'Old Journeyman Hatter' in his published reminiscences, and the President of the Edinburgh Trades Council, himself a joiner, told the Royal Commission on Housing, 'Properly speaking it is generally the Irish element, labourers and what not, who live in that locality, and I must confess that I do not come into communication with them as a rule.'[22] It was a far cry from 'brothers be for a' that.'

It is an open question as to how far the strength of Irish immigration into Scotland in the 1840s and later helped to drive even deeper wedges into the Scottish working class than had existed before, and to align the respectable skilled workers still more firmly with the middle classes as they drew their skirts aside from the world of the alien and unskilled Paddy. There is no reason at all to think that the Scots were unusually racist. Indian visitors to Scotland in the 1840s, for example, found their unfamiliar colour and exotic dress attracted crowds to stare at them and finger their clothes, but with none of the derision and hostility they encountered from the working class of London. Lithuanian immigrants to the Bellshill area of Lanarkshire from the 1880s found their strange names anglicized to epithets like 'Joe Gorilla' by their fellow workers, and were for a time ostracized as blacklegs and job-stealers—Keir Hardie himself gave evidence to a Select Committee on Immigration as to the menace of these 'hordes from the East' flooding into the iron-works and coal-mines. In a generation, though, they were very peace-fully integrated. So it was with Irish migrants, although their movement was on a very much more substantial scale in the west of Scotland and in Dundee in particular. At first they were distrusted, des-pised, treated as inherently comic, drunken and superstitious, and were the butt of Orangist attack both in the coal-fields and the cities. They did, however, integrate—by joining the trade unions, who first blamed them for coming over and taking Scottish jobs, by forming football clubs (albeit often rivals to Protestant ones), and by ultimately joining political parties with other working men. Certainly, in the perspective of one hundred years, the absorption of the Irish into the social fabric of Scottish life must be considered one of the achievements of Scottish his-tory. But if there was a time when this integration was seriously incom-plete, and when Scottish working men were likely to accept with less questioning the view of the Irish as a wastrel, contaminating element in Scottish life (which was certainly a commonplace opinion among the middle class), it was in these middle Victorian decades.

It would, however, be a great mistake to see the working-class leadership of the Gladstonian period as simply suborned by the political establishment and tricked into assuming a range of middle-class values calculated to cut them off from the body of the proletariat. The Scot-tish artisan believed in thrift, sobriety and education not because he was brainwashed by the upper classes but because these beliefs were functional in his life. They enabled his family to survive in the economic jungle of a society with minimum welfare provision. In fact, along with this working-class ethic of respectability went an emphatic rejection of middle-class condescension, exemplified when the secretary of the Edinburgh Typographical Society called a proposal to form a working men's club 'a hybrid between a soup kitchen and a penny reading room, with in all probability interesting old women in black mittens to talk in a goody-goody strain to the recipients of their bounty'.[23]

The same independence was shown in the artisan's reading habits. The skilled Scottish working man of the 1860s, 1870s and early 1880s was not going to read Marx, and few even followed the English and Scottish socialists of the Owenite and post-Chartist tradition. On the other hand, he was not excited by Thomas Chalmers or Samuel Smiles, whose *Self-Help* was handed round at a meeting of the Edinburgh Trades Council and declared to be unhelpful. Even Walter Scott got the cold shoulder from an avid proletarian reader like John Younger, the Border shoe-maker, who found his portrayal of common humanity impossibly unreal and condescending. On the other hand, working-class leaders might very well be prepared to accept Thomas Carlyle as an illuminating preceptor. His background of Scottish poverty and parental religious observance and sternness was the background from which many had come themselves. His anger against the squalor in which the 'rational' laws of political economy had engulfed so many in society was an anger they shared. To find so famous an intellectual attacking the prevailing political philosophy, on the grounds that it made a principle of neglecting the very evils that it should be the main function of government to eradicate, came as a flash of inspiration after the round of plausible middle-class lecturers who declared at meetings of the Mechanics Institutes that there could in nature be no alternative to *laissez-faire* and the iron laws of classical economics. Keir Hardie was one famous and attentive reader of Carlyle, but there were many others who found in him, as they found in his and their own Covenanting traditions, an inspiration to resist the intolerable.

The basic independence of the Scottish working-class mind can readily be seen in the labour politics of the day. The Trades Council of Glasgow proved itself very well able to organize the workers against class injustice in 1863, when it originated the national movement for the reform of the master and servant laws. The Trades Council of Edinburgh was not at all afraid in 1873 to lead the opposition to Duncan McLaren, local darling of the middle-class Liberals, for his part in the Criminal Law Amendment Act which had outlawed picketing—McLaren was described as 'a traitor to the working-class interest' at a great demonstration, with thirty-six bands and four gangs of pipers, called against him in the Queen's Park outside Holyrood.[24]

Individual Scottish trade union leaders demonstrated a similar blend of personal respectability and public toughness. This was exemplified by the life of Alexander McDonald, who became head first of the Lanarkshire miners, in 1863, then President of the newly-formed Miners National Association (the forerunner of the NUM), and ultimately the first Scottish working man to sit in Parliament (albeit for an English constituency). McDonald used his position to act personally as an apostle of self-improvement among the men, greatly deprecating drunkenness and ribaldry, however genuinely they might spring from working-class culture. In 1857, in Holytown, Lanarkshire, for instance, he was at a meeting organized by the *Glasgow Sentinel* to 'elevate the tastes of the workmen' and did not mince his words when 'two songs were sung of such a character as to call for a strong expression of indignation'. But equally McDonald was willing to question contemporary economic orthodoxy, to deny the middle-class assumption that miners should be no more than passive units in supply and demand, to recommend restriction of output by the workers to limit stocks and increase demand, and cautiously to sanction strike action on a rising market.[25] He looked for parliamentary allies wherever he could find them in the struggle for legislation to limit the truck system (that had obliged miners to shop at the company store) and improve safety in the mines, even when the best ally proved to be Lord Elcho, a Tory coal-owner and landlord from Fife whose personal friendship exposed McDonald to criticism both from Liberals and rank-and-file miners. In his day, McDonald was probably the best-known trade union leader in Britain, though he went down under a cloud in the 1870s due to what many regarded as his excessive timidity in opposing wage reductions during an industrial depression. To dismiss him, and labour leaders like him, as mere lickspittles of the bosses is fundamentally to misunderstand them. Co-operation they believed in, submission they did not.

Between about 1850 and the mid-1880s, therefore, the working-class radical tradition had clearly remained in the hands of moderates, whose ethos reflected and reinforced the intrinsic divisions within the working class rather than attempting to obliterate them. The working class at one level had not done badly from the State since the 1840s, thanks in no small degree to pressure from these leaders: the franchise had been twice extended, the secret ballot conceded, trade union picketing legalized, the protection of factory acts widened, universal public education introduced, and the standard of living improved. Nothing, however, had as yet shaken the distribution of effective political power and wealth from the hands of a narrow elite, and to be working class in Scotland was still to be exposed to a range of social experiences— appalling housing, bad health, poor schools, low incomes—that were generally regarded as inevitable and therefore unalterable. The challenge to those preconceptions was about to come from the socialists, but their message, when it came, would not be a new wine bursting an old wine-skin, but a blend in which the attitudes and traditions of the radical past would mix with and modify the new.

Perhaps, though, it was the notion that man's fate rested in his own hands and that he should act to do something about it rather than rest upon the vagaries of fate, God and the ruling classes that linked radical and socialist alike to the Enlightenment, and which most differentiates them from the twentieth-century mood that puts its trust so unheedingly in the 'experts' of a modern bureaucratic state.

CHAPTER XI

The Rise and Fall of Socialist Idealism

1

The demonstration of the Glasgow Trades against the House of Lords during the Third Reform Bill agitation of 1884 marked the visible apotheosis of working-class support for the Liberal Party and their Grand Old Man. Almost immediately afterwards, the Gladstonian ship ran into a hurricane of conflicting winds from right and left that all but tore the rigging of popular support from its masts.

In 1886, the split over the Irish question destroyed the Government when right-wingers led by Joseph Chamberlain refused to countenance the Prime Minister's plans for a very limited measure of Home Rule. In the ensuing elections, Chamberlain's Liberal Unionists carried away nearly a third of the Scottish Liberal seats. Scotland in general (and Glasgow in particular) remained more loyal to Gladstone than any part of England, but it was nevertheless a parting of the ways for many on the right who had come to regard the Liberals as a bad risk. Whig landowners like the Duke of Argyll were alarmed by the implications of land tenure reforms in Scotland as well as in Ireland. Some businessmen claimed to be worried that an independent Ireland might be used as a base by foreign powers for military adventures against British trade, and were perhaps realistically aware that a more aggressive naval policy than Gladstone's could bring valuable orders to the Clyde. Many churchmen considered Liberal backing for the Free Kirk's disestablishment campaign distasteful. The Liberal Unionists and their Conservative allies (they merged to form the Unionist Party in 1912) played on these creeping middle-class suspicions that Liberals were becoming softies and lefties sufficiently to gain an actual majority of Scottish seats, including all seven in Glasgow, during the Boer War in 1900. Although there was a great resurgence of the Liberals in 1906 in Scotland and elsewhere, their eventual position proved to have been seriously undermined by this slippage of trust on the right.

Even more significant in the long run was the revolt on the left, though when it first appeared in the 1880s, the rebels appeared to be puny in numbers, divided in doctrine and much easier to contain than the followers of Chamberlain. Some were agrarian radicals, some were unsatisfied Irish nationalist immigrants, and some were socialists whose novel creeds had percolated up from England, France and Germany, fusing with the native radical tradition to produce a characteristic and alarming mix, but not an immediately effective one, if potency is measured by votes in the ballot box.

In the Highlands, there was an instant and surprising success for agrarian radicalism in 1855, when the newly-formed Crofters' Party pledged to return the land taken from the people in the clearances, swept the north-west and returned four MPs in the first election after the Third Reform Bill. The Crofters' Party had grown directly out of the Highland discontent that had first erupted in riots in Skye in 1882, and owed much to the example of what the Irish had obtained for themselves in land reform by dint of agitation and organization in similar circumstances. The movement found effective external leaders in advanced Liberals and radicals like John S. Blackie, Professor of Greek at Edinburgh University, Gavin B. Clark, a Scottish doctor of socialist and nationalist sympathies living in London, and Charles Cameron, a Glasgow Liberal MP, all of whom combined enthusiasm for the Celtic cultural heritage with old anti-landlordism carried to new extremes. It chimed exactly with the Highlanders' own conviction that God had given the land to the people and the lairds had taken it from them. It was expressed in the slogans to be seen 'at any one of scores of crofters' meetings': 'The earth is mine ... The earth is the Lord's and the fulness thereof ... Woe unto them that join house to house, that lay field to field ... The earth he hath given to the children of men.'[1]

Despite their immediate success in the ballot box, and their equally instantaneous success in hard political terms in obtaining from Gladstone's short-lived ministry of 1886 the Crofters Act, which conferred on the Highlands most of the benefits of the Irish Land Act of 1881, the Crofters' Party died young, reabsorbed into the Liberals after 1892. The latter, by giving the crofters heritable security of tenure and a fair rents tribunal, showed themselves for once a sufficiently flexible and radical party to outflank the left. This was possible because, after the Duke of Argyll and other Whigs had left the party, there was little to be gained by placating landed grandees who were now almost uniformly a Tory group: conversely, the urban middle class, for whose votes Liberal and Tory were now competing on more equal terms than before, shared with the workers a traditional dislike of country land-lords that went back to the days of the Corn Laws and beyond. Any laird-bashing that took place in Ross and Cromarty was unlikely to lose votes in Cathcart. However it had to stop short of actual confiscation of property, which would certainly have seemed a bad precedent to the bourgeois in the towns.

In the Lowlands, the story was very different. Here the main opposition to the Liberals on the left came to be socialist, foreshadowed by the formation of the Scottish Labour Party in Glasgow in 1888 following Keir Hardie's unsuccessful intervention as an independent labour candidate at the Mid-Lanark by-election, in a constituency where he was a well-known miners' union leader but where he proved unable to collect more than a derisory 617 votes. That party merged with the Independent Labour Party (ILP) two years after the latter's foundation by Keir Hardie in Bradford in 1893: and the ILP in turn became the ally of the trade unions in founding the British Labour Party (to which it remained affiliated until 1932) in the opening years of the twentieth century. Scots played an exceptionally large part in all this, and the character, ethos and ideology of the original leaders is therefore a matter of importance beyond Scottish history.

The men who came together in Glasgow in 1888 were united at least in being distrustful of orthodox Liberals. The maverick among them was R. G. Cunninghame Graham, 'Don Roberto', landowner, littera-teur, dandy, wit, and returned adventurer from Latin America. In 1886 he had been elected as Liberal MP for north-west Lanarkshire; in 1887 he fell under the spell of the London socialists of the Social Democratic Federation (SDF) and found himself arrested for organizing a riot of the unemployed in Trafalgar Square. His championship of the under-dog in the House of Commons was described by another socialist as 'a species of inverted dilletantism', and Parliament found it hard to take him seriously.[2] After the mid-1890s, he passed from the political lime-light, only to surface again in 1928 as a co-sponsor of the Scottish Nationalist Party. It is not given to many to found two opposed political parties in their lifetime, but a concatenation of socialist and at least a degree of nationalist feeling was present in many labour activists of the day.

More typical of the early founders, if a good deal less fun, were Keir Hardie himself, Gavin B. Clark of the Crofters' Party, John Ferguson of the Irish National League, centred on Glasgow, and Robert Smillie of the Lanarkshire Miners. They shared the belief that the Liberal Party, at least for the moment, could not be relied upon to carry the torch any further for the working man, though some among them hoped that the foundation of the new party would itself be a sufficient tactic to bring the Liberals to their senses. In a sense, Liberalism had fallen victim to its own progressive ideology and the belief that one reform should always follow another. In the wake of the Third Reform Bill, for example, the Lib-labs of the Glasgow Trades Council called a meeting to discuss the next logical step in the onward march of the people, and decided in accordance with their traditions that it lay in fielding an increased number of respectable working-class candidates in Parliamentary and council elections. This, however, would have involved a sacrifice by the middle-class men who everywhere dominated the selection committees; they would have had to relinquish their grip on the levers of power, which they had no intention of doing. It was the experience of this impasse over class power that led some radicals to contemplate alternative solutions.

Being disillusioned with the existing Liberal Party did not, though, in itself, make the founding fathers of 1888 socialists, and much in their initial programme was simply old-fashioned extreme radicalism, such as the call for rigid control of the drink trade which headed their first agenda. Even their demand for land nationalization, which sounds socialist, owed more to the influence of the American agrarian radical Henry George, who had been given a rapturous reception in the Lowlands on his tour a few years earlier. Not until five years after its foundation did the party go as far as to proclaim its objective to be 'the co-operative ownership by the workers of land and the means of production'.[3] It was this small but vital step, this magic formula, that made them explicitly socialist and carried them away from the world of Tom Paine towards the world of Karl Marx.

It did not, however, carry them very far. Keir Hardie, Bruce Glasier, Ramsay MacDonald, and all the early Scottish leaders of the ILP came unequivocally to be socialists in the formal sense because they stood for the public ownership of the means of production. They were, however, what Bruce Glasier liked to call 'ethical socialists'. He had this to say about Hardie:

> I doubt if he ever read Marx or any scientific exposition of Socialist theory. He certainly had not done so before he avowed himself a Socialist. So far as he was influenced towards Socialism by the ideas of others it was as he himself has stated, by the Bible, the songs of Burns, the writings of Carlyle, Ruskin and Mill, and the democratic traditions in working class homes in Scotland in his early days. In the main, however, as with many of us, he derived his Socialism from his own thought and feeling, the plight of the workers and the state of the world. He was guided by religious, or perhaps I should say moral, convictions, rather than by philosophical theorising or scientific analysis of economic or social phenomena.[4]

What this meant in practice was that Hardie and his fellows projected a compelling image of concern for the plight of their fellow human beings combined with total faith in socialism as a remedy. Glasier went on to portray his hero at meetings uttering his 'familiar appeal' in a 'clear warm voice' with 'arms outstretched'. The Christian and Covenanting echoes were overwhelming:

> Come now, Men and Women, I plead with you, for your own sake and that of your children, for the sake of the downtrodden poor, the weary, sorehearted mothers, the outcast, unemployed fathers—for their sakes, and for the sake of our beloved Socialism, the hope of peace and humanity throughout the world—Men and Women, I appeal to you, come and join us and fight with us in the fight wherein none shall fail.[5]

Hardie's debt to the Scottish radical tradition of the earlier nineteenth century was every bit as clear as his dedication to the novelty of socialist evangelism. It was seen in his lifelong abhorrence of drink: as long as he was leader, no Labour MP was allowed in the bar of the House of Commons. It was seen in his outspoken dislike of royalty, and in his ardent pacifism during the Boer War and the First World War. Equally, it was seen in his emphatic rejection of violence against the established order at home. Leo Meillet, a refugee from the Paris commune teaching French at Edinburgh University, who once urged shooting the Principal of Glasgow University as a priority when the revolution came, on another occasion told a circle of sympathizers gathered at Revd Dr Glasse's house that 'the only bulwark for liberty and justice is a sea of blood between the poor and the rich'. The young Hardie spontaneously leapt to his feet to exclaim, 'It is not socialism, it is brute madness.'[6] Hardie, moreover, consistently deprecated the idea of any class war involving the concept of irreconcilable differences between the workers and the bourgeoisie, to Marx the very essence of true social perception, to Hardie a damaging and irrelevant myth. Hardie saw socialism in moral terms, as an alliance of all good men against the evils inherent in capitalism, and he believed it would be achieved not by revolution but by evolution, as more and more of all classes became convinced, through reason, of its rightness: the debt to the radical tradition was again clear.

In the hands of Bruce Glasier and Ramsay MacDonald the moral fervour of the ILP frequently deteriorated into anti-intellectualism and extreme wooliness. Even Hardie was better as street-corner orator than as Parliament debater, and he was worst of all in working out exactly what he meant by socialist policies. What, for example, was intended by that critical phrase the 'collective ownership of the means of production, distribution and exchange'? Hardie, fixated on his own background, 'seems to have thought—when he thought at all—of the pit owned by the village and run by an elected council of villagers'.[7] But if the message of the early apostles of the ILP lacked precision, it gained in breadth of appeal, for many could respond to their anger and commitment to a better world who would have fundamentally disagreed about the nature of the remedy or the means of attaining it.

By 1906, there is no doubt that most socialists in Scotland were members of the ILP, but there were also significant groups who represented alternative Marxist and revolutionary traditions, most importantly the branches of the Social Democratic Federation (SDF) which had existed since its foundation in London in the 1880s, and the Socialist Labour Party (SLP), which broke away from the SDF in Scotland in 1903 with the help of James Connolly, the Edinburgh-born leader of the Irish labour movement. The SLP became attracted to 'industrial unionist' ideas from France and America involving the notion of direct control by the workers of the industries which were taken over by the State, and the idea of a political strike to achieve the collapse of the capitalist system. Both preached class war and direct action, and despised the ILP for the tendency to collaboration and compromise that it inherited from the radical past.

We know now, with the historian's privilege of hindsight, that the formation of the Scottish Labour Party and of the ILP were portentous events for Scottish and British history. There is no doubt, too, that even in the 1880s, many middle-class people were already gravely perturbed by the rise of socialism. The churches in Scotland especially observed its moral seriousness as a challenge, and responded by turning their attention (to a degree unprecedented in earlier decades) to the problems of housing, destitution and human rehabilitation in the great cities. On the other hand, the socialists were the recipients of very few votes in Scotland before 1906. In municipal politics, ten 'Labour Stalwarts' were elected to the City Council of Glasgow by 1898 under the leadership of John Ferguson, but not all were socialists: they were identified with the Irish ethnic interest more than with the ILP, and not all voted together. They mostly lost their seats in 1901, and were not altogether remembered with affection even by those they tried to represent. The Catholic *Glasgow Observer* in 1908 recalled how 'the old Stalwart party ... elected on a democratic ticket, proceeded to scramble as quickly as possible to the Bailie's Bench, and there dissolved into gilded impotence.'[8] In Parliamentary terms, no seats at all were won by labour candidates and the showing of ILP candidates even at by-elections was often worse than in England.

Part of the reason for the early failure of the socialists was the relative weakness of the trade unions in Scotland, which were incapable of organizing support behind a chosen labour candidate. Part of it was the inability of the ILP leaders to carry the Irish, who were deterred by their priests from backing obvious socialists, and equally were often put off by the visible distaste of men like Hardie and Glasier for Irishmen, whom they were still openly inclined to regard as simple victims of superstition and popery: the Covenanting tradition had its disadvantages in uniting the workers of the world. And part of the explanation for their failure was simply the continuing strength of liberalism among Scottish craftsmen: despite everything, they still had a strong faith in the successors of Mr Gladstone and a belief that class collaboration within a framework of capitalism was a better way to improve the lot of the working class than the untried recipe of socialism. For these reasons, if not for others, many Scottish ILP leaders, like Keir Hardie, Bruce Glasier and Ramsay MacDonald, found their political careers flourished better in England and Wales than in their native land.

2

Between 1906 and 1922, British politics underwent a transformation and in Scotland gave birth to a myth. The transformation began in the north with the election of two MPs for the Labour Party (for Glasgow and Dundee) in the Liberal landslide of 1906, and culminated with the election of twenty-nine Labour MPs, plus a Communist and a left-wing Prohibitionist, in the second election after the First World War. By 1922, Glasgow was the city of the 'Clydesiders', of the fiery James Maxton and martyred John MacLean, having become with Sheffield the reddest city in Britain: 42 per cent of its electors voted Labour, while Birmingham and Liverpool could only muster 25 per cent. The myth was that the Clydeside workers, led by SLP shop stewards, enlightened by Marxist evening classes held by MacLean, and fired by the examples of the Bolsheviks, had come within an ace of revolution. William Gallacher, strike leader and Communist, blamed himself later for letting the opportunity slip during the riot in George Square in 1919: 'A rising was expected. A rising should have taken place. The workers were ready and able to effect it ...'[9]

Certainly the cataclysm of these years left the Liberal tradition in ruins and helped to bring Ramsay MacDonald, backed at a critical juncture by the Clydeside MPs, to the premiership of Great Britain in the first minority Labour Government of 1924. From there, through the twists of fortune of the ill-fated second minority Labour Government of 1929–31 and the black 1930s, the way led via the Second World War to the majority Labour Government of 1945–51. That Government more than any other was responsible for the rise of the modern collectivist state that relied on the mixed economy and the guidance of a bureaucracy of professional government-financed experts. It may have substantially improved welfare, but it was anything but revolutionary, radical, socialist or liberal—in the true senses of any of those words. Its ideology became an unchallenged consensus in British politics until the 1980s.

That, however, is to anticipate. Even before the First World War, there were clear signs that the beliefs that had sustained the radical craftsman of the nineteenth century were being stretched to breaking point. It had been axiomatic to the Victorian working-class Liberal that, however much masters and men might legitimately differ on the division of the income arising from their labour, there was a fundamental unity of interest in maintaining a successful capitalist mode of production. The sentiment was encapsulated in the Boiler-makers' song of 1872:

> Now 'tis true that capital
> All the risk must run
> Like a ship exposed to all
> Winds beneath the sun;
> Feels the first trade's ebb and flow,
> Must keen competition know.
> So 'tis just and meet
> Labour should co-operate,
> And help with all their might
> Masters to compete.[10]

The return for this for the skilled artisan was, firstly, high wages, which enabled him to have a chance of accumulating enough to enter the ranks of the middle classes, perhaps as a subcontractor employing a few men on his own account, and secondly, very often some guarantee of security as a key worker in times of slack trade that would bring unemployment for the less skilled. By the turn of the century, however, the scale and complexity of the ship-building and engineering shops along the Clyde made it difficult for ambitious workers to find a niche among the self-employed, and the uneven demand for ships, tied to trade cycles of feast or famine, exposed tens of thousands of skilled men to periodic bouts of unemployment in a manner that had scarcely been known since the 1840s. Furthermore, the overwhelming defeat of the Amalgamated Society of Engineers in the strike of 1897 deprived the men of much of their traditional control over the job on the work-floor. While this encouraged employers to introduce new machines and to attempt to speed up work, it was largely a hollow victory as it drove the men to antagonism and an elaborate defence of restrictive practices which was scarcely dismantled before the 1980s. The American Consul, who had a higher regard for the intelligence of Scottish workmen than he did for that of management, observed that the new pneumatic riveting machines that a Chicago firm was trying to sell at Scotstoun and elsewhere along the Clyde in 1902 were 'not favoured by the labor unions, and with native labor they accomplish little, if any, more than is accomplished under the present system'.[11] Alienated labour was plainly losing interest in helping 'masters to compete'. Nothing has been more catastrophic for the long-term health of British industry than the inability to pursue consensus in the work place. For this the employers' assumption that they could ride willy-nilly over their work force whenever economic circumstances gave them a temporary advantage is, in historic terms, largely responsible. For those who have been on the receiving end, the lessons of history are not quickly forgotten.

The unemployment crisis of 1907–8 proved to be the last straw for many Liberal loyalties. Glasgow was one of the worst affected places in the United Kingdom: 7000 people were dependent on a special relief fund by Christmas 1907, and *The Times* reported nine months later that over 16,000 in Govan were 'on the verge of starvation'. At a demonstration organized by the socialists that summer, 35,000 marched in the traditional radical manner, each organization carrying a banner or symbol of its trade and purpose, and the joiners bearing again their 1832 banner with the motto, 'They are unworthy of freedom, who hope for it from hands other than their own.'[12] What they heard from John Hill, the leader of the boiler-makers, was, however, a message of puzzled disillusion:

> Only a few years ago unemployment had no terrors for well-organized skilled trades ... Now the tables are turned. With improved machinery our craft is at a discount, and a boy from school now tends a machine which does the work of three men ... It is mostly machine-minders who are wanted and a line from some well-known Liberal or Tory certifying that you are not an agitator or a Socialist is the chief recommendation in the shipbuilding and engineering trades. Thus today we find the ranks of the unemployed largely recruited by men of intellect: men of genius, and men of high character and independent means.[13]

The older men might, in these circumstances, just add a pottery plate of Keir Hardie to the one of W. E. Gladstone already adorning the mantelpiece, but by the opening years of the twentieth century there was, for those who wanted to take advantage of it, a fully-fledged alternative political culture. The younger generation were offered a rich variety of red-blooded socialist things to do, especially in Glasgow. One might begin at a very tender age as a member of a socialist Sunday school ('There was a naming ceremony where a big crowd sang socialist songs ... four little girls put flowers on the baby for purity, and then a red rose was put on for revolution,'[14]) or join the Clarion Scouts distributing ILP literature (when two met, the password was 'boot' and the reply 'spur'), or subscribe to *Forward*, Tom Johnston's lively ILP newspaper founded in 1906, or attend one of the innumerable lectures and meetings in the Glasgow halls where the principles of the ILP, or the SDF, or the SLP, or the syndicalists, or the secularists, or the anarchists, were propounded. For the most serious-minded there were the evening classes of the Workers' Educational Association, and, most rigorous of all, those of John MacLean, Govan schoolteacher and member of the SDF, anti-militarist, revolutionary, whose teaching of 'Marxian economics' at times attracted classes of over a thousand. Then there was the artistic side, drawn from old connections with William Morris' Socialist League in the 1880s, which attracted men like the young poet Edwin Muir at the time of the First World War. *Forward* advertised piano lessons, and Hugh Roberton's Glasgow Orpheus Choir became in the 1930s the most famous amateur choir in the world; it was the most important manifestation of the cultural aspects of the ILP.

There was indeed, among the early twentieth-century Scottish socialists, a style and a fermenting energy which drew the young and uncommitted like bright lights. The sense that man should act to determine his own fate, that the future was in his own hands and immediately improvable, linked the early socialists to the mood of the older radical tradition at its most ardent. That socialism throughout the world was as yet an untried remedy added to its charms for the young. The proponents of different schools differed profoundly and often bitterly about the way to Utopia, so that a parliamentarian 'ethical' ILP socialist like Ramsay MacDonald 'laughed and wept at its rubbish' when he found an SLP pamphlet by Gallacher and J. R. Campbell on *Direct Action* on a Menzies bookstall in a Highland railway station.[15] But he would have been at one with the sentiments expressed in its introduction by J. S. Clarke:

The Revolutionary age in which we live marks not only a transition from capitalism to communism but also the greater transition from the semi-human to the wholly human ... Socialism is the only gospel on earth that makes for the spiritual emancipation of the human race.[16]

None of this meant that, at the outbreak of the First World War, the working class had gone socialist, still less that it had been converted to revolution, but it surely did mean that big cracks had opened up in the façade of Liberal hegemony. There were eighteen ILP councillors in Glasgow by July 1914, and the ablest among them, John Wheatley, had already taken two steps of the utmost significance for the future appeal of Labour in Scotland. Firstly, in 1906, he had founded a Catholic Socialist Society, later affiliated to the ILP, devoted to convincing his fellows of Irish faith and descent that, despite the hostility of the hierarchy, there need be no conflict between their religion and the new politics. Secondly, he had begun, with his pamphlet *Eight-Pound Cottages for Glasgow Citizens*, his campaign for good quality public-sector housing to replace the slums, with their appalling rates of ill health and infant mortality. The pamphlet commenced thus: 'Dr Chalmers, Chief Medical Officer of Health for Glasgow, has just issued his report for last year. Commenting on it the "Glasgow Herald" remarks that "it reflects a year of normal experience". In this case the normal is horrible.'[17] This understanding that 'the normal is horrible' in working-class experience, and the faith that something could be done by the working class to change it, was the key to the appeal of Wheatley's party.

The impact of the First World War on the burgeoning class-consciousness of the west of Scotland was complex and contradictory. Its immediate effect was to heighten class antagonisms for certain sectors of the population, but simultaneously to divide interests and opinions in such a way as to make solidarity more difficult. Socialists like Keir Hardie and Ramsay MacDonald in London, and John Wheatley, Tom Johnston and John MacLean in Glasgow, all continued to support the pledge of the Second International at Basle in 1913, that the working classes of the world should never fight in a European capitalist war. To their immense disconsolation, the outbreak of hostilities was welcomed with hearty patriotism by the overwhelming majority of British workers, by the trade unions, by sections of the Parliamentary Labour Party, and by sixteen out of eighteen Glasgow ILP councillors.

In the early days, it proved remarkably easy to raise volunteers from the Scottish working class: 'Men rushed to join the army hoping the war wouldn't be all over by the time they got to the front.'[18] Relative to population there was a bigger response to the call to the colours in Scotland than anywhere else in Britain. In Glasgow in September 1914, the Corporation decided to raise and equip two battalions from the tramway employees: within twenty-four hours, one in six—over 1000 men—had volunteered, and by the end of the year recruitment had reached 1756.[19] Most of them were subsequently killed at the Somme. Though anti-war speakers like John MacLean were given a hearing in the streets and halls of Glasgow that they would not have got in an English city, they certainly failed to sway the multitude.

The bulk of the workers left behind were involved in wartime production in the shipyards and engineering shops, the biggest concentration of munitions suppliers in Britain. Apart from a brief strike at Fairfields in August 1915, there was no industrial trouble in the shipyards during the war. It was among the engineers in factories like Beardmores, Weirs, Albion Motors, and Barr and Stroud that the main trouble arose.

The problems here were manifold. On the one hand there was a group of shop stewards who formed the militant Clyde Workers' Committee (CWC) to take unofficial action when their own unions backed away from confrontation, especially William Gallacher at Albion Motors, John Muir at Barr and Stroud and Arthur MacManus at Weirs, who had close links with the 'workers' control' ideology of the SLP: to them should be added David Kirkwood of the ILP at Beardmores, clearly not a revolutionary but equally involved in the notion of workers' control. Opposed to them was a group of industrialists, led by the young and aggressive William Weir, who saw the war as a chance to break the traditional work practices of the Clyde for ever and to introduce new methods, new machinery and new types of labour—even women. Pressing from above was the London Government, with Lloyd George as Minister of Munitions, anxious only to produce as much as possible to win the war in the shortest possible time. The Government made Weir munitions controller in Scotland in 1915. Caught in the middle were the engineers themselves, well-paid, skilled, contemptuous of mere labourers, conservative in their ways, highly organized, but already made to feel deeply insecure by the pre-war offensive of the employers on their trade. In addition, they were exempted from conscription for the trenches by virtue of the 'essential' nature of their war-work at home: but what if, through changes in the nature of their work and their replacement by women, they should lose that exemption? Could they then be sent off to die? Cheering from the sidelines were socialist propagandists of various persuasions ranging from John MacLean, who was urging them deliberately to sabotage the production of munitions to facilitate the overthrow of the capitalist warmongers, to Tom Johnston, who admitted the need to produce shells but warned the workers against being fooled and exploited by the boss class under the cloak of patriotic necessity.

The upshot was what Gallacher was to christen 'The Revolt on the Clyde', in effect a series of incidents mainly involving the engineers between 1915 and 1919. The most important of these were the 'tuppence an hour' strike in 1915, the struggles over the Clearance Certificates demanded under the Munitions Act before a man could leave his job, and over 'dilution'—i.e. the limited employment of women in certain mass-production munition jobs like making fuses and shells. It culminated in the disruption of a meeting held by Lloyd George to convince the CWC shop stewards and their sympathizers of the necessity and importance of dilution, followed by the suppression of Tom Johnston's *Forward* for reporting the incident accurately, and the deportation of the leading shop stewards to Edinburgh in February 1916. Thereafter there were no more troubles until after the end of the war.

There was, however, a dramatic postscript in January 1919, when the CWC called the 'forty-hour strike' in support of a claim for a shorter working week to avert postwar unemployment. The unsuccessful attempt to make this a general strike of the Glasgow workers, and a subsequent riot when the police charged a large demonstration of strikers in George Square who were thought to be interfering with the power supply for the tramcars, was enough to persuade the Secretary for Scotland that he was dealing with a Bolshevist rising (it was, after all, scarcely a year since the Russian Revolution). Next day, the citizens of Glasgow woke up to find six tanks in the Cattle Market, a howitzer at the City Chambers and machine-gun nests at the hotels and the post office: 'It was a strange experience to see ... soldiers who were not from the front but walking the streets to hold us in check.'[20] Emmanuel Shinwell, the seamen's leader, who spent a month in prison for allegedly inciting the crowd to riot, recalled that the troops 'had nothing much to do but chat to the local people and drink their cups of tea' while the officers 'complained about fraternization with the "enemy"'.[21]

But Glasgow was obviously not Petrograd, or even Berlin, and it never could have been. The only leader with any theoretical notion of how a revolution might be constructed was John MacLean, who had no effective party and spent much of his time in prison for preaching sedition. The shop stewards of the SLP, dedicated but few in number, had no political plans at all: revolutionaries in theory, they found it hard to discover how to be so in practice. The ILP never pretended to want revolution: Tom Johnston ended by urging the workers to work as hard as possible to get the war finished. As for the engineers themselves, they were not much admired by the rest of the working class and found it hard to resist the charge that in 1915 and 1916 their strikes were for narrow, sectional and unpatriotic ends.

The position of many ordinary working people was probably best mirrored in the attitude of David Kirkwood at the outbreak of war:

> I hated war. I believed that the peoples of the world hated war ... Yet I was working in an arsenal, making guns and shells for one purpose—to kill men in order to keep them from killing men. What a confusion! What was I to do? ... I resolved that my skill as an engineer must be devoted to my country. I was too proud of the battles of the past to stand aside and see Scotland conquered. Only those who remember 1914 can understand the struggle of mind and the conflict of loyalties which so many of us experienced.[22]

A little later he was exulting in the close relationship he had formed with Sir William Beardmore in organizing production at Parkhead forge; then he was working out, with the help of John Wheatley, a way to make the new production methods more acceptable to men and management alike; then he was deeply hurt at being banned by Sir William from a free run of the factory as shop steward; then uncomprehending about his arrest and forcible deportation to Edinburgh. When at last he was allowed to move back to Glasgow he was made department production manager in Mile-end Shell Factory 'with David Hanton, William Gallacher and wee MacManus as shop stewards':

> What a team! There was never anything like it in Great Britain! We organised a bonus system in which every one benefited by high pro-

duction. Records were made only to be broken ... In six weeks we held the record for output in Great Britain, and we never lost our premier position. Sir William Beardmore came often to see the system working ...[23]

This was no way for anyone to bring the capitalist system to its knees, but Sir William did buy Kirkwood 'the best hat in Glasgow' out of respect for his efforts.

The industrial struggles of the engineers in the history of Red Clydeside had little positive effect in turning the city red, and perhaps a negative one. It would, however, be a great mistake to leave the story there. As a whole, the First World War served as such an object lesson in the folly, remoteness, and even corruption of the rulers as to raise the class consciousness of the workers by several degrees—not, certainly, to the white heat of revolution but, undoubtedly, to a warm sense of disenchantment with those in power. This was fuelled, for one thing, by the inept management of the war by the generals and the politicians, which within twelve months of its outbreak had wiped out the popular enthusiasm of the opening campaign. Whether committed to the strategy of heavy slog over Flanders (like Haig) or to derring-do at the Dardanelles (like Churchill), their approach appeared simply to disregard the appalling list of casualties. It is still not known how many Scots died in the war. One well-argued estimate put the figure at 110,000, equivalent to about 10 per cent of the Scottish male population aged between sixteen and fifty, and probably to about 15 per cent of total British war dead—the sacrifice was higher in proportionate terms than for any other country in the Empire. Thirteen out of fourteen were privates and non-commissioned officers from the working classes.[24]

The anguish of war was countered in church by appeals to patriotic sentiment and other ecclesiastical bromides. The clerical Principal of Aberdeen University called it 'a sacrament, and a sacrament in the full sense of that name as we Scots have been brought up to understand it'. Its spiritual fruits were welcomed from the pulpit as an antidote to the 'fetid quagmire' of materialism, bringing together again to a common purpose the middle classes and the multitude, described by the Professor of Divinity at Edinburgh University as 'the slouching spectators of the football spectacle'.[25] Small wonder that after the war, attendance at church by the working classes was seen to have eroded even further than ever before.

The conduct of the war on the home front was equally insensitive. The prosecution and imprisonment of John MacLean, James Maxton and the shop stewards made martyrs out of nuisances. Tom Johnston wrote of MacLean's imprisonment in 1918:

> The bulk of the workers do not want a Socialist Revolution by any method, but go on rivet-hammering competitions, and scrambling for overtime, and regard the John Macleans as 'decent enough, but a bit off'. The blood of the martyrs is said to have been the seed of the church, and John Maclean's dramatic sacrifice may do more to shake up the brains of the working class than did all John Maclean's years of educative propaganda for Socialism.[26]

When MacLean was released from gaol, thousands cheered him through the streets of Glasgow: it did not make them revolutionary, but it was an expression of the popular sense of disgust at his persecution.

A more personal sense of injustice was aroused by the contrast between the sluggish increase in the rate of wages and the immediate jump in profits of the munitions-makers and anyone else who could cash in on the shortages. Thus at Clydebank the local rationing committee divided a consignment of 15 cwt. of margarine so that Clydebank and Dalmuir Co-operative Societies, with a membership representing 60 per cent of the local population, each received 1 cwt., while the convener of the committee, a grocer and a police judge selling from a single shop, awarded himself 8 cwt. Following protests, the convener was told by the Deputy Food Control Commissioner for the west of Scotland that he had made 'an error of judgement'.[27]

Most effective of all for the working-class education in class consciousness was the rent strike agitation of 1915 in which the housewives of Govan and Partick—and later women in other areas of the city—refused to accept the steep increases in rents imposed by factors taking advantage of wartime housing scarcities. Between 15,000 and 20,000 households were quickly involved: attempted eviction was resisted in the close-built fortress of the tenement closes by women of every political persuasion, Orange and Tory as well as Liberal and Labour, who defended their neighbours from the police and the factors' servants with a powerful mixture of physical force and moral outrage. Many of the families concerned had men at the front, a fact tellingly emphasized on the placards carried in the demonstrations: 'While my father is a prisoner in Germany, the landlord is attacking our home,' and, 'Our husbands are fighting Prussianism in France, and we are fighting the Prussians of Partick.' To the efforts of the local women, left-wing leaders of the suffragettes like Helen Crawfurd, ILP councillors like Andrew MacBride and Patrick Dollan, and the ILP lawyer Rosslyn Mitchell lent support and their own special skills. The Government, persuaded that total disruption of munitions production was imminent when the shipyards and engineering shops threatened to come out in support of the women, passed a Rent Restriction Act stopping increases during the remainder of the war.

All this in due time helped to provide an inspiration for Lloyd George's 'Homes fit for Heroes' postwar election slogan, seen by the Prime Minister as an insurance against Bolshevism: 'Even if it cost a hundred million pounds, what was that compared to the stability of the State,' he exclaimed at a Cabinet meeting after the George Square riots early in 1919.[28] The upshot was the Addison Act, providing State support for council housing. Its immediate outcome was a failure, which counted against Lloyd George at the subsequent election: but it laid the foundations for all government intervention thereafter, including Wheatley's more effective Housing Act introduced under the Labour Government itself in 1924.

As one reflective Glasgow ILP housing reformer, W. C. Anderson, remarked in 1915, through the rent strike the rule of the landlord had been suddenly challenged 'by hundreds of thousands of discriminating and undiscriminating minds'.[29] It is certainly no coincidence that the most effective attack of the war years had been launched not on the employer but on the landlord, who in a rural setting had long been the traditional radical bogeyman and was now translated into the bogeyman of the town. Even in Tom Johnston's *Forward*, the kind of language used against landlords was always far stronger than that used against businessmen, and the sales of his polemical history of *Our Noble Families*, purporting to expose the Scottish peerage as bandits and rackrenting monsters, were enormous among working-class readers, who were accustomed, in Glasgow, also to use the term 'laird' for their tenement landlord.

It has to be said, however, that any disenchantment with the rulers was not immediately visible in the first postwar General Election of 1918, when Labour took not more than six seats in Scotland, including only a single success in Glasgow, significantly at Govan, where the rent strike had centred. By 1922, however, there were twenty-nine Labour MPs, of whom ten came from the fifteen Glasgow constituencies and nine more from elsewhere in the west. The difference between the two elections is attributable partly to technical factors. The authorities in 1918 were inefficient in making arrangements for servicemen to vote and in completing the electoral register under the new Reform Act which, unlike 1884, really did concede manhood suffrage and in addition gave the vote to a substantial number of women in response to the suffragette agitation. Three out of four voters had never been on the roll before. Labour success was also due to the way the Government dissipated the support it had achieved in victory over the Kaiser by its failure to produce 'Homes fit for Heroes', by its failure to counteract rising unemployment after 1920, and by its continuing belligerence overseas and at home. The Cabinet's policy of fighting in Russia and Ireland, and the show of force in George Square, exasperated those who had endured and survived fighting the Germans in 'the war to end all wars'. Winston Churchill had in fact argued in Cabinet against sending troops to Glasgow in 1919, but in popular tradition he was the villain of the piece. Billy Kay remembered an Ayrshire upbringing after the Second World War:

> I recall reading with astonishment the school history books' unqualified praise for Churchill as Statesman, War Hero and Saviour of Britain. In my home there was unqualified hatred for him as the man who advocated the use of tanks and troops against the workers in Glasgow in 1919 and who sent the Scots regiments in to be slaughtered at the Dardanelles . . .[30]

Churchill lost his parliamentary seat in Dundee to the left-wing Prohibitionist Edward Scrymgeour in 1922, partly because the Irish vote turned against him and partly because women voted anti-drink.

It is indeed possible to argue that the main reason for the great increase in the Labour vote in 1922 was that the Irish, still mainly in unskilled jobs, had at last buried the hatchet with socialism and made common cause with the skilled workers of the ILP. From the Catholic viewpoint, the great advantage of Labour by then was that it was not opposed (as its municipal opponents were in Glasgow) to State provision for denominational schools under the 1918 Scottish Education Act. It became Labour policy, therefore, to subsidize separate Catholic schools, 'Rome on the rates' as their opponents called it. The patient work of men like John Wheatley and Patrick Dollan had at last born fruit.[31] By 1922, the working class was sufficiently united at the ballot box to return a phalanx of left-wing MPs.

3

The departure of the Clydesiders to Parliament in 1922 was accompanied by Messianic scenes in which the MPs publicly pledged themselves to a declaration drawn up by Rosslyn Mitchell to 'abjure vanity and self-aggrandisement' and to recognize 'that their only righteous purpose is to promote the welfare of their fellow-citizens and the well-being of mankind'. The ringing echoes of a tradition as radical as it was socialist were caught again in the mass singing of two Covenanting psalms, the 23rd and the 124th, 'Had not the Lord been on our side'. The crowd sang the Red Flag in a more modern mode as they made their way to St Enoch's Station, and James Maxton shouted, 'Don't hurry for the train—it'll all belong to the people when we come back.'[32]

Maxton died twenty-four years later, in the first year of the first majority Labour Government, which was indeed destined to nationalize the railways, though not in a way that made them in any effective sense 'belong to the people'. Of those who went with him to Parliament, the ablest, John Wheatley, died in 1930 after attaining distinction as Minister of Health in the minority Labour Government of 1924 and introducing a Housing Act that was to be the cornerstone of effective council-housing policy in the interwar years; his rival in intellect and political sagacity, Tom Johnston, had in 1946 just completed a wartime term in Churchill's Cabinet as Secretary of State for Scotland, which finally committed the Government of Scotland to a system of rule by committees and quangos responsible to London; David Kirkwood was about to become ennobled as Baron Bearsden; Rosslyn Mitchell had faded from public life, his only contribution to Parliament being an impassioned speech opposing the revision of the Church of England Prayer Book—Kirkwood's verdict, 'the speaker sat down famous',[33] was not widely shared. Maxton himself became the leader of an ILP disaffiliated on his insistence from the Labour Party in 1932, wrecked by its association with the Communists in a so-called 'Popular Front', and turned into a pointless rump with three MPs. The story of the 'Clydesiders' is not edifying.

Why did they fail? For one thing, they fell into a Parliamentary environment that was totally out of sympathy with their ideology and world view, and they allowed themselves to be overwhelmed by it. Maxton had told the crowds at St Enoch's Station that they 'would see the atmosphere of the Clyde getting the better of the House of Commons',[34] and for a time the Clydesiders deliberately tried to keep themselves apart, socially and politically, from what they regarded as a corrupting atmosphere of frippery and *bonhomie*: 'The dour Scot objects to any social intercourse,' complained Beatrice Webb, 'the private houses of rich members of the party are anathema, and any club to which these members and their wives belong is almost equally objectionable.'[35] Such self-denying ordinances could not last, however, and the end was exactly the reverse of Maxton's prophecy. The tone of their absorption as 'rough diamonds' at Westminster was exactly caught in two passages from Winston Churchill's pen. The first was the opening of his foreword to Kirkwood's autobiography of 1935:

> David Kirkwood has so many friends of all parties in the House of Commons and at large in the country that this engaging account of his pugnacious career will receive a warm welcome. Everyone thinks him a grand fellow, if handled the right way.[36]

The other was his final affectionate letter to Maxton during his last illness in 1946:

> I have been thinking a lot about you lately, and today David Kirkwood told me you had sent me such a charming message saying we were both good House of Commons men. But as I always say to you, 'the greatest gentleman in the House of Commons' . . .[37]

This was despite Maxton's stormy career, his denunciation of a Tory MP as a 'murderer' during a debate on the Scottish health estimates in 1923, and his long opposition to Churchill's own conduct of the Second World War. The most famous statesman and proponent of the British capitalist state in the twentieth century would never have used these tones had he thought Kirkwood or Maxton posed any threat to the world as he knew it.

Could the socialists have avoided the trap? Some of them did not see it that way: Tom Johnston, whom Churchill made Secretary of State for Scotland in the Second World War in the spirit of appointing to the post of gamekeeper a former poacher, had abandoned the Scottish radical and ILP tradition of self-help and self-made liberty in favour of the modern State's belief in the rule of the expert and the consensus of the well-informed. Beveridge and Keynes became his mentors, and committees 'representing all shades of opinion' but appointed on his recommendation, his preferred mode of governing Scotland—as it remains for Westminster and the Scottish Office to this day. The rule of the experts has been productive of much good, but it has little intrinsically to do with a man's right to control his own fate, with liberty, equality and fraternity, with socialism, or with anything else in the original pantheon of Scottish political idealism.

One way, in theory, in which the trap could have been avoided would have been to cut adrift from England and to form a Scottish Workers' Republic, on the model of what James Connolly was trying to establish in Ireland at the Easter Rising in 1916. This solution appealed to John MacLean at the close of the First World War, but his visionary schemes found no support at all from the Scottish electorate. The ILP, in theory, had also always espoused at least some measure of home-rule, and when George Buchanan introduced a Home Rule Bill for Scotland in 1924, Maxton declared with fine rhetoric at St Andrews Hall in Glasgow that he would 'ask for no greater job in life' than to make 'the English-ridden, capitalist-ridden, landlord-ridden Scotland into a Scottish socialist Commonwealth'.[38] However the home-rulers obtained no support in the House of Commons, little in the British labour movement, and scarcely more from the Scottish working class itself. The onset of depression in the 1920s killed what little faith the Scots had in being able to go it alone in the economic sense, and most socialists saw more hope for the future in gaining a new world through a Labour Government for the whole of Britain. Some left-wing Scots of independent mind, led by R. G. Cunninghame Graham coming round for the second time, R. E. Muirhead, small businessman and former ILP activist, and Hugh MacDairmid, maverick poetic genius, attempted to found a viable Scottish Nationalist Party (SNP) independent of Labour in 1928. They were joined by others less left-wing, led by John MacCormick, and when the SNP assumed its modern form in 1934, the original founders were largely edged aside. The new party had some appeal, and some value in stirring the establishment to pay more heed to Scotland in the later 1930s and 1940s than would otherwise have been the case, but made very little electoral mark.

Who then fell heir to the hard work of the Clydesiders and of the generations in the radical tradition before them? The unrecognizable remnants of the mantle of Elijah fell upon orthodox Labour, and in 1945, Scotland returned forty MPs to support Clement Attlee, as well as three ILP members, a Communist, and thirty Conservatives or National Liberals: there were no proper Liberals left. The Labour Government of 1945–51 was dedicated to expert solutions controlled from the centre, and, unlike Johnston, was indifferent to Scotland's traditions. Within Scotland the most powerful Labour politician in the 1930s was Sir Patrick Dollan, knighted in 1941 after having been leader of the Labour group on Glasgow Corporation for most of the period since 1922, and having drawn his skirts skilfully aside from James Maxton when he disaffiliated the ILP from the Labour Party in 1932. In 1933, a poor year for Labour nationally, Glasgow Council attained a Labour majority for the first time, largely because of divisions in the ranks of the right wing, the militant Protestants having fallen out with the middle-class alliance that they normally supported. Thanks to Dollan, once it obtained power, Labour never lost it in Glasgow again. It was Dollan, unemotional organizer, Catholic, party-machine man *par excellence*, who really understood the Scottish working-class voter of the years after 1920. He manipulated an electorate frightened by the immense scale of unemployment and industrial collapse, lacking the confidence for new adventure, distrustful of Tory and Liberal after the war, but nevertheless impressed by the practical energy of Wheatley in getting the Housing Act through in 1924 and even of Kirkwood in helping to get work restarted on '534', the hull that was to be the *Queen Mary*, in 1933. Meanwhile, the party kept its pledges to leave the Catholic schools with full State support. Labour in Scotland became synonymous with the defence of council housing, jobs in heavy industry and sectarian schools: it had nothing whatever to do with participatory democracy, enthusiasm for socialism or hope for the future.

In Christopher Harvie's phrase, 'the time of the "wee hard men" had come',[39] and the people who put them there had neither energy nor interest left to challenge them. The failure of the General Strike of 1926, followed by the defeat of the miners who held out afterwards for many starving months, and the lack of impact of the 'hunger marches' directed on London by the unemployed of Scotland and the north of England in the 1930s, had buried the tradition of direct action. So the radical tradition and socialist idealism did not end with the bang the

Thomas Chalmers in old age.

The great moral cause: ABOVE the temperance movement flanked by idealized Highlanders; BELOW the independent labour movement, flanked by Keir Hardie and Cunninghame Graham.

Outside the pub: ABOVE Springburn about 1900;
BELOW St Andrews 1910. The children are buying windmills.

Church and school: ABOVE ministers of Dunbarton Presbytery, at the time of the
Disruption of 1843; BELOW teacher, pupil–teacher and good little boys,
Anstruther, early twentieth century. There is no sign, in the country,
of the rickets that so afflicted slum children.

The coming of modern traffic: ABOVE Windmill Brae, Aberdeen, c. 1840;
the vegetable seller can set up her stall comfortably in the middle of the road;
BELOW Union Street, Aberdeen, in the early 1900s;
behind the tram on the left an early motor cab is about to pull out.

Boyish elegance: ABOVE the ideal in Argyle Street, 1884; BELOW the reality in Springburn, c. 1900.

ABOVE Markinch, Fife, 1897: open drains, bare feet, but in a small country town, straight legs. BELOW evacuees heading for the country at Dundee railway station, 1940: round every neck a name-tag, in every box a gas-mask.

Chartist plate of the period 1838–48.
The beehive was the emblem of labour before the hammer and sickle
and is portrayed here among symbols of prosperity and beauty.

Right had feared and the extreme Left had hoped for in 1919. It would have been a finely tuned ear that heard the whimper by 1945.

So what was the upshot of it all? The social historian has to be careful to avoid the sentimentality that has dogged the economic history of Scotland, where there has been much lament over the failure of the old heavy industries of the nineteenth century and less appreciation of the far better standard of living that the bulk of the population has come to enjoy since their final demise after the Second World War. The fruits of the collectivist State, of the rule of the expert, and of a policy of welfare determined from above and afar, are to be seen in the steadily improving quality of life for the Scottish people between the 1940s and the mid-1970s. If there is a message in this book, it is in how limited were the gains for most of the Scottish people between 1830 and around 1920, when heavy industry flourished and both radical tradition and socialist idealism attained their height. To say that they were limited is not to deny that some real gains in material welfare existed: we have tried to describe and delineate them. What was shocking to contemporaries, and is shocking to us, is how little one of the top two or three richest countries in the world did for its citizens until well on into the twentieth century.

The coming of the collectivist state, and its determination to turn over decision-making to the experts once it had been agreed that a combination of economic growth and welfare was to be the main aim of government, bears much of the credit for the improved state of Scottish welfare since 1945. However, it would be a blind observer of the Scottish scene who thought that Scotland today enjoys the vibrant popular political culture it enjoyed from the 1830s to the 1920s. Few today are as concerned as their forefathers were with the meanings of liberty or democracy, or would understand the meaning of the motto that the joiners of Glasgow carried on their banner in their demonstrations from 1832 to 1908. The Friends of the People, the Chartists, the Liberal Working Man, Keir Hardie and the Clydesiders shared a common belief that, at the close of the twentieth century, we are in danger of losing: by the exercise of political will, the people hold their own future in their own hands, and in the last analysis, no one can be blamed for our predicament but ourselves.

Notes, References and Further Reading

CHAPTER I: SCOTLAND IN THE 1830s AND 1840s

1. Quoted from Henry Cockburn's *Journal*, Vol. II, pp. 215–6 by Karl Miller, *Cockburn's Millenium* (London, 1975), p. 127
2. Alan B. Campbell, *The Lanarkshire Miners: A Social History of their Trade Unions, 1775–1874* (Edinburgh, 1979), p. 104
3. Quoted ibid.
4. Quoted from J. Murdoch, *A Guide to the Highlands of Speyside* (Forres, 1852), p. 324, by R. W. Butler, 'The Development of Tourism in the Highlands in the 18th and 19th Centuries', unpublished paper presented at the Annual Meeting of the Canadian Association of Scottish Studies, Montreal, June 1980
5. *Return showing the Total Annual Value of Real Property in each Parish for each County assessed to the Property and Income Tax for the year ending April 1843*, P.P. 1845, Vol. 38
6. *New Statistical Account* (Edinburgh 1845), Vol. VII, Argyll, p. 187
7. Ian Carter, *Farmlife in Northeast Scotland 1840–1914: The Poor Man's Country* (Edinburgh, 1979)
8. Quoted ibid., p. 33
9. Ian Levitt and Christopher Smout, *The State of the Scottish Working Class in 1843* (Edinburgh, 1979), Chapter 2
10. A. G. Bradley, *When Squires and Farmers Thrived* (London, 1927), p. 77
11. James E. Handley, *The Irish in Modern Scotland* (Oxford, 1974), p. 176
12. *Report of the Royal Commission on the Poor Laws (Scotland)* P.P. 1844, Vol. 21, p. 498
13. A. B. Campbell, op. cit., p. 134
14. James Taylor, *Journal of Local Events or Annals of Fenwick* (ed. T. D. Taylor, Ayrshire Archaeological and Natural History Society, 1970)
15. *Poor Law Report*, Vol. 22, p. 467
16. Norman Murray, *The Scottish Hand Loom Weavers 1790–1850: A Social History* (Edinburgh, 1978), p. 23

17. See, for a fuller account, T. C. Smout, 'The Strange Intervention of Edward Twistleton: Paisley in Depression 1841-3', in T. C. Smout (ed.) *The Search for Wealth and Stability: Essays in Economic and Social History presented to M. W. Flinn* (London, 1979)
18. *Report of the Select Committee on Distress in Paisley*, P.P. 1843, Vol. 7, p. 56
19. *Poor Law Report*, Vol. 21, p. 615
20. Ibid., Vol. 20, p. 612
21. Alexander Wilson, *The Chartist Movement in Scotland* (Manchester, 1970), p. 172
22. Quoted in A. Wilson, op. cit., p. 179
23. Ibid., Chapter 16
24. *Reports on the Sanitary Condition of the Labouring Population of Scotland* (House of Lords Papers, 1842, Vol. 28), p. 156
25. Ibid., pp. 8-9
26. *Poor Law Report*, Vol. 20, p. 119

Further Reading

A more detailed overview of the social plight of the working classes in this period is provided by Ian Levitt and Christopher Smout, *The State of the Scottish Working Class in 1843* (Edinburgh, 1979). Rural society then and later is discussed in Ian Carter, *Farmlife in Northeast Scotland 1840–1914* (Edinburgh, 1979) and James Hunter, *The Making of the Crofting Community* (Edinburgh, 1976). The handloom weavers are surveyed by Norman Murray, *The Scottish Hand Loom Weavers 1790–1850: a Social History* (Edinburgh, 1978), and the miners, very brilliantly, by Alan B. Campbell, *The Lanarkshire Miners: a Social History of their Trade Unions, 1775–1874* (Edinburgh, 1979). Much can be gleaned about the *mentalité* of Scotland from L. J. Saunders, *Scottish Democracy 1815–1840* (Edinburgh, 1950), a classic study of popular education. The best book on the Chartists is Alexander Wilson, *The Chartist Movement in Scotland* (Manchester, 1970), and the early history of social provision is surveyed by Thomas Ferguson, *The Dawn of Scottish Social Welfare* (Edinburgh, 1948).

The general histories of Scotland are valuable for this and later chapters. Relevant here, in particular, are Sydney and Olive Checkland, *Industry and Ethos: Scotland 1832–1914* (London, 1984); W. Ferguson, *Scotland 1689 to the Present* (Edinburgh, 1968); R. H. Campbell, *Scotland since 1707: the Rise of an Industrial Society* (2nd ed., Edinburgh, 1985); Bruce Lenman, *An Economic History of Modern Scotland 1660–1976* (London, 1977); A. Slaven, *The Development of the West of Scotland, 1750–1980* (London, 1975). A Marxist perspective is provided by Tony Dickson (ed.), *Scottish Capitalism* (London, 1980), of which Chapters 4–6 are especially stimulating.

CHAPTER II: THE TENEMENT CITY

1. *The Builder*, 1861, p. 293
2. Simone de Beauvoir, *Force of Circumstance* (London, 1968), p. 260

3. William Mitchell, *Rescue the Children* (London, 1886), p. 105

4. Quoted in T. Ferguson, *Scottish Social Welfare, 1864–1914* (Edinburgh, 1958), p. 104

5. Ibid., p. 104

6. S. G. Checkland, *The Upas Tree: Glasgow 1875–1975* (Glasgow, 1976), p. 20

7. R. Baird, 'Housing', in A. K. Cairncross (ed.), *The Scottish Economy* (Cambridge, 1954); R. G. Rodger, 'The Invisible Hand: Market Forces, Housing and the Urban Form in Victorian Cities', in D. Fraser and A. Sutcliffe (ed.), *The Pursuit of Urban History* (London, 1983), pp. 190–211. The latter paper also gives the most convincing account to-date of the effects of the feuing system

8. Brian Elliott and David McCrone, 'Urban Development in Edinburgh: a Contribution to the Political Economy of Space', *Scottish Journal of Sociology*, Vol. 4 (1980), p. 6

9. R. G. Rodger, 'Speculative Builders and the Structure of the Scottish Building Industry, 1860–1914', *Business History*, Vol. 21 (1977), p. 227

10. B. Elliott and D. McCrone, loc. cit., p. 15

11. *Report of the Royal Commission on Housing the Industrial Population of Scotland*, cd. 8731 (1917), p. 69

12. T. Brennan, *Reshaping a City* (Glasgow, 1959), p. 30

13. *The Builder*, 1861, pp. 421–2

14. E. Bredsdorff, *H. C. Andersen on England* (Copenhagen, 1954), p. 550

15. Quoted in Ian Adams, *The Making of Urban Scotland* (London, 1978), p. 155

16. G. Best, 'The Scottish Victorian City', *Victorian Studies*, Vol. 9 (1968), p. 334

17. R. G. Rodger, 'The Evolution of Scottish Town Planning', in G. Gordon and B. Dicks (ed.), *Scottish Urban History* (Aberdeen, 1983), p. 81

18. The complexities are well dealt with in G. S. Pryde, *Central and Local Government in Scotland since 1707*, Historical Association Pamphlet no. 45, 1960

19. G. Best, loc. cit., p. 335

20. *Autobiography of John McAdam* (Scottish History Society, 1980), p. 55

21. *The Builder*, 1859, pp. 701–2

22. I am grateful to Prof. G. K. Neville, Southwestern University, for this information from her unpublished research on Selkirk, and to Mr Stephen Patterson, St Andrews University, for the references to Fife. See *Twenty-second Annual Report of the Board of Supervision for Relief of the Poor (Scotland)*, 1867

23. John Butt, 'Working-class Housing in Glasgow, 1851–1914', in S. D. Chapman (ed.), *The History of Working-Class Housing* (Newton Abbot, 1971), pp. 57–92

24. I am indebted to Dr W. H. Fraser for this quotation, which is from R. E. C. Lond, *Fortnightly Review*, Jan. 1903. Dr Fraser's unpublished paper, 'Municipal Socialism and Social Policy' is the best account of municipalization in Scotland, and I am most grateful to the author for allowing me to use it

25. George Bell, *Day and Night in the Wynds of Edinburgh* (reprint, 1973), p. 4

26. Ibid., p. 10

27. Reported in *The Builder*, 1860, p. 667

28. *The Builder*, 1861, p. 349

29. Cited in John Whiteford, 'The Application of the Poor Law in Mid-nineteenth Century Glasgow', unpublished Edinburgh University Ph.D. thesis, 1982, p. 223

30. *Return by the Superintendent of Police* (Edinburgh, 1870)

31. J. Whiteford, op. cit., pp. 226–7

32. Bill Murray, *The Old Firm: Sectarianism, Sport and Society in Scotland* (Edinburgh, 1984), pp. 143–158. Dr Aaron Esterson, *pers. comm.*

33. Sean Damer, 'State, Class and Housing: Glasgow, 1885–1919', in Joseph Melling (ed.), *Housing, Social Policy and the State* (London, 1980), p. 82; Butt, 'Housing in Glasgow, 1851–1914', pp. 64, 68–9

34. Quoted in J. Whiteford, op. cit., p. 184

35. Thomas Thorburn, *Statistical Analysis of the Census of the City of Edinburgh* (Edinburgh, 1851), pp. 9–10

36. John Wheatley, *Eight-Pound Cottages for Glasgow Citizens* (Glasgow, 1908), p. 2

37. Brian Elliott and David McCrone, 'Property and Politics in Edinburgh: 1875–1975', in J. Garrard (ed.), *Middle-Class Politics* (London, 1978)

38. Quoted in Damer, 'State, Class and Housing', p. 83

39. Olive Checkland, *Philanthropy in Victorian Scotland* (Edinburgh, 1980), pp. 81–2

40. Enid Gauldie, *Cruel Habitations: A History of Working-Class Housing 1780–1918* (London, 1974), pp. 203–6

41. Quoted in John Butt, 'Working-Class Housing in the Scottish Cities 1900–1950', in George Gordon and Brian Dicks (eds), *Scottish Urban History* (Aberdeen, 1983), pp. 241–2

42. Sir William Y. Darling, *So It Looks to Me* (London, n.d.), p. 231

43. In Glasgow, 74,000 houses were built, 1920–1951: of these 0.3% had one room, 6% had four rooms, 4% had five rooms and 1.7% had more than five. Butt, 'Housing in the Scottish Cities 1900–1950', p. 258

44. Robert Grieve, 'In Retrospect: 40 Years of Development and Achievement', *The Planners*, May 1980, p. 62

45. H. W. Richardson, J. Vipond and R. Furbey, *Housing and Urban Spatial Structure: a Case Study* (Farnborough, 1975), p. 158. Some indication of the difference between Edinburgh and the other cities is given by the indices of dissimilarity between the highest and lowest class. In Edinburgh the figure is 71, compared to 54 in Chicago, 46 in Oxford, 44 in Oslo, and 53 in the Outer Metropolitan Area of Kent

46. Iain McLean, *The Legend of Red Clydeside* (Edinburgh, 1983), p. 233; S. G. Checkland, op. cit., pp. 39–40

47. Patrick Geddes, *City Development: A Report to the Carnegie Dunfermline Trust* (with an introduction by Peter Green) (Shannon, 1973), p. 32 of main text

48. S. G. Checkland, op. cit., p. 94

Further Reading

Urban history is a blossoming subject today, and Scotland has shared in the interest. Ian Adams, *The Making of Urban Scotland* (London, 1978) is a good introduction, and S. G. Checkland, *The Upas Tree: Glasgow 1875–1975* (Glasgow, 1976), though a small book is a classic. D. Englander, *Landlord and Tenant in Urban Britain, 1838–1918* (Oxford, 1983), Enid Gauldie, *Cruel Habitations: a History of Working-Class Housing, 1780–1918* (London, 1974), and M. J. Daunton, *House and Home in the Victorian City: Working-*

Class Housing 1850–1914 (London, 1983) are volumes on British problems, with extensive Scottish material. Much of the best writing on Scottish housing, however, is still scattered in the articles and essays by J. Butt, R. G. Rodger, B. Elliott and D. McCrone, and S. Damer, cited in the notes to this chapter. Public health can be approached through R. J. Morris, *Cholera 1832: the Social Response to an Epidemic* (London, 1976), O. Checkland and M. Lamb (eds), *Health Care as Social History: the Glasgow Case* (Aberdeen, 1982) and two older books by T. Ferguson, *The Dawn of Scottish Social Welfare* (Edinburgh, 1948) and *Scottish Social Welfare 1864–1914* (Edinburgh, 1958). For the demographic facts, M. W. Flinn (ed.), *Scottish Population History from the Seventeenth Century to the 1930s* (Cambridge, 1977) is indispensible. G. F. Best's 'Scottish Victorian Cities', *Victorian Studies*, Vol. 9 (1968), pp. 329–358, is valuable: Haldane Tait, *A Doctor and Two Policemen* (Edinburgh, 1982) is a helpful account of Littlejohn and his successors in Edinburgh's public health administration. The twists in administrative history are partially unravelled, at least, by G. S. Pryde, *Central and Local Government in Scotland since 1707* (Historical Association, 1960). The big subject of middle-class good works is tackled by Olive Checkland, *Philanthropy in Victorian Scotland* (Edinburgh, 1980).

Finally, it is worth seeking out in the nearest university or large public library at least two classic parliamentary papers of the period: *The Report on the Sanitary Condition of the Labouring Population of Scotland*, 1842, and *The Report of the Royal Commission on Housing in Scotland*, 1917. In case the reader is overwhelmed by gloom, however, and comes to believe that no human being could be happy in a tenement, he or she should turn to Molly Weir, *Shoes Were for Sunday* (London, 1970), the recollections of a very bouncy child brought up among the respectable poor of Glasgow in the interwar years.

CHAPTER III: LEAVING AND STAYING ON IN THE COUNTRYSIDE

1. *Report of the Royal Commission on Labour*, Parliamentary Papers 1893, Vol. 36, pp. 8–10, 117–8
2. Ibid., p. 13
3. Ian Carter, *Farmlife in Northeast Scotland, 1840–1914* (Edinburgh, 1979), p. 161
4. *Report of R.C. on Labour*, loc. cit., Part II, p. 8
5. Archibald Geikie, *Scottish Reminiscences* (Glasgow, 1904), pp. 226–7
6. Eric Richards, *A History of the Highland Clearances* (London, 1982), pp. 474–5
7. Elihu Burrit, *A Walk from London to John O'Groats* (London, 1864), p. 394
8. Eric Richards, 'Highland emigrants to South Australia in the 1850s', *Northern Scotland*, Vol. 4 (1982), pp. 28–9
9. *Papers on Sutherland Estate Management* (Scottish History Society, 1972), Vol. I, pp. 175–6
10. Quoted in E. Richards, loc. cit., p. 23
11. *Report to the Board of Supervision by Sir John MacNeill on the Western Highlands and Islands*, P.P. 1851, Vol. 26

12. Thomas Pennant, *A Tour in Scotland and Voyage to the Hebrides, 1772* (London, 1776), Vol. I, p. 365

13. Donald Macdonald, *Lewis: A History of the Island* (Edinburgh, 1978), p. 174

14. James Hunter, *The Making of the Crofting Community* (Edinburgh, 1976), pp. 132–3

15. *Report of the Royal Commission on the Condition of the Crofters and Cottars of the Highlands of Scotland*, P.P. 1884, Vol. 33, p. 709

16. Clive Dewey, 'Celtic Agrarian Legislation and the Celtic Revival: Historicist Implications of Gladstone's Irish and Scottish Land Acts 1870–1886', *Past and Present*, No. 64 (1974), pp. 30–70

17. J. A. Symon, *Scottish Farming, Past and Present* (Edinburgh, 1959), p. 295

18. Nigel Nicolson, *Lord of the Isles* (London, 1960), pp. 76–7

19. A. Geddes, *The Isle of Lewis and Harris* (Edinburgh, 1955), p. 275

20. N. Nicolson, op. cit., p. 151

21. For Ireland see Joseph Lee, *The Modernisation of Irish Society 1848–1918* (Dublin, 1973)

22. Adam Collier, *The Crofting Problem* (Cambridge, 1953), p. 64

23. Ibid., p. 75

24. *Report of the Royal Commission on the Depression of Trade and Industry*, P.P. 1886, Vol. 23, pp. 186–95

25. A. Geddes, op. cit., p. 285

26. A. Collier, op. cit., pp. 133–41

27. J. P. Day, *Public Administration in the Highlands and Islands of Scotland* (London, 1918), p. 296

28. A. Geddes, op. cit., pp. 84–5

29. *Report of the Royal Commission on Labour*, P.P. 1893, Vol. 36, pp. 8, 33

30. Andrew Purves, 'A Shepherd Remembers', *Journal of the Scottish Labour History Society*, No. 15 (1981), p. 26

31. A. Collier. op. cit.; R. Hutchison, 'Report on the Dietaries of Scotch Agricultural Labourers', *Transactions of the Highland and Agricultural Society*, 4th series Vol. 2 (1868); E. P. Cathcart, A. M. T. Murray and J. B. Beveridge, *Studies in Nutrition; An Inquiry into the Diet of Families in the Highlands and Islands of Scotland*, Medical Research Council, Special Report Series, No. 242 (1940)

32. *R.C. on Labour*, p. 10

33. James Littlejohn, *Westrigg: the Sociology of a Cheviot Parish* (London, 1963), Chapter VIII

34. Ibid., p. 146

35. Ibid., p. 151

36. David Buchan, 'The Expressive Culture of Nineteenth-Century Scottish Farm Servants', in T. M. Devine (ed.), *Farm Servants and Labour in Lowland Scotland, 1770–1914* (Edinburgh, 1984), p. 235

Further Reading

Writing on the social history of the Scottish countryside has been very unequally divided between the Highlands and the Lowlands. The Lowlands are represented only by two splendid and very different books: Ian Carter, *Farmlife in Northeast Scotland* (Edinburgh, 1979) and James Littlejohn, *Westrigg: the Sociology of a Cheviot Parish* (London, 1963). Much information on 'traditional' ways of rural life can, however, be gleaned from A. Fenton, *Scottish Country Life* (Edinburgh, 1976). A recent valuable collection of essays is T. M. Devine (ed.), *Farm Servants and Labour in Lowland Scotland, 1770–1914* (Edinburgh, 1984). The Highlands have attracted a wealth of excellent writing. Eric Richards, *The Highland Clearances* (London, 1982) would have been more read if it had not been so abominably printed: it is the only level-headed account of its subject. James Hunter, *The Making of the Crofting Community* (Edinburgh, 1976) is one-sided but scholarly and highly readable. There is one good article on the migrant labour economy: T. M. Devine, 'Temporary migration and the Scottish Highlands in the 19th century', *Economic History Review*, 2nd series, Vol. 32 (1979), pp. 344–359. V. E. Durkacz, *The Decline of the Celtic Languages* (Edinburgh, 1983) is essential for the decay of Gaelic. Older studies of great worth include J. P. Day, *Public Administration in the Highlands and Islands of Scotland* (London, 1918) (a much wider book than its title suggests); Adam Collier, *The Crofting Problem* (Cambridge, 1953); F. Fraser Darling, *West Highland Survey* (Oxford, 1955). Willie Orr, *Deer Forests, Landlords and Crofters* (Edinburgh, 1982) is useful on sporting estates. P. Gaskell, *Morvern Transformed* (Cambridge, 1968) is a case study of one remote area. Nigel Nicolson, *Lord of the Isles* (London, 1960) is a lively account of Leverhulme on Lewis. The extreme north is discussed in A. Fenton, *The Northern Isles: Orkney and Shetland* (Edinburgh, 1978). The differing perspectives of outsiders visiting the Highlands is discussed in C. Smout, 'Tours in the Scottish Highlands from the Eighteenth to the Twentieth Centuries', *Northern Scotland*, Vol. V (1983), pp. 99–121.

Finally, it is worth seeking out *The Report of the Royal Commission on the Employment of Women and Children in Agriculture*, volume of Scottish evidence, 1870, for Lowland social conditions, and, for the Highlands, *The Report of the Royal Commission on the Highlands and Islands of Scotland*, 1884 (the Napier Commission): both give a great wealth of local detail.

CHAPTER IV: A WORKING LIFE IN INDUSTRY

1. G. M. Thomson, *Scotland, that Distressed Area* (Edinburgh, 1935), pp. 4–6
2. Thomas Bell, *Pioneering Days* (London, 1941), pp. 72–3
3. Harry McShane, *No Mean Fighter* (London, 1978), p. 41
4. *People's Journal*, 14 Oct. 1922, quoted in William M. Walker, *Juteopolis: Dundee and its Textile Workers, 1885–1923* (Edinburgh, 1979), p. 40
5. *Forward*, 19 Oct. 1912
6. Billy Kay, *Odyssey: Voices from Scotland's Recent Past* (Edinburgh, 1980), p. 38
7. Kellog Durland, *Among the Fife Miners* (London, 1904), pp. 116–8
8. *Reports of the Schemes of the Church of Scotland* (1894), p. 810
9. R. Q. Gray, *The Labour Aristocracy in Victorian Edinburgh* (Oxford, 1976), pp. 106–7
10. *Reports of the Schemes of the Church*, p. 807

11. David Kirkwood, *My Life of Revolt* (London, 1935), pp. 57–9
12. H. McShane, op. cit., pp. 3–4
13. D. Kirkwood, op. cit., pp. 11–12
14. *Report of the Royal Commission on Labour*, Parliamentary Papers, 1893, Vol. 37 (I), p. 194
15. B. Kay, op. cit., pp. 40–1
16. K. Durland, op. cit., pp. 98–9
17. R. Q. Gray, unpublished paper, 'The Problem of Labour Aristocracy, Class Situation, Life-Styles and Working-Class Culture'
18. L. Llewelyn Lewis, *The Children of the Unskilled* (London, 1924), especially pp. 12–16
19. T. Ferguson and J. Cunnison, *The Young Wage-earner: a Study of Glasgow Boys* (Oxford, 1951), pp. 42–3
20. Ursula R. Q. Henriques, 'An early factory inspector: James Stuart of Dunearn', *The Scottish Historical Review*, Vol. 50 (1971), pp. 18–46
21. W. H. Marwick, *Economic Developments in Victorian Scotland* (London, 1936), p. 140
22. T. Bell, op. cit., p. 21
23. Abe Moffat, *My Life with the Miners* (London, 1965), p. 16
24. A. Campbell, 'The granting of certificates of fitness to children and young persons for employment in factories and workshops', *British Medical Journal*, 1902, Vol. 2, p. 756
25. Quoted in W. M. Walker, op. cit., p. 83
26. A. Moffat, op. cit., p. 16
27. T. Bell, op. cit., pp. 21–5
28. R. H. Tawney, 'The economics of boy labour', *Economic Journal*, Vol. 19 (1909), p. 520
29. Ibid., pp. 525–6
30. T. Ferguson and J. Cunnison, op. cit., pp. 14–16
31. R. H. Tawney, loc. cit., pp. 521–2
32. L. L. Lewis, op. cit., p. 75
33. *Disinherited Youth* (Carnegie United Kingdom Trust Report, Edinburgh, 1943), p. 13
34. D. J. Robertson, 'Labour turnover in the Clyde Shipbuilding Industry', *Scottish Journal of Political Economy*, Vol. I. (1954)
35. Sylvia Price, 'Labour mobility in Clyde Shipbuilding, 1889–1913', unpublished paper presented to a conference on shipbuilding in Britain and Scandinavia, Gothenburg, November 1982
36. J. H. Treble, 'The seasonal demand for adult labour in Glasgow, 1890–1914', *Social History*, Vol. 3 (1978), pp. 50–3
37. All the above illustrations are drawn from the *Reports of the Royal Commission on Labour*, Parliamentary Papers 1893, Vol. 32 (for Fife miners); Vol. 33 (for transport workers); Vol. 34 (for chemical workers and shop assistants)
38. K. Durland, op. cit., p. 88
39. *R.C. on Labour*, op. cit., Vol. 32, p. 455
40. K. Durland, op. cit., p. 51
41. T. Bell, op. cit., p. 25

42. Sylvia Price, 'Riveters' earnings in Clyde Shipbuilding 1889–1913'. *Scottish Economic and Social History*, Vol. 1 (1981), p. 56

43. T. Bell, op. cit., pp. 64–5

44. Edwin Muir, *The Story and the Fable* (London, 1940), pp. 163–4

45. Robert Smillie, *My Life for Labour* (London, 1924), p. 17

46. H. McShane, op. cit., pp. 19–20

47. *R.C. on Labour*, P.P. 1892, Vol. 36 (1), p. 66; K. Durland, op. cit., p. 75

48. R. Smillie, op. cit., p. 23

49. P. S. Bagwell, *The Railwaymen* (London, 1963), p. 146

50. D. Kirkwood, op. cit., p. 122

51. Ibid., p. 261

Further Reading

A readiness to generalize about the conditions of nineteenth-century labour has seldom been matched by eagerness to examine what work was like, and what attitudes the working classes really held. One honourable exception to this rule is certainly A. B. Campbell, *The Lanarkshire Miners* (Edinburgh, 1979); another is W. M. Walker, *Juteopolis: Dundee and its Textile Workers, 1885–1923* (Edinburgh, 1979). Both treat work as a background to studies of union history, and a similar approach informs J. Hinton, *The First Shop Stewards' Movement*, which is useful for the background to Clyde engineering. Generally, however, the reader is forced back to contemporary sources. Kellog Durland, *Among the Fife Miners* (London, 1904) is a remarkable outside view of a mining community. Various working-class autobiographies provide, in their early pages, informed inside views—for example, on the engineers, Harry McShane, *No Mean Fighter* (London, 1978) and David Kirkwood, *My Life of Revolt* (London, 1935); on the miners, Abe Moffat, *My Life with the Miners* (London, 1965) and Robert Smillie, *My Life for Labour* (London, 1924); on foundry-workers, Thomas Bell, *Pioneering Days* (London, 1941). Patrick Macgill, *Children of the Dead End* (London, 1914), is an effective autobiographical novel about a navvy's life in Scotland. The pages of the government blue books contain an enormous amount of information: the *Report of the Royal Commission on Labour*, 1893, is an especially good example. Other very useful studies for various aspects of this chapter are R. Q. Gray, *The Labour Aristocracy in Victorian Edinburgh* (Oxford, 1976), which is most illuminating on respectability; Stuart Macintyre, *Little Moscows* (London, 1980), on interwar Fife and the Vale of Leven; R. H. Tawney, 'The economics of boy labour', *Economic Journal*, Vol. 19 (1909); and J. H. Treble, 'The seasonal demand for adult labour in Glasgow, 1890–1914', *Social History*, Vol. 3 (1978); J. Melling, '"Non-commissioned officers": British employers and their supervisory officers', *Social History*, Vol. 5 (1980). Lastly, it should not be overlooked that oral history provides a treasure-house of evidence on the nature of work: much has been taped, but little exists transcribed and analysed between hard covers. However, Billy Kay's two collections, *Odyssey: Voices from Scotland's Recent Past* (Edinburgh, 1980) and *Odyssey: Voices from Scotland's Recent Past, the Second Collection* (Edinburgh, 1982) along with Paul Thompson, *Living the Fishing* (London, 1983), illustrate what might be done.

CHAPTER V: THE REWARDS OF LABOUR

1. E. Cramond, 'The Economic Position of Scotland', *Journal of the Royal Statistical Society*, Vol. 75 (1911–12); L. M. Cullen and T. C. Smout (eds), *Comparative Aspects of Scottish and Irish Economic and Social History 1600–1900* (Edinburgh, 1977), p. 14. See also note 4

2. A. D. Campbell, 'Changes in Scottish Incomes, 1924–1949', *Economic Journal*, Vol. 65 (1955)

3. C. H. Feinstein, *National Income, Expenditure and Output of the United Kingdom, 1855–1965* (Cambridge, 1972)

4. R. Dudley Baxter, *National Income of the United Kingdom* (London, 1867), p. 56. I have telescoped some of his categories to make the table more comprehensible, and the numbering 1–6 is not in the original

5. Clive Lee, 'Modern Economic Growth and Structural Change in Scotland: the Service Sector Reconsidered', *Scottish Economic and Social History*, Vol. 3 (1983), pp. 5–35

6. *Labor in Europe and America* (Washington, DC: Government Printing Office, 1876). The US consular reports for Scotland are available in xerox form in Edinburgh University Library

7. R. H. Campbell, *The Rise and Fall of Scottish Industry, 1707–1939* (Edinburgh, 1980), Chapter 4; E. H. Hunt, *Regional Wage Variations in Britain, 1850–1914* (Oxford, 1973)

8. S. F. Price, 'Riveters' Earnings in Clyde Shipbuilding, 1889–1913', *Scottish Economic and Social History*, Vol. 1 (1981), pp. 42–65

9. R. G. Rodger, 'The Invisible Hand: Market Forces, Housing and the Urban Form in Victorian Cities', in D. Fraser and A. Sutcliffe (ed.) *The Pursuit of Urban History* (London, 1980), pp. 190–211

10. Carnegie United Kingdom Trust, *Disinherited Youth* (Edinburgh, 1943), p. 6

11. Edwin Muir, *Scottish Journey* (edn. Edinburgh, 1979), pp. 2, 139

12. A. D. Campbell, 'Income', and D. J. Robertson, 'Wages', in Cairncross, *Scottish Economy* (Cambridge, 1954).

13. E. Llewelyn Lewis, *The Children of the Unskilled: an Economic and Social Study* (London, 1924), p. 9

14. Gavin McCrone, *Regional Policy in Britain* (London, 1969), p. 163

15. Stuart Macintyre, *Little Moscows* (London, 1980), p. 126

16. Abe Moffat, *My Life with the Miners* (London, 1965), p. 57

17. C. B. Gunn, *Leaves from the Life of a Country Doctor* (London, 1935), p. 38

18. W. L. Mackenzie, *Scottish Mothers and Children*, Vol. III of the Carnegie UK Trust Report on the Physical Welfare of Mothers and Children (Dunfermline, 1917), p. 169

19. J. B. Russell, *On the Prevention of Tuberculosis* (Glasgow, 1896), pp. 43–4, 53

20. *Report of the Committee on Scottish Health Services* (Edinburgh, 1936), Cmd. 5204, pp. 14–15, 200–204

21. Quoted in W. Leslie Mackenzie, *The Medical Inspection of School Children* (Edinburgh, 1904), pp. 142–3

22. Dugald Baird, 'Environment and reproduction', *British Journal of Obstetrics and Gynaecology*, Vol. 87 (1980), pp. 1057–67
23. William Mitchell, *Rescue the Children* (London, 1886), p. 84
24. W. L. Mackenzie, *Scottish Mothers and Children*, op. cit., p. 181
25. Ibid., p. 183
26. James Ewan, *The School Health Service, Glasgow* (Glasgow, n.d.)
27. *Family Diet and Health in Pre-War Britain*, Report to the Carnegie Trust from the Rowett Research Institute (Dunfermline, 1955), p. 58
28. W. L. Mackenzie, *Medical Inspection*, op. cit., pp. 167, 209
29. E. P. Cathcart et al., *The Physique of Man in Industry*, Medical Research Council Industrial Health Research Board Report, No. 71 (HMSO 1935)
30. Ian Levitt and Christopher Smout, *The State of the Scottish Working Class in 1843* (Edinburgh, 1979), Chapter 2
31. *Glasgow Municipal Commission on the Housing of the Poor, Minutes of Evidence*, Vol. I (1903), pp. 337–8
32. David Kirkwood, *My Life of Revolt* (London, 1935), p. 52
33. W. Mitchell, op. cit., pp. 101–3
34. *Report of the Committee on Scottish Health Services*, p. 95
35. Helen Corr, 'The schoolgirl's curriculum and the ideology of the home, 1870–1914' in *Uncharted Lives; Extracts from Scottish Women's Experiences* (Glasgow Women's Studies Group, 1983), pp. 74–97
36. John Boyd Orr, *Food, Health and Income* (London, 1936), p. 5
37. *Family Diet and Health*, pp. 41–5
38. Ibid., pp. 7–8

Further Reading

Careful research on the Scottish standard of living has yet to be undertaken, but economic historians have interested themselves in certain aspects of the problem for their own purposes. Ian Levitt and Christopher Smout, *The State of the Scottish Working Class in 1843* (Edinburgh, 1979), R. H. Campbell, *The Rise and Fall of Scottish Industry* (Edinburgh, 1980), and E. H. Hunt, *Regional Wage Variations in Britain, 1850–1914*, together with the articles by Lee, Rodger and Price cited in notes 5, 8 and 9 to this chapter, represent the main corpus of modern work into wages before the First World War. Levitt and Smout, and R. H. Campbell's chapter 'Diet in Scotland: An Example of Regional Variation', in T. C. Barker, J. C. Mackenzie, J. Judkin (eds), *Our Changing Fare* (London, 1966) discuss food in the same period. For the interwar years, A. D. Campbell, 'Changes in Scottish Incomes 1924–1949', *Economic Journal*, Vol. 65 (1955), is indispensable, as are chapters by himself and others in A. K. Cairncross (ed.), *The Scottish Economy* (Cambridge, 1954). S. Macintyre, *Little Moscows* (London, 1980) is revealing on poverty in small communities in this period. The numerous investigations of doctors, nutritional scientists and school medical inspectors working on height, weight, food and income are a fascinating mine of information for the first half of the twentieth century. The pioneers in this field were D. N. Paton, J. C. Dunlop and E. M. Inglis, *A Study of the Diet of the Labouring Classes in Edinburgh* (Edinburgh, n.d.);

Dundee Social Union, *Report on Housing and Industrial Conditions and Medical Inspection of School Children* (Dundee, 1905); D. E. Lindsay, *Report upon a Study of the Diet of the Labouring Classes in the City of Glasgow* (Glasgow, 1913). The Reports to the Carnegie UK Trust cited, and the Special Reports of the Medical Research Council (e.g. No. 13 on munitions workers, No. 87 on miners, No. 218 on foodstuffs, No. 242 on the Highlands and No. 289 on miners and clerks in Fife) are especially noteworthy, and can be obtained on inter-library loan if you have problems finding them locally. The general outlines of the fall in child mortality are dealt with in M. W. Flinn et al., *Scottish Population History from the Seventeenth Century to the 1930s* (Cambridge, 1977), and further medical information is in David Hamilton, *The Healers* (Edinburgh, 1981).

CHAPTER VI: DRINK, TEMPERANCE AND RECREATION

1. The calculations are approximate. They are arrived at from data in G. B. Wilson, *Alcohol and the Nation* (London, 1940) and I. Donnachie, *A History of the Brewing Industry in Scotland* (Edinburgh, 1979). For whisky, the annual consumption of proof gallons is multiplied to take account of the fact that the average strength of whisky is 30 per cent under proof and 100 gallons of proof spirit makes 143 gallons of 'selling' spirit (Wilson, pp. 2–3): the sum is then multiplied by 8/52 to find a weekly per capita consumption in pints, and multiplied again by 5/3 to take account of the fact that 40 per cent of the population was under 14. Beer consumption statistics are harder to come by: Donnachie p. 119 gives a figure for 1830 of 326,000 barrels, and 36 gallons were in the standard barrel. Thereafter production in Scotland grew rapidly, reaching 2,000,000 barrels around 1900 (equivalent to about 5 pints a head) but apparently well over half of this was consumed outside Scotland and imports of English beer did not compensate. This figure had fallen to 1,000,000 by 1930, when the same market conditions pertained.

2. Brian Harrison, *Drink and the Victorians* (London, 1971), p. 314

3. John Dunlop, *The Philosophy of Artificial and Compulsory Drinking Usage in Great Britain and Ireland* (London, 1839), p. 6

4. G. B. Wilson, op. cit., p. 258

5. Anon., *Doings of a Notorious Glasgow Shebeener: How He Made his Drink, with Numerous Drink Recipes* (n.p., n.d.), pp. 2–3. This pamphlet is in the Mitchell Library, Glasgow, and I am grateful to Dr Daniel Paton for bringing it to my attention

6. *Glasgow, 1858: Shadow's Midnight Scenes and Social Photographs*, with an introduction by J. F. McCaffrey (Glasgow, 1976), pp. 98–9

7. George Bell, *Blackfriar's Wynd Analyzed* (Edinburgh, 1850), p. 17. This pamphlet and its companion, *Day and Night in the Wynds of Edinburgh* (Edinburgh, 1849), were reprinted in facsimile with an introduction by G. H. Martin (Wakefield, 1973)

8. Sir Archibald Geikie, *Scottish Reminiscences* (Glasgow, 1904), p. 312

9. James Devon, *The Criminal and the Community* (London, 1912), p. 69

10. Quoted in James E. Handley, *The Navvy in Scotland* (Cork, 1970), p. 335
11. Quoted in Norman Longmate, *The Waterdrinkers* (London, 1968), p. 153
12. Andrew L. Drummond and James Bulloch, *The Church in Victorian Scotland* (Edinburgh, 1975), p. 27
13. *The Abstainers Journal* (Glasgow, 1853), pp. 28–9, 166–8
14. *Report of the Royal Commission on the Scottish Poor Law* P.P. 1844, Vol. 20, p. 113
15. Quoted in James E. Handley, *The Irish in Scotland, 1798–1845* (Cork, 1943), pp. 247–8
16. Quoted In Elspeth King, *Scotland Sober and Free* (Glasgow, 1979), p. 6
17. Ibid., p. 11
18. *Edinburgh Juvenile Temperance Union Monthly Pictorial Tract* (n.d., ca. 1860)
19. About 2.34 proof gallons per year in 1825–9, and 2.40 in 1845–9
20. *Testimonies and Statistics in Reference to the Working of the Public Houses Act* (Glasgow, 1857), pp. 43–4
21. James Stirling, *Failure of the Forbes Mackenzie Act* (Glasgow, 1859), p. 22
22. *Glasgow Shebeener*, op cit., pp. 4–5
23. Arthur Sherwell, *The Drink Peril in Scotland* (Edinburgh, 1903)
24. Kellog Durland, *Among the Fife Miners* (London, 1904), pp. 153–4
25. David Lewis, *Britain's Social State* (Glasgow, 1878), p. 102
26. E. King, op. cit., p. 16
27. Ibid., p. 24
28. Ian Donnachie, 'World War I and the Drink Question: State Control of the Drink Trade', *The Journal of the Scottish Labour History Society*, No. 17 (1982)
29. A. Sherwell, op. cit., pp. 13–14
30. Carnegie United Kingdom Trust, *Disinherited Youth* (Edinburgh, 1943), pp. 101–2
31. I am greatly obliged to Roberta Scott for this information, from her forthcoming book, *Dunbarney: A Parish with a Past*, Chapter 7
32. Thomas Bell, *Pioneering Days* (London, 1941), p. 17
33. Lynne Jamieson, 'Growing up in Scotland in the 1900s', in *Uncharted Lives: Extracts from Scottish Women's Experiences, 1850–1982* (Glasgow Women's Studies Group, 1983), pp. 20–1
34. [William Walker], *Glaiska Fair* (Glasgow, n.d.), p. 4
35. Olive Checkland, *Philanthrophy in Victorian Scotland* (Edinburgh, 1980), p. 140
36. J. Devon, op. cit., pp. 86–7
37. Morris Marples, *A History of Football* (London, 1954), p. 92
38. H. H. Almond, 'Football as a Moral Agent', *Nineteenth Century*, Vol. 34 (1893), pp. 902–3
39. W. W. Beveridge, 'Scottish Football: its Early Days', in N. L. Jackson, *Association Football* (London, 1899), p. 225; 'Queen's Park', ibid., p. 314; J. E. Handley, *The Celtic Story* (London, 1960), p. 14
40. M. Marples, op. cit., p. 179; N. L. Jackson, op. cit., p. 241
41. Paul Fussell, *Class, Style and Status in the USA* (London, 1984), p. 115
42. 'Reports of the Committee on Non-Church Going' in *Reports on the Schemes of the Church of Scotland*, 1891–3
43. Bill Murray, *The Old Firm: Sectarianism, Sport and Society in Scotland* (Edinburgh, 1984), pp. 76–8 and especially Chapter 7

44. Tony Mason, *Association Football and English Society 1863–1915* (Brighton, 1980), pp. 154–7

45. Abe Moffat, *My Life with the Miners* (London, 1965), p. 20

46. Wray Vamplew, *The Turf: a Social and Economic History of Horse Racing* (London, 1976), p. 205

47. T. Mason, op. cit., p. 198

48. *Report of the Select Committee of the House of Lords on Betting*, P.P. 1902, Vol. V; Carnegie United Kingdom Trust, *Disinherited Youth* (Dunfermline, 1943), p. 109

49. David A. Jamieson, *Powderhall and Pedestrianism* (Edinburgh, 1943), p. 125

50. K. Durland, op. cit., p. 129

51. Billy Kay, *Odyssey: Voices from Scotland's Recent Past* (Edinburgh, 1980), p. 79

52. *Disinherited Youth*, op. cit., p. 105

53. Ibid., pp. 101, 104, 107

54. D. J. Robertson, 'Consumption' in A. K. Cairncross (ed.), *The Scottish Economy* (Cambridge, 1954), p. 177

Further Reading

The best account of Scottish drinking and its temperance opponents is, unfortunately, still unpublished: D. N. Paton, 'Drink and the Temperance Movement in Nineteenth-century Scotland', Ph.D. thesis, Edinburgh, 1977. There is, however, an excellent illustrated pamphlet published from the People's Palace, Elspeth King, *Scotland Sober and Free* (Glasgow, 1979), commemorating the temperance cause. On the drink problem itself, G. B. Wilson, *Alcohol and the Nation* (London, 1940) directs itself to Britain with ample treatment of Scotland. It is an indispensable compendium of factual information on consumption, licensing, etc. Most contemporary accounts of the slums and of working-class life emphasize the drink question. Two reprinted examples are George Bell, *Blackfriars' Wynd Analyzed* (Wakefield, 1973), and *Glasgow, 1858: Shadow's Midnight Scenes and Social Photography*, with an introduction by J. F. McCaffrey (Glasgow, 1976).

Recreation has been even less studied than drink, but the important topic of the interrelationship between sectarian violence and football in Glasgow is discussed in Bill Murray, *The Old Firm: Sectarianism, Sport and Society in Scotland* (Edinburgh, 1984). Writing on Scottish sport, especially football, has not had a very strong dimension in social history, though Bob Crampsey, *The Scottish Footballer* (Edinburgh, 1978) is an exception to the rule. Unfortunately, it is very brief. See also John Rafferty, *One Hundred Years of Scottish Football* (London 1973), John Hutchinson, *The Football Industry* (Glasgow, 1982), Tony Mason, *Association Football and English Society* (Brighton, 1980).

CHAPTER VII: SEX, LOVE AND GETTING MARRIED

1. T. C. Smout, 'Aspects of Sexual Behaviour in Nineteenth-Century Scotland', in A. A. MacLaren (ed.), *Social Class in Scotland: Past and Present* (Edinburgh, 1976), p. 56

2. James Boswell, *The Life of Samuel Johnson ... to which is added the Journal of a Tour to the Hebrides*, ed. P. Fitzgerald (London, 1897), p. 593

3. Ralph Wardlaw, *Lectures on Female Prostitution* (Glasgow, 1843), pp. 57–8; *Social Evils and Problems*, edited for the Church of Scotland Commission on the War by W. P. Paterson and D. Watson (Edinburgh, 1918), p. 68

4. Alfred C. C. List, *The Two Phases of the Social Evil* (Edinburgh, 1861)

5. *Statistical Account of Scotland*, Vol. VI (1793), p. 612

6. Olive Checkland, *Philanthropy in Victorian Scotland* (Edinburgh, 1980), p. 239

7. William Tait, *Magdalenism: an Inquiry into the Extent, Causes and Consequences of Prostitution in Edinburgh*, second edition (London, 1842), pp. 2–10

8. R. Wardlaw, op. cit., pp. 31–2

9. Isabella L. Bird, *Notes on Old Edinburgh* (Edinburgh, 1869), pp. 22–3

10. *Glasgow; 1858: Shadow's Midnight Scenes and Social Photographs*, with an introduction by John F. McCaffrey (Glasgow, 1976), p. 60; John Dunlop, *Autobiography* (London, 1932), p. 99; [William Walker], *Glaiska Fair* (Glasgow, n.d.), p. 5; A.C.C. List, op. cit., p. 4

11. William Logan, *The Great Social Evil* (London, 1871), pp. 107–10

12. W. Tait, op. cit., pp. 2–3, 237, 245–7

13. Patrick MacGill, *Children of the Dead End* (London, 1914), p. 264

14. Edwin Muir, *Scottish Journey* (edn. Edinburgh, 1979), p. 264

15. *Synapse* (the Journal of the Edinburgh University medical students), 17, No. 2, p. 11

16. Free Church General Assembly Proceedings, 1864, *Report of the Committee on Houses for the Working Classes*

17. Ibid., 1863

18. See W. Cramond, *Illegitimacy in Banffshire* (Banff, 1888), pp. 44–50 for this and similar comments

19. *Fourth Report of the Royal Commission on the Employment of Women and Children in Agriculture*, P.P. 1870, Vol. 13, p. 80

20. George Seton, *The Causes of Illegitimacy* (Edinburgh, 1860), p. 38

21. John Walker, *The Scottish Sketches of R. B. Cunninghame Graham* (Edinburgh, 1982), p. 59

22. W. Cramond, op. cit.

23. J. M. Strachan, 'Immorality of Scotland', *Scotsman*, 20 May, 2 June, 7 June 1870

24. D. K. Cameron, *The Ballad and the Plough* (London, 1978), p. 125

25. T. C. Smout, loc. cit., pp. 75–6

26. W. A. Smith, *Lewsiana* (edn. 1886), p. 79

27. *Fourth Report ... Agriculture*, p. 66

28. *Social Evils and Problems*, pp. 95–104

29. Carnegie United Kingdom Trust, *Disinherited Youth* (Edinburgh, 1943), pp. 107–8

30. E. Muir, op. cit., pp. 18–19

31. *Disinherited Youth*, p. 104

32. Stuart Macintyre, *Little Moscows* (London, 1980), p. 138

33. Paul Thompson *et al.*, *Living the Fishing* (London, 1983), pp. 251–2

34. R. Q. Gray, *The Labour Aristocracy in Victorian Edinburgh* (Oxford, 1976), pp. 112, 119–20

35. Lynn Jamieson, 'Growing up in Scotland in the 1900s', in *Uncharted Lives: Extracts from Scottish Women's Experiences, 1850–1982* (Glasgow Women's Studies Group, 1983), pp. 26–7

36. Mollie Weir, *Shoes Were for Sunday* (London, 1980), pp. 117–18

37. S. Macintyre, op. cit., p. 138

38. James Littlejohn, *Westrigg: the Sociology of a Cheviot Parish* (London, 1963), p. 119

Further Reading

The issues of prostitution, illegitimacy and marriage are discussed by myself at somewhat greater length in 'Aspects of Sexual Behaviour in Nineteenth-Century Scotland', in A. A. Maclaren (ed.), *Social Class in Scotland: Past and Present* (Edinburgh 1976), and in 'Scottish Marriage, Regular and Irregular', in R. B. Outhwaite (ed.) *Marriage and Society: Studies in the Social History of Marriage* (London, 1981): see also the chapter on illegitimacy in M. W. Flinn (ed.), *Scottish Population History from the Seventeenth Century to the 1930s* (Cambridge, 1977). There is a vigorous exchange of views between myself and Ian Carter in *The Scottish Journal of Sociology*: see Carter 'Illegitimate births and illegitimate inferences', Vol. I (1976), pp. 125–135 and Smout 'Illegitimacy: a reply', in Vol. II (1977), pp. 97–104. K. Boyd, *Scottish Church Attitudes to Sex, Marriage and the Family, 1850–1914* (Edinburgh, 1980) is an important survey of the problem from the viewpoint of the various churches.

The history of the family, and of child upbringing and the place of the woman within and without the home, is so neglected in Scotland as to verge on becoming a historiographical disgrace. A beginning has been made by Paul Thompson et al., *Living the Fishing* (London, 1983), which raises very important questions about the relationship between child-rearing and the economic success of communities that are not even touched on here. Women's history will no doubt develop in Scotland as elsewhere: a useful start has been made with *Uncharted Lives: Extracts from Scottish Women's Experiences, 1850–1982* (Glasgow Women's Studies Group), which comes closer to the nerve than the helpful, but rather conventional, survey by Rosalind Marshall, *Virgins and Viragos* (London, 1983). Stuart Macintyre, *Little Moscows* (London, 1980) gives a good, if brief, picture of miners' womenfolk in Fife, and Joseph Melling, *Rent Strike* (Edinburgh, 1983), though primarily about political action, is full of insights about women's life in the tenements. There is still a great deal to be written on Scottish women's experience in an exceptionally male-dominated society.

CHAPTER VIII: CHURCHGOING

1. S. J. Brown, *Thomas Chalmers and the Godly Commonwealth in Scotland* (Oxford, 1982); Bernard Aspinwall, *Portable Utopia: Glasgow and the United States, 1820–1920* (Aberdeen, 1984), p. 7

2. B. Aspinwall, op. cit., p. 2

3. Quoted in C. J. A. Robertson, 'Early Scottish railways and the observance of the Sabbath', *Scottish Historical Review*, Vol. 47 (1978), p. 153. Italics in the original

4. W. M. Haddow, *My Seventy Years* (Glasgow, 1943), pp. 11–12

5. Arthur Geddes, *The Isle of Lewis and Harris* (Edinburgh, 1955), pp. 290–1

6. Henry Cockburn, *Journal* (Edinburgh, 1874), Vol. II, pp. 21–2

7. R. W. Ensor, *England, 1870–1914* (Oxford, 1936), p. 138

8. A. C. Cheyne, *The Transforming of the Kirk* (Edinburgh, 1983), p. 61

9. Norman Maclean, *Death Cannot Sever* (London, 1932), pp. 63, 107–8, 154–5. The remark of Mill is cited in Cheyne, *The Transforming of the Kirk*, p. 73

10. James Smith, *Domestic Scenes* (Glasgow, 1847)

11. Quoted in S. J. Brown, op. cit., p. 274

12. Except where otherwise stated, the quotations in the following paragraphs are drawn from the 'Report of the Committee on Non-Church Going', in *Reports on the Schemes of the Church of Scotland*, 1890–6

13. I. R. Govan, *Spirit of Revival* (London, 1938), p. 47

14. J. M. Lang, *The Church and its Social Mission* (Edinburgh, 1902), quoted in D. J. Withrington, 'The Churches in Scotland, c.1870–c.1900: Towards a New Social Conscience', *Records of the Scottish Church History Society*, Vol. 19 (1977), p. 168, fn. 21

15. Quoted in D. J. Withrington, loc. cit., p. 162

16. A. L. Cheyne, op. cit., pp. 177–8

17. John Highet, *The Scottish Churches: a review of their state 400 years after the Reformation* (London, 1960), p. 205

Further Reading

Although most church history has been written from the standpoint of ecclesiastical rather than social history, there is much that can be gleaned from the standard books. A. L. Drummond and J. Bulloch have a trilogy, *The Scottish Church, 1688–1843* (Edinburgh, 1973); *The Church in Victorian Scotland, 1843–1874* (Edinburgh, 1975); *The Church in Late Victorian Scotland, 1874–1900* (Edinburgh, 1978): in the last two volumes there is a good deal of social history. J. H. S. Burleigh, *A Church History of Scotland* (Oxford, 1960) provides a useful overall survey, and A. C. Cheyne, *The Transforming of the Kirk* (Edinburgh, 1983) discusses the intellectual response of the church to the new challenges of Victorian Scotland with great insight. S. J. Brown, *Thomas Chalmers and the Godly Commonwealth of Scotland* (Oxford, 1982) is an outstanding biography of Scotland's most distinguished nineteenth-century cleric. The Disruption of 1843 cries out for comprehensive treatment: A. A. MacLaren, *Religion and Social Class: The Disruption Years in Aberdeen* (London, 1974) is a rare example of the work of a sociologist who has, with great skill, worked on church history. The twentieth-century Scottish churches have been examined by another sociologist, John Highet, in *The Scottish Churches; a review of their state 400 years after the Reformation* (Glasgow, 1960). The Catholic tradition is best surveyed in David McRoberts (ed.), *Modern Scottish Catholicism* (Glasgow, 1979). Finally, the relationship between the churches and social reform movements can be gauged in Olive Checkland's *Philanthropy in Victorian Scotland*

(Edinburgh, 1980), Stewart Mechie, *The Church and Scottish Social Development, 1780–1870* (London, 1960), and in an important article by D. J. Withrington, 'The Churches in Scotland, *c.*1870–*c.*1900: towards a new Social Conscience', *Records of the Scottish Church History Society* Vol. 29 (1977), pp. 155–68.

CHAPTER IX: THE AIMS AND FAILURES OF EDUCATION

1. Quoted in H. C. Barnard, *A Short History of English Education from 1760 to 1944* (London, 1947), pp. 65–6
2. *Wealth of Nations* (Everyman edition), Vol. II, pp. 269–70
3. *Essays on the Principle of Population* (Everyman edition), Vol. II, p. 213
4. J. D. Myers, 'Scottish Nationalism and the Antecedents of the 1872 Education Act', *Scottish Educational Studies* Vol. 4 (1972), p. 75
5. Quoted in W. M. Humes and H. M. Paterson (eds), *Scottish Culture and Scottish Education, 1800–1980* (Edinburgh, 1983), pp. 31, 63–4
6. R. D. Anderson, 'Education and the state in nineteenth-century Scotland', *Economic History Review*, second series Vol. 36 (1983), pp. 518–34
7. Quoted in H. Hutchison, 'Church, state, and school in Clackmannanshire, 1803–1872', *Scottish Educational Studies* Vol. 3 (1971), p. 31
8. Quoted in D. J. Withrington, 'Towards a national system, 1867–72: the last years in the struggle for a Scottish Education Act', *Scottish Educational Studies*, Vol. 4 (1972), p. 122
9. Robert Somers, *An Inquiry into the State of Schools and Education in Glasgow* (London, 1857), p. 11
10. Quoted in James M. Roxburgh, *The School Board of Glasgow, 1873–1919* (London, 1971), pp. 52–3
11. John Boyd Orr, *As I Recall* (London, 1966), pp. 35–9
12. R. D. Anderson, *Education and Opportunity in Victorian Scotland* (Oxford, 1983), pp. 8–9
13. Quoted in R. D. Anderson, op. cit., p. 136
14. Ibid., pp. 138–9
15. Ibid., p. 152
16. Ibid., p. 269
17. Lyon Playfair, MP, addressing the House of Commons on the 1871 Education Bill, quoted in Anderson, *Education and Opportunity*, p. 108
18. George Davie, *The Democratic Intellect* (Edinburgh, 1961); H. M. Knox, *Two Hundred and Fifty Years of Scottish Education* (Edinburgh, 1953); James Scotland, *The History of Scottish Education* (London, 1969)
19. A. S. Neill, *A Dominie in Doubt* (London, 1921), p. 16
20. W. S. Humes and H. M. Paterson, *Scottish Culture and Scottish Education, 1800–1980* (Edinburgh, 1983), p. 198
21. V. Durkacz, 'Gaelic education in the nineteenth century', *Scottish Educational Studies*, Vol. 9 (1977), p. 19

22. J. M. Roxburgh, op. cit., p. 53

23. Ibid., p. 199

24. Helen Corr, 'The sexual division of labour in the Scottish teaching profession, 1872–1914', in Humes and Paterson (eds), *Scottish Culture and Scottish Education*, pp. 137–50

25. James Grant, *History of the Burgh Schools of Scotland* (Glasgow, 1876), p. 465

26. W. Boyd, *Education in Ayrshire through Seven Centuries* (London, 1961), p. 177

27. Quoted in R. D. Anderson, op. cit., p. 164

28. George Crichton, *An Educational Address delivered at the opening of the enlargement to Kinning Park School*, 1887, quoted in Roxburgh, *School Board of Glasgow*, p. 177

29. L. R. Moore, 'The Aberdeen Ladies Education Association', *Northern Scotland*, Vol. 3 (1979–80), p. 147, footnote 1

30. Adam Collier, 'Social origins of a sample of entrants to Glasgow University', *Sociological Review*, Vol. 30 (1938), p. 276. See also Anderson, *Education and Opportunity*, pp. 308–319; Ian J. McDonald, 'Untapped Reservoirs of Talent?—Social Class and Opportunities in Scottish Higher Education, 1910–1960', *Scottish Educational Studies*, Vol. I (1967), pp. 52–9

31. H. M. Paterson, 'Incubus and Ideology: the Development of secondary schooling in Scotland, 1900–1939', in Humes and Paterson, *Scottish Culture and Scottish Education*, p. 208

32. Quoted in R. D. Anderson, op. cit., pp. 250–1

33. A. S. Neill, *A Dominie's Log* (London, 1915), pp. 11–12

34. Quoted in H. M. Paterson, loc. cit., pp. 208–9

35. A. F. B. Roberts, 'Scotland and infant education in the nineteenth century', *Scottish Educational Studies*, Vol. 4 (1972), pp. 39–45

36. J. Scotland, op. cit., Vol. 2, p. 80

37. J. Bowie, *Penny Buff: a Clydeside School in the Thirties* (London, 1975), pp. 37, 109

Further Reading

Writing on the history of education has been very uneven. On the one hand there have been general histories of the Scottish school system, of which the latest is James Scotland, *The History of Scottish Education*, 2 vols. (London, 1969); on the other hand there are detailed studies of particular aspects of education. George Davie, *The Democratic Intellect* (Edinburgh, 1961) was a pioneering investigation into the nineteenth-century universities: his conclusions have been enlarged, and partly altered, by R. D. Anderson, *Education and Opportunity in Victorian Scotland* (Oxford, 1983), which also deals comprehensively and brilliantly with secondary education. The latter author has also contributed a stimulating article on the provision of elementary education, 'Education and the state in nineteenth-century Scotland', *Economic History Review*, second series, Vol. 36 (1983), pp. 518–34. Regional studies of education generally give short shrift to the nineteenth century, and shorter still to the period after 1872, but J. M. Roxburgh, *The School Board of Glasgow, 1873–1919* (London, 1971) is a notable exception. The problem of Gaelic education in the nineteenth century is dealt with in V. E. Durkacz, *The Decline of the Celtic Languages* (Edinburgh, 1983) and more briefly in an article in *Scottish*

Educational Studies, Vol. 9 (1977)—a journal, which, incidentally, seldom passes a year without publishing some good article on educational history. A useful collection of essays, strongly tending towards the critical in a tradition where older contributions were largely self-congratulatory, is W. M. Humes and H. M. Paterson (eds), *Scottish Culture and Scottish Education, 1800–1980* (Edinburgh, 1983). This collection also contains some shrewd chapters on the twentieth century, which most books tend to skate over somewhat lightly. There is, however, one example of a balanced and sober comparison with another twentieth-century system in G. S. Osborne, *Scottish and English Schools: a Comparative Survey of the Past Fifty Years* (Pittsburgh, 1966): not all the comparisons there between Scotland and England are unfavourable to the northern partner in the Union.

There are not many good books about what it was actually like to teach in a Scottish school, but A. S. Neill, *A Dominie's Log* (London, 1915) and Janetta Bowie, *Penny Buff: a Clydeside School in the Thirties* (London, 1975) are certainly two of them.

CHAPTER X: THE WORKING-CLASS RADICAL TRADITION TO 1885

1. Quoted in H. W. Meikle, *Scotland and the French Revolution* (Glasgow, 1912), p. 93. The references in lines 3 and 4 are to flax hecklers and bakers
2. John Millar, *Observations Concerning the Distinction of Ranks in Society* (London, 1771), pp. 184–5
3. Karl Miller, *Cockburn's Millennium* (London, 1975), pp. 107–8
4. Quoted in Fiona Montgomery, 'Glasgow and the struggle for parliamentary reform, 1830–1832', *Scottish Historical Review*, Vol. 61 (1982), p. 140
5. Norman Gash, *Sir Robert Peel* (London, 1972), p. 646
6. Alexander Wilson, *The Chartist Movement in Scotland* (Manchester, 1970), pp. 102–3
7. Robert E. Duncan, 'Artisans and proletarians: Chartism and working-class allegiance in Aberdeen', *Northern Scotland*, Vol. 4 (1981), p. 61
8. A. C. Cheyne, *The Transforming of the Kirk* (Edinburgh, 1983), pp. 20–2
9. W. Aiton, *A History of the Rencounter at Drumclog* (Hamilton, 1821), pp. 97–9, quoted in J. D. Young, *The Rousing of the Scottish Working Class* (London, 1979), p. 59
10. See John Younger, *Autobiography* (Kelso, 1881), p. xxii
11. Hugh Miller, *My Schools and Schoolmasters* (edn. Edinburgh, 1907), pp. 40–1
12. *The Minutes of Edinburgh Trades Council, 1859–1873*, ed. Ian MacDougall (Scottish History Society, 1968), p. 356
13. *Autobiography of John McAdam, 1806–1883*, ed. Janet Fyfe (Scottish History Society, 1980), p. 79
14. See the thesis cited in note 19, p. 98
15. T. Paine, *Rights of Man* (Thinker's Library edn, 1937), pp. 145–8

16. Quoted in Stewart J. Brown, *Thomas Chalmers and the Godly Commonwealth in Scotland* (Oxford, 1982), p. 275

17. See note 13 above: the quotations are from J. McAdam, op. cit., pp. 17, 157, 190, 176

18. *Glasgow, 1858: Shadow's Midnight Scenes and Social Photographs*, ed. J. F. McCaffrey (Glasgow, 1976), p. 40

19. Joan M. Smith, 'Commonsense thought and working-class consciousness: some aspects of the Glasgow and Liverpool labour movements in the early years of the twentieth century', unpublished Edinburgh University Ph.D. thesis, 1981, pp. 188–9. I am most grateful for permission to cite this passage.

20. George S. Pryde, *Scotland from 1603 to the Present Day* (Edinburgh 1962), p. 207

21. Neal Blewett, 'The franchise in the United Kingdom 1885–1918', *Past and Present*, No. 32 (1965), pp. 27–56

22. Quotations from Robert Q. Gray, *The Labour Aristocracy in Victorian Edinburgh* (Oxford, 1976), pp. 98–9

23. Ibid., p. 140

24. *The Minutes of Edinburgh Trades Council*, pp. xxxiv–xxxv

25. Gordon M. Wilson, *Alexander McDonald, Leader of the Miners* (Aberdeen, 1982), pp. 85, 127–8

Further Reading

The standard political history of Scotland for the nineteenth century is still W. Ferguson, *Scotland 1689 to the Present* (Edinburgh, 1968). It is particularly strong on the period of early radicalism, to 1820. J. D. Young, *The Rousing of the Scottish Working Class* (London, 1979) argues for a genuine revolutionary and nationalist tradition in Scottish radical politics but his findings have not been generally accepted, certainly not by this author. Tony Dickson has edited two books, firstly *Capital and Class in Scotland* (Edinburgh, 1982), in which the editor's own contribution on Paisley is outstanding, and secondly *Scottish Capitalism* (London, 1980). In both, the sections on the nineteenth century present Scottish history from a left-wing perspective that reveals a good deal. Specific aspects of the story are dealt with by Henry Meikle, *Scotland and the French Revolution* (Glasgow, 1912)—still not surpassed as a monograph on the classic Paineite period; Alexander Wilson, *The Chartist Movement in Scotland* (Manchester, 1970); R. Q. Gray, *The Labour Aristocracy in Victorian Edinburgh* (Oxford, 1976); A. B. Campbell, *The Lanarkshire Miners* (Edinburgh, 1979); G. M. Wilson, *Alexander McDonald, Leader of the Miners* (Aberdeen, 1982). See also Ian Macdougall (ed.), *Essays in Scottish Labour History* (Edinburgh, 1978), W. H. Marwick, *A Short History of Labour in Scotland* (Edinburgh, 1967), and W. H. Fraser, 'The Glasgow cotton spinners, 1837', in J. Butt and J. T. Ward (eds), *Scottish Themes* (Edinburgh, 1976). Important articles include W. M. Roach, 'Alexander Richmond', *Scottish Historical Review*, Vol. 51 (1972); Fiona Montgomery, 'Glasgow and the Struggle for Parliamentary Reform, 1830–1832', *Scottish Historical Review*, Vol. 61 (1982); K. J. Cameron, 'William Weir and the origins of the "Manchester League" in Scotland, 1833–39', *Scottish Historical Review*, Vol. 58 (1979).

Much of the best writing has unfortunately remained unpublished in the form of

Ph.D. theses. Particularly important are Fiona Montgomery, 'Glasgow Radicalism 1830–1848', Glasgow University, 1974; I. G. Hutchison, 'Politics and Society in Mid-Victorian Glasgow 1846–1886', Edinburgh University, 1974; Joan M. Smith, 'Commonsense thought and working-class consciousness: some aspects of the Glasgow and Liverpool labour movements in the early years of the twentieth century', Edinburgh University, 1981. Finally, the flavour of the respectable Victorian working man is well conveyed in two publications of the Scottish History Society, *The Minutes of Edinburgh Trades Council, 1859–1873* (1968) and *The Autobiography of John McAdam, 1806–1883* (1980).

CHAPTER XI: THE RISE AND FALL OF SOCIALIST IDEALISM

1. J. Hunter, *The Making of the Crofting Community* (Edinburgh, 1976), p. 159
2. B. Glasier, *James Keir Hardie, A Memorial* (Manchester, n.d.), p. 28
3. David Howell, *British Workers and the Independent Labour Party, 1888–1906* (Manchester, 1983), p. 148
4. B. Glasier, op. cit., p. 62
5. Ibid., p. 68
6. Laurence Thompson, *The Enthusiasts* (London, 1971), p. 40; B. Glasier, op. cit., p. 57
7. L. Thompson, op. cit., p. 89
8. Quoted in Iain S. McLean, *The Legend of Red Clydeside* (Edinburgh, 1983), p. 186
9. William Gallacher, *Revolt on the Clyde* (London, 1936), p. 234
10. Quoted in E. J. Hobsbawm, *Labouring Men* (London, 1964), p. 320
11. T. C. Smout, 'American consular reports on Scotland', *Business History*, Vol. 23 (1981), p. 307
12. Joan Smith, 'Commonsense thought and working-class consciousness: some aspects of the Glasgow and Liverpool labour movements in the early years of the twentieth century', unpublished Edinburgh University Ph.D. thesis (1981), pp. 320–3. I am very grateful to the author for permission to cite this work
13. Quoted ibid., p. 324
14. Harry McShane, *No Mean Fighter* (London, 1978), p. 31
15. David Marquand, *Ramsay MacDonald* (London, 1977), p. 234
16. Quoted in Ray Challinor, *John S. Clarke: Parliamentarian, Poet, Liontamer* (London, 1977), p. 15
17. John Wheatley, *Eight-Pound Cottages for Glasgow Citizens* (Glasgow, n.d.), p. 1
18. H. McShane, op. cit., p. 62
19. W. R. Scott and J. Cunnison, *The Industries of the Clyde Valley during the War* (Oxford, 1924), p. 176
20. H. McShane, op. cit., p. 107
21. E. Shinwell, *I've Lived Through It All* (London, 1973), p. 46
22. David Kirkwood, *My Life of Revolt* (London, 1935), p. 82
23. Ibid., p. 168

24. Christopher Harvie, *No Gods and Precious Few Heroes: Scotland 1914–1980* (London, 1981), p. 24; Duncan Duff, *Scotland's War Losses* (Glasgow, 1947), pp. 42–7

25. P. C. Matheson, 'Scottish War Sermons, 1914–1919', *Records of the Scottish Church History Society*, Vol. 17 (1971), pp. 203–13

26. Quoted in Iain McLean, *The Legend of Red Clydeside* (Edinburgh, 1983), p. 151

27. J. Kinloch and J. Butt, *History of the Scottish Co-operative Wholesale Society Limited* (Glasgow, 1981), p. 277

28. M. Swenarton, *Homes Fit for Heroes: the Politics and Architecture of Early State Housing in Britain* (London 1981), p. 78

29. Joseph Melling, *Rent Strikes: People's Struggle for Housing in West Scotland, 1890–1916* (Edinburgh, 1983), p. 114

30. Billy Kay, *Odyssey: Voices from Scotland's Recent Past* (Edinburgh, 1980), introduction

31. I. S. McLean, op. cit., pp. 176–201

32. R. K. Middlemas, *The Clydesiders: a Left-Wing Struggle for Parliamentary Power* (London, 1965), pp. 112–13

33. Only they may be Mitchell's words. He is suspected of having ghosted Kirkwood's autobiography, *My Life of Revolt*, from which the quotation comes, p. 239

34. I. S. McLean, op. cit., p. 204

35. B. Webb, *Diaries 1924–32* (London, 1956), p. 12

36. D. Kirkwood, op. cit., p.v.

37. Quoted in R. K. Middlemas, op. cit., p. 279

38. Quoted in M. Keating and D. Bleiman, *Labour and Scottish Nationalism* (London, 1979), p. 81

39. C. Harvie, op. cit., p. 106

Further Reading

Keir Hardie has been the subject of three biographies in the past decade: K. O. Morgan, *Keir Hardie, Radical and Socialist* (London, 1975); Iain McLean, *Keir Hardie* (New York, 1975); Fred Reid, *Keir Hardie, the Making of a Socialist* (London, 1978)—the last is particularly perceptive in its examination of the links between Scottish radicalism and socialism. Much can be gleaned about the specifically Scottish scene in David Howell, *British Workers and the Independent Labour Party, 1888–1906* (Manchester, 1983), Walter Kendall, *The Revolutionary Movement in Britain 1900–1921* (London, 1969), and James Hinton, *The First Shop Stewards' Movement* (London, 1973). Iain McLean, *The Legend of Red Clydeside* (Edinburgh, 1983) is persuasively unromantic, but perhaps too much belittles what happened—see R. J. Morris, 'Skilled workers and the politics of the "Red" Clyde', *Journal of the Scottish Labour History Society*, No. 18 (1983). This periodical contains many good articles on this period. Joan Smith's thesis, cited for Chapter X, is detailed and penetrating on alterations in class consciousness, and Joseph Melling has also contributed substantially to the debate in 'Scottish Industrialists and the Changing Character of Class Relations in the Clyde Region, c.1880–1918' in Tony Dickson (ed.) *Capital and Class in Scotland* (Edinburgh, 1982), in his own edited volume, *Housing, Social Policy and the State* (London, 1980), and in *Rent Strikes: People's Struggles for Housing in West Scotland, 1890–1916* (Edinburgh, 1983).

Scottish Labour history since the First World War has not been so intensively studied, but W. Knox, *Scottish Labour Leaders, 1918–1939* (Edinburgh, 1984) is a collection of concise biographies prefaced by a highly stimulating introduction. Stuart Macintyre, *Little Moscows* (London, 1980), provides detailed studies of the Vale of Leven and the Fife coal-field; M. Keating and D. Bleiman, *Labour and Scottish Nationalism* (London, 1979) and H. J. Hanham, *Scottish Nationalism* (London, 1969) are most useful. R. K. Middlemas, *The Clydesiders: a Left-wing Struggle for Parliamentary Power* (London, 1965) is somewhat superficial but nevertheless not yet replaced. For the General Strike in Scotland, see Jeffrey Skelley (ed.), *The General Strike, 1926* (London, 1976). *The Bulletin of Scottish Politics*, No. 2 (1981) contains two relevant articles: C. Harvie, 'The Age of Tom Johnston' and T. Gallagher, 'Catholics in Scottish Politics'. See also I. S. Wood, 'John Wheatley, the Irish and the Labour Movement in Scotland', *Innes Review*, Vol. 31 (1981). C. Harvie, *No Gods and Precious Few Heroes: Scotland 1914–1980* is very well informed on the political scene, casting a jaundiced eye over Labour, and most other, Scottish politicians.

Many figures on the left wrote their autobiographies, sometimes apparently mainly to conceal how left-wing they had once been, or to alter the story to their liking in other ways. Thomas Johnston's *Memories* (London, 1952) is a good example of the first, William Gallacher, *Revolt on the Clyde* (London, 1936) an even better example of the second. More honest and enjoyable, though in very different ways, are David Kirkwood, *My Life of Revolt* (London, 1935) and Harry McShane (with J. Smith), *No Mean Fighter* (Edinburgh, 1978). Finally, anyone with access to the pages of *Forward* (e.g. in the Mitchell Library, Glasgow) will gain a very good insight into the culture and outlook of the Labour movement in the early twentieth-century Scotland.

Index

T. C. Smout

A History of the Scottish People 1560–1830

'By far the most stimulating, the most instructive and the most readable account of Scotch history that I have read . . . this splendid work carries us from Knox to Neilson, from the hot gospel of Calvin to the hot-blast smelting process – and incidentally seeks to explain the change. For always, in following this lucid narrative, we see an original mind at work, questioning and explaining as well as illustrating.

The illustrations, incidentally, are original and delightful too. The whole book has delighted me. I cannot praise it too highly.' Hugh Trevor-Roper, *Sunday Times*

'This is a fine history of Scotland. It combines rich and deep scholarship with an elegant and lucid style . . . No one who professes an interest in Scotland can afford to miss reading it.' *Times Literary Supplement*

'This remarkable book leaves the reviewer with little to say except that all Scots, and even Englishmen who are interested in Britain's development, should read it. It is admirably proportioned, based on vast reading, and brings all the main topics together.' *Economist*

FONTANA PRESS